King William's War

French batteries bombard the English fleet during the siege of Quebec, 1690. (*National Archives of Canada*)

The First Contest For North America, 1689–1697

King William's War

MICHAEL G. LARAMIE

WESTHOLME
Yardley

Westholme Publishing, LLC
904 Edgewood Road
Yardley, Pennsylvania 19067
Visit our Web site at www.westholmepublishing.com

ISBN: 978-1-59416-288-6
Also available as an eBook.

Printed in the United States of America.

For my mother, Priscilla Boissoneault,
and my grandmother Althea Decato.

Contents

LIST OF MAPS

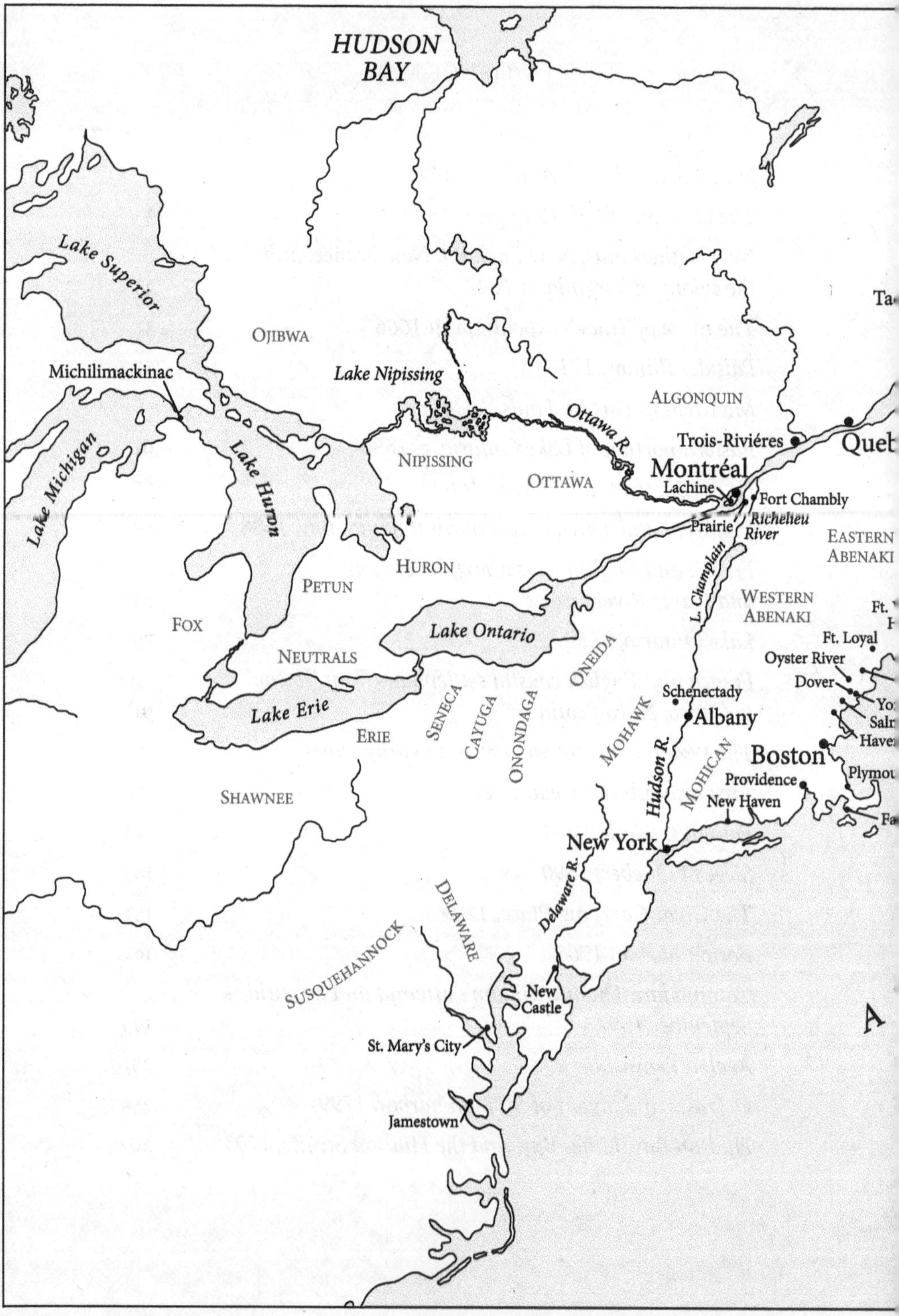

HUDSON BAY
Lake Superior
OJIBWA
Michilimackinac
Lake Nipissing
ALGONQUIN
Ottawa R.
Trois-Riviéres
Lake Michigan
Lake Huron
NIPISSING
OTTAWA
Montréal
Lachine
Fort Chambly
Prairie
Richelieu River
EASTERN ABENAKI
HURON
PETUN
L. Champlain
WESTERN ABENAKI
FOX
Lake Ontario
Ft. Loyal
NEUTRALS
ONEIDA
Oyster River
Dover
Schenectady
Lake Erie
SENECA
CAYUGA
ONONDAGA
MOHAWK
Albany
ERIE
Hudson R.
MOHICAN
Boston
Providence
SHAWNEE
New Haven
New York
Delaware R.
DELAWARE
SUSQUEHANNOCK
New Castle
St. Mary's City
Jamestown

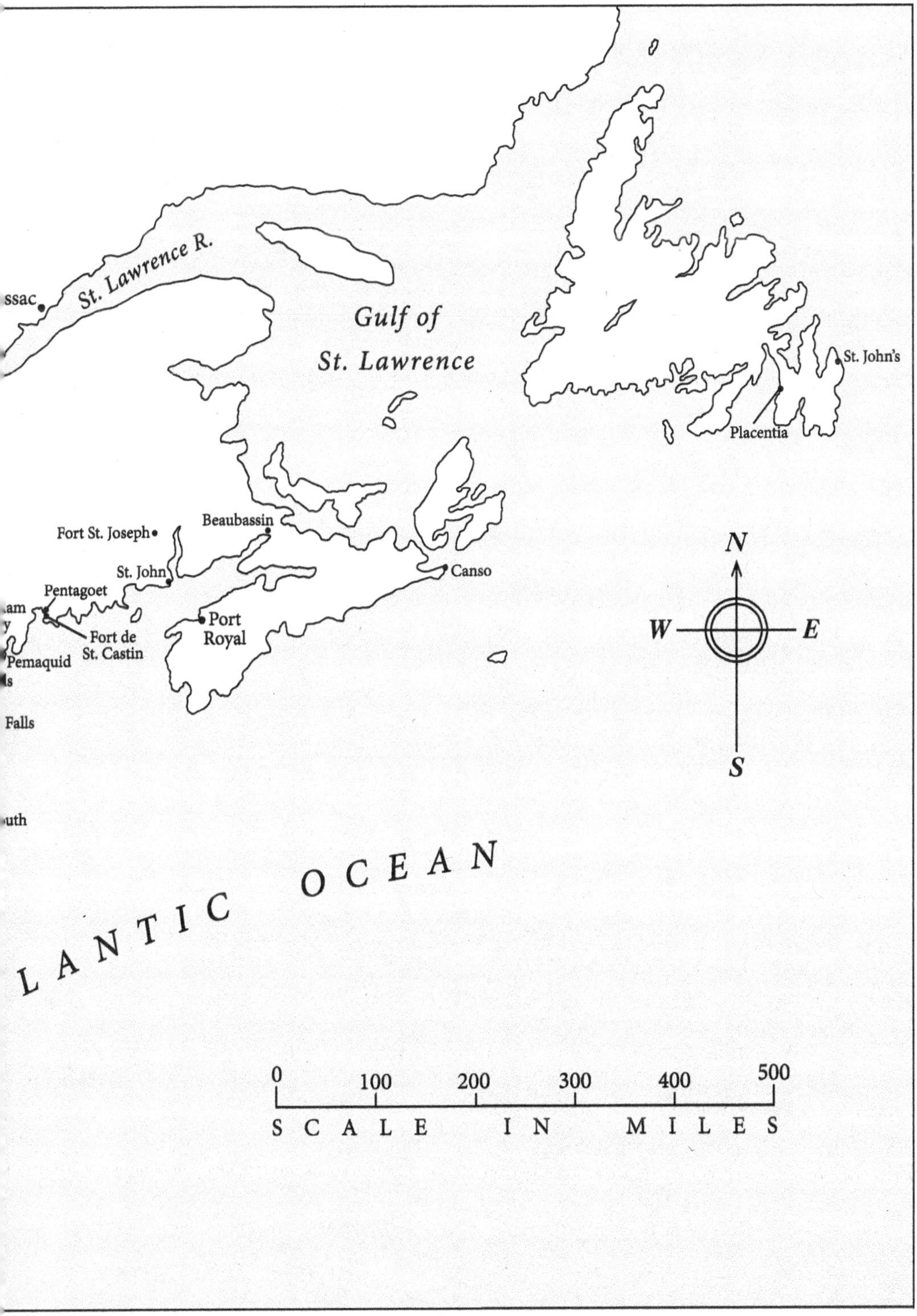

ssac
St. Lawrence R.
Gulf of
St. Lawrence
St. John's
Placentia
Fort St. Joseph
Beaubassin
St. John
Pentagoet
am
y
Fort de
St. Castin
Pemaquid
s
Port
Royal
Canso
N
W
E
S
Falls
uth
LANTIC OCEAN
0
100
200
300
400
500
SCALE IN MILES

Preface

King William's War is the first of two books, with a companion volume on Queen Anne's War planned to follow. The two conflicts may, in many ways, be thought of as one conflict with a five-year pause; thus with this break included, France and England were at war from 1688 to 1715. The European part of these conflicts, known as the War of the League of Augsburg and the War of Spanish Succession, was punctuated by battles like Steenkirk, Blenheim, and Malplaquet—any one of which dwarfed the scale of colonial military involvement. Although much can be found on these conflicts fought in Europe, the same cannot be said for their colonial components.

Certainly King William's War was markedly different from its European counterpart. Smaller populations and the vast areas upon which these numbers were scattered dictated as much. Manpower shortages, supply nightmares, and transportation issues on the frontier dominated the conflict on both sides and proved just as challenging as defeating the enemy, but these aside, there were even greater distinctions that dictated the character of the conflict in North America. King William's War was actually three conflicts. The first of these was a long-running feud between the Iroquois Confederacy, New France, and New France's native allies. Fueled by English guns and money as well as the confederacy's desire to divert the French fur trade toward their English trading partners in Albany, this conflict had started with the opening pages of the French colony. To the east another conflict would be captured under the banner of King William's War. The pro-French Wabanaki of Maine, Nova Scotia, and New Brunswick had previously fought a war with New England. English expansion and French urgings, aided by foolish moves and political blunders on the part of New England, erupted into a second Wabanaki war on the eve of King William's War. Thus, these two proxy wars fought by the English and the French through their native allies officially became one with news of a declaration of war between France and England in 1689.

While much has been said and written on the last French and Indian War (1754–1763), or the Old French War as it is sometimes stylized, very little has been said on the colonial conflicts that preceded it. Yet the foundations for this last war, which resulted in the conquest of Canada, are readily seen in the first contest between the two colonial powers in King William's War. The patterns of these conflicts for the next seventy years, and the goals and objectives of both sides are laid here, as well as the fermenting attitude that the two colonies could not coexist. Throw in a change of monarchs, witch trials, pirates, questionable decisions by both crowns and colonial leaders, treasure hunters, adventurers, explorers, a seventeenth-century military jack-of-all-trades by the name of Pierre Le Moyne d'Iberville, as well as the original American ranger in Major Benjamin Church, and you have a recipe for an unusual and seldom told story. I hope it strikes your interest as well.

Part One

New Worlds

French soldiers, far left, and their Algonquin allies attack an Iroquois fort along the Richelieu River in 1610. (*Library and Archives of Canada*)

CHAPTER ONE

The Beaver Wars

On September 18, 1609, a small Dutch vessel named the *Half Moon* dropped anchor near modern Albany, New York. The vessel better known for its captain, Henry Hudson, had spent several weeks sailing up the narrow waters of the Great North River, which the Hudson River was known as for many years to come. Hudson's journey had come to an end at Albany. Although the river extended north for many more miles small boats sent forward reported "it to be at an end for shipping," having "found but seven foot water, and unconstant soundings." It was but one of many disappointments for the explorer who had previously charted Chesapeake Bay and the Delaware River in search of the elusive Northwest Passage. With another dead end before him, a few days were spent trading for beaver and otter pelts with the local Mahican before Hudson retraced his steps, never to return to the river that would one day bear his name. Although the explorer would not know it, this short and seemingly benign event was to have a profound impact on the future of North America.

News of the discovery and the promise of the lucrative fur trade attracted a number of Dutch vessels to the area over the next few years, and as each vessel returned with more furs the decision was reached to erect a permanent establishment at this location. In the summer of 1614 small bands of Mahican watched from the banks of the river as a handful of Dutch traders erected Fort Nassau on Castle Island. The region's first fort was an unassuming structure built like many early North American forts—by men with little or no formal training in the art of military fortification. In its completed form the stronghold was nothing more than a square palisade, measuring fifty feet to a side with an eighteen-foot-wide moat dug about its perimeter and a drawbridge at the main gate. Inside this stockade sat a thirty-six-by-twenty-six-foot trading house, which not only harbored the trade goods but acted as the living quarters for the dozen or so traders who occupied the post. A pair of light cannon sat within the fort's parade ground for defense, while eleven *pierriers*, small swivel guns designed to fire rock projectiles, lined the structure's walls.

As it was, Fort Nassau's days were numbered. The low-lying Castle Island, while seemingly an excellent defensive choice, was subject to the annual ravages of the Hudson River. In the spring of 1617 the fort was so badly damaged by floodwaters that its occupants were forced to abandon the structure and build a new one on the west bank of the river a few miles south of the old site.[1]

In 1624 the second Fort Nassau was replaced by a larger structure to better accommodate the burgeoning fur trade. Fort Orange, as it was called, was moved back up the river almost opposite the old Fort Nassau on Castle Island. A four-bastioned structure measuring 150 feet to a side, it was of earth and wood construction. A pair of fifteen-foot parallel walls, made in the same fashion as Fort Nassau, were erected, tracing out the fort's perimeter. At this point the walls were braced with cross members and the intervening space between them was filled in with earth, most likely taken from the moat that surrounded the fort on three sides. A rampart or walkway was then fashioned in the area between the two walls by placing planks on horizontal cross members, which were then secured to the palisades on either side. It is not clear exactly how thick the walls of Fort Orange were made, but given that one citizen who had a dwelling within the fort petitioned to cut a door in the curtain wall to allow easier access to his home, one suspects that they were thinner rather than thicker. Protruding diamond-shaped bastions were placed at each corner of the structure to allow the defenders to sweep the walls with gunfire and serve as firing platforms for the fort's eight large stone firing guns.

While bands of Mahican watched in curiosity, and soon began frequenting Fort Orange to trade their pelts for European goods, other visitors arrived as well. Foremost among these tribes were the Mohawk and their Iroquois brothers. Clustered in fortified villages stretching from the Mohawk River in the east, through the reaches of upper New York, to the northeastern shores of Lake Erie, the Iroquois, or "the people of the long house" as they were known, were a confederacy of five nations: the Mohawk, the Oneida, the Onondaga, the Cayuga, and the largest and most western tribe,

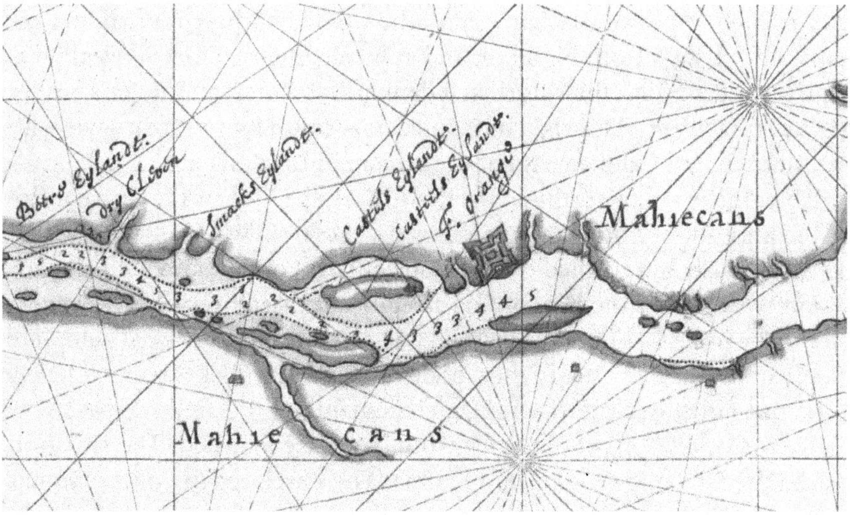

Detail from a Dutch map circa 1639 showing the location of Fort Orange along the North (Hudson) River. The remains of Fort Nassau can be seen on the northern edge of Castle Island just to the left of Fort Orange. The cartographer has noted that "Mahiecans"—Mahican Indians—dominate both sides of the river. (*Library of Congress*)

the Seneca. Bound by a military and trade alliance the Five Nations was among the most successful and powerful native confederations in North America. They were also a people at a crossroads.

The establishment of New France in 1609 had brought a new adversary. The founder of the French colony, Samuel de Champlain, had, for obvious geographical reasons, allied himself with the Iroquois's traditional northern enemies, the Huron and the Algonquin. The result was a string of defeats for the Iroquois, who had nothing to counter the influence of French firearms. Elsewhere, the Iroquois were beginning to encounter similar problems. Their enemies to the south, the Susquehannock, had established trade connections with the English of Virginia, while to the east the Mahican had developed a source of European goods not only from the Dutch at Fort Orange but from the English settlers of the Massachusetts Bay colony as well. Although at the moment this arrangement was hardly an iron ring, it was clear to the Iroquois leadership that one day it would be if they did not act and establish their own direct link to European goods.

With a path agreed upon, the Iroquois secured their southern border with the Susquehannock via peace delegations and gifts. This left only one task to execute their plan. In 1622 a Mohawk delegation approached the French and their Algonquin allies with overtures of peace. The proposition immediately appealed to Champlain, who wanted nothing more than a reliable flow of furs from his allies, and at his insistence a formal treaty was signed in 1624. With their northern flank now secure, the Iroquois, under Mohawk leadership, launched the confederacy into a four-year struggle with the Mahican to obtain control of the upper Hudson valley.[2]

The conclusion of hostilities in late 1628 left the Mohawk in firm control of the area about Fort Orange. Strangely, the Mohawk-Mahican conflict never seriously interrupted the fur trade at Fort Orange, and with the cessation of hostilities the flow of furs steadily increased over the next generation. The increase in trade, however, was not without its price. There were plenty of beaver and otter in the woodland and Finger Lakes region of New York, just not enough to sustain Dutch demand.[3]

By 1640 the Mohawk hunting grounds were exhausted. The situation placed the Dutch in a political dilemma. There were plenty of Indian nations with furs for sale, particularly the Canadian ones; the problem was that the Iroquois had no intention of giving these nations access to Fort Orange. Nor were the Dutch in a position to open a direct trade route to these tribes, for even attempting to do so would bring the wrath of their Iroquois trading partners down upon the infant colony. For the Iroquois the situation was worse. At the moment they were able to obtain their furs from their western brothers, but this was only a stopgap measure. The furs they so desperately needed lay just out of their reach, within the domain of the tribes of the Great Lakes and Canada. The Iroquois initially pursued a peaceful path toward obtaining the object of their desire. On several occasions the Huron and upper lake tribes were approached in hopes of forming a trading alliance, but in each instance a treaty never materialized. The failure was due in part to French influences, but fundamentally it had more to do with the fact that these tribes were no more interested in trading through a middleman than the Iroquois were.[4]

With the Huron proving uncooperative the Iroquois approached the French in early June 1641. A delegation of nearly five hundred Iroquois arrived before the town of Three Rivers carrying with them two French prisoners. The leader of the delegation called for peace between the French and the Iroquois and for an opening of trade between the two nations. As a symbol of their true intentions the Iroquois promptly returned the French prisoners. When Governor Charles Hualt de Montmagny arrived a few days later the matter had become clearer. Although the Iroquois wanted peace with the French and wished to erect trading posts in both countries, effectively ending the commercial rivalry between the two, such a peace was not to include the French Huron and Algonquin allies.

The sincerity of the delegation was soon in doubt when a number of Iroquois warriors seized several Algonquin canoes and made their occupants prisoners, although they had openly stated that they would refrain from any such actions during the negotiations. The Iroquois then insisted that the French provide them with guns to demonstrate their friendship. When Montmagny rejected the idea of abandoning New France's allies, and then refused to provide the requested firearms, matters quickly degenerated. The Iroquois became enraged that "Onontio had not given them arquebuses to eat," and began taking an aggressive posture, even going so far as showering arrows upon the French vessels anchored before Three Rivers. At that point "the Governor resolved to give them arquebuses to eat, but not in the way that they asked," one chronicler of the event noted. Montmagny ordered the cannon and swivel guns aboard the small craft to fire on the Iroquois position across the river. The Iroquois soon took flight and eventually escaped a French pursuit under the cover of darkness.

It was a poor attempt to split the French from their allies but hardly a setback for the Five Nations. If they could not obtain what they wanted through diplomacy, then they would obtain it through other means. War parties soon began raiding the Huron and upper lake tribes' trade routes to Montreal, but this was merely a preliminary step toward the complete conquest of this trade.

In this new approach the Iroquois had allies. If the Dutch did not directly encourage the Iroquois, they certainly facilitated their efforts. Although there were severe punishments in place for selling firearms to the natives, between 1643 and 1645 the warriors of the longhouse obtained no less than four hundred Dutch-made muskets. The matter was in part a by-product of a 1640 decision to remove the Dutch East India Company's fur trade monopoly. The aim was to promote free trade and encourage settlement in New Netherland. In this regard it succeeded but not in the fashion that was hoped. Instead of attracting settlers who might supplement their income with the occasional foray into the fur trade—but who in general would be more concerned with occupations that would expand the agricultural and industrial base of the colony—the act created an influx of individuals lured by the quick returns and high profits associated with the fur trade. This in turn made the existing ban on selling firearms to the natives almost impossible to enforce. The author of the "Journal of the New Netherlands," observed the net effects on one of the communities near Fort Orange:

> The inhabitants of Renselaerswyck who were as many traders as persons, perceiving that the Mohawk were craving for guns, which

> some of them had already received from the English, paying for each as many as twenty beavers and for a pound of powder as much as ten to twelve guilders, they came down in greater numbers than was their wont where people were well supplied with guns, purchasing these at a fair price, thus realizing great profit; afterwards they obtained some from their Heer Patroon for their self-defence in time of need, as we suppose. This extraordinary gain was not kept long a secret, the traders coming from Holland soon got scent of it, and from time to time brought over great quantities, so that the Mohawk in a short time were seen with firelocks, powder and lead in proportion. Four hundred armed men knew how to use their advantage, especially against their enemies dwelling along the river of Canada, against whom they have now achieved many profitable forays where before they derived little advantage; this causes them also to be respected by the surrounding Indians even as far as the sea coast, who must generally pay them tribute.[5]

For their part Dutch traders had argued for years that there were plenty of other sources from which the natives could obtain firearms. New England traders routinely sold muskets to their Mahican allies, the French traded and sold weapons to their Canadian allies, and the traders of New Sweden even went so far as to sell small cannons to their Susquehannock trading partners and instruct them in their use. So why should Dutch traders suffer by banning the sale of such items?

It was, of course, a practical economic argument, but the sudden upsurge of firearms into the Mohawk camp indicated more than simple disregard of company regulations in order to appease the traders of the region. There was also another element at work. Although the restrictions did not differentiate between native nations, there was clearly a distinction. In 1642 a series of conflicts broke out between the Dutch and the Delaware-speaking river tribes along the lower Hudson valley. The matter quickly became perilous for the sparsely inhabited colony, and on several occasions its inhabitants were forced to abandon their villages in order to seek shelter within the confines of New Amsterdam. Fort Orange, however, was spared from the violence, primarily due to its location within Mohawk territory and its trade connections to the Five Nations. In fact, the sale and distribution of firearms to the Mohawk during this period seems to have had the tacit approval of the governor of New Holland, William Kieft.[6] Given the weak position of New Netherland, Governor Kieft had decided to make firm allies of the Iroquois in hopes of using their influence and military might to hold the other native threats to the colony in check. If the Mohawk then wanted to use these weapons to obtain their furs from neighboring tribes, well then so much the better for the Dutch. In either case Kieft could pursue his policy and if need be shift blame for the whole thing on renegade traders or the policies of a foreign colony, several of whom were known to be hostile toward New Netherland.[7]

Kieft's approach bore quick fruit, for not long after a substantial number of guns were in Mohawk hands they struck at the governor's enemies under the auspices of laying tribute on these tribes. Nor was the meaning lost when the Mohawk sat beside the Dutch during the peace negotiations a few years later. Although Fort Orange had not been affected by the conflict, it was not clear what would happen to it if New Netherland were to collapse. With their sights set on conquering the western fur trade, the Mohawk wanted no uncertainties surrounding this vital post. Peace between the Dutch and the River Indians was the easiest means of securing this goal—a peace motivated by the threat of full-scale Mohawk intervention if need be.[8]

Armed with Dutch muskets the Iroquois began slowly choking off the supply of furs to Montreal. A parade of war parties were launched toward the Ottawa River, the traditional trade route from Lake Huron to Three Rivers and Quebec, such that one party would relieve the next, making any voyage down this waterway the likely target of an Iroquois ambush. The banks of the St. Lawrence were another favorite target of Iroquois war parties, either by way of Lake Ontario or the Lake Champlain-Richelieu River corridor. In response to the latter, Governor Montmagny erected a fort at the mouth of the Richelieu River in August 1643. Built in a simple palisade fashion the fort was besieged almost the day it was completed by 350 Iroquois warriors. Supported by cannon fire from the small vessels in the river the French garrison beat off the attack, but it soon became clear that any thoughts the French entertained toward cutting one of the Iroquois's primary invasion routes into New France with the erection of this stronghold was misguided. The fort and its small garrison were strong enough to defend themselves but were too weak to close the Richelieu River to Iroquois war parties who simply took their canoes out of the water and bypassed the structure. Nor were the Huron and Algonquin villages safe refuge as raids against these locations pointed out, and with the establishment of Montreal in 1642, the Iroquois added yet another target to their list.[9]

By 1644 Iroquois efforts were beginning to take their toll on New France and its allies. "The Iroquois," Jesuit father Hierosme Lalemant wrote to his superiors in France,

> have closed all the passages and avenues of the River that leads to Kebec [Quebec]; and of those whom the necessity of obtaining goods from France had compelled to close their eyes to these dangers, many have fallen therein. Most of the others have come back entirely naked, or pierced with arquebus balls, after having escaped seven or eight times from the hands and the cruelties of those barbarians. There was no less desolation throughout the country. Nearly every day, unfortunate women were killed in their fields.
>
> The villages were in a state of continual alarm, and all the troops that were raised in good numbers to pursue the enemy over the frontiers were defeated and routed; captives were taken by hundreds, and frequently we had no other couriers and bearers of these dismal tidings but poor unfortunates who had escaped from the midst of the flames, whose half-burnt bodies and mutilated fingers convinced us, more than their words, of the misfortune that had fallen on them and on their comrades.

The Algonquin, frequent targets of the Iroquois efforts, had abandoned their homes and hunting grounds to seek refuge with the Huron, who were also beginning to feel the strain of constant warfare. Although Lalemant was speaking specifically about the Huron, his words reflected the state of the French colony as well. The fur trade was in shambles, and the constant "hit and run" raids had left Montreal, Three Rivers, and the smaller French villages that dotted the shores of the St. Lawrence in a state of constant alarm. Crops went unattended for lack of troops to guard those tending to the fields, and now famine, an enemy far more feared than the Iroquois, was beginning to take hold.[10]

Although New France and her allies scored a number of successes during this period they were too few and too small in scale to dissuade the enemy. Nor was it possible to launch a major offensive against the Iroquois that might have halted the onslaught. First, given the lack of intelligence as to the enemy's numbers it was not clear what kind of force was required to achieve these ends. Second, it was not clear where such a strike should fall. Third, and perhaps more importantly, was the lack of resources available by the colony. The entire population of the country at this time was no more than 1,200 souls. Even should sufficient numbers and resources be gathered for a campaign, and the colony's native allies convinced to join in a like fashion, it would leave both parties vulnerable should the attack miscarry. Simple risk analysis dictated that the best course of action was to conserve their resources in what was turning into a war of attrition.

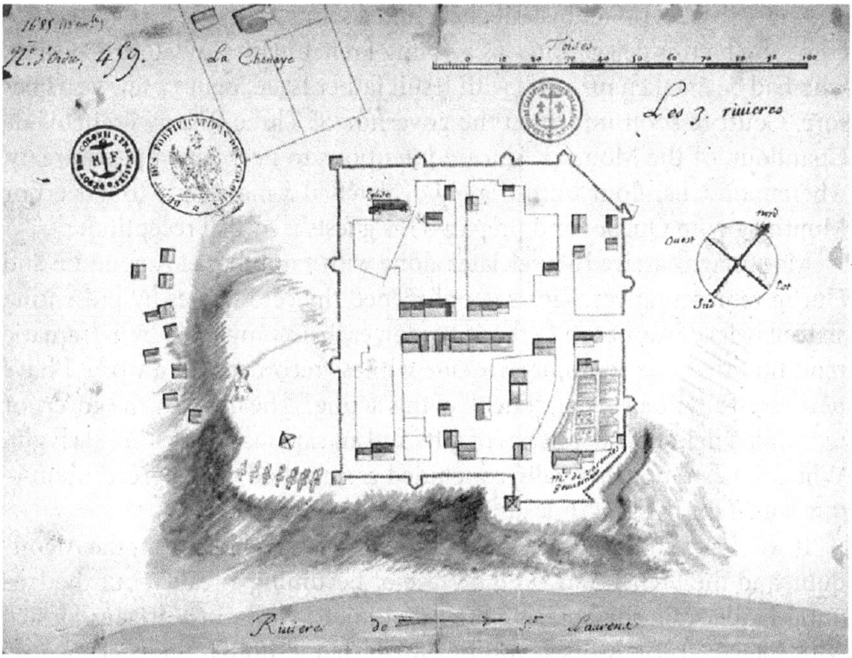

A plan of Three Rivers, 1685. Founded in 1642 and located on the north bank of the St. Lawrence River between Montreal and Quebec, Three Rivers would quickly become the third largest town in New France. (*Library and Archives of Canada*)

By the spring of 1645 both the French and their Huron and Algonquin allies were looking for peace. An opportunity presented itself in May when a Huron war party returning from a recent foray delivered a pair of Mohawk prisoners to Montmagny "to do with as he thought best." After a brief discussion with his allies Montmagny released one of the prisoners and dispatched him with an invitation for the Mohawk to come to Three Rivers and discuss peace. The gesture proved fruitful when the prisoner and a Mohawk delegation arrived at Three Rivers on July 5, 1645. When the canoe carrying the Iroquois ambassador, Kiotseaeton, beached itself before the walls of the town he courageously stepped ashore. "My brothers, I have left my country to come and see you," he shouted to the apprehensive French watching from the fort's ramparts. "I was told, on my departure, that I was going to seek death, and that I would never again see my country. But I have willingly exposed myself for the good of peace. I come therefore to enter into the designs of the French, of the Huron, and of the Algonquin. I come to make known to you the thoughts of all my country."

The words set off an instant cheer and a salute from the fort's guns. Accompanying this delegation was a young Frenchman, Guillaume Couture, who had been taken prisoner with Jesuit father Isaac Jogues a few years before. Couture soon informed the governor of Three Rivers, Francois de Chanflour, of the Mohawk' sincere intentions to negotiate a peace treaty, whereupon Chanflour immediately dispatched a messenger to Governor Montmagny in Quebec and prepared his guests a cordial reception.

Montmagny arrived a week later along with a number of Algonquin and Huron representatives. Kiotseaeton opened the ceremonies by presenting sixteen belts of wampum to the governor, each accompanied by a dramatic rendition that was so impressive one witness recorded, "In a word, I have never seen anything better done than this acting." The next day the governor responded in kind with a series of gifts and an explanation behind each gift. When the ceremonies finally concluded a truce had been agreed upon—one which for the first time also included the French allies.

It would seem that peace between the Mohawk, the Huron, the Algonquin, and the French was on the verge of becoming a reality, but the Iroquois had not finished playing their diplomatic cards. In a private council with the governor, Kiotseaeton put forth that although the peace would publically include the Algonquin, the Mohawk wished to include a secret provision that excluded them. Montmagny initially rejected the idea, but in a second meeting the next day a number of Jesuits convinced the governor to accept Kiotseaeton's proposal. The only stipulation to the agreement, which was clearly an attempt on the part of the Jesuits to recruit converts, was that Christian Algonquin were to be excluded. Strangely, exactly how the Iroquois were to tell the difference was never discussed.

Kiotseaeton and his delegation departed for Mohawk territory the next day, accompanied by a pair of Frenchmen who were to deliver the governor's message to the tribe's sachems. Both sides agreed that once emissaries had contacted all parties to inform them of the peace proceedings they would meet again at Three Rivers in the fall to finalize the treaty.

For Montmagny the event was a double-edged sword. In the short term the colony, and its allies, desperately needed peace to recover its strength, and for the first time the terms of this peace included at least part of New France's allies. In the long term, however, the governor was skeptical. Thus far only the Mohawk had come forward, implying that the rest of the confederacy had not changed their attitude. No mention had been made of a commercial arrangement between the two sides, and without this it was difficult to see how any agreement, whatever the terms, could last. Nor was such an agreement, even if it should come to fruition, in the best interest of the colony. What the Iroquois could not take by force they were likely to achieve by diplomacy. A trade arrangement between the French and the Iroquois would allow the latter to slowly assume the role of middlemen between the Huron and the Algonquin, not only through coercion and threats or, in the case of the betrayed Algonquin, by direct force, but by introducing the pro-French tribes to the cheaper Dutch goods at Fort Orange. On the other hand, if the Five Nations were to continue their current military assault they might well accomplish the same results. In either case, it left the Iroquois in control of the fur trade and New France isolated. For the moment, peace was the priority, but Montmagny was under no illusions; it was nothing more than a reprieve in what was to be a long struggle.

As agreed upon, the representatives from each nation arrived at Three Rivers during the late summer and fall of 1645. The Mohawk ambassadors were the last to arrive in mid-September a few days after Montmagny. With a hundred Huron and Algonquin warriors about him Montmagny met with the nine Mohawk representatives in an event never seen before in New France. Apprehension soon gave way to accord as both sides exchanged prisoners and presented gifts backed by dramatic orations, which were made even longer as the interpreters echoed the speeches in four different languages. Last to go before the council was an Algonquin chief by the name of Jean Baptiste Atironta. Atironta called upon the Mohawk to follow the provisions of the treaty, and then in a bold shout he concluded the ceremony with, "It is done. We are brothers."

It would seem that peace between the Mohawk, Huron, and French had finally been realized, with the Algonquin the secret losers. Representatives were dispatched to each nation and it was agreed that trading posts would be set up within Mohawk territory and at Three Rivers to soothe the commercial rivalry between the two powers. And although the remaining elements of the Iroquois Confederacy were not included in the treaty, the Mohawk ambassadors had promised to speak with the other nations in an attempt to negotiate a larger agreement in the future.

Politically the Mohawk had achieved a commanding victory at the expense of New France's need for peace. Through their war of a thousand cuts they and their Iroquois brothers had weakened the French colony and its allies and then preyed on this weakness in dictating peace terms that divided their enemy's alliance. The path before the Mohawk was filled with both military and political opportunity. They could honor the peace terms while the remaining elements of the confederacy continued their attacks. This left the Mohawk free to work the political elements of Iroquois policy by further dividing the French-Huron-Algonquin alliance through the agreed-upon trade arrangements. In the meantime their Iroquois brothers to the west could militarily strain the French alliance until, in one fashion or another, it broke or until the Mohawk decided to reject the peace treaty and reenter the fray.

As it was both Iroquois political and military plans would prove fruitful. The fall of 1645 and much of 1646 was calmer for New France and her allies. The Mohawk held firm to their word and refrained from their attacks. It was true that the other elements of the confederacy continued with some sporadic efforts, but the reprieve made for a much more manageable situation. The fur trade increased and the crops were planted and harvested with little interference. On September 12, 1646, eighty Huron canoes loaded with beaver pelts pulled ashore at Montreal. The largest fur convoy ever seen in New France had proceeded to Montreal unmolested in what was viewed as a product of the new peace treaty. With the arrival of the fur convoy a general feeling of relief took hold in the French colony. "This peace, together with the trade which the country now has," wrote Father Isaac Jogues, who had just returned from his appointment as one of the French representatives to the Mohawk, "causes a notable change in its appearance, an increase in the number of inhabitants, and greater comfort in all respects." Jogues, who had but a month to live, would never see the frightening times that lie ahead.

The early indications of storm clouds came from a Huron war chief by the name of Tandihetsi. In January 1646, Tandihetsi, who had a number of relatives among the Algonquin, warned these tribes of "the secret of his country" and urged them to assemble at Three Rivers for a council to discuss this matter. He made clear the secret provisions of the previous years' peace treaty and warned that three hundred Mohawk were planning on striking the Algonquin villages within a few months. A number of Algonquin heeded his call, but with little proof and both the Mohawk and, more importantly, the French discrediting Tandihetsi's testimony, the matter was soon dropped. Still, the event did little to promote harmony within the French alliance.

Even with the secret provisions of the 1645 treaty in force the Mohawk refrained from attacking the Algonquin. Instead they promoted the peace treaty and abided by its conditions. In the spring of 1646 Father Jogues, who had previously been captured and tortured by the Mohawk, returned to the people who had tormented him. Jogues, and another previous captive, Couture, acted as French representatives to the Mohawk. The father was to establish a mission within Mohawk territory from which trade could be carried on between the two nations. For their part the Mohawk treated

A Huron warrior, left, and an Iroquois warrior sketched by Louis Nicolas, a Jesuit priest, in 1670. (*New York Public Library*)

Jogues as an honored guest and listened closely to his proposals that the tribe should bring the other Iroquois nations into the peace treaty by restricting their access to Montreal and Fort Orange.

The Mohawk took Jogues's comments to heart because from their perspective the success of a French trade mission in their homeland not only accomplished Iroquois goals but put the Mohawk at the head of the confederacy. This tribe, because of its easternmost position, which placed its borders against New France to the north and New Netherland on the southeast, considered itself the door to the Iroquois nations. The burgeoning fur trade at Fort Orange, which they controlled, and the supply of Dutch firearms and powder that came from this, reinforced this belief. If they could now augment this position with access to the French fur trade it was clear that they would ascend to the head of the confederacy. Thus, although the ultimate goal was for the Iroquois to control access to the French and the Dutch fur markets, within the Mohawk nation itself there was another goal—that of becoming the middlemen to the rest of the Five Nations.

In fact, this approach explains why the Mohawk, when presented the opportunity, were so quick to negotiate a separate peace when they of all the

Iroquois nations had suffered most at the hands of the French. By securing peace with New France and her allies, or at least some of them, the Mohawk accomplished two ends. Militarily, their Iroquois brothers were still engaged, keeping alive the threat of a larger war that New France could ill afford, and diplomatically, with the possibility of a broader conflict still looming before them, both New France and her allies would turn to the Mohawk to remove this threat by convincing the rest of the Five Nations to enter into a larger peace treaty.

In exchange for securing this peace the Mohawk would be in a position to extract concessions from the French. These concessions would center about excluding other tribes from the French fur trade and the need to use the Mohawk to funnel European goods toward their Iroquois brothers in order to maintain the peace. In the end the Iroquois would grow stronger, which would make New France even less desirous of an open rupture with the Five Nations and more agreeable to concessions that concentrated the fur trade even further into Iroquois hands. With the fur trade under Iroquois control the Five Nations would then be in a position to force both the Dutch and the French into a bidding war. And at the center of all of this would be the ultimate middlemen, the Mohawk.

With this approach in mind it is not difficult to see why the Mohawk refrained from attacking the Algonquin and kept to the terms of the peace treaty. As long as French trade passed through their hands they could reserve any attack on the Algonquin, using it later to coerce and intimidate the Huron and any other tribe (all while not violating the terms of the treaty) should they attempt to bypass trade with the Mohawk. And once this French trade was established, nothing stopped them from negotiating another secret arrangement with the French, under the threat of a wider war, to punish other tribes who refused to cooperate—a fact that would be clearly demonstrated when they destroyed the Algonquin while the French watched and did nothing.

It was a remarkable plan, worthy of the machinations of any court in Europe, but at its heart was the newly enacted trade agreement with the French. Without this, the plan would quickly crumble. Unfortunately for the Mohawk, two elements disrupted their ambitions. The first was the fur fleet that arrived at Montreal in September 1646. Although it was agreed under the peace treaty that the Mohawk would have access to this commerce, not a single fur in the record haul found its way to them. The conclusion seemed clear; the French and their allies had no intention of living up to the commercial terms of the peace treaty. This event might have been smoothed over and the French reminded of the consequences of such ac-

A French fisherman and a trapper drawn by Carel Allard, c. 1690. (*New York Public Library*)

tions short of a resumption of hostilities, but a second element diverted this path: the political interests and jealousies of the remaining members of the confederacy. The Oneida, Onondaga, Cayuga, and Seneca had watched the Mohawk efforts closely while still carrying on their war to capture the fur trade. Certainly political pressure had been brought to bear on the Mohawk to break the treaty and return to the warpath, but until the French or their allies had violated the treaty the Mohawk put aside such pressures in lieu of obtaining the tribe's greater goal. Now with clear evidence of French duplicity before them, these pressures tipped the balance. The treaty was discarded and the tribe's direction shifted back toward war.

Of course, Father Jogues and his fellow ambassador Jean de Lalande knew nothing of this change of heart. The Jesuit had returned to Quebec in the summer of 1646, and after a few months' stay, he and his companion were but a few days' journey from their Mohawk mission when they encountered a large Mohawk war party on their way to strike at Fort Richelieu. The two, now treated as captives, were carried back to the Mohawk village of Osseronon by the expedition. Although a popular figure within the tribe it was not enough to spare Jogues's life. Before any objections could be raised, both he and Lalande were assassinated on October 18 and their bodies thrown into the Mohawk River.

With the reentry of the Mohawk into the conflict the question now became where and when the Iroquois should strike. The confederacy would certainly return to its old tactics and shut down the fur trade to New France, but for the moment the Iroquois briefly turned their attention to Fort Orange. Kieft had been replaced by Governor Peter Stuyvesant, an old soldier and the former governor of Curacoa. "Wooden Leg," as the Mohawk began calling him after his artificial appendage, began his tenure on a curious note by attempting to stop the illegal sale of guns to the natives. Several individuals were accused and arrested for being involved in the contraband trade, but few were actually punished. The issue had become too confused to enforce a coherent policy. For a moment the Mohawk and their Iroquois brothers pondered the motives of the Dutch aristocrat but only for a moment. Whatever his public display, Stuyvesant found himself under orders to continue the arms trade with the Mohawk so as not to upset these valuable allies. There was really little choice given that the new peace treaty between the Mohawk and the French not only threatened to shift the fur trade north if the flow of guns did not continue but also opened up the very real possibility that their trading partners might turn on the colony if this should happen.[11]

The Huron, upon learning in the spring of 1647 that the peace treaty was no longer in place, turned to direct peace negotiations with the Onondaga. In fact the Huron, which like the Iroquois was a confederacy of four nations, did not seem overly alarmed by the resumption of hostilities with the Mohawk. On the surface this was understandable. During the peace a great deal of wealth and goods had made their way into the Huron Confederacy. Nor were the Huron a weak opponent. Although perhaps not as aggressive as their adversaries, their numbers roughly matched those of the Iroquois, and if the allied Algonquin were counted their numbers actually surpassed those of the Iroquois. They were also equipped with firearms through their French allies, although the price the French demanded for these weapons limited the number in the tribe's hands. Taken together this helped redefine Huron strategy. First they would approach the Onondaga with overtures of peace in hopes of politically dividing their opponents. This would be followed by the old principle of encircling the Iroquois through cementing an alliance with the Susquehannock. It was a sound plan and strangely effective enough to cause the demise of the Huron nation.

The Huron overtures to both the Susquehannock and the Onondaga bore fruit. The Susquehannock were pleased to renew their old alliance with the Huron, a tactic that had been used before to moderate the ambitions of the Five Nations. The Onondaga were also interested in what the Huron had to say. This smaller Iroquois tribe was not as heavily involved in the ongoing conflict, nor were they in the position to accept the losses involved in a protracted military operation. Also, just like the Mohawk, an Onondaga-sponsored truce with the Huron and the French elevated the tribe's status within the confederacy, while a prolonged war did nothing but weaken their position.

The initial response on both fronts to the Huron efforts had the net effect of pushing the Huron leadership closer toward complacency. A false sense of security took hold of the tribe's attitude toward the conflict. This was further reinforced by the seemingly difficult logistics encountered by their enemy. Given the distances involved and the time required to cover these distances, a large Iroquois army could not in any practical form mask its movements from the Huron scouts. Thus, ample warning would always be forthcoming should a large-scale invasion be mounted against the Huron villages. This coupled with the ongoing diplomatic efforts and the strength of the Huron Confederacy seemed to squash any fears another conflict might bring.

The Huron, however, had miscalculated their adversaries' fear. Seizing or blocking the French fur trade was one thing, but as the Mohawk and Seneca looked toward the developing situation they soon realized that this was now a secondary consideration. The renewal of the Huron-Susquehannock alliance coupled with the influence the Huron maintained over the Neutral nations of the west had now encircled the confederacy, posing a threat to its very existence. Just as importantly, diplomatic efforts had swayed the Onondaga toward neutrality, and news now reached both tribes that the Cayuga were also interested in peace negotiations with the Huron. If this effort reached fruition, how long would it be before the Oneida followed suit? A politically divided confederacy would leave an isolated Mohawk in the east and an isolated Seneca in the west, both vulnerable and unable to come to the assistance of the other and both encircled by their enemies. For these two tribes the matter was no longer about the fur trade but the future of the confederacy.

The Mohawk and Seneca were in a difficult position. The Dutch were more than happy to provide weapons and materials but showed no interest in becoming involved in a conflict with New France while the participation of the Onondaga, the Cayuga, and even the Oneida was questionable at best. Neither tribe wavered from the task before them, however, and throughout 1647 and 1648 both Seneca and Mohawk war parties descended upon the St. Lawrence and Ottawa valleys, looking to reestablish their former blockade. In this regard they met with mixed results. The Seneca scored some success against the Huron when they raided the frontier village of St. Joseph, but a large Mohawk war party to the east was defeated in the vicinity of Three Rivers when it tried to intercept a Huron fur fleet. Perhaps the best gauge of the Seneca and Mohawk efforts over this period can be seen in the number of furs reaching New France in 1648. A large Huron fur fleet of some 60 canoes and 250 men reached Three Rivers in July, while the fur trade at Tadoussac, farther down the St. Lawrence, exceeded its previous year's totals.

For the leadership of the Mohawk and Seneca it was clear that their current efforts had failed to stem the flow of furs reaching New France, nor was it sufficient to alter Huron policy toward the confederacy, even though efforts by the two tribes had cut off communications between the Huron, the Neutral nations, the Onondaga, and the Susquehannock. What was required was a more perilous undertaking, one that would strike at the heart of the Huron Confederacy and eliminate the Huron from the equation once and for all. After some debate it was agreed that two large war parties, one Seneca and the other Mohawk, would both strike at the main Huron villages near Georgian Bay. With a plan agreed upon there was still a logistical matter to overcome. The Huron were correct in their assessment that any large Iroquois army moving north would be seen long before it reached Huron territory, thus leaving the Huron ample time to prepare a defense. To deal with this problem it was agreed that Mohawk and Seneca forces would move north in the fall of 1648, conduct their normal raiding operations, and then winter in the area. This would leave both forces in a position to strike at the Huron early the next spring, when they least expected such an attack.

The destruction, or perhaps better stated dispersion, of the Huron nation began on March 16, 1649, when a joint Seneca-Mohawk war party, nearly a thousand strong, fell upon the Huron village of St. Ignace. The surprise was near total and only a handful of Huron escaped into the snowy night to warn the nearby village of St. Louis three miles to the northwest. Leaving a small detachment to secure their prize the Iroquois war party marched on St. Louis the next morning. Warned by the survivors of the previous night's attack most of the inhabitants had fled, but some eighty Huron braves chose to defend the town's walls. Their heroic defense blunted the Iroquois attack, but in the end it was simply overwhelmed, and by noon St. Louis was in flames.

With this the Seneca and Mohawk retired to St. Ignace and prepared for their next operation. A half dozen miles away lay the strategic Huron town of St. Marie, a fortified mission and trading center that housed several thousand Huron. It was agreed, after detachments returned from scouting the village, that this would be the next target. But as the Iroquois assembled for their trek on the morning of March 18, 150 Huron warriors launched a counterattack on St. Louis. The brazen move caught the Iroquois off guard, and the rest of the day was consumed in fighting off this effort, which whittled the Huron detachment down to only a handful of survivors.

While the inhabitants of St. Marie abandoned their homes, and the Huron braves within the village prepared for the oncoming onslaught, the Seneca and Mohawk sachems held council within the confines of St. Louis. The Huron counterattack, pressed home with reckless abandon, had rattled the Iroquois chieftains. They were deep within Huron territory, and now fears that the Huron were massing for a larger stroke derailed their plans to assault St. Marie. Thinking better of their position, the Iroquois war party departed the morning of March 19, but not before they tied their prisoners to the structures within St. Ignace and then put the town to the torch. Some seven hundred Petun, allies of the Huron, pursued the retreating Iroquois war party for several days but always at a distance for fear of being outnumbered and short on supplies.

The Seneca-Mohawk offensive had dealt the Huron a severe blow, burning two villages and killing some three hundred warriors at their own loss of perhaps half that number, but militarily it was hardly a death blow, and certainly as they made a hasty retreat south, the Seneca and Mohawk must have felt that they had missed an opportunity to crush their enemy. But as fate would have it, fear would complete what they could not.

Although the threat was gone, panic took hold. The Iroquois attack, on a scale never seen before, had struck at the heart of the Huron nation during a season in which warfare was not conducted. The tales of horror continued to magnify as they spread from one village to another, and although militarily little had been lost, any sense of security was shattered. The Huron were no longer safe, for the men of the longhouse would be back, of this they were all sure. The psychology of flight ruled supreme and was the only option left in the minds of most. Father Ragueneau at St. Louis attempted to quell the rumors with reason, but it had little effect. One by one over the next two months the Huron burned their villages, a task that would have taken five times the number of Iroquois warriors that burned just two, and abandoned their homelands. Some took refuge with the Neutral nations, others with the Ottawa and Petun. A few hundred undertook the long trek to Quebec to become known as the Huron of Lorette, the only members of a once-mighty tribe to still bear its name. Some, resigned to their fate, surrendered to the Iroquois, but the bulk, some eight thousand in number, retreated to the Jesuit mission on nearby St. Joseph Island (today Christian

Island). Ragueneau, realizing that the barren isle could not sustain its new population, urged a migration north toward the Ottawa, but the Huron were not interested in his words. Here many spent the summer in perpetual fear having "postponed death rather than prolonged life, by living either in the woods on a few bitter roots and wild fruits." Although the Jesuit fathers distributed what supplies they had among the refugees, nothing could prevent the impending misery that winter brought. "It was a frightful thing to see," one Jesuit recorded, "instead of men, dying skeletons, walking more like shadows of the dead than like bodies of the living. . . . Many who, aided by our alms, escaped the scourge of hunger, were attacked by a contagious disease, which in a few days made great slaughter, especially among the children. There remained nothing but war to ruin them altogether, and this failed not; and thus they were at the same time smitten with all three scourges."[12]

By spring what little was left of the original eight thousand departed the isle and scattered to the four points of the wind. The Huron nation was no more.

CHAPTER TWO

New France and New Netherland

However surprised the Iroquois might have been by the sudden collapse of the Huron Confederacy, it did not translate into hesitation. In the fall of 1649 the warriors of the longhouse shifted their attention toward the Petun and the Neutral nations. The first of these, the Petun, had no intention of going without a fight. News of an advancing Iroquois force reached the Petun homeland in early December. Not waiting to share their neighbor's fate a large Petun war party left the village of St. Jean to intercept the Iroquois. It proved a fatal mistake when two days later the Iroquois detachment they sought fell upon the town. When the Petun war party returned they found the village a smoldering ruin, and after a brief delay to gather together what was left, the remainder of the tribe, like the Huron, abandoned their homelands before the Iroquois onslaught.

The Neutral nations were simply a victim of geography. They posed no real threat to the Iroquois, and although most of their trade was conducted with the Huron, they showed little sympathy toward the latter when they sought refuge from their enemies. Although the Neutrals were not hostile to the Iroquois, they occupied a strategic position south of the Petun, between Lake Ontario and Lake Erie, which blocked the confederacy's westward expansion toward the fur-rich territories of the upper Great Lakes. An obvious target, all that was required was an excuse on the part of the Five Nations to begin the conquest. Several were fabricated in quick order, and by the spring of 1651 Mohawk and Seneca war parties were striking at the villages of the Neutral nations. The Neutrals struck back at the nearby

Seneca, burning one of the Seneca's frontier settlements and massacring its inhabitants, but it was already too late. By the summer of 1652 the Neutrals had gone the way of the Huron and the Petun, seeking shelter where they could find it with nearby tribes.

For New France all indications were that 1653 would bring a dark shadow down upon the colony. Their traditional allies and trading partners to the west had been routed, and for the last five years not a single fur fleet had descended the Ottawa nor reached Montreal. The small towns and hamlets along the St. Lawrence were under constant threat, calling into question their meager defenses and prompting plans for their evacuation. Even the defenses of the larger towns were suspect. The previous year a party of Oneida and Mohawk had routed a detachment of French near the outskirts of Three Rivers. The governor of the town, Duplessis Bouchart, and two other defenders fell in the skirmish while more than a dozen were captured. Nor were Quebec and the fledgling settlements of Montreal any exception, as Mohawk war parties pressed upon both in a running barrage of raids and false alarms that left the fields untended and the citizens sleepless. It seemed clear to all that the Iroquois were massing for a final push that would drive the French into the sea.

Instead, the opposite occurred. News first reached the colony in the spring of 1653 that the Seneca were interested in brokering a peace. The recent destruction of the Huron, Petun, and Neutrals had alarmed the Seneca's western neighbors the Erie, or Cat nation as they were known, and the latter had launched a series of attacks in a preemptive effort to dissuade Seneca expansion in their direction. According to the reports, it seemed the Cayuga were also interested in a truce. Such rumors were reinforced in late June when a party of sixty Onondaga arrived before the gates of Montreal. They came "to learn whether the hearts of the French would be inclined to peace." A portion of the delegation was whisked off to Quebec to treat with the new colonial governor, John de Lauson, while the remainder departed to speak with the Oneida with the intent of convincing the latter to join in the negotiations.[1]

If Lauson was skeptical of the colony's good fortune, this was soon set aside as the Oneida, agreeing to the peace proposal, dispatched an embassy to Montreal. As a gesture of their sincerity, the Oneida representatives informed the town's governor, Paul de Maisonneuve, that six hundred Mohawk had recently set out with the intention of capturing and burning Three Rivers. Maisonneuve immediately forwarded the information to Quebec, whereupon Lauson arranged a rude surprise for the raiders, killing a good number of them and capturing several of their sachems.[2]

The military setback, and the political pressures brought to bear by the remaining members of the confederacy, convinced the Mohawk to join the peace accord. By the first week of September ambassadors from each of the Five Nations had arrived in Quebec, and by early November the treaty had been signed. For the denizens of New France the turn of events was nothing short of stunning. "It is the Iroquois that have made peace," one French chronicler concluded. "Or, rather, let us say that it is God; for this stroke is so sudden, this change so unexpected, these tendencies in Barbarian minds so surprising, that, it must be admitted, a genius more exalted than that of man has guided this work."[3]

Indeed, the turn of events was puzzling. Within a few months the entire Iroquois Confederacy, on the verge of annihilating New France, had reversed its stance. The reasons for this are unclear. Certainly the Seneca, faced with a potential war with the Erie, had the best reasons to seek peace. The Cayuga, influenced by their more powerful brothers, seemed to have simply followed suit, but the reasons for remaining elements of the confederacy to seek peace are not clear. The Mohawk were clearly pressured into the arrangement, and the Oneida convinced after the subject was first broached. This leaves the Onondaga at the heart of the question. This is the same nation that proved so receptive to Huron peace overtures, which forced the Mohawk and Seneca to take more drastic action toward the Huron. The reasons for the Onondaga peace initiative, including threats posed to the tribe by the Erie and Susquehannock, the military commitment and smaller size of the tribe, the opening of trade, and political opposition to what they viewed as Mohawk attempts to lead the confederacy, certainly played a part in opening a dialog with the French, but another reason played an important role as well—fear for their Dutch trading partners.

The late 1640s proved a prosperous time for New Netherland. The end of the ruinous wars under Kieft had allowed the colony to expand and return to some sense of normalcy. At Fort Orange, which had seen little change from these conflicts, the Iroquois wars of expansion had led to an explosion in the fur trade. These wars had also led to an increased Iroquois demand for firearms and powder, which the Dutch traders were more than happy to accommodate. All, however, was not well in New Netherland. Although Iroquois successes had led to a steady stream of furs, it also created a number of problems. First, Iroquois demands for firearms were putting a strain on the supply in New Netherland, such that it became necessary for the government to begin to supply these weapons. Second, the enemies of the Iroquois, looking to launch raids into the Mohawk homelands, had approached Governor Stuyvesant to ask for permission to cross the Hudson during these raids. Stuyvesant had politely refused, but the matter made it clear that one day the Iroquois's enemies might view the Dutch as their enemies as well. There were also many older unresolved issues with local tribes that periodically exploded into violence and threatened to engulf the colony in another general conflict. Lastly, and perhaps most importantly, the English colonies of New England were beginning to press on the northeastern borders of New Netherland.

In mid-1652 the first of three wars broke out between the Dutch and the English. In New Netherland the immediate effects were not military in nature but economic. English coastal and high seas raiders began seizing merchant vessels, slowly cutting into the supply line from Holland and the export of furs. For the traders at Fort Orange this translated into a shortage of muskets and powder, so much so that they convinced Stuyvesant to release firearms from the armory at Fort Amsterdam for trade with the Iroquois, lest the latter turn to the English.

By 1654 matters took a turn for the worse when a dubious paper began to circulate, claiming that the Dutch planned to incite an Indian uprising against the English inhabitants of the Connecticut River valley. The paper, along with a few well-placed words from leading English colonists, reached the ear of Lord Protector Oliver Cromwell. Cromwell responded by dispatching four frigates and two hundred troops under the command of Captain John Leverett and Major Robert Sedgwick to assist the New Englanders in the subjugation of New Netherland. The English fleet reached Boston in June, where it found a populace more than willing to assist in the conquest. The muster drums were beat and corner criers called upon the men of New England to join the crusade against the Dutch. By mid-July the efforts had netted 633 volunteers, including a troop of horse, which, along with the necessary supplies, were loaded onto the English warships.[4]

The news set off a panic throughout the Dutch colony. The defenses of New Amsterdam had been supplemented by a palisade and shallow ditch a few years before, but otherwise little had been done to strengthen the defenses of the town. Stuyvesant set crews to work repairing the dilapidated shell of Fort Amsterdam, but it had to be done secretly so as not to alarm the inhabitants, most of whom it was known would not fight against such overwhelming odds. There were also problems within the colony. The English residents of Long Island, who were almost as numerous as the Dutch of the region, were known to be sympathetic to their country's cause and might openly revolt at any time. With only a hundred soldiers to man a crumbling fort, and a militia unlikely to answer a call to arms, New Amsterdam appeared doomed.

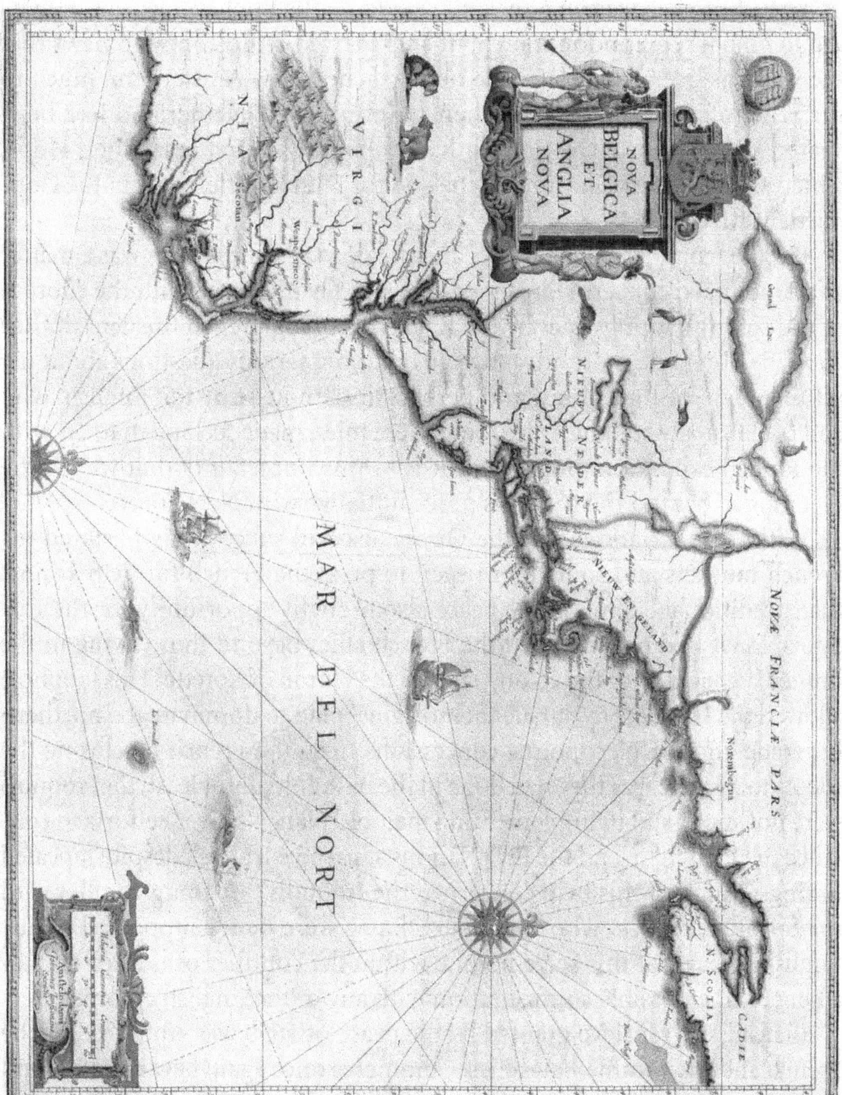

A 1647 map published in Amsterdam showing the boundaries between New Netherland, New England, New France, and the colony of Virginia. (*Library of Congress*)

Luck, however, was on Stuyvesant's side. As the English fleet was preparing to embark, a London merchant ship arrived at Boston with news that the war was over. A day later the news reached New Amsterdam, much to the relief of the residents and their governor. New Netherland had been spared but at a cost. The English had previously seized Fort Good Hope, which signaled the beginning of the end for Dutch settlements in the Connecticut River valley.[5]

For the Iroquois, Dutch affairs and the shortage of firearms was a matter of pronounced concern. Firearm prices steadily increased with the rupture of the colony's supply lines by the English, making French firearms, if they could be obtained, more attractive. In addition, serious questions about the ultimate fate of the colony, and perhaps its conquest by the English, who had traditionally supplied the Iroquois enemies, made seeking markets with the French even more important. It is in this uncertainty that we see the real motive behind the Iroquois peace initiative with New France.

Within a year and a half the Onondaga had successfully bartered for French muskets and soon after began to press the French for help against their traditional enemies. The peace also brought opportunity for the Iroquois, for it had not included the French allies beyond those living in the immediate vicinity of the colony, such as the Huron of Lorette. This loophole allowed the Iroquois to pursue their original plan to dominate the northern fur trade and force economic concessions from the French by closing the routes to Montreal as they had done in the past. Initially at least, the Iroquois were not successful in implementing their old plan. Nor were efforts to convince the French to lend the Five Nations assistance fruitful, despite repeated urgings. Much of this help concerned the Iroquois's ongoing conflict with the Susquehannock, who the French knew were being supported by the English. Clearly at this stage no one within the confines of the colony saw a benefit in a possible confrontation with any of the English colonies.

Instead, the reprieve granted by the peace of 1653 was embraced by the French and their immediate allies. Commerce once again began to flow and the fields were tended to with far less consternation, but as with the previous peace treaties, such an arrangement was short-lived. Although the Iroquois had successfully destroyed the Huron fur monopoly, they had failed to divert it toward themselves. Instead, the Ottawa, located north of the Huron homelands and much harder for the warriors of the longhouse to reach, happily filled this economic vacuum. In 1654 and again in 1656 large fur fleets descended the Ottawa River hauling their profitable cargo ashore at Montreal, and as in the aftermath of the previous peace treaty in 1645, the Iroquois were once again excluded from this trade.

By the summer of 1656 it was clear to even the Onondaga that the peace was a failure. Control of the northern fur trade still eluded them, and although they had granted the French peace they were still unable to secure commercial concessions from them to gain access to this trade. Matters with the Erie and even the Susquehannock had been settled, with the Iroquois victorious in both cases. With these two conflicts resolved, and a stable Dutch source of firearms reestablished, it was time to return to the old path. Soon raiding parties were scouring the upper St. Lawrence and Ottawa Rivers, severing the peace and once again cutting the flow of furs to New France.

The termination of the 1653 peace accord came as no surprise to the French. In reality the raiding had never really stopped, but the scale and frequency of the attacks had decreased. The colony had used the time allotted to it to increase its numbers and bolster its defenses, but even so, some of the darkest days of the settlement lay ahead. For New France's native allies, who had not been included in the treaty, the attacks increased in focus and fury. Between 1656 and 1665 the Five Nations launched no less than forty expeditions against the French and some thirty more against her allies. Montreal and Three Rivers found themselves in a perpetual state of siege, and the fur trade had devolved to a shadow of its former self. "I would almost as soon be besieged by Goblins as by the Iroquois," one observer noted. "The latter are hardly more visible than the former."[6]

The end result was a large swath of Iroquois-controlled territory running from the Ottawa River in the east to the shores of Lake Michigan in the west. But all was not well with the Five Nations. By the mid-1660s a series of events had drained Iroquois resources. They began with a series of military setbacks. In 1661, two Mohawk expeditions were defeated, the first by Mahican-led forces and the second by the French-allied Ottawa. The latter, coupled with more determined French resistance, were able to use their victory to expel the Iroquois from the lower Ottawa River valley and reestablish direct communications with their French allies. A new conflict with the English-armed Western Abenaki in 1663 fared poorly as well, and raids against Algonquin New England tribes spawned a series of counter raids that penetrated deep into the Mohawk heartland. Resources were also being drawn away as the Five Nations resumed their long struggle against the southern Susquehannock and Delaware tribes, who began intercepting Seneca trading parties bound for Fort Orange and struck with such ferocity that the Cayuga were forced to move farther north.

As severe as the military toll was on the Five Nations, far more damaging was the arrival of European plagues in 1662. There are few records from the time to give an accurate tally of the devastation wrought on the Iroquois nations, but the fact that Jesuit missionaries recorded baptizing three hundred dying infants in one village during the height of the epidemic gives a sense of its scope. If these events were not enough, two more were forming that would alter the future of the confederacy.

The late 1650s and early 1660s were a trying time for New Netherland as well. Having narrowly avoided an English invasion in 1655 Governor Stuyvesant turned his attention toward colonial rival New Sweden on the Delaware River. The two colonies had been arguing over land claims and trade for over a decade before Stuyvesant finally decided to settle the issue with force. The tiny Swedish colony, which numbered no more than a few hundred, surrendered in a few weeks and became part of New Netherland. This matter had no sooner been settled when the specter of another Indian war struck the Dutch. Reminiscent of Kieft's conflicts, a dozen tribes along the lower Hudson River, many still embittered by the previous conflicts, unleashed their fury on the colony. Once again settlers found themselves abandoning their farms and villages as nearly two thousand natives drove them into the confines of New Amsterdam.

Realizing that the colony could not afford another Indian conflict Stuyvesant negotiated a peace that restored some sense of calm. It was an unsteady arrangement, and four years later it was broken when five hundred Esopus braves launched an attack on the village of Esopus and its outlying communities. Panic once again ensued, but this time the Dutch responded with a military expedition of their own, which brought the tribe to the peace table the next year. It was perhaps too optimistic to believe that the treaty would hold. On June 7, 1663, the Esopus Indians, still smarting under their past differences with the Dutch, once again launched a surprise attack on the village of Esopus. While the bulk of the male population of the town tended to their fields, a large number of natives entered the village under the pretext of trading with the settlers. The normal routine of the day was soon shattered by war whoops and the sound of gunfire. Ambushes were laid for the men returning from the fields while the town suffered the wrath of the onslaught. Those left in the village eventually rallied and drove off the attackers but not before thirty of their number lay scattered among the ruins, many burnt beyond recognition, while another thirty-four, primarily women and children, were led away into captivity. The Dutch response to the Second Esopus War was much different than the first. The scale and scope of the massacre at Esopus left no questions as to the aim of the outcome—that being the total elimination of the Esopus Indians and their allies. The fact that the Esopus Indians had broken the Mohawk-Mahicanbrokered peace treaty politically isolated the tribe, which facilitated the effort, and by the end of the year the task had been accomplished.[7]

For the two thousand or so Dutch settlers of Orange, as the village about the fort became known, the fury of the Esopus Wars was a removed distraction. Safely nestled within Mohawk territory, they had little to fear from the southern river tribes, who had no intention of provoking their much stronger Iroquois neighbors. The problems these settlers faced were more of an economic nature. Iroquois setbacks directly translated into falling fur profits. Still, this was viewed in the light that 1663 had proved an exceptionally difficult year for the colony. The year had begun with an earthquake that rattled the Hudson valley and was followed by unusually heavy rains that flooded the river and carried away the already-sown crops. A smallpox epidemic was next, striking just before the outbreak of the Esopus conflict.

With the turn of the new year hope once again returned to the Dutch colony. The smallpox epidemic had subsided, and when the spring rains came it was clear that the deluge of the previous year would not return. Reports also arrived that a massive Seneca war party was bound for the Susquehannock homelands, an event that would certainly reverse the falling fortunes of the Iroquois. Optimism took hold and it seemed that opportunities abounded. That is until news arrived that an English fleet was bearing down on New Amsterdam.

Stuyvesant had heard rumors that things were not well between Holland and England, but he did not know until word of the English fleet reached him that war had once again broken out between the two nations. The governor, who was at Fort Orange at the time, raced down the Hudson for New Amsterdam, calling out the militias of the towns along the way and ordering them to rendezvous at Fort Amsterdam. Most nodded at the orders but did little else. A war between New Netherland and the English colonies was one-sided enough, but with Old England now involved no one was interested in participating in such a lopsided affair.

The governor reached New Amsterdam in time to watch the English fleet, which consisted of three frigates, a brig, and a number of support vessels carrying three hundred troops, drop anchor before Manhattan. With little in the way of time before him Stuyvesant began organizing a hasty defense. The town's militia was called out and every third man within the limits of New Amsterdam was ordered to begin work on the city's defenses with spade, shovel, or wheelbarrow. Carriages were hurriedly constructed for eight cannon that were to be added to Fort Amsterdam's current complement of fourteen, while on the land side of the island work was started on a trench and a crude breastwork.

On September 2, after having seized Staten Island, the English commander, Major Richard Nicolls, demanded the surrender of New Amsterdam. A parley ensued over the next few days in which representatives, acting on the governor's behalf, presented legal arguments as to the validity of Dutch claims to the colony. Nicolls politely listened to their assertions and when it came time for his response he informed the delegates with a shrug that such arguments were reserved for heads of state. As far as he was concerned his king had ordered him to seize New Amsterdam and that was his intention. Searching for an opening the envoys replied, "Friends will be welcome if they come in a friendly manner." Nicolls, however, irritated with the delays responded sarcastically, "I shall come with my ships and soldiers, and he will be a bold messenger, indeed, who shall then dare to come on board and solicit terms." When the dejected Dutch deputies threw up their arms and asked, "What, then, is to be done?" Nicolls ended the meeting with, "Hoist the white flag of peace at the fort, and then I may take something into consideration."[8]

Nicolls's response left Stuyvesant in a precarious position. Fort Amsterdam was a dilapidated structure incapable of surviving more than a few cannon shots before collapsing, and mounting only a few light brass cannon it was doubtful whether it could even damage the English warships, which bore ten times as many guns of a much larger caliber. Not that it would matter: the master gunner had estimated that there was only enough powder for a day's firing. The fort's company of 150 soldiers could be counted on to fight, but the 250 or so militia of New Amsterdam had refused to risk their lives in such a one-sided affair. All work on the city's defenses had stopped and not a single burgher would answer the call to arms. Still, Stuyvesant was determined to resist. An old soldier, he was loathe to give up without a fight. The cannon were loaded and the smell of lit matches drifted on the fine autumn breeze as several leading citizens pleaded with the governor not to undertake such a folly. Perceiving that Stuyvesant was determined to resist, Nicolls began landing troops below Breukelen on September 4 and ordered a pair of frigates to take up firing positions before the fort. Surveying the warships from a vantage point in one of the angles of the fort the governor finally bowed to the hopelessness of the situation and signaled for the Dutch flag to be replaced with a white one.[9]

A few days later the English sailed up the Hudson and placed a similar summons before the commander of Fort Orange, who consented without delay. The only resistance encountered throughout the colony was at New Amstel on the Delaware River. A pair of English frigates and one hundred English regulars arrived before the settlement and convinced all but the fort's commander, Governor Alexander d'Hinoyossa, and his thirty-man garrison to accept their terms. D'Hinoyossa's small fourteen-gun wooden fort was quickly pounded into submission by a few broadsides from the thirty-six-gun frigate HMS *Guinea* before the fort and its storehouses were pillaged and the tiny Dutch garrison was led off to captivity.[10]

By mid-September the conquest was complete. New Netherland was no more. For the Iroquois, who quietly watched the proceedings, it was a disaster. True, they had signed a treaty of friendship with the English shortly after the surrender of Fort Orange, but this had simply been done for expediency and to allow trade to continue at the fort. The Five Nations had few dealings with the English, and most of these were not good. It was the English of Massachusetts and Connecticut who provided guns to their Mahican and Western Abenaki allies, and it was the English of Maryland and Virginia who armed the Susquehannock and even went so far as to provide troops to guard the Susquehannock villages while their warriors raided the confederacy.

Throughout the longhouses of the Five Nations the winter of 1664 was filled with arguments and conversations as to the nature of their new alliance. For the moment the English, still at war and too few in number to risk altering the status quo, had allowed the Dutch to continue their trading activities at Fort Orange, but this might change once they grew stronger. And what then? What if the English decided in favor of the Five Nations' enemies and refused to trade guns and powder to the Iroquois? What would become of them then? To make matters even more confusing, rumors were that a Dutch fleet was preparing to retake New Amsterdam. Should the Iroquois treat with the English and the Dutch return, would there be repercussions? Just as importantly, would there be repercussions if they didn't?

In August 1665 Iroquois representatives traveled to Albany, as Orange was now known, to meet with Governor Nicolls and Mahican representatives. Nicolls was interested in hammering out a peace treaty between the two nations, and although some efforts were successful along these lines, the Five Nations were more preoccupied with rumors reaching them from New France.

CHAPTER THREE

The King's Hand

THE IROQUOIS SIEGE OF NEW FRANCE reached a breaking point in 1662. After untold years of conflict and numerous pleas and letters from ranking members of the colony, the matter finally came before King Louis XIV and his council. Europe's most powerful king did not focus his typically distracted attention on the subject so much for love of his colonial subjects but because his financial minister, Jean-Baptiste Colbert, had infused the monarch with talk of mercantilism and the profits it would bring to Louis's coffers. Canada, he was informed, if fostered correctly, was a source of revenue Louis could draw upon to finance his ambitions in Europe. There were a number of administrative changes required to accomplish this task, Colbert pointed out, such as placing the colony directly under royal control, but these were trifling obstacles to be left to the finance minister's capable hands. Of immediate concern was the Iroquois threat. If this were not removed the administrative matters would be for naught, and New France would never achieve her true potential.

The king was soon sold on the plan. In late 1662 he ordered the dissolution of the *Compagnie de la Nouvelle-France* and substituted his own authority in the form of the Royal Council of Quebec, which would administer the colony. The following year Louis appointed Lieutenant-General Alexandre de Prouville, the Marquis de Tracy,[1] to oversee the establishment of a royal government and its necessary infrastructure in New France.

Tracy was given vice regal powers to accomplish this task, which, coupled with the marquis's stature, demonstrated the importance Louis placed on the undertaking. In keeping with these actions, Louis placed no less importance when it came to choosing the troops bound for Canada, and in January 1665, one of the premier standing units in the French army, the Carignan-Salières Regiment, was selected for the task.

Transferring some 1,100 men and their supplies across the Atlantic was no simple task for the small and poorly equipped French fleet. A lack of ships meant that the regiment would have to be dispatched in detachments over the course of several months. The first detachment set sail for Canada in mid-April, but it would not be until late May that the last eight companies, along with the newly appointed governor, Daniel de Remyde Courcelle, and the new intendant of Canada, Jean Talon, departed La Rochelle. The supply ship *Jardin de Hollande*, the last vessel assigned to the expedition, finally followed suit nearly a month later.[2]

The regiment and Tracy, whose first mission was to secure French possessions in the Caribbean, arrived at Quebec throughout the summer of 1665 to the repeated celebrations of the denizens of Quebec. In July, with barely a third of his troops in place, Tracy embarked on a course of action. The marquis forwarded detachments to Three Rivers and Montreal to bolster the garrisons of these towns and then turned his attention to a favorite Iroquois invasion route—the Richelieu River. Here he planned four forts, the first at the site of old Fort Richelieu, followed by three more extending south to the outlet of Lake Champlain. As more troops arrived over the course of the summer and fall Tracy forwarded them to the Richelieu to pursue these objectives. By late October three-quarters of his objectives had been achieved. At the former site of Fort Richelieu a new stronghold called Fort Sorel was raised, while farther south Fort Chambly was erected at the head of the Chambly basin, followed by Fort St. Therese a dozen miles farther south. The season was too advanced to construct the last fort envisioned in the chain of posts, but a site had been scouted near the outlet of Lake Champlain and work would start on this the following spring.

These actions brought about the desired effect. The Iroquois had closely monitored the influx of soldiers into the colony and their actions along the Richelieu. Something had dramatically changed with their French enemies, and news of this quickly spread through the Five Nations. In December, Seneca, Cayuga, and Onondaga envoys arrived at Quebec to investigate this new and alarming trend. Tracy carefully crafted the scene as the representatives arrived in the colonial capital. Formations of troops marched to and fro or were stationed in large numbers along the envoys' path. Soon the Iroquois ambassadors found themselves before the stern marquis and his council, flanked by the blue uniforms of Tracy's personal guard and surrounded with the unfamiliar pageantry of a European court.

The Iroquois, somewhat taken back by the projection of power, presented their customary gifts and made note of the prisoners they had returned as a sign of their goodwill toward the French. Finally, in typical Iroquois fashion, the Onondaga war chief Garakontie stood before the marquis and delivered a speech "full of good sense and of an eloquence that had no savor of barbarism." He called upon the French to accept the Iroquois offer of friendship and to end the deaths of so many Frenchmen and Iroquois alike. He offered his condolences for the French recently slain at the hands of his countrymen and concluded with a reminder of all he had done for the French and how deep his bond of friendship was with them.

Tracy accepted the envoys' gifts and presented his own. He also accepted the offers of peace and pledged as much on his part but not without reminding those present that he did so only because he wished to, not because he must. As a sign of his good faith, the marquis then released three Iroquois prisoners to the delegation. So long, he said, as they respected the French and their allies they would not suffer the consequences of the king's arms, and peace would prevail between them. With the proceedings shifting in his favor, the marquis then demanded to know why the Mohawk and Oneida had not sent representatives. Garakontie and his companions made excuses for their eastern allies, but Tracy would have none of it. The king's favors and good graces, he warned them, would only extend to those present. As the Mohawk and Oneida had not deemed it necessary to show themselves, he was not obliged to temper his conduct toward them in any fashion. The delegates nodded quietly at the viceroy's parting words and, having achieved what they sought, returned to their respective villages with news of the agreement.[3]

Certainly the resurgent strength of New France played an important role in the decision of the Seneca, Cayuga, and Onondaga to seek peace, but other elements played into this as well. The confederacy's strength had been tapped by years of conflict and the ravages of disease, and the war against the Susquehannock was not going well. Many of the Cayuga villages had been driven to the shores of Lake Ontario by Susquehannock raids, and the Seneca had been forced to deploy nearly half of their military strength just to escort their furs to Fort Orange. Coupled with the conquest of New Netherland, the uncertain relations with the new English rulers, and their questionable ability to continue to supply the Iroquois with firearms, there was little choice but to seek peace with the French.

As Tracy had pointed out to the Iroquois delegates, the Mohawk and Oneida had elected not to participate in the peace proceedings. Much of this had to do with their position within the confederacy and their long-running animosity toward New France. The Susquehannock located farther south and west posed little threat to the Mohawk, and as a result this tribe had refused to participate in the ongoing conflict. Instead, the Mohawk and many of the Oneida still favored the original plan of forcing the French into an economic basis for peace. Although this approach deviated from that of the western elements of the confederacy, the reasons for it were clear; success would give the Mohawk a lead role within the confederacy. Revenge also seems to have had a role in the decision. The long conflicts with New France, starting with Champlain's original efforts, had fallen mostly upon the Mohawk, which certainly created a generational animosity toward the French.

Thus far Tracy had shown a great deal of patience in dealing with the Iroquois. He had rattled his saber before the Five Nations while allowing them time to formulate a political response. As a result, diplomacy and threat of force had yielded him an agreement with the westernmost tribes while still leaving his options open. Excuses had been made for the Oneida and the Mohawk, claiming that neither had been informed nor given time to send envoys to the peace proceedings. It seems that a little more patience might have brought these last two tribes into the peace accord, but when it came to the Mohawk Tracy's course was different. This may have been because he understood that they were the real force behind the conflict and therefore a blow should fall upon them regardless of what transpired. Or it may have been that with the western members of the confederacy falling in line, he felt a message needed to be sent to demonstrate French resolve. Whatever the case, after showing a great deal of restraint, Tracy succumbed to the urgings of Governor Courcelle and made the unusual move of authorizing a winter expedition against the Mohawk villages.

European military doctrine typically avoided winter campaigns, particularly those in unfamiliar territory. The wisdom behind this became clear when Courcelle, with a force of some five hundred Canadians and regulars, set out from Fort St. Therese in late January 1666. The impatient governor, not waiting for his tardy native guides and ignoring the brutal Canadian winter which had already extracted a toll on his force during the preliminary march from Quebec to Fort St. Therese, pushed forward with the 150-mile march to the Mohawk villages.

The column slowly worked its way down the frozen length of Lake Champlain, huddled together along the tree lines at night to provide at least some measure of shelter against the cold. At length, they reached Ticonderoga and crossed over to Lake George.[4] They moved down the icebound waterway past the snow-splattered bluffs of what would become known as Sabbath Day Point and Rogers Rock to the head of the lake. At this point, even the rudimentary knowledge of the Canadians ran out. Still, the column pushed forward into the upper Hudson valley.[5]

The expedition crossed the upper Hudson River, perhaps near the Great Falls, and entered what was known as the Kayadrossera Mountains. Here, in this neck formed by the upper Hudson to the north and east and the Mohawk River to the south, the column became hopelessly lost. Days were spent floundering through the snow in one direction only to retrace their steps in order to try another direction. The march, now nearly three weeks long, began taking its toll. Every day more soldiers fell out of the ranks or lay motionless under their blankets when the haggard column set out again the next morning.

Finally, on February 20, a number of crude cabins were sighted. Courcelle didn't bother to investigate and launched an immediate attack on the hamlet. For their part, the troops who had suffered the hardships of three weeks in the frozen wild didn't fail to carry out his orders. Pent-up anger over their misfortunes overcame reason, and the occupants of the cabins became the focus of their wrath. The victims were a boy and three old women. A few others were taken captive when the troops came to their senses, and to Courcelle's horror, one of them informed him that he was on the outskirts of Schenectady in New Netherland.[6]

Matters soon deteriorated. A few dozen Mohawk who had come to Schenectady to trade set out to investigate the gunfire and soon began skirmishing with Courcelle's vanguard. After scoring a brief success the Mohawk quickly broke off the engagement when the main body of the French army moved forward. Courcelle was putting his army in order and tending to his casualties when another misfortune befell the expedition. The burgomaster of Schenectady arrived on the scene and informed Courcelle that he had entered the territories of James, the Duke of York. To the governor's surprise he had strayed into New Netherland. But to make matters worse, New Holland had recently been seized by the English, meaning that his troops had inadvertently attacked an English settlement. The burgomaster then informed Courcelle that Schenectady was undefended and that if he wished, he could occupy the village without opposition.

Given the state of his troops this was the last thing Courcelle wanted. Instead he negotiated a release of his prisoners and asked the burgomaster if he could purchase supplies. The latter were obtained at a steep price, and the next evening the French army turned north and began their trek back

A portion of a 1688 French map showing the route taken by Tracy's expedition in 1666 (the dotted line from the bottom of Lac du Sainct Sacrement). The Mohawk (Anniez) villages can be seen to the west of Orange (Albany), while the forts constructed along the Richelieu River during the fall of 1665, and Fort La Motte on the Ilse La Motte in Lake Champlain can be found to the northwest of Iroquois territory. (*Library of Congress*)

to Fort St. Therese. The governor's native guides, some thirty Algonquin warriors, appeared before the beleaguered detachment a day later which greatly simplified the march home. Even so, for many it was too much. Falling behind they either succumbed to the elements or were picked off by small Mohawk detachments that followed the strung-out column. Some four hundred survivors passed through the gates of Fort St. Therese two weeks later. The folly of the venture, which accomplished nothing other than alarming the English, was clear. Over one hundred men had perished; far more than any that would have fallen in most Mohawk raids.

Even so, the expedition did accomplish one thing. For the first time the French had been strong enough to attempt a strike on the Mohawk villages. This fact only cemented the position of the Seneca, Cayuga, and Onondaga. Further, it brought the Oneida to Tracy's doorstep early that summer. They too wanted peace with the French. The Mohawk, however, even though they sent emissaries, remained fickle toward the idea. Enough so that Tracy decided that another expedition was required to convince them of the error of their ways. The matter also became more precarious in the sense that, although he could not prove it, the marquis suspected collusion between the Mohawk and the newly installed English rulers of New York, as New Netherland was now called. Were this the case, Tracy wanted to make clear to the Mohawk that they would find no safe haven in such an arrangement but, at the same time, not provoke a conflict between the two colonies.

The matter became clearer when in early August 1666 a letter arrived from France informing the marquis that England and France were formally at war. As a result, the king presented two possibilities to his North American deputy: either secure neutrality with New York or attack them using the resentments of the recently annexed Dutch to aid him in this effort. No mention was made of the Mohawk, but it was clear to Tracy that the actions of this tribe were coupled to those of New York. If the marquis chose neutrality with New York, he left the English free to employ their Mohawk allies as intermediaries to carry the war to Canada. The government of New York could then formally claim peace while still carrying out its aims against the French. On the other hand, an invasion of New York could only be accomplished by first neutralizing any threat the Mohawk might pose to an attacking force's rear. Thus, each path brought him to the doorstep of the Mohawk.[7]

This time Tracy would personally lead the expedition. It would be conducted in the fall, a far more conducive time of year for such operations, and it would employ the largest force New France had ever put into the field: some six hundred Canadians, six hundred regulars, and one hundred

Algonquin warriors. A pair of small cannon were even to be brought to hammer down the walls of the Mohawk villages if necessary. The entire force, loaded into small boats and canoes, would sail up the length of Lake Champlain and Lake George, allowing for a much faster and easier march than Courcelle's expedition and, if they were lucky, an opportunity to catch the Mohawk by surprise.

Although the troops were scheduled to rendezvous at Fort St. Anne on September 28 and set out for the Mohawk homelands in one force, a number of the contingents were inevitably delayed. Governor Courcelle, however, "yielding to his customary impatience to gain the scene of action," had already departed with an advance force of four hundred men before Tracy was able to leave with the main body on October 3. The rear guard, under the command of Captains Berthier and Chambly, followed a few days later, and by October 5, the flotilla of three hundred boats and canoes was working its way up the rain-swept length of Lake Champlain.

Unlike Courcelle's previous effort, Tracy's march encountered few problems, even with the intervention of heavy autumn rains. Led by their Indian guides, the troops disembarked at Ticonderoga and carried the boats, canoes, and supplies, including the two small cannon, through the damp fall foliage over to the choppy waters of Lake George. From here the detachments, now reformed into one group, advanced quickly up the length of the lake into the upper reaches of the Hudson valley. When the army crossed the upper Hudson waterway, it became apparent that any element of surprise they had hoped for was gone. Mohawk scouts were seen signaling each other from distant mountaintops and on occasion fired a few ineffective long-range shots at the column or shouted insults down upon the Frenchmen.[8]

A few days out from the Mohawk villages, a brief skirmish occurred between a party of Mohawk and a number of Algonquin scouts. The Mohawk broke off the engagement almost as quickly as it had started, but it was enough for Tracy to accelerate the pace of the march. Although his presence might be known, there was still a chance to launch an attack before the enemy could bolster their defenses. Within striking distance of his goal, the general ordered a forced march on the night of October 15, and by dawn the little army found itself arrayed before the first of the Mohawk villages.

What they expected to find was a small hamlet of huddled longhouses perhaps surrounded by some crude defensive outworks. What they found instead amazed them and in Tracy's mind lent credence to his theory of collusion between the Mohawk and the government of New York. Before them lay what appeared to be the work of a military engineer: a veritable wooden fortress of triple palisades, at least eighteen feet in height, with bastions arranged at each corner. Within this fortification lay as many as twenty longhouses, each with a storeroom packed to the ceiling with maize and beans in such quantities that it was estimated it could feed the entire population along the St. Lawrence for two years. There were even casks of water stored throughout the fortress to fight fires should the village be attacked and firing platforms constructed along the length of the stronghold's walls. The Mohawk "castles" were truly an impressive sight.

As the army arrayed its ranks, a number of Mohawk braves hooted and hollered at the French from a safe distance, but all quickly scattered when the army advanced on the village to the steady beat of the drum. Once again the French were surprised but this time because they found the entire complex deserted. Still hoping to catch the Mohawk, Tracy ordered an advance on a second village half a dozen miles away, but this one proved to be deserted as well.[9]

Empty-handed, the marquis held a council of war to consider his next move. Although there were certainly more, the two Mohawk villages that had been seized were the only ones known to the French. As the officers debated what to do, an Algonquin camp follower, a woman who had previously been captured by the Mohawk, approached Courcelle and informed him that there were two more villages a short distance to the west. Courcelle ordered the troops forward and, true to her claim, the detachment found another deserted "castle" an hour or so later. It was late in the day, but at the insistence of their guide, Courcelle and his men set out for another village a short distance away.

This village, known as Andaraque, was the largest of the four, and unlike the others was not completely deserted. Two old women, an old man, and a small child were found huddled within its confines, which like the other "castles," was stocked with the fruits of a bountiful harvest and the personal belongings of its inhabitants. The fortress also held more gruesome undertakings. Scattered about the cinders of a large fire lay the half-tortured, half-burnt remains of a number of Mohawk captives. It was a poignant reminder for those who had lost sight of the expedition's purpose among its hardships.

The captives informed Courcelle and Tracy that the Mohawk retreating from the other villages had planned to make a stand at Andaraque, but the number of French before them and the beat of their drums squashed whatever courage they possessed. Panic soon took hold, and the whole had fled into the woods, leaving their homes and personal belongings behind. The story, which became the official French line, is interesting but unlikely. The

Governor Daniel de Remy de Courcelle (left) and Lieutenant-General Alexandre de Prouville, the Marquis de Tracy. (*Library and Archives of Canada*)

abandoning of their villages was a deliberate choice on the part of the Mohawk and when considered was the only logical decision that could be arrived at. The scattered positioning of the villages meant that they could not support one another in the event of an attack. Nor were the Mohawk interested in fighting a stand-up European-style battle, which would have heavily favored the French and probably would have led to the destruction of their tribe. With no time to ask for help from the English or their confederate allies, and the likelihood that neither would have been willing to intervene, this left only one choice: flight. In doing so they would sacrifice their homes in exchange for the survival of the tribe and the opportunity to fight again another day.[10]

In their haste to arrive at a decision, the Mohawk had severely underestimated the position of Tracy's army as well as their own options. The French were hundreds of miles from their nearest base with no supplies other than what they carried and in hostile and unfamiliar territory with no likelihood of reinforcements. Had the Mohawk defended their "castle" walls or, better yet, had they launched an aggressive guerilla campaign against the isolated French column, they would have certainly placed Tracy's command in a dire, if not desperate, position. While one force delayed the main French army, another could have been sent to overwhelm Tracy's rear guard at the head of Lake George with the goal of destroying the rows of neatly gathered boats along the rocky shore. With his retreat cut, Tracy's force would have been open to an endless series of hit-and-run raids as his detachment blazed a trail home through the primeval forest that lined the two lakes. Like a pack of wolves wearing down a bear, the Mohawk could have slashed at the column, allowing it no rest or respite, until the time was right to strike the death blow. Certainly the Mohawk would have lost their homes under such a plan, but as it was, these fixed targets were doomed anyway. The only question, then, became at what price they would be sold. Fortunately for the French the price was cheap. "Certain it is that there is a miracle in all this," Mother Marie de l'Incarnation wrote in her diary. "For if the Iroquois had held firm, they would have caused our army great difficulty and delayed it considerably—fortified and armed as they were and bold and proud as they are."[11]

Although Tracy had captured four Mohawk villages, in doing so he had failed to achieve the decisive military victory he had been seeking. This now left the marquis with a difficult decision. Before him lay New Amsterdam, or New York as it was now called. With its ice-free ports and protected harbors, it was a prize that would transform the nature of the French position in America. Should he seize such a jewel, he would cut the Mohawk off from their Dutch and English trading partners, which would ultimately bring them into the French fold and open all of the Iroquois country to New France. It would give the colony a year-round port from which it could be supplied and reinforced from Europe with ease, while driving a wedge between the English colonies and checking the expansion of New England at the same time. Many of the general's officers, knowing that a state of war existed between the two countries, urged him forward. Thanks to his recent acquisitions, the army was well supplied and had suffered nothing in the way of casualties. The English were known to be weak, the Mohawk were scattered, and the recently conquered Dutch populace would certainly rise up in support of the French.

For an instant the image of the Fleur-de-lis fluttering over the island of Manhattan flitted through the Marquis's mind but only for an instant. He was too tried and practiced a soldier to gamble the fate of his little army and the safety of the colony on such a venture. The Mohawk were hardly defeated, and if he advanced there were no guarantees that the Dutch would come to their aid. Tracy shook his head. No, the risks were too great. The army would return to Canada.

At dawn on October 17, the forest echoed with the sound of rolling drums as the entire detachment was formed up before the village of Andaraque. Captain Jean-Baptiste DuBois, acting under the authority of the intendant, read the official act of possession before the army, which claimed all the settlements, the lands about them, and the items found therein property of the French crown. A cross bearing the royal arms of France was then erected nearby with its completion being punctuated by the cry of "*Vive le Roi*." Mass was said, and with the ceremonies completed the Iroquois village was set ablaze before the army paraded off to the east. The remaining three villages were dealt with in like fashion, leaving them all flickering cinders and ash by the time the army reached their boats at the head of Lake George.[12] By early November the makeshift armada had reached Fort St. Anne, and by the middle of the month the detachments had redeployed to their normal duty stations.[13]

For all those involved, the expedition was hailed as an unparalleled success. Although the Mohawk had not been chastised on the field of battle, many felt that hunger and the trials of winter would exact an even greater toll on the homeless tribe. "Have not a doubt," one Jesuit recorded in his journal, "that almost as many will die of hunger as would have perished by the weapons of our soldiers."[14] It did not prove to be the case. The Mowhawk recovered quickly from the loss of their villages, building new ones farther south, closer to their Dutch and English allies. They also seem to have just as quickly obtained a supply of food either from hidden caches or from their confederate allies, for no records exist to show that they suffered any unusual hardships that winter. Among the towns and villages of Canada, however, all this was cast aside. An air of optimism swept across the countryside and many looked forward to years of peace and prosperity.[15]

As it turned out they would have it. The next spring Iroquois delegations began arriving at Quebec, and this time they included the Mohawk. Tracy demanded the release of all prisoners, and the Iroquois assented. Jesuit missionaries were sent to each Iroquois village, and French fur traders were established in these same villages to redirect trade away from the Anglo-Dutch posts and back toward Canada. Specific hunting territories were established for all tribes, and hostages were given to the French to assure that the Iroquois would abide by the treaty. Satisfied with the conditions, the marquis signed a formal peace treaty with the Iroquois in July 1667, which, with a few isolated exceptions, was to bring peace to New France for almost eighteen years.[16]

CHAPTER FOUR

The French and the Five Nations

For the French, peace with the Iroquois led to the next steps in Colbert's plans to develop the colony. Through liberal land grants and monetary incentives the minister of the marine enticed over four hundred soldiers of the Carignan-Salières Regiment to remain in the colony. This alone was a large boost to the fledgling population, but it also served the purpose of stiffening the core of the colony's militia. Colbert then backed this population increase by sending hundreds of additional colonists from France. Among these were a large number of young women, known as the king's girls, who quickly found husbands in the colony. The result was a population explosion. In 1662 the colony numbered some 2,500 souls, but by 1674, a few years after Colbert's measures were enacted, it had jumped to nearly 7,000 inhabitants, many of whom were children.[1]

The influx of settlers, coupled with the peace, led in turn to an increase in cultivated lands within the colony and the start of a number of industries, such as fishing and logging. Colbert was particularly interested in the latter of these pursuits. The young French navy relied on the Baltic states for its masts. With the wealth of timber in Canada this need could easily be met by the new colony. In addition, with this abundance of wood, there was no reason to believe that shipyards wouldn't become a main staple of the colony as well. Efforts were made to recruit immigrants versed in these trades, but few were willing to leave France, and those who did demanded extraordinary compensation to do so. As to the other industry, fishing, the waters of the New World teemed with opportunities—opportunities that would not only go a long way toward sustaining the colony but that also translated into exports that would feed the growing populations of Europe. Additional efforts were begun as well. Manufacturing of shoes and hats was started, cattle and sheep were dispatched to the colony in hopes of fostering ventures in beef and wool, surveys were launched in search of mineral deposits, and the first brewery was opened, which acted as an outlet for the surplus grain produced by the settlers.

For the moment, however, the most important industry of Canada saw an immediate impact from peace with the Five Nations. With the Iroquois threat removed the native fur fleets, some from tribes who had never ventured to the colony, once again returned to the shores of Montreal. After almost a decade of stunted profits the year after the signing of the peace accord with the Iroquois saw a record 550,000 livres' worth of furs shipped to France. With the profits to be had it did not take the merchants of Montreal long to realize that going to the source of the furs avoided competition and allowed them to pick and choose from the merchandise. Soon waves of expeditions to the native villages of the "high country" were being sponsored by wealthy Montreal merchants. The men who made up these expeditions were known as *coureurs de bois*. Hardy adventurers, these souls braved marauders, traveled hundreds of miles by canoe, lived among the tribes they traded with, learned their language, and often adopted their ways and customs in order to secure the furs they sought. This lucrative occupation soon drew hundreds of able-bodied men away from the development of the colony. The problem became severe enough that Colbert passed directives to the governors of New France to restrict the practice, but once started it proved impossible to stop.

The demand for furs soon pushed the boundaries of New France as *coureurs de bois* traveled farther and farther west in search of new sources. Some of this was under the guise of exploration, but at its heart was always the profit of the fur trade. Nor were just merchants involved in this practice. In 1673 the new governor of the colony, Louis de Baude, Count de Frontenac, organized an expedition to erect a fort near the outlet of Lake Ontario. The rationale behind this fort was to keep the Iroquois in check, particularly in terms of preventing them from enticing the Canadian tribes to bypass the French and trade at Albany. Certainly something could be said for this argument, but the real motives behind the erection of Fort Frontenac were monetary. By placing the fort near the headwaters of the St. Lawrence it would be in a position to intercept much of the native trade that would have otherwise gone to Montreal. It also served as a staging point and supply depot for traders heading west, and under Frontenac's control it guaranteed the governor and his associates, men such as Sieur de La Salle, an ample portion of the profits arising from this traffic.[2]

The erection of Fort Frontenac drew the ire of Montreal merchants, who eventually vented their anger to Colbert. The minister of the marine did not directly accuse Frontenac of promoting his own financial interest through the construction of the fort, but he did chastise the governor for not stopping the expansion of the colony via the actions of the *coureurs de bois*. Allowing such behavior, he reiterated, drained valuable manpower away from the colonial industries that he was pushing so hard to establish. In the same vein, however, Colbert recognized the need to explore the frontier, particularly in terms of finding a western seaport that would link the colony to France during the winter months. Coupled with this he understood in certain instances the necessity to secure these territories in the name of the king, but "as a general rule," he informed Frontenac,

> Should the countries of which you take possession be necessary to the trade and traffic of the French and be open to discovery and occupation by any other Nation that may disturb French commerce and trade. But when such a category does not exist, his Majesty is always of opinion that you may and ought to leave the Savages at liberty to bring you their peltries, without giving yourself the trouble of going so far in search of them.[3]

The king, fearing for the safety of the colony, and looking to avoid costly defense expenditures, made the matter clearer in a later letter to the governor.

> In regard to new discoveries, you ought not to turn your attention thereunto without urgent necessity and very great advantage, and you ought to hold it as a maxim, that it is much better to occupy less territory and to people it thoroughly, than to spread oneself out more, and to have feeble colonies which can be easily destroyed by any sort of accident.[4]

Neither the king or Colbert, nor strict ordinances and licensing conditions put in place by the government against traveling to the native territories, had the desired effect. For one, the profits far outweighed the risks. Second, the *coureurs de bois* had become something like ambassadors among the dozens of tribes that fell within the French economic and military sphere. Removing this influence, which typically prevented these tribes from turning to the Iroquois and English for trade and oftentimes prevented open conflicts between tribes bound to French interests, was neither

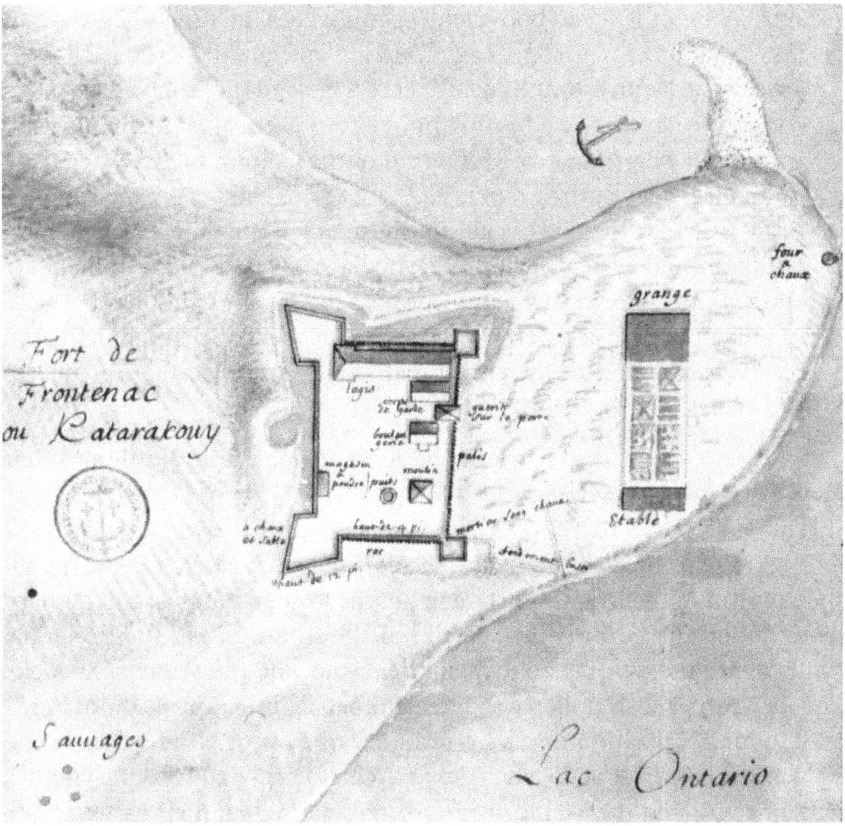

A plan of Fort Frontenac, c. 1685. (*Archives Nationales d'Outre-Mer, Aix-en-Provence, France*)

wise nor feasible. Lastly, Frontenac and his replacements, when they were not involved in profiting from such arrangements, had to walk a fine line with limiting these activities. The Iroquois and the traders at Albany were more than happy to buy furs and did not care where they came from, thus threats of draconian punishments designed to prevent these activities had the net effect of driving the *coureurs de bois* and the tribes they dealt with into the hands of the English. By 1679 the matter had spiraled out of control. The intendant of the colony, Jacques Du Chesneau, who occupied a position second only to that of the governor, informed the minister of the marine that,

> I recur, My Lord, to what relates to the disobedience of the *Coureurs de bois*, and I must not conceal from you that it has at length reached

> such a point that everybody boldly contravenes the King's interdictions; that there is no longer any concealment, and that even parties are collected with astonishing insolence to go and trade in the Indian country. I have done all in my power to prevent this misfortune, which may be productive of the ruin of the Colony. I have enacted ordinances against the *Coureurs de bois*; against the merchants who furnish them with goods; against the gentlemen and others who harbor them, and even against those who have any knowledge of them and will not inform the justices nearest the spot. All that has been in vain, inasmuch as several of the most considerable families in this country are interested therein, so that the Governor lets them go on, and even shares in their profits.[5]

Whether anyone liked it or not, the genie was out of the bottle and New France was expanding west.

The 1667 peace treaty with New France and the disruption of trade through Albany brought on by the Second Anglo-Dutch War also brought about a shift in the Iroquois's state of affairs. Coupled to this, and perhaps more important from the perspective of the Iroquois, was their ongoing conflict with the Susquehannock, the Mahican, and the Western Abenaki. The new pro-French policy was merely practical in nature and not based on a sudden realization that long-term harmony with New France would be in the best interest of the confederacy. With the powerful Susquehannock to their south and the Mahican and Abenaki poised on their eastern flank it made little sense to continue to provoke the French and their allies to the north. The matter was exacerbated by the English seizure of New Netherland in 1664. The new English governor of New York, Colonel Richard Nicolls, wished to continue good relations with the Iroquois, but finding himself with too few troops to watch over a newly conquered territory, fearing an attack by a Dutch fleet, and perhaps suspecting an attachment to the Dutch on the part of the Five Nations, it was next to impossible if not questionable to maintain the flow of firearms and trade goods that the Iroquois sought.

The necessity to secure a supply of firearms and trade goods while minimizing their military commitments pushed Iroquois policy toward the French, but such an arrangement was always viewed as temporary. French failure to militarily support the Iroquois when asked only solidified this outlook in the minds of the Five Nations. Clearly, if the French wanted a lasting relationship they would be willing to come to the aid of the confederacy, but this was not the case. As the years passed and French influence, primarily via the activities of the *coureurs de bois*, spread to the tribes farther west it became apparent that all the French wanted was the Iroquois out of the way so that they could reach other markets. By the mid-1670s the sachems of the longhouses eyed French movements with concern. Coupled with the military post at Fort Frontenac and a newly erected post at Niagara, the colony's contact with the Miami and Illinois tribes had now erected a northern arch about the Five Nations, threatening to flank them with an alliance of unfriendly nations. What the Iroquois required was an end to their current conflicts so that they could address this matter before it became too late.[6]

In 1676 the opportunity came. First, the Third Anglo-Dutch War had secured New York for the English, stabilizing the uncertain status of Albany and bringing forth a new English governor by the name of Edmund Andros who sought closer ties with the Five Nations. More importantly, Andros's first step toward this goal was to provide the Iroquois with a steady supply of firearms. Second, the Susquehannock conflict came to a sudden end, not by the hand of the Iroquois but when a number of English traders launched a surprise attack on their one-time allies and scattered them. Third, King Philip's War, a native rebellion that started in New England in 1675 and raged throughout these northern colonies for the next three years also created another opportunity. At Andros's request Mohawk war parties aided the New England colonists by attacking Philip's forces. This move was to pay dividends when the treaty that ended the war also included a lasting peace treaty between the Iroquois and the New England allied Mahican. At the same time the Abenaki, who had also proved a threat to the eastern boundaries of the confederacy, became embroiled in a conflict with the New England colonies, which removed yet another potential enemy.[7]

The change of Iroquois fortune was soon reflected in the confederacy's attitude toward New France and her allies. With their enemies gone and a secure supply of English firearms behind them, the Five Nations returned to their original plan of redirecting the fur trade toward Albany and establishing themselves as the gatekeepers of this trade. Of first concern were French penetrations into the west, particularly among the Illinois and Miami tribes. Led by La Salle and his companions the French had established trading relations with these nations, but the construction of a few trading posts did not concern the Iroquois as much as the appearance of the *Griffon*, a small bark La Salle had built on Lake Erie during the summer of 1679. Until now one of the most effective and efficient methods the Iroquois had employed to divert the fur trade from the French had been to intercept the native fur fleets on their way to Montreal and Fort Frontenac.

The work of the *coureurs de bois* had complicated this approach but not to the point that they couldn't be overcome with a concerted effort. However, the sight of the forty-five-ton vessel armed with seven small cannons plying the lakes below Niagara Falls threatened this strategy. It clearly demonstrated that the French were willing to go to the source of the furs and handle the transportation themselves. Several vessels of this type were already on Lake Ontario, and armed like the *Griffon* they had little to fear on the open waters. If left unchecked, the French could build fleets of these ships to transport their furs east. Coupled with well-manned fortifications at key staging points such as Niagara and Fort Frontenac, they would seriously undermine any Iroquois threat to their transport and communications lines.

The implications were clear. The Iroquois would have to strike at the tribes who provided the furs before it was too late. The Illinois would be first. Occupying an area along the Illinois River to the confluence of the Mississippi, the Illinois were a confederation of twelve tribes, with contemporary estimates placing their numbers at nearly twenty thousand in some sixty or so villages. A war with this tribe would be a major undertaking on the part of the Iroquois and particularly the Seneca, who would bear the brunt of the effort due to their westward location. The thought of a prolonged conflict, after having borne so many, instilled hesitation in the Iroquois. In September 1680, an Iroquois force of five hundred warriors moved against the main Illinois villages along the Illinois River. Although their effort was well timed in the sense that most of the Illinois warriors were away hunting, the Iroquois were reluctant to attack and instead sent emissaries to the Illinois requesting a parley. The Illinois used the time to send their women and children down river while La Salle's friend Henri Tonty met with the Iroquois. When an agreement could not be reached the Illinois warriors on hand and a few Frenchmen, a force roughly equal to the Iroquois but armed primarily with bows and arrows, crossed the Illinois River and launched an attack on the Iroquois. The ferocity of the attack, coupled with Tonty's embellishment as to the size of the Illinois force, led to a truce, which allowed the Illinois to withdraw from the area. The Iroquois crossed the river the next day and followed the Illinois's slow withdrawal south. Peace negotiations continued for the next few days until the Iroquois launched an attack on one of the lagging Illinois columns. The skirmish was brief and the Iroquois, after having captured several hundred women and children, contented themselves with burning an Illinois village and venting their frustrations on the most helpless elements of their enemies before retreating east.[8]

Pais des Ilinois, "the Illinois country," 1718. The location of Fort St. Louis is denoted by "le Rocher" in the right center portion of the map. (*Archives Nationales d'Outre-Mer, Aix-en-Provence, France*)

The half-hearted Iroquois effort accomplished little. In fact, it caused more harm than good. The Illinois were roused, and the French-Illinois relationship solidified. To make matters worse, on their way back the war party attacked and burnt a Miami village. The plan had been to take advantage of the Miami-Illinois rivalry by using the Miami to help destroy the Illinois before then turning on the Miami, but now this plan was in ruins. Instead the Illinois and the Miami were both pushed toward the French and toward an alliance against the Iroquois. Through the efforts of La Salle and the leaders of several displaced New England tribes who had fought against the English in King Philip's War, a grand council was convened in Miami territory during the spring of 1681 which sealed an Illinois-Miami alliance and incorporated other tribes with grievances against the Iroquois, including the previously mentioned New England ones.

All that remained was to bind this confederation to New France. La Salle did this by calling for a French fort to be built in the heart of Miami country. Construction began on Fort St. Louis of the Illinois in the winter of 1682. "The Rock," as the fort became known, was built on a two hundred-foot stone outcropping along the south bank of the Illinois River, not far from the Illinois village of Kaskaskia, which had been destroyed by the Iroquois a few years before. With two-hundred-foot cliffs covered by the river on three sides Fort St. Louis was in a position of natural strength. The land side, which was the only means to access the fort, was covered by a twenty-two-foot palisade, which incorporated a *cheval de frise* along its length to discourage any attempt to scale the wall. An earthen redoubt backed this wall for additional protection. The rest of the fort's perimeter, which was some six hundred feet in circumference, was covered by a shorter fifteen-foot palisade. Completed in the spring of 1683 Fort St. Louis immediately attracted a large number of natives to the site, and by early 1684 there were some 3,500 natives living near the foot of the fort, most of whom were Illinois, Miami, and Shawnee. As La Salle had hoped, the new stronghold quickly became the nerve center for his anti-Iroquois alliance, while representing French commercial and military commitments to this effort.[9]

The Iroquois turned to diplomacy in an attempt to reverse the consequences of the foolish attack on the Miami. Emissaries were dispatched to the Miami to lure them away from involvement in any alliance against the Five Nations. These ambassadors preyed on the Miami's commercial rivalry with the Illinois and called La Salle's motives into question. This was not the first time such a message had been presented to the Miami, and although it had made some headway in the past, this time the Miami were not interested, and when La Salle arrived, the frightened Iroquois ambassadors departed in the middle of the night, which only bolstered La Salle's reputation among the Miami. It was an unfortunate turn of events for the leadership of the Iroquois Confederacy. Together the Illinois and Miami could muster some three thousand warriors. Added to some five hundred additional warriors from the other contingents of La Salle's new confederation and led by the French, such a force posed a powerful obstacle to Iroquois westward expansion.

From 1681 to 1682 Iroquois raids into Illinois territory continued, albeit at a reduced scale. In part this was because the Iroquois had turned their attention north toward the Ottawa and Potawatomi, who alone provided New France with two-thirds of its fur trade. The death of a Seneca chief in an Ottawa village was all the pretense the Five Nations needed to turn their focus toward two of New France's vulnerable allies. Soon peace overtures and implied threats, punctuated by an occasional raid, seemed to be making inroads toward detaching these tribes from the French interest. For Frontenac and New France the turn of events was alarming. If something wasn't done to check the Iroquois, the Illinois would be dispersed and the Ottawa and Potawatomi involved in a war that would severely disrupt the fur trade.[10]

The colony could not sit idly by while the Iroquois threatened such economic ruin. Even with the evidence before him Frontenac responded in a cautious manner and did not take the matter as seriously as might be thought. This was in part because for almost ten years the governor had kept the peace between the western nations, making him believe that all it required was a little diplomacy. His response to the exploits of the Five Nations was to reassure his western native allies and then summon the Iroquois to a conference in Montreal. Here he could smooth over the problem with a liberal number of gifts and a few trade concessions. If this did not work, "Five or six hundred soldiers," he wrote the king, "would very soon dispel all these different ideas, and it would be necessary only to show them, and promenade them through their lakes, without any other hostile act, to ensure ten years' peace."[11]

It was a reasonable initial approach to the problem, but it failed to capture the clear change in Iroquois attitudes after their victory over the Susquehannock. The Five Nations listened to Frontenac's request for a conference and then balked at its location. They would meet with the French and their allies but in Iroquois territory at La Famine on Lake Ontario. Of course, Frontenac, needing to reassure his allies of French strength, refused. By early fall it was finally agreed that the meeting would take place at Fort Frontenac, but because of the lateness in the year, it would not be until the next spring.[12]

With the recall of Frontenac in 1682 on charges that he had abused his authority, the problems of New France fell to newly appointed governor Joseph Antoine le Febvre de La Barre. La Barre had spent the bulk of his career in the French navy. In 1664 he commanded a French squadron that carried the Marquis de Tracy to the West Indies and was instrumental in helping the marquis fulfill his task of securing French possessions in the Caribbean. With Tracy's departure for Canada, La Barre was appointed governor of Guiana and a few years later was promoted to the rank of lieutenant general. During the Second Anglo-Dutch War La Barre commanded the French West Indies squadron with questionable results. When news of the declaration of war reached La Barre in 1666, he seized the initiative and quickly captured the English-controlled islands of St. Kitts, Antigua, and Montserrat. La Barre then joined forces with a Dutch squadron, which had likewise been successful in securing a number of English-held islands, and attacked an English fleet commanded by Captain John Berry near Nevis. Superior numbers did not help La Barre, who was accused of showing a lack of courage and having taken flight at a crucial stage. The Dutch and French fleets parted ways shortly after the dismal defeat, and not long after La Barre found himself trapped in St. Pierre's Bay, Martinique, by a newly arrived English force under Sir John Harman. Harman besieged the French forts and La Barre's squadron for over a week, ultimately ending in La Barre's decision to scuttle his ships, which all but handed control of the Caribbean back over to the English. The disaster did not seem to affect La Barre's reputation, in part because the Treaty of Breda, signed a few months later, returned the state of the West Indies to prewar status. During the Third Anglo-Dutch War La Barre was once again at sea in command of French warships. He was cited for his bravery on several occasions and served with distinction in both the French Atlantic and Mediterranean fleets. Thus, although La Barre had served in administrative posts in the French West Indies for a brief time, his appointment as governor general of Canada in early 1682 came as something of a surprise, given his primarily naval background.[13]

La Barre had little time to acclimate himself to Canada before the matter of Iroquois expansion and the threat it posed to the colony came before him. In October 1682 he called together the leading civilian, military, and religious leaders of the colony to discuss the issue. First, it was clear that the situation was more pressing than the new governor had thought. Frontenac's peace initiative with the Iroquois was a dismal failure. The Iroquois had simply used these diplomatic efforts as subterfuge to cover their real aims. One participant after another testified to the Iroquois efforts to destroy the Illinois.

Once the Illinois were conquered the Five Nations would turn on the Miami and the Ottawa with the aim of expelling the French from the region west of Lake Ontario, while at the same time inducing the French to believe that a negotiated settlement was just within reach. There was more, but the governor had heard enough. "The object of their enterprise," he later informed the French court, "is to destroy all the Nations in alliance with us, one after the other, whilst they keep us in uncertainty and with folded arms; so that, after having deprived us of the entire fur trade, which they wish to carry on alone with the English and Dutch established at Manate [Manhattan] and Orange, they may attack us isolated, and ruin the Colony."[14]

The matter seemed clear enough, but the question as to how to respond now hung in the air. There were only two paths before the colony: a lasting peace treaty or military action. Although the Iroquois could be enticed into a peace treaty via French trade concessions and annual gifts, such an arrangement was almost certain to fail. The Five Nations had signed numerous treaties in the past and had broken each as soon as it was in their interest to do so. These treaties had been nothing more than maneuvering room for them to resolve side issues before returning to their ultimate goal of becoming masters of the fur trade. Just as important, there was another element working against a lasting peace treaty: the English. Under the guidance of New York governor Edmund Andros, efforts had been made to lure the *coureurs de bois* to Albany, an action Frontenac had considered a major threat. More importantly, under the New York governor a steady supply of firearms and powder was available to the Iroquois. Although there had been no overt action on the part of the English that would trigger a direct confrontation between the two colonies, the council was in unanimous agreement "that the English have omitted nothing for four years to induce the Iroquois, either by a great number of presents or by the cheapness of provisions, and especially of guns, powder and lead, to declare war against us."[15]

This left only a military solution, which La Barre had favored from the outset. The governor's councilors agreed, but such an approach was fraught with questions and perils. The first question was where to attack. The Seneca, it was pointed out by La Barre, were at the heart of the current problem, so they would be the target. The matter then became where and when. The "where" was the easier of the two questions. An attack would be launched from Fort Frontenac across Lake Ontario with the aim of destroying the primary Seneca villages along the south shore of the lake. The "when" was more difficult. First, it involved raising the necessary forces. It was estimated that a thousand men, mostly militia, would have to be employed in the field for several months. To support this effort, supplies would

A detail from Jean Baptiste Louis Franquelin's 1688 map, "Carte de l'Amerique Septentrionale," showing the area from Montreal in the upper northeast to Fort St. Louis in the far west. Also indicated is the distribution of the French allied Illinois, Miami, and Mascoutens (Fox). The Potawami occupied the region between Lake Michigan and Lake Erie, while to the north, the Ottawa stretched from the upper peninsula well past the northern shores of

have to be accumulated at Fort Frontenac, and the garrison of this fort as well as the supporting forts along the upper St. Lawrence would have to be bolstered. Once this was accomplished a fleet of canoes carrying half of the army would depart Fort Frontenac followed by the rest of the army in three small vessels stationed at the fort. The two forces would land along the southern shore of Lake Ontario and then march on the Seneca.

There were no objections to the plan other than that it would take over a year to put in place. First, funds were necessary to procure and transport the supplies. Second, three small barks would have to be built at Fort Frontenac to facilitate the movement of the army. Next, the militia would have to be called out, which placed the expedition in the late spring or early sum-

Lake Huron. The Iroquois had previously secured the area between Lakes Huron, Erie, and Ontario, but were unable to secure the far reaches of the Ottawa River, which became one of the primary fur routes to Montreal. French expansion onto Lake Ontario, including Fort Frontenac, further obstructed Iroquois efforts to cut French fur routes via the waterway. (*Library of Congress*)

mer to avoid interfering with planting or the harvest. Lastly, to support the campaign and guard the approaches to Canada while the army was on the frontier, some three hundred to four hundred soldiers would have to be sent by the king, assuming he agreed to the expedition.[16]

La Barre transmitted his plan and his requests to France for approval and implemented what measures he could to secure the frontier. Reinforcements were sent to the Ottawa and Potawatomi, while envoys were sent to the Iroquois to engage them in dialog with the intent of holding their attention while preparations for the expedition proceeded. La Barre's fear of a major Iroquois offensive against the Ottawa and Potawatomi did not materialize over the course of 1683, and although the two tribes' loyalty seemed to waiver, no doubt due to the idea of gaining access to the cheaper goods provided by the English at Albany, in the end they were not interested in letting the Iroquois act as middlemen for this trade, and hence they stayed firm to the French alliance.

The French court was not initially swayed by La Barre's call for military action, having been convinced by the recently returned Frontenac that a negotiated settlement was the course to pursue. Eventually, however, the king agreed that "as circumstances may arise in a country so distant as Canada which would oblige it to be proclaimed, he empowers the said Sieur de la Barre to begin it, provided he certainly finds himself in a condition to terminate it advantageously in a year's time." Although the response was short on his request for troops and munitions, at least La Barre was granted the money he needed to proceed.[17]

Making no inroads to the north in the spring of 1684 the Iroquois made one last attempt westward. A war party of some two hundred marched into the Illinois country and at once stumbled upon fourteen Frenchmen on their way to trade with the Illinois. The French party was quickly captured and their goods, valued at some fifteen thousand livres, plundered. Buoyed by this success, the war party advanced to the Illinois River and launched an attack on Fort St. Louis. Henri-Louis Baugy, who La Barre had recently appointed to take command of Fort St. Louis, had been warned of the war party's intentions and prepared a rude reception for them. The Iroquois, hoping to surprise the garrison, immediately launched a frontal attack, which was easily repelled. After skulking about the fort for six days, occasionally sniping at its occupants, the Iroquois war party withdrew, with small detachments of Illinois and Miami warriors in pursuit. It was another failed attempt on the part of the Iroquois to break the French-Illinois-Miami coalition, and this time there were to be consequences.

The attack, coupled with concerned letters from the posts in the Illinois and lake country, set La Barre in motion. He would proceed with his expedition even without the troops he had requested from France. Orders were sent to Sieur du Lhut and Olivier de La Durantaye in the "high country" to gather together as many *coureurs de bois* and allied warriors as possible and rendezvous with the army on Lake Ontario. While the militia was being called out, La Barre wrote Governor Thomas Dongan of New York, who had replaced Andros, notifying him of French intentions. La Barre informed Dongan that he had been ordered by the French court to maintain cordial relations with the English and understood that James, the Duke of York, had issued a similar directive. He then pointed out to the New York governor that his grievances and efforts were only directed at the Seneca and the

Cayuga, who he held responsible for the attack on Fort St. Louis. He requested that, in keeping with both sovereigns' wishes, Dongan forbid all arms and ammunition sales to the Seneca as well as punish those who would transfer them such merchandise. Lastly, La Barre politely informed Dongan that, "If you have any cause of complaint against their conduct, you can advance it now, and I shall consider your interests as those of the King my master."[18]

The French governor was caught off guard by the reply. Dongan informed La Barre that there must be some confusion given that the Iroquois were English subjects, but not to worry,

> I intend forthwith to go myself to Albany on purpose, and there send for the Indyans and require of them to do what is just in order to a satisfaction to your pretences, if they will not, I shall not unjustly protect them, but do for your Governmt all that can be reasonably expected from and in the mean time for to preserve and continue a good amity between us I think it convenient, and desire of you that no act of hostility be committed; such differences are of so weighty a concern that they are most proper to be decided at home and not by us.[19]

From here matters only degenerated between the two leaders. La Barre had no intention of allowing Dongan to interfere with his expedition, nor did he accept the idea that the Iroquois were English subjects, while Dongan made the case that the French governor was about to launch an attack into English territory, which was in direct violation of their kings' mutual mandates. After a few rounds of accusations and recriminations the correspondence came to a halt.

Although nothing but a war of words, the correspondence did offer Dongan an opportunity. As he promised La Barre, the Iroquois sachems were summoned to Albany, although not to discuss problems with the French but to provide an explanation as to why they had raided the Maryland frontier. Nonetheless, Dongan used the occasion to warn the Iroquois and press the idea that the Iroquois were English subjects. To his delight the Iroquois, fearing an open rupture with the French and their allies, were willing to declare themselves English subjects and put all their land under the protection of King Charles II. In return the governor urged the Iroquois to hold fast against La Barre's efforts and pledged to do what he could for them, even going so far as to give them copies of the Duke of York's coat of arms to be placed at the head of their villages. In securing this much from the conference Dongan had pressed the limit of New York's claims in an attempt to check French westward expansion, but in reality there was little he could do in terms of direct involvement. Letters from the Duke of York's secretary, Sir John Werden, made clear the extent of Dongan's powers. "Encourage the Indians all you can," he informed the governor, "but not so as to vex your European neighbours. It will be impossible to get the French to give up trading with them, so we must try by our good dealing to make them prefer to trade with us rather than with the French." A few months later Werden was even clearer in terms of the governor's relations with New France. "Use your prudence," he wrote Dongan, "without shocking the Governor of Canada, to discourage the trade of the French with the Indians by attracting the Indians to trade with us."[20]

For La Barre the maddening correspondence with Dongan was nothing more than an unpleasant distraction. More important tasks now filled his mind. Although his numbers were closer to eight hundred than the projected one thousand, the effort to assemble this force at Fort Frontenac was of a scale not seen since Tracy's expedition in 1666. Strings of canoes loaded with supplies traced the upper St. Lawrence as far as La Galette. At this location the supply canoes transferred their cargo to the newly constructed bark, the *Le Generale*. The canoes then returned to Montreal to collect another load while the bark pressed on to Fort Frontenac. Moving the troops proved even more trying. There was a shortage of canoes and a need to build larger flat-bottom vessels to carry the army's field gear, and many of the troops were inexperienced when it came to navigating the perils of the river. Native guides helped alleviate this last problem, but the logistics coupled with a southwest wind delayed the governor's advance to Fort Frontenac by several weeks.

By early August 1684 the bulk of the French army had reached Fort Frontenac. With his forces now gathered about the stone citadel La Barre was buoyed by the arrival of Charles Le Moyne along with several hundred allied warriors, but because the contrary winds had interfered with the passage of the *Le Generale* a shortage of flour stalled any plans to advance across the lake. Although of concern, the delays were not the foremost thoughts in the governor's mind. A letter had reached him a few weeks earlier from Father Lamberville that the Onondaga were in favor of peace and that they had convinced the other tribes to allow them to negotiate a treaty between the French and the Five Nations. If this was not pursued, Lamberville warned the governor, the Iroquois would consider an attack on the Seneca an act of war against the confederacy. After all the prior considerations on the matter La Barre should have dismissed the news, but there were good reasons to consider this new course of action. First, his army was ill-sup-

Detail of the eastern portion of Lake Ontario from a seventeenth century French map. Fort Frontenac ("Katarakouy") is at the bottom or north end of the map. La Famine (Salmon River), and the various paths to nearby Iroquois villages, including the major Onondaga settlement of Techiroguen, can be seen on the south shore of the lake. (*Library of Congress*)

plied, ill-trained, and uncertain of the size of the threat before them. Second, since no reinforcements had arrived from France, these troops represented the bulk of Canada's defenses. Should something go awry, be it the loss of the army or a widening of the conflict as Lamberville had warned, the colony would be vulnerable to a counteroffensive. Lastly, it had been eighteen years since the French had openly warred with the Iroquois, and at that time they did not have far-flung posts scattered about the Great Lakes to defend. The logistics and communications issues involved in accomplishing this task might be beyond the capabilities of the colony.[21]

Against the advice of many and the backdrop of rumors that the governor had given up on a military solution, La Barre dispatched Le Moyne to entreat with the Onondaga. While he waited at Fort Frontenac for word of Le Moyne's mission, supply shortages and illness struck the French army.

An idle amateur army is never a good thing. Food shortages and persistent rumors only made things worse. The wet campground about the fort was hardly ideal, and soon an epidemic of influenza had taken hold. Some relief came on August 21 when a number of canoes arrived, having transferred the contents of the bark to their holds. La Barre wasted no time in ordering bread and biscuits made, and the next day, hoping to prevent a complete loss of his forces to the epidemic, he dispatched two-thirds of his army to La Famine, a small bay on the south shore of Lake Ontario a short march from the main Seneca villages.

Four days later, one of Le Moyne's sons arrived with news that, although Dongan had forbade the Onondaga from negotiating with the French, they agreed to meet with La Barre at La Famine to conclude their talks. It was the news the governor had been waiting for. After seeing to some final details and assigning a garrison to the fort, La Barre and the remaining elements of the army set sail for La Famine a few days later.

For the French army matters were little better at La Famine. Supply shortages abounded and if anything the campgrounds at La Famine were worse than those at Fort Frontenac. This did little to prevent the spread of illness among the ranks. Over 150 men had been struck down by fever, which when added to those left at Fort Frontenac had reduced the army by nearly a third. At the rate things were proceeding there would be no French army if the Iroquois did not arrive soon.[22]

Mercifully, the Onondaga, Oneida, and Cayuga representatives arrived on September 3. The next day a grand ceremony was held to commence the talks. French drums rolled and presents were exchanged to long orations speaking to the goal of peace between the two parties. With the preliminaries concluded Hateouati, who spoke for the Iroquois, asked a gravely ill La Barre why he sought to break the peace between the French and the Five Nations. The pillaging of the French convoy in the Illinois country had not resulted in any deaths and certainly was not reason enough to go to war.

Reparations would be made, Hateouati assured him, which should solve the matter. La Barre accepted the gesture and asked that the Iroquois also return a number of native prisoners they held.

Hateouati, well aware of the state of the French army and the dire circumstances the governor had placed himself in, avoided the request and pressed his advantage. "Why the army?" he asked. Certainly no good would come of this. "I pray," he told La Barre, "you return to Quebec, so that your children may sleep in peace." And from now on, he continued, they should meet at La Famine; Fort Frontenac had too many grasshoppers, which interrupted the Iroquois sleep, and Montreal was too far for them to travel.

To Hateouati's delight La Barre agreed to both requests. He would leave the next day, and from now on they would meet at La Famine. With the advantage quickly swinging in his favor the Iroquois spokesman made clear the confederacy's position. They would cease warring with the Ottawa and Miami, but "regarding the Illinois, I am at war with him; we shall both of us die fighting."[23]

La Barre accepted this statement, although doing so undermined one of the principle reasons behind the expedition. As with the other Iroquois demands, he really had little choice. His army was in ruins. If the Iroquois chose to attack, most, if not all, of it would fall before their onslaught, which in turn would leave the colony open to attack. The number of sick was multiplying at such a rate that when the French embarked the next day it proved difficult to find enough healthy men to load the sick into the canoes. Nor were there any supplies left even if he had wanted to stay. Provisions were so scarce that there was "no more than the trifle of bread I had brought them."

The wreckage of La Barre's army returned to Fort Frontenac while orders were dispatched to Durantaye, who had assembled some 150 French and 550 Ottawa at Niagara, to dismiss his forces. The news infuriated Durantaye, who had gone to great lengths to convince the Ottawa and several other tribes to join the effort. The Illinois, hearing word that the French and their allies had decided to attack the Seneca, had promised over one thousand warriors who had yet to arrive. Now, by ringing the bell but not seeing the venture through, the French appeared as questionable allies.

La Barre, whose health had deteriorated even further, did not wait for his army and departed for Montreal with news of the treaty. There was widespread condemnation of the governor's treaty throughout the colony. Many who had questioned his intentions from the outset now seemed convinced that they had been right all along. The intendant, Meulles, had previously warned the minister of the marine that "I can find no disposition whatsoever in the mind of M. le General to wage war with the Iroquois; I believe that he will content himself with going by canoe to Cataracoui [Frontenac]. . . and then have the Seneca come in order to treat for peace with them and so trick the people, the intendant, and if one dare say it, His Majesty." Now, as the details of the treaty reached him, Meulles penned another letter to the minister informing him that there was almost universal disbelief throughout the colony. As opposed to chastising the Seneca, "he grants them all they ask."[24]

In Paris there was a similar reaction. La Barre's concessions were not acceptable, nor, after some consideration, was La Barre.

CHAPTER FIVE

Rivals to the North

It took the French court over a year to recall La Barre. The order, when it came, spoke to the governor's ill health as the reason for his dismissal, but no one was confused as to the actual reasons. The man chosen to replace La Barre was Jacques-Rene Brisay, the Marquis de Denonville. Denonville was from an old French family of lower nobility, although his father, Pierre, had done much to change his families fortunes, rising to the position of one of the king's councilors before eventually being appointed a major general in 1668. As his eldest son, Jacques-Rene inherited the title marquis and entered the army at an early age. By twenty-six he had obtained a captaincy in the Regiment Royal and three years later was made a captain in the Queen's Dragoons. Denonville served throughout the Dutch War of 1672, quickly rising in rank until he eventually purchased the regiment in 1675, obtaining the rank of colonel in the process. News of his talents reached the highest levels, and upon the conclusion of the conflict he was appointed inspector general of dragoons. A few years later, in 1683, he was promoted to brigadier general. A devout and pious man by nature, Denonville was known for his bravery and, more importantly, his organizational skills and attention to detail. Considered one of the best military officers in France, this alone would have seemed sufficient qualifications for the post of governor general of Canada, particularly given the martial efforts that would be required to reverse the damage done by La Barre, but Denonville possessed another trait that may have been more telling in his selection; he was honest almost to a fault. Given the confusion that surrounded the affairs of New France and the myriad opinions and partial truths that reached Versailles, perhaps this last element was the deciding factor in his appointment.[1]

Denonville's orders, issued to him on March 10, 1685, made clear the king's intentions "to secure the quiet of Canada by a firm and solid peace; but in order that such a peace be permanent, the pride of the Iroquois must be humbled, the Illinois and other allies who have been abandoned by Sieur de La Barre must be sustained, and the Iroquois must from the outset be given, by a firm and vigorous policy, to understand that they will have everything to dread if they do not submit to the conditions it will be his pleasure to impose on them." The king had left it to the marquis's discretion on how best to proceed. A peaceful settlement was preferred, which of course promoted trade and profited all, but if this was not possible then Denonville was free to use whatever resources were at his disposal to bring the Iroquois around by force of arms. As for the English, and in particular the governor of New York who seemed to be supporting the Iroquois efforts, Denonville was directed to maintain cordial relations with his colonial counterparts, "but if the latter, contrary to all appearances, excite and aid the Indians, they must be treated as enemies when found on Indian territory, without, at the same time, attempting anything on territory under the obedience of the King of England." He was also to be aware of English pretensions in Acadia (Nova Scotia). Reports were that the government of Massachusetts had seized several long-standing French posts in this area and had yet to explain their actions.[2]

To carry through with this task the king gave Denonville five hundred troops of the Free Companies of the Marine, but unlike in the past where the designated companies had been simply transferred from their stations in the various ports in France, the marquis was free to recruit what was essentially a battalion of colonial marines. It is something of a testimony to Denonville's reputation that he had no problems raising the troops in question. In fact, many of the senior noncommissioned officers were regular officers who had been placed on half-pay with the army reductions that followed the Dutch war. While the troops were being recruited and marshaled at La Rochelle, the new governor used the time to become thoroughly acquainted with the affairs of New France. What he found depressed and confused him, but he convinced himself that these matters would be clearer once he arrived in Quebec.

With the logistics addressed the marquis set sail for Canada, dropping anchor at Quebec on August 1, 1685. After a brief tour and meetings with the colony's senior officials, he was convinced that matters were in fact far worse than he had imagined. The lure of the fur trade had stripped the colony of precious resources and returned little in the way of permanent measures toward securing it. Added to this, the expansion brought on by this trade had stretched colonial military resources, making the defense and security of these remote posts nearly impossible. Nor were the current fortifications within the heart of the colony adequate. The only post worth mentioning was Quebec, but even here the fortifications had been neglected. At Three Rivers the wooden palisade that surrounded the town was in disrepair and without gates. Between Three Rivers and Montreal Denonville found "not a solitary spot affording the semblance of shelter from an enemy," while Montreal was just as bad, "there being nothing to stop a determined enemy from raiding and burning the town."[3]

There were numerous other problems to contend with as well, ranging from the ill conduct of the populace associated with the fur trade to matters of establishing industries, such as iron foundries. All of these, however, paled in comparison to those concerning foreign threats to the colony. First among these were the Iroquois. Of all the native nations "they are the most powerful by reason of the facility they possess of procuring arms from the English," the marquis informed the French court. "Their large purchases of arms and ammunition from the English, at a low rate, have given them hitherto all the advantage they possess over other tribes." At the moment the question was not whether the Iroquois would attack New France; this seemed unlikely. Instead the Iroquois appeared content to take advantage of the terms of La Barre's peace treaty by concentrating on breaking the Franco-native trade alliance. Once this was done and they had diverted the fur trade to Albany, they could then turn their efforts toward the colony. Backed by English guns and money, New France would face dire days without a major intervention on the part of the king. In Denonville's opinion the only way to prevent this catastrophe was to strike against the Iroquois in order to secure the trade alliance.

While the Iroquois were a direct threat, the English concerned the French governor just as much. "It is well to consider whether the English are not equally, if not more to be feared," he wrote the minister of the marine, "and whether we must not take as much care to protect ourselves against them." To the south, New York supplied New France's native enemies and fueled their ambitions while New England tested the colony's resolve by pressing English claims in Acadia. To the far north another English threat was gathering at James Bay. The establishment of several English trading posts in this disputed area, Denonville pointed out, "will be more injurious to us than in the direction of Acadia: For if their establishments continue as they have

A map of Hudson Bay and the Hudson Straits as they were in 1662 before the founding of the Hudson Bay Company. (*T. S. Drage, Account of a Voyage for the Discovery of a Northwest Passage, Vol. II, 1749*)

begun at the three places on that Bay which they actually occupy, and on the river Bourbon or Port Nelson, we must expect to see all the best of the Beaver Trade, both as to quality and quantity, in the hands of the English."[4]

With external threats posed on all sides it was in the northern direction that the marquis first took action. Over the course of the winter Denonville planned an expedition against the English posts on James Bay. To command this effort the governor turned to a marine captain, Pierre de Troyes, who had sailed to Quebec with the marquis. Denonville ordered Troyes to take a small force, march north, and occupy posts on the shores of the bay. For diplomatic reasons, no mention was ever made of the English or of seizing the existing English posts along the bay. Instead the orders focused on arresting illegal traders and those associated with them "wherever they may be found." If in Troyes's opinion this required seizing a fort to accomplish his task, so much the better as far as the governor was concerned.[5]

Troyes's expedition, which was poorly cloaked in the guise of a law enforcement matter, was hardly the first military act along James Bay. In fact, the short history behind the establishment of European trading posts in this area was filled with treachery and conflict. After the initial voyage of discovery by the ill-fated Henry Hudson, a number of English vessels visited this area between 1612 and 1632. As such, the English were quick to claim sovereignty over the region. The French countered that all of these voyages had been conducted in search of the elusive Northwest Passage, with Hudson and James Bays being nothing more than waypoints for these expeditions. If not, then why had no posts or permanent settlements been erected to support these territorial claims? Nothing was resolved, and for four decades questions regarding claims to this vast uncharted area received little attention and even less debate.

In 1668 this changed, primarily due to the efforts of two French adventurers, Medard Chouart des Groseilliers and Pierre-Esprit Radisson. In 1659 the two men were among some of the first *coureurs de bois* to travel to the shores of Lake Superior. The pair traded with the Petun and wintered with the Sioux in upper Minnesota, returning to Montreal the following year with three hundred canoes filled with furs and news of trading opportunities to the west. Groseilliers followed this lucrative venture with another expedition the following year. It was during this time that he first heard news of Hudson Bay and the prosperous beaver opportunities that existed among the tribes in the area. After another expedition, which proved so profitable that it put him at odds with the traditional fur-trading establishment, measures to limit the *coureurs de bois* and other private traders were put into effect by the colonial government. The ultimate aim, of course, was to promote the practice of having the tribes bring their furs to Montreal, thus keeping the manpower of the colony at work improving the settlement. Groseilliers was fined and had a portion of his furs confiscated. The trader argued against such a policy but to no avail. He then turned to his brother-in-law Radisson for advice and it is likely that Radisson, after hearing of Hudson Bay, convinced Groseilliers to seek money in France to finance an expedition.

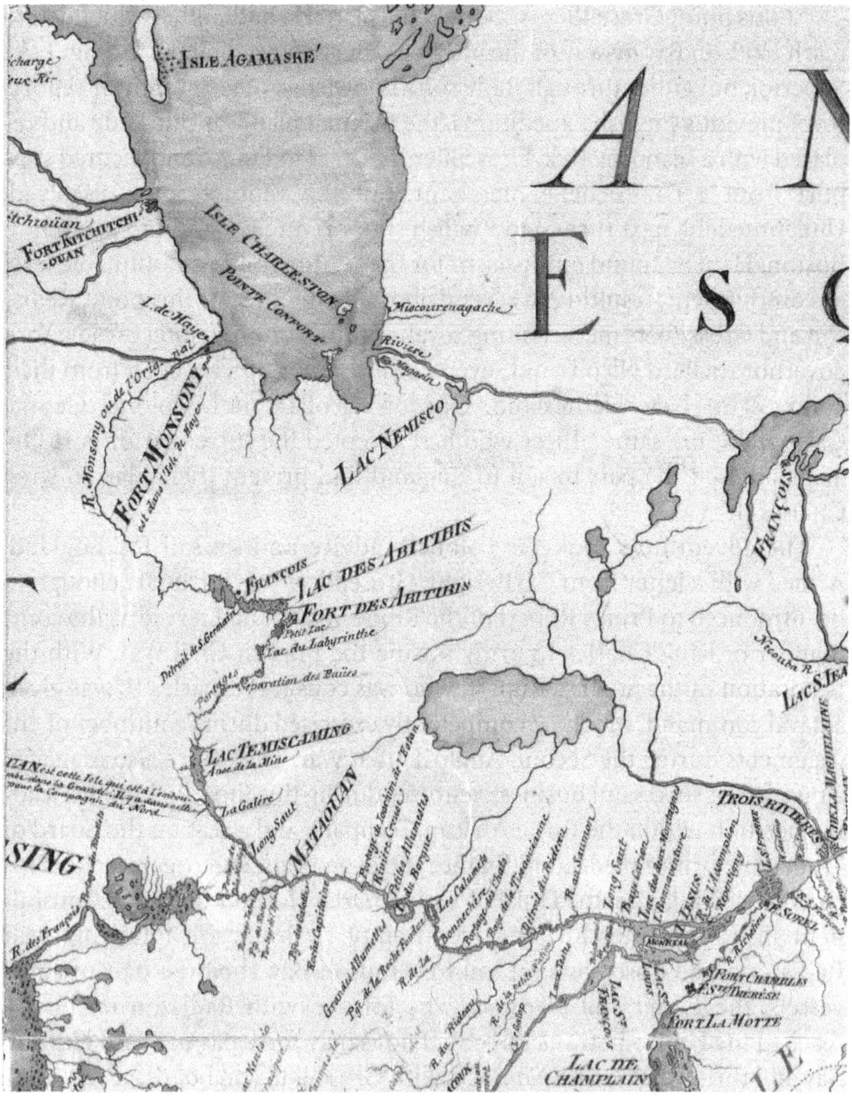

A section of Franquet's 1688 map of North America showing the region from Montreal and Three Rivers, north to James Bay. The three posts on James Bay are shown with their French names. The post marked "magasin" on the southeast side of the bay is Rupert's House, while the two posts on the west side of the bay are Fort Monsony (Moose Fort) and Fort Kitchitchi (Fort Albany). One can trace Troyes's 1686 expedition up the Ottawa River to Lake Abitibis (Lake Abitibi) and down the Abitibi River to James Bay. (*Library of Congress*)

At this point Groseilliers modified his plan. He had initially intended to reach Hudson Bay by way of the interior waterways leading north from Lake Superior, but either through Radisson's knowledge of geography or reports from previous English expeditions, the original plan was put aside and replaced with a seaborne trek. Groseilliers traveled to France and secured support from a La Rochelle merchant, but the venture soon dissolved. Undaunted, he next turned to English support and soon found himself in Boston. Here he found enthusiasm for the venture but a questionable level of commitment, resulting in several aborted attempts. At this point Radisson and Groseilliers met a visiting royal commission consisting of New York governor Richard Nicolls and several of his senior officers fresh from their conquest of New Netherland. One of Nicolls's staff, Colonel George Cartwright, the same officer who had accepted the surrender of Fort Orange, advised the pair to sail to England and present their plan to King Charles II.[6]

The adventurers took the colonel's advice and set sail for England. Armed with a letter from Cartwright, Groseilliers was fortunate enough to be introduced to Prince Rupert of the Rhine. Rupert had served as the commander of King Charles I's army during the English Civil War. With the restoration of the Stuarts, Rupert, who was cousin to Charles II, was given a naval command, which he competently exercised during a number of engagements during the Second Anglo-Dutch War. The prince also managed a number of successful business ventures during this time, including a leading position within the Royal African Company and a seat on the Board of Trade. The prince pledged to finance the expedition and organized a company of which James, the Duke of York, Charles II, and Rupert were prominent investors. After an abortive attempt in 1667, the following year Radisson and Groseilliers set sail for Hudson Bay aboard a pair of small vessels, the *Eaglet* and *Nonsuch*. The former, with Radisson on board, reached the Hudson Straits but could not safely force passage into Hudson Bay and turned back. The *Nonsuch*, with Groseilliers on board, successfully navigated the hazardous narrows and made landfall at the mouth of what is now known as the Rupert River at the southern end of James Bay. Groseilliers built a small trading post on the site and later that fall sent the *Nonsuch* back to England loaded with furs. The next year Radisson arrived onboard the *Eaglet* with news that the *Nonsuch* had delivered her cargo and that the investors were so happy that they had purchased a third ship to help carry on the trade at the post.

Radisson was not boasting of the enthusiasm shown by Rupert and his investors. A charter was quickly drawn up asking Charles II for a patent granting a trade monopoly in Hudson Bay. Charles granted the patent in May 1670, which gave the Company of Merchant Adventurers trading into Hudson Bay, exclusive commercial rights in the area, police powers, administrative power, and the power to make war and peace with any native tribe in the region. As for the region itself, it was simply described as all lands whose waters emptied into Hudson Bay.[7]

When news reached Quebec of the English trading post on Hudson Bay it did not take long for the French to object. They disputed English claims and asserted their own, which in general were weaker. In 1671, the intendant of New France, Jean Talon, sent Jesuit father Albanel toward James Bay with orders to ascertain the English position on the waters, to determine the prospects and possible location for a French trading post, and to convince the natives in the area to trade with the French. Reports of this French probe spurred Hudson Bay governor Charles Bailey to build a second trading post at the mouth of the Moose River in 1673. The new location was better suited for security reasons and, it was hoped, would stymie French trading efforts. The company's main operations were shifted from Fort Charles, or Rupert's House as it became known, over to this location not long after news reached Bailey that the French had erected a trading post farther up the Moose River.

Even with the threat of a rival French commercial presence lurking on the horizon the next few years found the profitable Hudson Bay Company expanding its operations. Supply vessels began regularly arriving, unloading their trade goods before filling their holds with beaver destined for England. Rupert's House was expanded. A rendezvous site was erected on Charlton Island to coordinate shipping and receiving with the two trading posts on James Bay, or factories as the English referred to them. The cartographers were busy as well, making navigational maps and attempting to chart the extent of the company's grant. Another post was added as well. Governor Bailey erected Fort Albany in 1674 on the north bank of the Albany River near its outlet into James Bay. Its purpose followed the governor's thinking that posts should be built at the mouth of all the rivers emptying into James Bay. This would entice more trade by providing better opportunities for the region's tribes to bring their furs to market.[8]

By 1679 neither Groseilliers nor Radisson was in the employment of the Hudson Bay Company. The English expansion had begun to alarm New France. The *Compagnie du Nord*, the French equivalent of the Hudson Bay Company, desperately needed to establish their claims and challenge the English traders in the disputed region. The question was, who would lead this effort? The governor of New France, Louis de Buade, the Count Frontenac, believed he had an answer. In the fall of 1673 he dispatched Father

Albanel to James Bay to dissuade the tribes of that area from trading with the English and to "sound out Des Groseilliers, if he meets him, and to try to find out whether he can bring him back to our side."[9]

After a series of setbacks, Albanel, bearing a letter from Frontenac to Governor Bailey, reached Rupert's House on August 30, 1674. Bailey correctly assessed Albanel's real mission to incite dissent among the local tribes against the English and had him arrested and sent to England. In England Albanel met with Groseilliers and Radisson. He found a receptive audience in the two men, and both returned to French allegiance in 1675. Groseilliers returned to Three Rivers the following year while Radisson offered his services to the French navy.

In 1679, after having lost his possessions in a shipwreck, Radisson began seeking support to establish a French trading post along the shores of Hudson Bay. Although there was interest, his questionable credibility made support difficult to come by in the French court. Fortunately for Radisson, Charles la Chesnaye, the head of the *Compagnie du Nord* threw his support behind the adventurer's plan, which convinced the minister of the marine to listen. In the end the crown supported the idea but not to the point that they were willing to finance the venture. Needing financial backing, Radisson turned to the Jesuits, who agreed to finance the operation, as it offered new opportunities to spread the gospel to the tribes of the region.

With Jesuit backing Groseilliers and Radisson reunited in Canada to lay out the logistics of the expedition. The government of New France did not officially sanction the plan, although it was clear that they supported the goal of disrupting English trade in the region and undermining any territorial claims that might be argued at a later date. Instead, the expedition was under the banner of the *Compagnie du Nord*. This did little to change the objectives. It was agreed that a new post would be erected, and if opportunity presented itself, the English posts were to be seized under the argument that they were on land belonging to King Louis.

Setting out in two small and well-used vessels, the *St. Pierre* and the *St. Anne*, Radisson and Groseilliers's force numbered some thirty traders and sailors. After a rough voyage both vessels rendezvoused in Hudson Bay, near the mouth of what would be called the Nelson River on August 27, 1682. After selecting a site on the Hayes River the two crews set to work constructing a fort while scouting parties were sent upriver. To the surprise of both Radisson and Groseilliers they stumbled upon a New England-sponsored trading post, which had arrived two weeks earlier.

Radisson, who knew several members of the New England delegation, warned them off by telling them they were on French-claimed land. Not

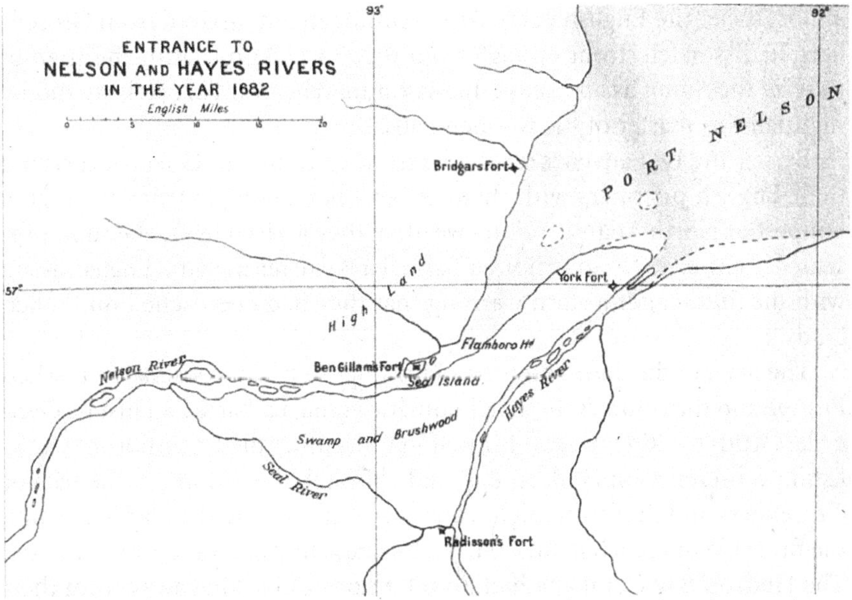

French and English Hudson Bay forts along the Nelson and Hayes Rivers in 1682. (*Agnes Laut, The Adventures of England on Hudson Bay, 1914*)

long after, he had a bigger problem. An English vessel had entered the Nelson River carrying the new governor of the Hudson Bay Company, John Bridgar. A standoff of sorts occurred, with Radisson claiming that this was French land and that significant French reinforcements were arriving soon. Bridgar was not convinced, and once the French party moved off, he began constructing Fort Nelson, the fourth Hudson Bay Company post.[10]

Over the course of the winter Groseilliers and Radisson worked on completing Fort Bourbon, while the New Englanders under Benjamin Gillam spent the time erecting a fine fort mounting six cannon. Governor Bridgar had been busy as well, spending his time on overseeing the construction of Fort Nelson. The proximity of the three competitive parties and their aspirations to control trade in the region almost guaranteed that the peace would not last long. Radisson and Groseilliers, fearing the commercial implications with the coming of spring, seized the New England post. When news reached Governor Bridgar at Fort Nelson, he was at first surprised to hear that a New England party had encamped nearby. Although the New Englanders were likely interlopers on Hudson Bay Company territory he sent a relief party, in part to capture the New Englander's brig *Susan*, as Bridgar's ship, the *Prince Rupert*, had not survived the winter ice. The venture backfired as Radisson, expecting such a move, laid a trap and captured almost the entire English party. After reinforcements arrived from Groseilliers, Radisson felt strong enough to go after Fort Nelson. Using the attempt to seize the *Susan* as an excuse, Radisson marched on Fort Nelson and by nightfall was master of the wooden palisade.

By fall the two adventurers had agreed to return to Quebec, carrying their English prisoners with them. After a harrowing journey through a tempest of North Atlantic sailing weather, they arrived in Quebec and presented themselves to Governor La Barre. La Barre released the English along with the *Susan* after a stern warning that they had encroached on French lands.[11]

The news of the duo's conquest of the English trading posts soon reached Europe and the colonies. In the diplomatic arena, La Barre had just received orders from the king to exert himself in preventing the English from establishing a presence on Hudson Bay, and although the actions on the part of Groseilliers and Radisson might cause some stir, it would go far in keeping the fur trade in French hands. On the business front, it was another matter. The Hudson Bay Company had no intentions of backing away from their claims, nor were they interested in allowing the *Compagnie du Nord* to infringe upon their trade. There was simply too much money at stake.

For a solution to their current problem the Hudson Bay Company turned to an unlikely source, Radisson. Radisson's enterprise, although in line with French policy, had made him a questionable figure in the minds of the French government, which now faced something of a diplomatic incident that had to be resolved. As such, there was no expedition given to Radisson the following year. It was at this point that the Hudson Bay Company came to recruit Radisson back into their ranks. Feeling that he had been treated unjustly, Radisson once again became an employee of the Hudson Bay Company.

Delighted, the company purchased and equipped three vessels and gave Radisson directive to reestablish the trading post at Fort Nelson. When Radisson arrived with his little fleet off the Nelson River in 1684 he was surprised to find two vessels at anchor, one of which carried the new governor of the Hudson Bay Company, William Phips. With such a force behind him, Radisson quickly convinced the French commander at Fort Bourbon, his nephew, that any resistance was futile. Fort Nelson, much to the complaints of the French, was now back in Hudson Bay Company's hands.[12]

The merchants of Montreal noticed a decline in furs from 1684 and 1685 and suspected that a good portion of their trade was being taken to the English trading posts on James Bay. Coupled with the issues associated with Fort Nelson the new French governor, Denonville, sought to address these problems by sending Captain Troyes to arrest the interlopers on the French claimed lands, particularly Radisson, who had changed allegiance one too many times.

Troyes organized his party of thirty marines and seventy-eight Canadians over the winter and early spring of 1686. His officers consisted of three Le Moyne brothers, Iberville, St. Helen, and Marincourt, the first two of whom were to play prominent roles in the French and English conflicts to come. The planned path to James Bay called for ascending the Ottawa River and, after navigating around the waterway's obstacles, pressing on to Lake Temiskaming. From here they would portage over to Lake Abitibi where they would construct a small stockade fort as a rendezvous point should the expedition go wrong. The party would then descend the Abitibi River to its conjunction with the Moose River and from the Moose River sail to James Bay.

Troyes left Montreal in March 1686, and almost three months later, after a grueling trek in which only one man was lost, he was within striking distance of Moose Fort. The English stronghold was a typical palisade fort, with curtain walls some 18 feet high and 130 feet in length. Four bastions occupied the corners of the fortification, constructed with earth packed between two rows of stakes, making them much more difficult to batter down. The fort was also defended by a dozen cannon. Fortunately for the attackers, the garrison was only a little over a dozen men.

Without cannon to conduct a siege, there was only one way to secure Moose Fort—by storm. Still possessing the element of surprise Troyes launched an attack on the post the morning of June 21, 1686, and within a few minutes he had overrun the stronghold. Leaving forty men behind to secure his prisoners and the fort, the French commander set off across the bottom of the bay for Rupert's House. By July 1, he was in position. His scouts confirmed that the English post looked like a smaller version of Moose Fort but without the cannon. Troyes watched the fort for two days and when no activity was noticed he attacked at dawn on July 3. The handful of surprised Hudson Bay Company employees at Rupert's House immediately surrendered. Iberville Le Moyne, who launched an attack on an English vessel lying at anchor before the fort, had a much harder time. A brief firefight broke out, leaving four English dead before the vessel surrendered. Thus far Troyes had seized two English posts without any French casualties and hardly any opposition.[13]

Troyes was particularly delighted to have taken the schooner *Craven*. He immediately loaded a few small cannon found at Rupert's House onboard and sent it to Moose Fort to gather up the guns found there while he and his men returned to the fort by canoe. By late July Troyes had sent the *Craven* north toward Fort Albany while his troops canoed up the west shore of the bay. Fort Albany was built much like Moose Fort but in low-lying ground that was prone to flooding. Some two-dozen cannon bristled from the firing platforms on the fort's four bastions while others were mounted behind the fort's gates to prevent any opponent from forcing entry in this fashion. As impressive as it may have looked for a frontier fort, Troyes was not dissuaded by the strength of the English post. After encircling the structure the marine captain called upon the fort's commander, Governor Henry Sloughter, to surrender. When Sloughter refused Troyes ordered several batteries to be erected, and on the next morning, July 26, he gave the order to open fire. His troop's gunnery and their rate of fire was not impressive, but it did not have to be. As Troyes suspected, after a few hours of cannonading Sloughter lowered his colors and surrendered the fort.

In a little over a month Troyes had seized the Hudson Bay Company's three posts on James Bay, essentially crippling English operations in the area. He and Iberville had contemplated moving on Fort Nelson as well, but a suitable pilot could not be found for the captured English ships, so the idea was abandoned. Troyes returned to Quebec with his prisoners and some fifty thousand beaver pelts to show for his efforts, leaving Iberville and forty men to oversee the three captured posts. James Bay was now firmly in French hands, but the question remained as to whether or not they could hold on to their gains.[14]

CHAPTER SIX

Denonville's Expedition

Before Troyes even departed Denonville turned his attention to greater matters—those concerning Iroquois threats to destabilize the west. After seeing the status of the colony firsthand and reviewing the information through interviews with colonial officials, what the governor found worried him. To the west, the Seneca were still attacking French-allied tribes and, disgusted with La Barre's treaty, the Great Lakes tribes were on the verge of breaking their alliance with the colony. In addition, New York was pressing its claims over all lands south of the Great Lakes through its links to the Iroquois. The weak and scattered French colony was besieged, and it seemed only a matter of time before the entire situation erupted into a general conflict. Should this happen, Denonville wrote the minister of the marine, nothing short of a miracle could save New France.

Denonville was convinced that "war with the Iroquois is inevitable, and if we do not make it against them, they will declare it after they will have done all in their power to rid themselves of the Indians who are friends of the French." Denonville also rightly assessed that the real threat was not just the Iroquois but also New York and its policy of exciting the confederacy to act against the French. For the French leader there seemed only two ways to save the colony. The first called for Louis XIV to buy the colony of New York. This, the governor argued, "would make us masters of the Iroquois without a war." The second approach was to deal the Seneca a major blow. Doing so would not only undermine the intrigues of New York but would bring the disaffected lake tribes back into the French fold. As might be expected Louis was not interested in buying anything, which left only the second course of action. But at the moment the colony was too weak to do anything. Denonville needed time to organize an expedition. "The only thing which I think I can do at present" he wrote regarding the Iroquois, "is to seek to temporise and spin out as well as can be done, seeking to negotiate until next year."[1]

The governor also ended up spending a significant amount of time exchanging quarrelsome letters with Dongan in regard to the Iroquois and English involvement with them. The two parties argued the merits of their cases, traded insults, and made threats. Both were correct in assessing the other's motives, and neither seemed willing to yield.

By the summer of 1687 Denonville was ready to attack the Seneca. Louis had sent both troops and money along with instructions to take whatever steps were necessary to subdue the tribe. "If war must be waged," The king informed him, "it is necessary to take good measures to promptly exterminate that nation and avoid prolonging the war." In June the militia was called out, and some 930 answered the rolls led by some of the more famous families in New France. When added to the colonial troops on hand, some 1,800 French and 300 allied Indians departed for Fort Frontenac. It was a sizeable army, greater than anything seen to date in the colony, and there was every belief that it would be reinforced by tribes allied to the French. Added to this were some eight hundred Troupes de la Marine who arrived at Quebec days before the army set off from Montreal. Denonville was relieved to see the reinforcements, who he left behind to see to the defenses of the colony.

Dongan had received news of the expedition and warned the Iroquois who, upon hearing the numbers involved, pleaded for his help. He gave them powder and shot but could do little else. The governor had recently received instructions from the king to maintain cordial relations with New France. A treaty signed in Europe had left matters in America in the hands of a court-appointed commission, and James, now king, did not want to jeopardize these proceedings. The representatives of the Five Nations were desperate enough to assert their English citizenship but to no avail. The New York governor warned them not to negotiate with the French, but otherwise his hands were tied.[2]

As the French army in 350 canoes and bateaux moved upriver from Montreal to La Galette (Ogdensburg, New York) the governor executed a plan which worked well but that he would later regret. At the end of the French and Iroquois negotiations the previous year Denonville had invited the principal Iroquois sachems to meet with him the following summer at

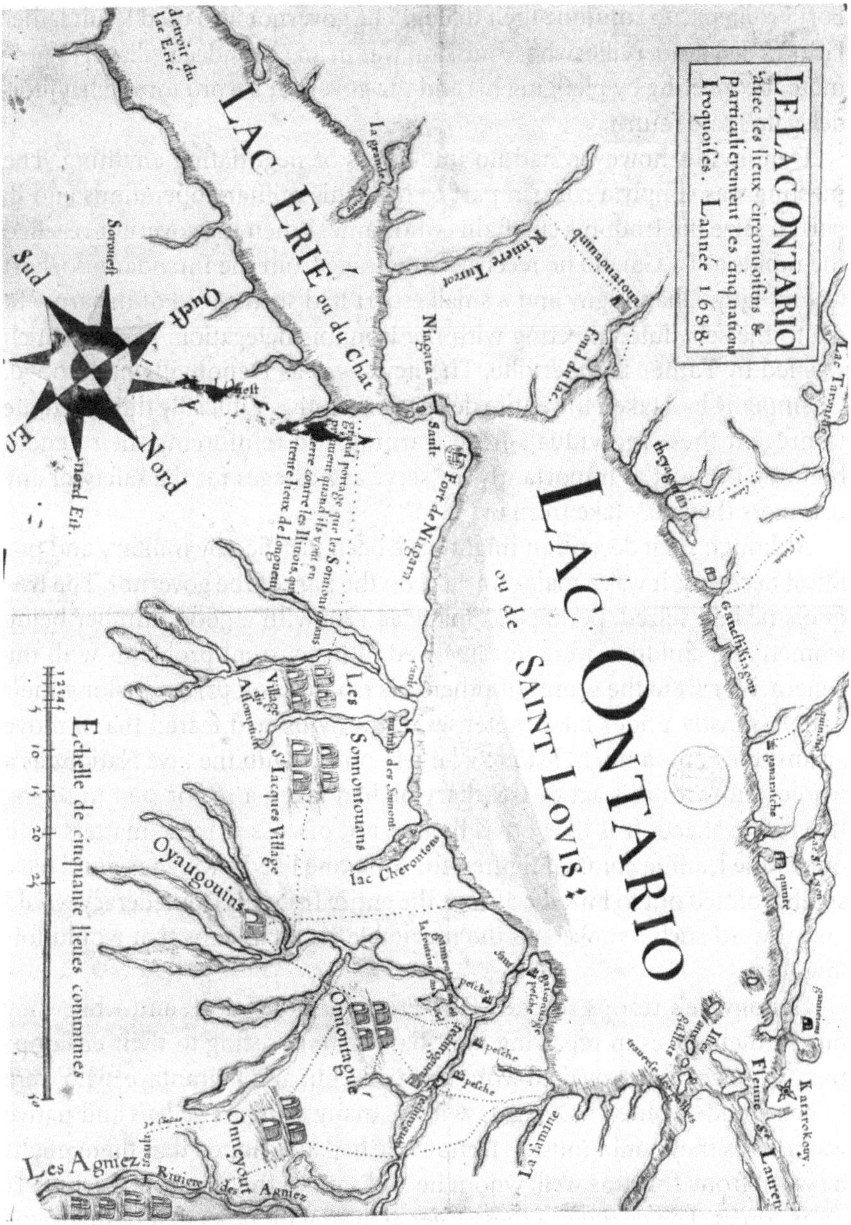

A 1688 map of Lake Ontario. Fort Frontenac, also called Katarokouy (Cataraqui) because it sat at the mouth of the Cataraqui River, is in the upper right hand portion of the map near the headwaters of the St. Lawrence. Fort Niagara is likewise located at the western end of the lake. The map also shows the Onondaga (Omontague) villages to the east, and the Seneca (Sommontouns) villages along the south-central portion of the lake. (*Library of Congress*)

Fort Frontenac to continue their dialog. The governor also used Jesuit father Jacques de Lamberville, whose mission was in an Onondaga village, to promote the meeting by pledging his and the governor's word for the Iroquois delegate's safe return.

Denonville, however, had no intentions of negotiating anything. The meeting was simply a ruse, in part to mask his military operations and in part to seize the Iroquois chieftains who came. When the governor reached the rapids at La Galette he received a message from the Intendant Bochart Champigny. Champigny and a small escort had sped ahead of the army to see to the scheduled meeting with the Iroquois delegation, part of which was led by Father Lamberville. The news was as Denonville had hoped. Champigny had taken the entire delegation captive. Officially this was done to prevent these individuals from warning and reinforcing their Seneca brethren but just as importantly to "serve as hostages for the safety of any prisoners they may take from us."[3]

Although such deception might have been justified by military and political necessity, it was a major mistake on the part of the governor. The Iroquois he had seized, perhaps as many as 120, with a good number being women and children, were not involved in his current problems with the Seneca. Nor were the scores of others his troops took prisoner along their march, mostly under false pretenses. Denonville had feared that a move against the Seneca might lead to a larger conflict with the Five Nations as a whole, and with this act of treachery he had taken a major step to seeing this fear realized. It is likely that he had not discussed these matters with one of the leading colonial figures, for someone like Le Moyne would have surely pointed out to him the affront the entire Iroquois Confederacy would take toward such a move and the inevitable repercussions that would follow.

Denonville's troops reached Fort Frontenac on July 1, and while they busied themselves in repairing their bateaux and seeing to their encampments, the governor awaited word from du Lhut and Durantaye, who were to have rendezvoused at Niagara with as many *coureurs de bois* and native warriors as they could muster. Denonville had also hoped that there might be word from Tonty as well, whom he had sent to the Illinois to secure yet more forces. The next day a messenger arrived with news that both groups were at Niagara with some 180 Frenchmen and 400 allies, waiting on the supplies Denonville had promised them. The marquis was pleased to hear the report, as he had already dispatched a small bark loaded with munitions and supplies to Niagara, but there was troubling news as well. Durantaye had seized two English trading parties on the Great Lakes bound for

Michilimackinac. For the moment they, and their Iroquois escorts, were being held prisoner.[4]

The presence of these trading parties was worrisome news to the governor. Du Lhut and Durantaye had difficulties convincing the Ottawa of Michilimackinac to join the expedition, in part because of Iroquois peace overtures, and now the governor had in his hands some sixty Englishmen and their Iroquois guides. Denonville clearly understood that with their cheaper goods, if these English traders were allowed access to the high country they would undermine the fragile array of Franco-native alliances. He also understood that it was forbidden by treaty, and as such he ordered the two parties and their Iroquois guides arrested and their cargoes impounded. Their fate would become a matter to be settled with Governor Dongan.[5]

Denonville ordered the army into their boats on July 4 and, after a storm-strewn voyage, arrived at the designated rendezvous point, Irondequoit Bay, on July 10. When a quick reconnaissance of the south shore showed no signs of the enemy the governor ordered the army to land. A few hours later, to the delight of all, Durantaye's forces were seen on the horizon. The following day was spent erecting field fortifications and landing supplies. The marquis's army reflected the stratum of Canada. Members of the king's government, colonial regulars, Canadian militia, led by the gentry of the colony, as well as bands of native allies dressed in their scalp locks and war paint swirled about the landing site. The French numbers soon increased as well, as several hundred Ottawa who had initially declined Durantaye's request changed their minds and paddled to the rendezvous.

Satisfied with the arrangements, on the afternoon of July 12 Denonville detached four hundred men to guard the camp and marched south in three columns toward the Seneca village of Gannagaro. After a dozen miles without incident the army encamped for the evening under the watchful eyes of a double guard and then resumed their trek the next morning. Late that afternoon, after a sweltering march through the forest, the French army descended a ridge a little over a mile from the Seneca village. The vanguard, consisting of three columns of *coureurs de bois* and native allies under Durantaye, du Lhut, and Tonty had just caught a glimpse of the fields about the town through the thinning trees when the woods to their right erupted in a volley of three hundred muskets. The initial shock had fallen upon Tonty and his detachment of Illinois and Ottawa warriors. Tonty's lieutenant and several of his men fell to the hail of musket balls as the Seneca raised a war whoop and charged.

A second smaller volley soon followed in front of the French advance guard as another 150 Seneca warriors launched their assault to complete the trap. The ambush, however, had been sprung too soon. Mistaking the tail of the vanguard for the end of the main French column, the Seneca on the French right had opened fire at, to make matters worse, too great a distance. Tonty's troops recoiled under the shock but responded well to the surprise and quickly returned fire. The governor of Montreal, Louis-Hector de Callières, who was in command of the advance guard in the centermost column, then ordered his men and the 260 mission Indians on his left flank to attack. In the dense forest the battle quickly became a confused melee. Flashes of muskets, war whoops, drifting clouds of smoke, and figures darting from tree to tree became the order of the moment.

To the rear the sound of the fighting sent a shiver through the dense formations of Canadian militia and blue-coated regulars. "Had you but seen, Sir," one witness wrote of the incident, "what Disorder our Troops and Militia were in amidst the thick Trees, you would have joined with me, in thinking that several thousands of Europeans are no more than a sufficient number to make head against 500 Barbarians." The nervous formations soon merged with one another into greater and lesser groups. With the sound of fighting seemingly nearer, and a panicked force of 1,800 with no man able to see more than a few dozen paces in any direction, the inevitable happened. Someone fired. Soon patches of men were firing at random or in some cases upon one another. A battalion of militia near the front of the French lines broke but was quickly rallied by veteran captains such as Philippe Valrenne, who would later fight one of the most contested battles of the conflict. The firing was brought to an end by hoarse shouts and the threat of the sword. With a shaky ordered restored, Denonville ordered the drums to sound the charge, and the army advanced toward the fighting.

It was not necessary. The French advance guard, which significantly outnumbered the attacking Seneca, struck back after absorbing the initial attack and had all but broken Seneca resolve. When the sound of French drums echoed throughout the forest it finished the job. The warriors of the longhouse, many of them just boys, as a good number of the village's warriors were on raiding parties or hunting, broke and fled. Some reportedly went so far as to throw away their arms "to escape under favor of the woods."[6]

Although pressed by his allies, Denonville made no attempt to pursue the retreating Seneca. His army had marched in unusual heat all day, fought a skirmish, and just as importantly had no idea what lay before them. Rest was called for and the troops set about making camp while the two dozen or so dead and wounded were attended to, including Father Jean Enjalran, who was wounded by a musket ball in the opening volley. Twenty-seven Seneca dead and trails left by wounded warriors covered the battlefield, im-

Political adversaries New York governor Edmund Andros (left), and the governor of New France, the Marquis de Denonville (right). Although the administrations of the two men were markedly different in their approach to internal problems, both took a similar aggressive stance toward westward expansion. (*New York Public Library/National Archives of Canada*)

plying that the enemy seemed to have suffered more casualties in the brief but decisive encounter.[7]

After being delayed the next morning by heavy rains, the French army marched on Gannagaro only to find smoldering ruins. Denonville spent the next few days demolishing the village's palisade walls, destroying the nearby cornfields, and rounding up fugitives to interrogate. On the morning of the nineteenth, the governor marched on the village of Totiakto approximately twelve miles to the west. The Seneca had fled and burned this village as well. The army spent the next few days laying the surrounding countryside to waste. All the livestock was killed, old crops were burned, and the new crops were hacked down with an angry glee. By now Denonville had spoken with enough captives to realize that the Seneca had fled. Just like with Tracy and the Mohawk a generation before, the Seneca had sacrificed their villages to avoid a pitched confrontation with the French. Turning back toward the landing site, the army destroyed a small village a few miles from Totiakto. While the well-practiced work of destroying the nearby crops proceeded, one French soldier handed the marquis an English coat of arms that had been posted near the entrance to the village. The document had been issued by Dongan, which no doubt reminded the governor of his bitter correspondence with his New York counterpart.

Satisfied that little more could be done, Denonville gave the order for the army to return to its boats. By July 30, the force had embarked and arrived at Niagara where Denonville put his men to work erecting a stockade fort. With the fort finished and a garrison in place under the command of Troyes, the governor released the militia on August 2. The next day he departed Fort Niagara and, after making a few defensive preparations at Fort Frontenac, by late August he was back in Montreal.

The expedition was a partial success. The Seneca were not destroyed, as they had successfully avoided a major engagement, but at the very least they had been humbled. This was enough to bring the allied tribes back into the French fold, but there were other complications. During the campaign two English trading parties were captured on the lakes. There was little choice but to do so. Both were sponsored by New York and both were intent on establishing a trading post at Michilimackinac near the outlet of Lake Superior. Given the rebellious state of the French tribes in the area, and the proliferation of cheap English goods that would have followed, not seizing the traders would have ended in an open break between the French and their native allies.[8]

Attacking the Seneca was bad enough, but the seizure of Englishmen incensed Dongan. The governor, who was meeting with the representatives of the Five Nations at the time the news arrived, informed them that as English subjects they must obey his commands and make no treaty with the French without his consent. He urged them to make peace with the lake tribes and expel the French from the west. The Iroquois, still smarting from the attack, agreed. "We will fight the French," they informed the governor, "as long as we have a man left." Dongan then turned his anger toward Denonville. He demanded the release of the English traders and their goods. Denonville refused, claiming that, by providing arms to the Seneca, Dongan had violated the recent treaty. The pair exchanged a series of counterarguments, which culminated in a number of threatening letters, but neither was prepared to budge.[9]

Denonville's actions were in accordance with his instructions and seemed to be within the scope of his directives. Dongan's conduct, however, is much harder to justify. The governor claimed the Iroquois as English subjects yet continually urged them to attack the French and provided them with the arms necessary to do so. Had these been the English citizens of Albany, there would have been open war, but since it was the Iroquois, the English governor could feign ignorance or simply say he would look into their conduct when the French complained. Dongan wanted to play both sides of the fence, and the French weren't buying it. He had managed to draw the Iroquois within his jurisdiction but only to the point of a direct confrontation with New France.

For New France, the following year proved nearly catastrophic. After a massive undertaking, Denonville had ultimately failed to undermine the Seneca's military strength and his seizure of the neutral Iroquois had raised the entire Five Nations against him. Roving bands of Iroquois kept most of the colony fort-bound, leading to a disastrous harvest, a collapse in the fur trade, and widespread economic ruin. In an attempt to secure some form of peace, the governor was forced to demolish Fort Niagara and return the English traders and Iroquois taken during his expedition. There was a moment of hope when Dongan was recalled, but this faded quickly when his replacement, Edmund Andros, the former governor, continued Dongan's aggressive policies.

With little choice, Denonville sued for a more permanent peace with the Iroquois and met with them in Montreal. The Five Nations, who held the upper hand in the negotiations, were initially indifferent to the idea. Their spokesman harangued the French for their misguided actions and broken promises. He then openly threatened Denonville, saying that they knew the weakness of the French and that the Five Nations could exterminate them whenever they chose to do so. Even so, the Iroquois spokesman concluded, in the interest of peace the Iroquois were willing to bury the hatchet. A treaty of neutrality was signed until a more permanent agreement could be concluded some time later that year when the delegation returned to Montreal. But the delegation never returned, under the excuse that Governor Andros would not allow it.[10]

For Denonville, a lifelong soldier, there seemed only one answer to the whole problem: the destruction of the Iroquois. He wrote to the minister of the marine in France with a plan to attack both the Mohawk and Seneca simultaneously. This time, however, the French would occupy the Iroquois villages and use them as staging points to continue the attacks on these tribes throughout the year. Forts would be built to support these efforts, the last of which was projected to be at the end of Lake Champlain. The plan was bold and beyond the capabilities of the colony. Several thousand men would be involved, many of whom would have to stay in the field throughout the year. The plan was also certain to bring the colony into a direct military confrontation with New York. The king agreed that three or four thousand men could accomplish the task, but at the moment he was not interested in provoking the English. Thus the project was set aside.[11]

But Denonville was not finished with the idea. He sent the governor of Montreal, Callières, to France to explain the perilous position of the colony and to lay an even more ambitious plan before the king: the conquest of New York. The argument was simple. The English were the real enemy. It was they who incited the Iroquois to attack Canada and supplied them with the weapons and means to do so. It was they who had violated the neutrality treaty, and it was they who made territorial claims to the ruin of the commerce of New France. With New York in French hands, the Iroquois would have no choice but to join the French cause. This would lead to complete control of the American fur trade. New England would be isolated and New France would possess not only a fine year-round harbor but land more fertile as any in Canada as well.

The plan called for 600 militia and 1,400 colonial troops to march on Albany by way of the Lake Champlain and Lake George route. The expedition would build a stockade fort at the head of Lake George, where two hundred of their number would be left to guard the larger boats and barges. The remaining 1,800 soldiers would haul their canoes and supplies through a dozen miles of swamp-laced forest to the reaches of the upper Hudson. From there they would proceed directly for Albany, leaving a small detachment to secure the hamlet of Saratoga along the way. The defenses of Albany were estimated to be some 300 militia and 150 regulars, who garrisoned the old fort on the western edge of the town. A fourteen-foot wooden palisade surrounded the village, but this would not prove much of an obstacle to 1,800 determined men. Albany would be summoned to surrender, and in the unlikely event that it refused, it would be stormed. In either case it would quickly be in French hands. Two hundred men would be left to garrison the town, while the rest of the expedition procured whatever water transportation it could find and, with the cannon seized from Fort Albany, proceed downriver to Manhattan. The town of New York had some four hundred militia under arms and one hundred or so regulars manning Fort James. If history was any indicator, most of the militia would refuse to fight, and the defenses of Fort James were known to be poor. Upon arriving at Manhattan, the expedition would coordinate with two French men-of-war, which would enter the harbor and cannonade the English fort while the troops on the landside stormed the town.[12]

The scheme was audacious and, to make it more appealing to the king, cheap. Denonville and Callières only asked for the use of two men-of-war and the replacements needed to bring the colonial troops up to full strength. The rest of the manpower would come from Canada. The bateaux and canoes needed for the expedition along with the other necessary supplies were already on hand from the previous campaigns.

This time Louis took notice. He was pleased with the cost of the venture and the benefits it would bring, but its timing was the root cause of his interest. In England the Glorious Revolution had deposed King James and placed the Dutchman William of Orange on the throne of England. Louis realized that it would only be a matter of time before William drew England into the league of nations arrayed against him. In Europe war between England and France was likely but not yet certain. Louis ordered the logistics for the expedition to be pushed forward but wrote Denonville that until an open rupture existed between the two countries nothing else could be done.[13]

CHAPTER SEVEN

Acadia and New England

FRENCH ACADIA, or Nova Scotia as it would later be called, was no less immune to the growing Anglo-French tensions than Hudson Bay or the western frontier. In fact, tensions had run high along this isthmus since its settlement by the French in 1604. After abandoning the initial colony in 1607, a second effort was made at Port Royal in 1610 under the leadership of Jean de Biencourt de Poutrincourt. Poutrincourt's fledgling colony eked out an existence and lived without incident next to its Micmac neighbors for the next few years. In 1613 their peaceful existence was shattered when Captain Samuel Argall, Pocahontas's famous captor, launched an assault on Port Royal. Argall was under orders from England to prevent the French from establishing a colony in Acadia. Over the course of two voyages he leveled the Jesuit mission of St. Sauveur in modern-day Maine, demolished the old French colonial position at St. Croix, and burned Port Royal to the ground, scattering its inhabitants. Argall's campaigns very nearly ended the French settlement in Acadia. Port Royal was partially rebuilt, but Poutrincourt soon departed while Charles La Tour and a number of other enterprising individuals abandoned Port Royal not long after to pursue their fortunes in the fur trade. La Tour built a small fort at Cape Sable named St. Louis, and from here he and others carried forth their business.[1]

In 1621 Sir William Alexander, the future Earl of Sterling, was granted a Royal Charter over Nova Scotia, an area roughly comprising modern-day Nova Scotia, New Brunswick, and the northwest section of Maine. Alexander had yet to exploit his royal grant, but with the fall of Quebec in the spring of 1629 he saw his opportunity. He easily obtained permission from King James I to sponsor colonies in Acadia, partly with the intention of securing the crown's new possessions by occupation, which always carried great weight in such matters. By midsummer two Scottish colonies were formed, one at Port Royal and a second at Baliene on Cape Breton Island. La Tour, seeing that Cape Sable was the only major holding still in French hands, appealed to France for help.

Aid was forthcoming as was an appointment for La Tour who, after building a fort at the mouth of the St. John River named Fort St. Marie, helped successfully guide the French colony through the Anglo-French War. With the signing of the Treaty of Saint-Germain-en-Laye in 1632, Acadia was once again French. Governor Isaac de Razilly, acting on behalf of the *Compagnie de la Nouvelle-France*, officially took possession from the Scots in the fall of 1632 and established his post at Port Royal. La Tour and Razilly had demarcated zones of responsibilities as directed by the *Compagnie de la Nouvelle-France*. Razilly was to administer to Port Royal and the St. Croix area, while La Tour was concerned with the region about his headquarters at Fort St. Marie. The arrangement seemed to work, trade flourished, and the colony grew. In 1635, however, Razilly died and left his holdings in the company to his brother Charles. Charles was not interested in leaving France to see to his brother's business interests in Acadia, so he recruited his cousin Charles D'Aulnay to see to the task.[2]

It was not long before La Tour and D'Aulnay began to clash. The matter became an open quarrel over D'Aulnay's handling of business transactions that had long been settled between Razilly and La Tour. Soon, D'Aulnay was petitioning the company to have La Tour removed. Using his influence at court, D'Aulnay obtained a set of very general orders from the king concerning La Tour's return to France as an excuse to attack and capture Fort St. Marie. The event would set off a violent feud between the two men that would last almost a decade. La Tour obtained support from the vice admiral of France, but when his relief vessels arrived at St. John he found that D'Aulnay had erected a blockade of the post. Undaunted, La Tour sailed to Boston and hired four ships along with a number of soldiers to force a passage into St. John. When D'Aulnay received reports of La Tour's fleet in the Bay of Fundy he retreated to Port Royal. La Tour followed, and when D'Aulnay refused to negotiate, La Tour backed by his own men and some 350 English mercenaries attacked and quickly defeated D'Aulnay's forces. The governor was quick to complain to the king, insinuating that La Tour was a traitor, in league with the English, and had incited open rebellion. La

Tour's reputation was severely damaged. D'Aulnay took advantage of La Tour's absence in early 1645 and once again besieged Fort St. Marie. Although he was driven off, the governor returned a few months later and was successful in capturing the post.

D'Aulnay's death in a boating accident in 1650 brought La Tour back to France. For the last several years he had worked with the governor of New France in Quebec and with the Jesuit missionaries there. The support of these two important branches of the colony proved crucial as he made his case before the king, calling for an inquest to clear his name. In the end the king exonerated him and restored his position in Acadia. It was not the end of La Tour's experiences in Nova Scotia, but it was the end of the civil war that raged between the two leaders, which, beyond the blood and treasure lost on both sides, proved divisive enough that it stunted the growth of the colony.[3]

A few years later on July 14, 1654, La Tour found himself once again immersed in conflict. Gazing out upon the St. John roadstead he saw a number of warships flying English colors. The English force, under the command of Captain John Leverett and Major Robert Sedgewick, had originally sailed to Boston as part of a plan to attack New Amsterdam, but the expedition was called off at the last moment when news arrived that the First Anglo-Dutch War had come to an end. This did not, however, end Sedgewick's mission in America. Leverett had aligned his interests with those of New England, which saw a commercial and military threat posed by French Acadia. Using an element of his orders, which called upon him to make reprisals against French commerce in response to attacks on English vessels by French privateers, he sailed for Acadia. After mounting a brief defense, there was little La Tour could do but comply with Sedgewick's demand to surrender. La Tour's fort mounted a few cannon but was not a match for one of the English warships, much less their combined might. After putting up a show of resistance, Port Royal followed suit. Penobscot followed shortly thereafter, and for the next thirteen years Acadia was occupied by the English. It is interesting to note that the decision to seize Acadia came at a time of peace between France and England and was not officially ordered by the lord protector, but Cromwell hardly objected to the new acquisitions, viewing them as bargaining pieces in future negotiations.[4]

Acadia was returned to France in 1667 with the Treaty of Breda that brought an end to the Second Anglo-Dutch War. Although the colony was returned, its actual boundaries were not specified, which would soon lead to more problems on the peninsula. In fact, it was argued soon after the agreement was signed that, while LaHave and Cape Sable were in Acadia,

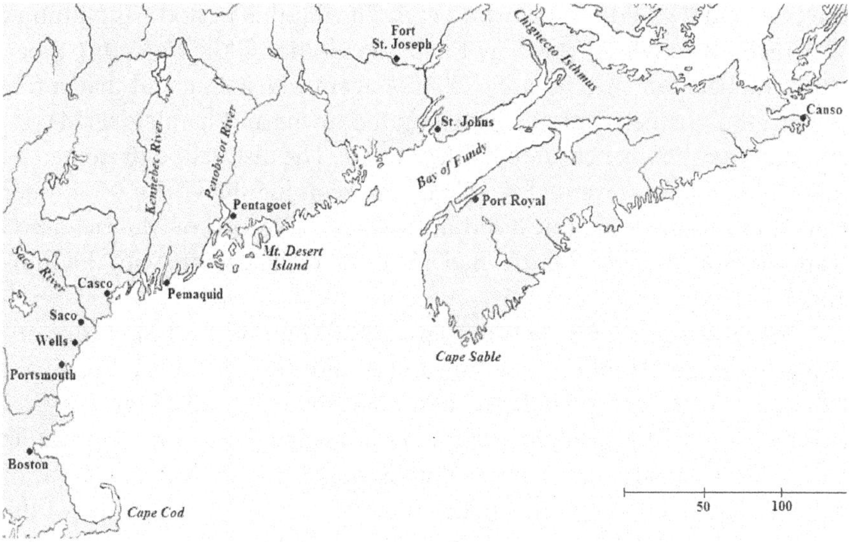

French and English coastal settlements from Boston to Canso, Nova Scotia. Disputed territorial claims and old animosities would make this one of the most contested regions during King William's War. (*Author*)

Port Royal and St. John were in the Scottish settlement of Nova Scotia and as such were not covered by the treaty.[5]

With the return of the colony there were administrative changes as well, brought on primarily by Talon and placed into effect with the arrival of the Marquis de Tracy.

The elements of New France were to be administered by royal rule. No longer would the *Compagnie de la Nouvelle-France* reign over the actions of the colony. Acadia would get its own royal governor who would be subordinate to the governor of New France in Quebec. The colony's first governor, the Chevalier Andigne de Grand-Fontaine, established himself not at Port Royal but at Penobscot. The fort at Port Royal was too decayed, and the latter location was better suited toward maintaining communications with Quebec. In 1670 Grand-Fontaine officially took control from English governor Sir Thomas Temple, who reported to the government of Massachusetts that he had surrendered "Pentagoet (Penobscot), St. John, Port Royal containing the whole country under my command" and that, according to the agreement. the border between the French and English colonies was to be the Penobscot River.

A few years later, in 1674, the Dutch under Captain Jurriaen Aernoutsz attacked and captured Acadia, but the resulting occupation and claims to the peninsula would not last two years. During this period King Philip's War raged throughout the New England colonies. Philip, a Wampanoag chieftain, had launched a native alliance against New England that sorely pressed the northern colonies, turning the towns and hamlets of Massachusetts and Connecticut into battlegrounds. The distraction presented by the conflict likely prevented Acadia from becoming the victim of another New England invasion, but it did not stop the colonists of Massachusetts from claiming that the French "had a hand in the late warre with the Indians."[6]

There was some truth to this accusation. When skirmishing broke out along the Maine frontier between settlers and the pro-French Wabanaki Confederacy that occupied the area, rumors circulated that a French officer led the natives. The individual in question was the Baron Jean-Vincent de St. Castin, an ensign stationed at Penobscot before the Dutch invasion of Acadia. The young baron met with Frontenac in 1674, at which point the governor directed him to convince the Abenaki and the other tribes throughout Acadia to take up the French cause. Castin took well to the task, eventually becoming an adopted Abenaki and marrying the daughter of a Penobscot chieftain. Although the Wabanaki Confederacy was sympathetic to Philip's cause, they had their own concerns about New England expansion into their territories, which meshed nicely with St. Castin's cause. Encouraged by Castin, in 1675 they attacked the Maine frontier, burning English settlements between Casco and the Saco River and raiding others as far south as Wells. The following year was a repeat of the first, eventually reaching the point that the Maine frontier settlements, which at the time were under the jurisdiction of New York, were abandoned, including Fort Pemaquid.[7]

Governor Andros responded the following year by sending a large force to Pemaquid to rebuild the fort there. The first detachment with four armed vessels proceeded directly to the fort while a second detachment carrying some two hundred colonial troops disembarked at Black Point when they saw signs of enemy activity. Before the expedition realized what had happened a sharp firefight broke out. Some sixty English casualties were counted when the engagement was finally broken off. Even with these losses Andros was successful in erecting and reinforcing Fort Charles at Pemaquid, thus maintaining New York's claim to the area. The Treaty of Casco the next year brought an end to the First Abenaki War, but for their part the Abenaki had stifled English expansion into Maine.[8]

The conflict had stopped, but the root causes of it still remained. While tensions remained high along the New England frontier, they did not suppress Massachusetts's interest in the growing Acadian fur trade or the New England fishing fleets that descended upon the area. For the next several years this last issue became the primary point of contention between Acadia and Massachusetts. At one point, after several French vessels were seized, the governor of Acadia demanded a French frigate to drive away the English interlopers. Acadia's capital was shifted back to Port Royal in 1684 with the arrival of Governor Francois-Marie Perrot, but progress was slow when it came to repairing the old fortifications. It would not be until Perrot's replacement, Louis-Alexandre des Frische de Mennenval, arrived in 1687 that more concerted efforts were undertaken to rebuild the fortifications of Port Royal, but even these were not finished by the start of King William's War.

In 1686, Andros returned to the American colonies, this time as governor of the Dominion of New England. He had been recalled to England due to complaints about his governorship of New York, but was exonerated of any charges against him. Not long after his appointment, the settlements along the coast of Maine were transferred to Massachusetts's care, which proved uneventful until problems began to resurface with the Abenaki in the spring of 1688. Andros responded by reinforcing the frontier, but what was perhaps more telling was when, knowing that Castin was away, he foolishly raided the baron's trading post at Penobscot and "plundered Castin's house and fort; leaving only the ornaments of his chapel to console him for the loss of his arms and goods." The governor couched the action as a search for contraband goods tied with illegal trade between the colonies, but at its heart he was clearly looking to punish Castin for what he saw as French involvement in his current border problems.[9]

A similar mentality was applied to the Abenaki. At Saco a local magistrate, Benjamin Blackman, seized and imprisoned sixteen natives under the pretense that they had been involved in killing cattle. The seizure brought an immediate response in the form of a raid on New Dartmouth (Newcastle, Maine), in which several English families were carried off. The Abenaki informed their prisoners that the raid was in retaliation for Blackman's actions and the attack on Castin's post. Castin was particularly enraged at what had transpired and promised his native allies all the French powder and ball they required. After this, it took very little on Castin's part to push the Abenaki toward retaliation. Attempts were made to hold peace talks and exchange prisoners, but the Abenaki were silent. "By their discourse and all their actions they Shew that they Intend War with us, & we Question not but that there is a Strong Combination with them and the French against us, and are afraid that the Captives are Carryed to the French & Indians at Penobscutt," the commander of Fort Falmouth informed the New England governor.[10]

In November, Andros responded by reinforcing Pemaquid with seven hundred troops to repair the fortifications and overawe the natives. Further attempts were made to hold peace talks, but nothing materialized. The remainder of the fall and winter passed in a guarded peace. Andros was confident that the defensive measures he had enacted in the area would hold, but this trust would prove to be misplaced.

Part Two

Grand Alliance

CHAPTER EIGHT

The Glorious Revolution

THE STUARTS PROVED TO BE A TROUBLED MONARCHY. Charles I had lost a war to parliament and paid for it with his head. His son, Charles II, proved a capable king when he returned from exile in 1664, but the delicate transition back to monarchy and personal distractions prevented him from being anything more. Charles's brother James, the Duke of York, became king upon his brother's death in 1685. James II's reign was perhaps the most troubled of all the Stuarts. It was certainly the shortest. Although James had held the position of lord high admiral, a post in which he had honorably served through the last two Anglo-Dutch Wars, he was considered less capable than his brother. There had been opposition to his reign from the start, primarily due to his earlier conversion to Catholicism. James's brutal retribution on those who had supported an uprising by his Protestant nephew and Charles II's popular but illegitimate son, the Duke of Monmouth, did little to help his reputation, while his marriage to the daughter of Louis XIV and his financial dependence on his father-in-law further diminished his image. His pro-French and pro-Catholic stance, coupled with his desire to create an absolute-style monarchy, had made many in England question their new king. When James produced a Catholic heir, the kingdom had seen enough.

English Protestant leaders extended the crown to James's eldest daughter, Mary, and her husband, William, the Prince of Orange, both Protestants. Seizing the opportunity William landed at Brixham on November 5, 1688, at the head of fifteen thousand Dutch, Danish, and German troops. Almost immediately prominent Protestants began to defect to William's cause, including James's younger daughter, Anne, and John Churchill, the future Duke of Marlborough. Within James's army there was wide-spread defection as well, and although he still possessed a force large enough to confront William, James instead opted to flee to France. Unfortunately, he was captured in Kent not long after. For simple political reasons William had no desire to keep James around, and as such, he was quietly allowed to "escape."[1]

News of the Glorious Revolution and the coronation of William III in February 1689 did not reach the American colonies until spring, but when it did it set off a political firestorm in New England. Charles II and his brother James's attempts to institute royal rule over the daily lives of New Englanders had been met with scorn and disdain. Had not the founders of the colonies left to avoid this, people asked. Was not life on the frontier difficult enough without all the problems of Old England as well? Up until the 1660s New England had, for all practical purposes, existed outside of English rule. As a good period of this time includes the upheaval of the English Civil War it is perhaps understandable why the English government did not play a greater role in the colony's life. But even when Cromwell assumed the mantle of protector he did little to interfere with the New England governments and, in fact, sent warships and troops to help deal with colonial threats. It was not until Charles II rejected the old charters in 1684 that Yankee ire began to show itself. Matters simply became worse under James II, as his open Catholic connections added yet another dimension to the Puritan outrage.

James looked to continue his brother's work and assert royal control over the American colonies. To accomplish this he formed the Dominion of New England in 1686, which also encompassed New York and New Jersey. He then placed Andros, who had served him well as governor of New York, in charge. The powers granted to Andros were viceroy-like; taxation, justice, commerce, and military affairs all fell within his prerogative. The people of New England recoiled at the new system, which swept away their representative assemblies. Charges of corruption and injustice were leveled at Andros and his advisors. For his part Andros did not overstep his authority, although it would have taken a large stride to do so. As far as he was concerned the king's wishes were to be realized whether the populace liked it or not. Protestors who argued the lack of representation in matters of levied taxes were immediately arrested, and traditional New England town meetings, which he claimed just promoted dissent, were limited to once a year.[2]

Thus, when news of the flight of James and the ascension of William and Mary to the throne of England arrived, it was met not only with delight but

King William III and Queen Mary II. (*Scottish National Gallery/Royal Collection*)

with opportunity. New Englanders had opposed royal rule from the outset and were still angry over the loss of their assemblies. Fueled by rumors of Papist plots and the heavy-handed tactics, Andros himself, a Catholic and longtime subordinate of James, was arrested in Boston on April 18, 1689, after a short standoff. The fortifications of Boston were taken without a shot the next day, leaving the revolutionary council not only in control of the city but all of New England. Andros was imprisoned and a letter of congratulations was sent to the new Protestant king, explaining the actions of the revolutionary council and their allegiance to William's cause. Then, to the delight of most, the old colonial charters were reinstituted throughout New England. While the long-term political and social repercussions of the Glorious Revolution would change the interactions between New England and the mother country as well as contribute to the development of a New England identity, the immediate impact was on the defense of the colony.[3]

Andros may have proven an inept politician, but the same could not be said for his military leadership. An officer in the Royalist Army during the English Civil War, he had proven proactive, and although he made some mistakes, such as destroying Castin's fort, he had demonstrated a competent approach in dealing with threats posed to New England. Replacing Andros's leadership in terms of the defense of the colony would be difficult. However, the matter would not be resolved at this point, as questions of loyalty and religion migrated down to the lower ranks of the colonies' militias. Soon the process had escalated to foolish levels as the need for control demanded by the restored assemblies approached that of what they had deposed.

The garrisons of the frontier forts also used the moment to revolt against the officers appointed over them by Andros. In June, Lt. John Jordan at New Dartmouth (Newcastle), Maine, was arrested by his men for acts of "cruelty and tyranny." It was also claimed that the lieutenant had attempted to convince his men to defend the fort "against the Boston dogs" who had seized the governor. The following month on July 23, the Revolutionary Council of Safety in Boston decided to withdraw the troops Andros had posted on the frontier for fear of their disloyalty to the new government. A trio of colonial officers "now abroad in the army to Eastern," was ordered "to dismiss Major Brockholes, Macgregory, Lockhart, Lieutenant Weems, Captain Manning, and Ensign Smith from their present command in the Army, and send them to Boston."[4]

The effect on the frontier garrisons was frightening and predictable. When Andros arrived he had brought two companies of regulars with him. Many of these men were assigned to bolster the frontier posts. With the governor and their commanding officers' arrests and their unit's recall, most simply deserted, leaving garrisons like the one at Fort Pemaquid with less than a score of men to defend its walls. Nor were matters improved by the void created by the imprisonment of Andros's staff. Logistics, raising the militia, and the basic forms of government, such as the courts, customs, and revenue collection, were suddenly thrown into the lap of the Council of Safety. The result was confusion and chaos.

Many of the frontier posts went without supplies and no replacements or reinforcements were sent forward. Arguments over positions and their powers, lack of legislative experience, and a general lack of leadership at this crucial time led one witness to comment that "New England, which yesterday was united and formidable, is divided into about ten little independent kingdoms, each acting as if it knew no superior power." Another wrote that, "Every man is a Governor." Soon the folly would come to fruition as the Wabanaki attacked and ravaged the Maine frontier. Panic struck New England, which was ill-prepared to handle a major conflict, and all braced for the raids that would surely follow. Andros's secretary, Edward Randolph, a prisoner alongside the governor, wrote New York lieutenant governor Francis Nicholson of the situation. "I know not how this country can be preserved from utter destruction through these internal dissensions unless the King send a good force to restore order."[5]

Nicholson could sympathize. The Glorious Revolution quickly swept through New York and New Jersey. These two colonies had long been against being included in the Dominion of New England, and New York City in particular suffered economically under the arrangement. When news of King William's coronation and the governor's imprisonment arrived from Boston, it set off uprisings in Long Island. "Having read the declaration published at Boston on 18 April, we, having like them at Boston groaned under arbitrary power, think it our bounden duty to use all lawful endeavors to secure the forts at Albany, New York, and elsewhere, pending further orders from the English Parliament." Armed with this document a detachment of men from Suffolk and the surrounding communities marched on Fort James.[6]

The twenty-nine-year-old Francis Nicholson, serving in his first official post as Andros's lieutenant governor, was able to negotiate an uneasy truce with this force but feared it was only a matter of time before the situation boiled over. "Several of them with the assistance of some ill-affected and restless spirits," he informed the Board of Trade in mid-May, "used all imaginable meanes to stir up the Inhabitants of this City to sedition and Rebellion, But we have hitherto prevented their dangerous designs, but know not how long we shall be able to resist their further attempts." There were also other concerns complicating the situation. First among these were rumors of a war with France. Fort James was in no condition to resist any kind of attack, being in a state of ruin after years of neglect. To pay for the stronghold's repairs Nicholson turned to another problem. The revolutionary zeal was beginning to manifest itself when it came to customs and duties. A number of New York merchants refused to recognize the authority of the New York customs agent to collect taxes, pointing to his association with James and now regarding the entire act as being illegal until news arrived from King William on how to proceed. Nicholson called together all parties and agreed that until directions arrived from England all monies collected from customs and duties would be used to repair Fort James.[7]

For the next few weeks rumors and secret meetings abounded, but there were no overt moves toward rebellion. On May 31, Nicholson provided the revolutionaries with their opportunity. In a dispute with Lt. Henry Cuyler, who was in command of a detachment of the city's militia, Nicholson leveled a pistol at Cuyler's corporal, a man the governor considered a troublemaker and scoundrel. "He afterwards said," Cuyler testified, "that there were so many rogues in the town that he was almost afraid to walk in the streets, and that before it should go longer on in this manner he would set the town on fire."[8]

Such wild words from an associate of Andros, and a former representative of the deposed King James, provided all the sparks required to start the fire. A crowd of protestors and part of the city's militia began gathering at the residence of council member Captain Jacob Leisler. Leisler was a prominent citizen and one of the richest men in New York. He had signed on as a soldier in the Dutch West India Company in 1660 and arrived in New Amsterdam that summer. When his enlistment expired, Leisler turned to the quick profits of the fur trade and was very successful, which allowed him to branch into other profitable ventures. Respected and well liked by the inhabitants of New York, Governor Dongan appointed Leisler to several civil posts within the colony and made him a captain of militia on September 10, 1684.[9]

After speaking to the people's grievances and rallying the crowd in the name of King William, several of Leisler's supporters led the group forward against Fort James, where Lt. Governor Nicholson and his council were meeting. The fort was in such a state that there was little to stop the mob from entering, and within minutes the parade ground was filled with armed men. There were some tense moments, but in the end, given the lopsided numbers, there was little choice. On the afternoon of May 31, 1689, Nicholson relented and handed over control of the fort. Then, as agreed upon, he arranged passage to England on the first vessel he could find.

With Nicholson and his staff gone a revolutionary council was convened, which named Leisler commander of Fort James. One of the first orders of business for Leisler and the new council was to draft a letter to the king, professing the current government's loyalty to William and explaining why Nicholson was removed from his post. The former lieutenant governor's comments concerning putting the town to the torch were, of course, purposely misconstrued to place Nicholson, a "pretended Protestant," alongside Andros as an enemy of the king, leaving the revolutionary leaders and the citizens of New York with no choice but to act in order to preserve their liberty, property, and religion.

For his part Leisler accelerated the repairs to Fort James, which he renamed Fort William Henry in honor of the new king. It was no simple matter, but work progressed well enough that Leisler turned his thoughts toward securing the rest of New York. Most of this did not prove difficult, but Albany and its council were not so quick to yield control to Leisler and his *ad-hoc* band. Instead, an uneasy cooperation developed between Leisler and the Albany party led by Robert Livingston, one based on the immediate threat posed by the French. This workable truce became more difficult later in the year when Leisler, seizing mail intended for Nicholson, loosely interpreted one letter from Whitehall as royal confirmation of his position as lieutenant governor of New York.[10]

Leisler's relationship with Albany would come to loggerheads the following year, but in the meantime the change in government brought about a state of confusion in regard to the defense of the colony, just as it had in New England. Many of the troops brought by Andros deserted, adding to the already critical manpower shortage along the frontier. Money was available at first from what was taken in by Nicholson's government, but it soon became in short supply with the needs thrust upon New York as news of war with France called the safety of both Albany and New York City into question. More importantly, the undercurrent of distrust between Leisler's revolutionary party and its political opponents colored far too many decisions and called the unity of the colony into question at the precise moment that it was needed the most.[11]

The Glorious Revolution also struck to the south in Maryland but in a far milder form. Protestant zeal and rumors of a Popish plot circulated through the colony, leading to a number of disturbances and several political confrontations with the governor, Lord Baltimore, but little came of it. London responded to the colony's complaints by replacing Baltimore with Lionel Copley, although this did little to solve the problem. Farther south in Virginia and the Carolinas the revolution had even less of an effect and little bearing on the leadership and conduct of these colonies in prosecuting the upcoming conflict with France.

CHAPTER NINE

The Wabanaki and the Iroquois

In April 1689, the Abenaki returned to the warpath. Their first target was Saco Falls and the nearby farms. While small raids continued for the next several months, a more important target, Dover, New Hampshire, came to the forefront. It was not so much the town that was the focus of the attack as it was the town's leader, Major Richard Waldron. Waldron had a checkered history with the tribes of the area. During King Philip's War, Waldron had maintained a peace treaty with the Dover and Penacook tribes of southern New Hampshire. The move insulated this area during the conflict, and both sides maintained the peace as promised. Although the Penacook abided by their end of the treaty, in the fall of 1676 several hundred refugees from King Philip's War in Massachusetts fled north to seek this tribe's protection. It was a difficult and conflicting choice for the Penacook, as it violated the terms of the treaty with Waldron, which called for them not to harbor any enemies of the English, but at the same time native tradition called for such acts. Word of this reached the governor of Massachusetts, who sent two companies to the area to seize the fleeing rebels. When the troops arrived at Dover in early September they found several hundred Penacook accompanied by Philip's refugees engaged in trading with Waldron. Although the natives had brought their weapons, there were no indications of anything but peaceful activity.

Captains Sill and Hawthorne presented their orders to Waldron and informed him that they were going to seize the refugees by force. Waldron, who had seen his share of fights and was sure that he would see another large one if the officers carried through with their plan, presented an alternative. He would stage a mock fight between his native visitors and the troops. Once the tribesmen fired, the armed English would be free to seize them. The plan worked perfectly. Not suspecting any foul play the natives assumed their role in the sham fight and fired their muskets into the air as part of the production. Once they did the Massachusetts troops swooped in and seized almost all of the unsuspecting natives. The refugees were sorted out, and some two hundred in all were sent to Boston. Seven of these refugees were hanged for their part in the war, while the rest were sold into slavery. The Penacook and the other southern natives who were known to be friendly were given back their arms and sent on their way.[1]

Over a decade had passed since the incident, but it was not forgotten by those who it was perpetrated upon. Reminders of this deceit came from the Wabanaki, who were interested in pushing back against the English. Together, a wide group of native warriors assembled to seek their revenge on Waldron, and to accomplish this task they would employ a sham of their own.

On the evening of June 27, 1689, pairs of native women approached each of Dover's five garrison houses. There were three houses on the north side of the town (Otis, Heard, Waldron) and two on the south side (Peter Coffin and his son). These fortified two-story homes more resembled blockhouses than dwellings. Thick wooden walls and firing ports were supported by barred doors and a seven-foot wooden palisade that circled the structure. These houses, a necessity on a hostile frontier, served as nightly shelter for the settlers. The women asked for shelter for the evening. As it was raining outside, nothing was thought of the request, and the visitors were given accommodations in four of the five houses, including Major Waldron's, where he gave his consent over the objections of several townspeople.

Lying in the woods just outside of the town were several hundred Penacook and Wabanaki warriors led by the war chiefs Mesandowit and Kankamagus. The rainy evening all but assured that they would go unnoticed as they watched for signs of activity. In the early-morning hours they saw what they were looking for. The women had slipped away unnoticed and opened the doors to the garrison houses. The signal was given and the warriors rushed forward. Waldron's house was one of the first stormed. The old major barely had time to throw on a pair of pants and draw his sword when the intruders were upon him. With sword in hand he cleared the attackers from his room and forced them out into the hallway. At this point Waldron turned to go back for his pistol and musket when a young warrior struck him in the back of the head. He was then tied to a chair and placed upon the dining room table. At this point the offended wreaked their vengeance upon the old man, subjecting him to a lengthy torture before finally contenting themselves by making him fall upon his own sword.[2]

Several of the other blockhouses fell quickly as well. In Coffin Sr.'s garrison the inhabitants were spared but the house was pillaged. Otis's house fell just as fast. Otis and several others were killed, but the bulk of the inhabitants were taken prisoner. At Heard's house the defenders were more fortunate. One of the garrison, William Wentworth, was awoken by a barking dog and got up to investigate. He arrived at just the instant the attackers were preparing to enter the opened door. Wentworth managed to outrace the attackers and close the door, bracing it from repeated attempts to break it down while he raised the alarm. The effort allowed the garrison to fight off the attackers. At the younger Coffin's house they had refused to allow the women to stay the evening so, locked down, the blockhouse easily repelled a few half-hearted assaults. It was not until his assailants brought Coffin's father forward and threatened to kill him that the doors to Coffin's house were opened and its occupants seized.

With the fighting over, Mesandowit and Kankamagus placed the captives in one house and pillaged the town in search of booty. Half a dozen homes were put to the torch, as well as the nearby mills. It was a catastrophic few hours for Dover. Twenty-three of its citizens lay dead in the wet autumn night, while another twenty-nine were led off into captivity. The war party departed the next morning. Not long after a letter arrived from Boston warning Waldron of an imminent attack. Relief followed a few days later in the form of fifty men from nearby Ipswich, but by then the Wabanaki and Penacook braves were long gone.[3]

A month later the French and the Wabanaki launched a far more ambitious plan. This one was aimed at capturing Fort Charles at Pemaquid. In this they were inadvertently aided by the change in government that came with the Glorious Revolution. The turmoil resulted in over half the garrison of Fort Charles having left or been recalled to testify as to their loyalty to King William. The French and their allies were well aware of this and took advantage of their opportunity.

Led by Castin and Jesuit father Peter Thury, who had recently built a mission at Penobscot, some three hundred Wabanaki took to their canoes. Following the coast the war party set ashore at New Harbor along Pemaquid Neck. The dozen or so homes in this area were deserted. The next day, August 2, scouts brought in a trio of English prisoners captured along the New Harbor road. Under the threat of death one of these men, John Starkey, informed Castin and Thury that half of the garrison of Fort Charles had gone

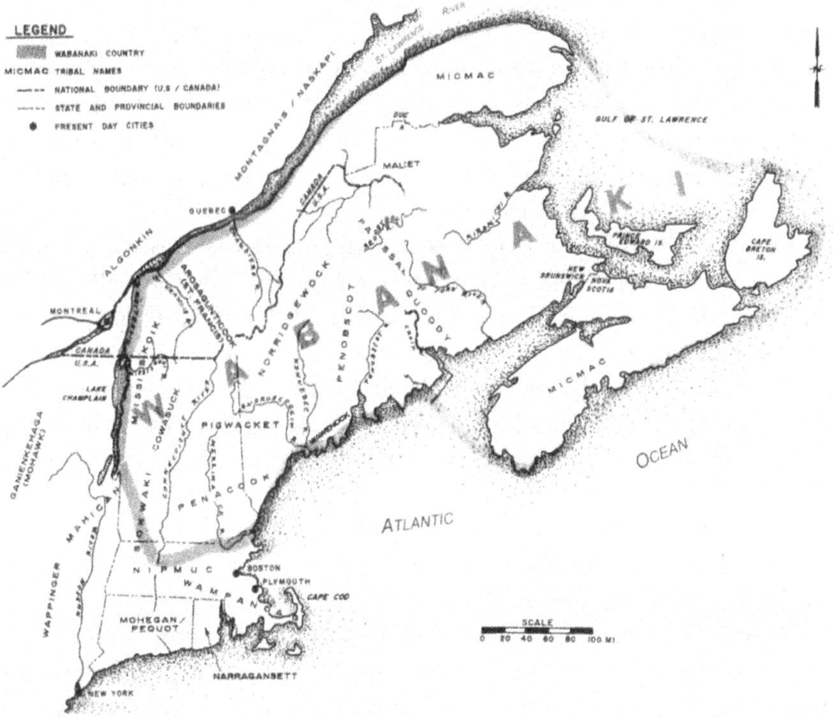

The Wabanaki Confederacy and nearby tribes. The Wabanaki Confederacy consisted of the Western and Eastern Abenaki, the Mi'kmaq (Micmac), the Passamaquoddy, and the Maliseet. In this map the Eastern Abenaki are represented by the Penobscot and the Norridgewock (Kennebec), who are but two of eleven tribes that make up the Eastern Abenaki. Likewise, several of the fourteen Western Abenaki tribes, the Penacook being the most prominent of these, are shown covering western Maine, New Hampshire, Vermont, and parts of modern day Quebec. This pro-French confederacy would fight alongside their allies until the conquest of Canada at the end of the last French and Indian War in 1763. (*Stacy Morin*)

to Pemaquid Falls to help gather the harvest and that the men of the nearby village were out in their fields as well. Armed with this intelligence Castin laid out a plan. Half of the raiders would attack Fort Charles and the nearby town while the other half proceeded to Pemaquid Falls to ambush any reinforcements that might come to the aid of the fort. The plan may have been one of the best executed during all of King William's War.

Castin led the forces against the town and the fort. Creeping as close as possible without being seen, they suddenly burst upon the open ground. Although the townsfolk were caught by complete surprise, Fort Charles was not. The fort's commander, Lt. James Weems, ordered his garrison to fire on the advancing Wabanaki warriors but to little avail. The attackers were simply too fast and too determined. The town was quickly cut off from the fort and its inhabitants either seized or killed. Despite Weem's use of the fort's cannon, the Wabanaki secured several stone houses near the fort. From there they poured a fusillade upon the stronghold's defenders. The attacking warriors were also quick to discern a large rock not far from one of the fort's walls. A number of braves secured the boulder and began to pour fire down on the fort from this location.[4]

It was a nearly impossible situation for Weems. His garrison of fourteen men was insufficient to effectively man the cannon along the walls, and it was too small to deal with a possible threat to different parts of the fort's perimeter. Within the first few hours of the siege several of his troops had been killed or wounded, making the defense of the structure even more difficult. Around sunset a barrel of gunpowder "was accidentally exploded by the firing of a cannon." The flash temporarily blinded the fort's commandant but did not deter him. As the sun went down the fear was that the enemy would scale the fort's walls. To prevent this he ordered his men to occasionally throw a grenade over the wall to discourage anyone from storming the fortifications.

The occasional thump of an exploding grenade and sporadic firefights took place over the course of the night until at daylight the Wabanaki resumed their barrage in earnest. For Weems the situation was coming to a head. Over half his garrison had been killed or wounded and he was being attacked along two fronts. "Towards eleven o'clock," he later wrote of his decision, "there being no Christian within a hundred miles of the fort, relief being hopeless, and the surviving men worn out with fatigue, the lieutenant on their solicitations and those of the women and children, agreed to negotiate for surrender on condition of life."[5]

Weems, the garrison, and the civilians within the fort were allowed honors of war. They marched out of the stronghold with their arms and possessions and boarded a small sloop that had been captured by the attackers. Within a few days they were in Boston telling their story.

The other element of the attack proved successful as well. Thomas Gyles, who had taken half of the fort's garrison to Pemaquid Falls, heard the cannon from the fort. Gyles told his son John that he hoped it was good news, perhaps even the arrival of the reinforcements Lt. Weems had requested. No sooner had the sound of the cannon faded when it was replaced by a scattered volley from the nearby woods and a rising yell from forty Wabanaki braves. With a quick surge it was over. Thomas Gyles and several others fell attempting to repel the attack, while the rest, including John Gyles, were captured and eventually carried back to Penobscot.

As the men in the fields responded to the alarm and made their way back to the fort they rushed into ambushes set by Castin and Thury's troops. Few, if any, of the English reached their objective, and not long after, the Wabanaki warriors were fanning out, burning down houses and farms as they went. When it was over Fort Charles lay in Wabanaki hands; some two-dozen farms and homes had been destroyed and perhaps as many as two hundred English settlers had been slain or captured—all at the cost of one slightly wounded Abenaki brave. The following day Castin burned Fort Charles before he and his war party sailed back to Penobscot aboard a pair of captured English sloops.[6]

The news of Pemaquid, coupled with the raid on Dover, set off alarms throughout New England. Residents east of Falmouth abandoned their lands upon hearing the reports and congregated at Fort Loyal. The Maine frontier was in shambles. Small bands of Wabanaki probed the English settlements, looking for their next opportunity. The new government of Massachusetts, which had in large part been responsible for the lack of a proper garrison at Fort Charles, was paralyzed. "We have much division among us," one correspondent informed the Board of Trade. While another wrote to his friend that "We are in great confusion and without any government."[7]

After raiding Dover, bands of French and Indians attacked Scarborough and Exeter, New Hampshire, as well as Saco, Maine. Local militia rallied to the cause, but they were too few in number to guard the frontier or take offensive action in an attempt to thwart further attacks. In coping with the assaults a stream of requests for aid were sent to the Massachusetts government. Confusion eventually gave way to action. Volunteers were called for and drafts made out of the colony's militia. Two expeditions were organized. The first, which set out from Dover in late August, consisted of six hundred militia under the command of Major Jeremiah Swayne. Swayne's orders were to seek out and attack the Wabanaki while securing the frontier by aiding threatened garrisons in the area. Given that it was autumn and that many of the men in small towns along the coast would be needed to bring in the harvest, this last task was of primary importance.[8]

Swayne spread his detachment across the coast from Haverhill to Casco. Two companies were sent to the latter location to reinforce the garrison there and cooperate with the second planned expedition, while the rest were scattered in detachments throughout the Massachusetts-New Hampshire frontier. It was of course impossible to defend the entire frontier from Haverhill, Massachusetts, to Falmouth, Maine, with six hundred men. Proof of this came when a sizable French and Indian war party struck Oyster River (Durham), New Hampshire. From the nearby woods the raiders had surveyed the town for three days. To their delight, on the morning of September 13, 1689, they watched as several dozen soldiers marched out of the town headed south. The attackers gave the detachment time to move off and then executed their plan. As at Pemaquid, some of the raiders concentrated on the men tending to their fields, while the rest would attempt to seize one of the town's garrison houses, which they noted were lightly defended. In both cases they were successful. The men harvesting corn were caught by surprise and a number fell before reaching their firearms. One of the garrison houses, defended only by a pair of boys, made a determined stand before falling to the war party.

When news of the attack reached Captain Andrew Gardner, who with a detachment of his company had left Oyster River earlier that day bound for Dover, he immediately turned his troops around. By the time they reached the site of the attack it was far too late. Some eighteen settlers, many women and children, either lay dead or had been led away into captivity. There was little to be done but issue orders that garrison houses had to have a minimum complement of defenders at all times and to order the troops and colonists to stay vigilant.[9]

The second expedition launched by the New England colonies was under the command of Major Benjamin Church. Church was a well-known officer from King Philip's War who had organized the first true ranging company, which emulated many native tactics and styles of wilderness fighting. Church's force of 250 men, which was half Mohegan and half colonial recruits, would sail directly for Falmouth and from there launch offensive operations against the hostile tribes in the area. When Church's force reached Casco Bay on the evening of September 20, his plan was to use information he had just obtained to launch an attack on a nearby Wabanaki village. The next morning, an hour after sunrise, these plans were quickly tossed aside when a dozen shots could be heard coming from a farmhouse near the base of the Falmouth Peninsula, a little over a mile and a half away.

Church consulted with Captain Nathaniel Hall, who was in command of Fort Loyal, having just arrived a few days before with part of Swayne's troops. Church, with his detachment and a portion of the fort's garrison, moved forward to investigate. Unfortunately, Church soon found out that a good number of his native allies had been issued the wrong ammunition for their muskets. These forces did not advance with the major as the garrison searched for suitable ammunition to equip them. To the surprise of Church and his men the detachment's vanguard under Captain Hall immediately came into contact with a force of four hundred French and Indians near the outskirts of an orchard. When the two sides began to trade fire Church moved forward with the rest of his force.

It was now the attackers' turn to be surprised. After having watched the town and fort for several days the sudden influx of English troops caught the French and Indian force off guard. Strung out across a field and an orchard that one participant would recall "was a pritty convenient place for [a] skirmish," a heated exchange took hold for the next several hours as both sides probed and tested the strength of their opponent. Five hours into the engagement Church gathered together a small force and had them circle around to fall on the enemy's flank. The plan worked and the French and Indian war party broke and retreated into the forest. Short on ammunition and his men exhausted, Church did not bother to pursue. The defenders had lost eleven killed and as many wounded but had likely saved Fort Loyal.[10]

Church accomplished little after this skirmish, which is sometimes called the Battle of Deering Oaks, nor did Swayne have any better luck farther south. Wherever possible Swayne reinforced garrisons, which in some cases, like Saco, had been depleted by politics or neglect to less than a quarter of their established complement. It was not enough to prevent handfuls of raiders who struck at isolated targets throughout the fall, but by November, Massachusetts was satisfied that the crisis had passed. Both Church and Swayne were ordered to fill out the frontier garrisons from their ranks and discharge the rest.[11]

In New England there had been serious talk regarding recruiting the Mohawk to help fight the Wabanaki Confederacy. The idea appeared feasible and agents were dispatched to Albany, but when they arrived they found the Iroquois preoccupied with other issues, for problems were brewing on the Canadian frontier as well. On August 4, 1689, the Iroquois shattered their treaty of neutrality with New France. The four hundred or so inhabitants of La Chine, a bucolic village six miles below Montreal, slept as a summer thunderstorm pelted their dwellings with rain and hail. The blackened skies and sweeping lines of rain concealed what lurked within the nearby tree line. Had anyone been looking, the occasional streak of lightning would have revealed grimly painted figures as they softly darted from cabin to cabin, slowly enveloping the hamlet. But no guard had been posted that evening. A discharge of thunder reverberated across the landscape and faded. Seconds later it was replaced with the screeches and war whoops of 1,500 Iroquois braves as they burst upon the village. It was the worst massacre Canada would ever see. Men, women, and children were hacked down as they rose from their beds. The rolling thunder occasionally masked the screams and cries of the bewildered as the neatly lined homes were set ablaze. A few fought back and a few fled into the wet night, but most found themselves engulfed by their frenzied attackers. The Iroquois were nothing if not efficient at such business. Within the hour two hundred souls lay sprawled upon the drenched ground, bound to torture stakes, or wrapped by the wind-blown flames that burned like beacons along the shore of the St. Lawrence.[12]

There were three stockade forts nearby: Remy, Roland, and La Presentation. In addition to these strongholds there was an encampment of two hundred soldiers located a few miles farther north. Around four o'clock that morning these troops were alarmed by the sound of the fort's cannon. Not long after, a breathless fugitive from the massacre entered the camp with news of what had transpired. The troops were put under arms but did not march, because their commander, an able young captain named Subercase, was in Montreal visiting Governor Denonville and his wife. Subercase returned around noon on the fifth and immediately ordered his men forward. Joined by one hundred militia, the detachment arrived at the smoldering ruins of La Chine about an hour later. A French surgeon who had escaped informed the captain that the Iroquois were encamped in a cluster of woods about a mile and a half away. Drunk on captured brandy and occupied with the spoils of their victory they were an inviting target. Subercase, now reinforced by the garrisons of the forts, moved down the length of his troops, shouting at them in hoarse tones, raising their ire, and boiling over their thirst for vengeance. When they were ready, he led his men forward, sword in hand. Had he been allowed to attack there was a good chance he would have recovered the French captives and dealt the unprepared Iroquois a serious defeat. But as the column entered the tree line, a voice from the rear ordered a halt. It was the Chevalier de Vaudreuil with orders from Governor Denonville to take no risks. All troops were to assume a defensive posture until further notice. Subercase exploded. Surely the governor did not understand the circumstances, he argued. They must attack now, before the Iroquois recovered their wits. But Vaudreuil was firm. His orders were clear. There was to be no attack. Hot words passed between Vaudreuil and Subercase, but in the end the captain had no choice but to obey. The attack was called off, and the troops returned to Fort Roland where Vaudreuil had gathered together another five hundred soldiers and militia.

The next morning, the Iroquois, having recovered from their celebration, attacked eighty men trying to cross from Fort Remy to Fort Roland. The detachment was cut to pieces in full sight of the latter fort, which did nothing to aid the hopelessly outnumbered Frenchmen. Only a handful of the original number managed to fight their way back to the safety of Fort Remy. The terror-stricken inhabitants of Montreal prepared for an attack, but the Iroquois satisfied themselves by burning the surrounding countryside. Those lucky enough to reach a fort were safe, but their homes, barns, and crops were put to the torch. Those not lucky enough suffered the fate of the citizens of La Chine. For a week the warriors of the longhouse roamed unopposed about Montreal, while the traumatized defenders huddled behind their fortifications, looking on in disbelief. Finally satisfied with their take of 120 captives, the Iroquois took to their canoes and sailed past the fortifications of Montreal, giving a shout to the defenders for each captive in their midst. But they had one more task to perform. With no fear of retaliation the force leisurely disembarked on the south bank of the St. Lawrence and set up camp. The inhabitants of Montreal spent a wretched night watching the flickering fires across the river, knowing that each held one of their friends, family, or countrymen at its core.[13]

CHAPTER TEN

Three Wars, One Name

Louis XIV did little for his colony on the eve of the War of the League of Augsburg. He could have sent a brigade of troops, money, and a dozen ships, but he did not do any of these. When war between France and a league of nations that included England began in June 1689, the king consented to Callières's plan for the capture of New York. In addition he entrusted the plan, along with the colony, to the old governor, Count Frontenac. It was a fortunate decision for New France, for although the count had many faults, indecision in military matters was not to be counted among them.

There would be neither troops nor money to support the count. He would have to make do with the resources Canada already possessed—resources that, unable to bring the Iroquois to bay, now had to face a war with the English colonies. But Louis was willing to make a token gesture. He gave the count his instructions and a pair of frigates to execute Callières's plan. The king placed high hopes on the capture of the city and had even gone as far as to minutely detail the count's actions once the conquest was complete. Had he wished, he could have sent a dozen warships and four thousand regulars to seize the town outright. The forces employed would have had no effect on the coming conflict in Europe one way or the other, and the monies spent would have been trifling compared to what was to be laid out for one campaign in Flanders. Under the leadership of a man like Frontenac, history might have been much different. But the king's ambitions and focus lay elsewhere. Instead, he parted with an aging count and a pair of frigates while he and his royal entourage contemplated the fruits of their future conquests among the pleasures of Versailles.[1]

As might be expected, Callières's plan was doomed from the outset. The season was already too far advanced when the frigates bearing Callières and the new governor pushed out of La Rochelle. The contrary winds impeded the passage to the point that it was mid-September by the time the vessels reached Chedabucto in eastern Nova Scotia. The delay had ruined any chance of executing the plan, not that Frontenac had ever held much stock in its prospects. Even so, he paced the deck of the vessel, disappointed in having lost the opportunity to try.

When he reached Quebec on a late October night he passed through the torch-lit streets and greeted throngs of citizens who had come out to welcome him. For many he was a symbol of hope, a leader of resolve and conviction, the Iron Count. For others, such as the Jesuits, he was an old enemy returned, a menace armed with royal decree. At the moment he was concerned with neither. Officials briefed him in half whispers of the events at La Chine and elsewhere as he climbed the pathway to the upper parts of the town. The count nodded at their words as he paused to greet an old friend or shake hands with an important enemy. He spent the better part of the next several days in meetings before departing for Montreal, despite the onset of heavy rains.[2]

In Montreal he found confusion, near panic, and incessant fear. He met with Denonville and found things worse than he had been told. The town and surrounding countryside were in a state of siege, although no one had a clear picture of exactly where besiegers were or how many they numbered. The populace and local garrisons were exhausted from the constant false alarms, and the converted Iroquois at the nearby missions were daily expecting an assault that would sweep them out of existence. To make matters worse, in hopes of appeasing the Iroquois Denonville had ordered Fort Frontenac destroyed. The count was furious over the order, but by the time he rescinded it the task was complete, or at least partially so. The three vessels belonging to the fort were sunk and the fort's cannon thrown in the nearby waters. In his haste, however, the fort's commandant set charges along the walls and pushed off downriver. Explosions were heard some time after, but as it turned out only a portion of the fort had been damaged. Frontenac fumed over the act, which all but signaled the abandonment of Canada's western allies.[3]

There was a glimmer of hope to play upon. In November a detachment of twenty-eight *coureurs de bois* under the command of two established leaders, Greysolon du Lhut and D'Ailleboust de Mantet encountered a pair of Iroquois canoes carrying twenty-two warriors in the Lake of Two Mountains. Du Lhut and Mantet placed themselves between the enemy canoes and the rising sun, which spoiled the initial Iroquois volley. While the warriors of the longhouse attempted to reload, the French closed the distance and delivered a devastating fire at point-blank range. Eighteen of the enemy were killed outright. As their canoes floundered, one made his escape by swimming ashore, while the remaining three were captured and handed over to the Huron and Ottawa.

The victory proved brief, for in mid-November the Iroquois returned, this time attacking La Chesnaye. One hundred and fifty warriors fell upon the hamlet and burned everything in sight. It was a smaller recreation of La Chine. Twenty settlers were killed and the rest were led away into captivity. The news set off a wave of terror that rippled through the lower colony. Garrisons and citizens slept on their firearms. What little trade and commerce that still existed stopped, leaving the streets of Montreal all but vacant. The atmosphere was such that the sight of a few Iroquois would have been enough to push most of Lower Canada over the edge.[4]

The devastation and general mood of the colony left the new governor in a difficult position. It was clear that the colony was too weak to make war, but his real fear was that it was too weak to make peace. Some semblance of strength was necessary not only to convince the Iroquois to make peace but to prevent a wholesale defection of the western tribes from the French cause. With nothing but his reputation to draw upon, the governor used just that. Frontenac, the great Onontio who had raised Fort Frontenac, whose words had brought the Iroquois council fires to that place, whose speeches still rang in the ears of the Iroquois sachems, would bluff.

Frontenac did possess one resource—a famous Cayuga war chief named Ourehaoue. Ourehaoue was among the Iroquois captured by Denonville in 1687 and sent to man the prison galleys in France. His loss had enraged the Iroquois to such a point that Denonville requested his and the other surviving captives be returned. Ourehaoue was given a fine French coat and placed on the frigate with Frontenac. During the voyage the two became fast friends. Frontenac now used this friendship to draw the Iroquois into negotiations. He sent three of the captive Iroquois to the Onondaga with a message from the war chief stating that he and "the great Onontio" had returned. He would be released as soon as the sachems of the tribes came to Montreal to speak with them both. They had nothing to fear, for Onontio did not blame them for their actions. "He looks upon you as foolish children," the war chief informed them. "He blames only the English who are the cause of your folly."[5]

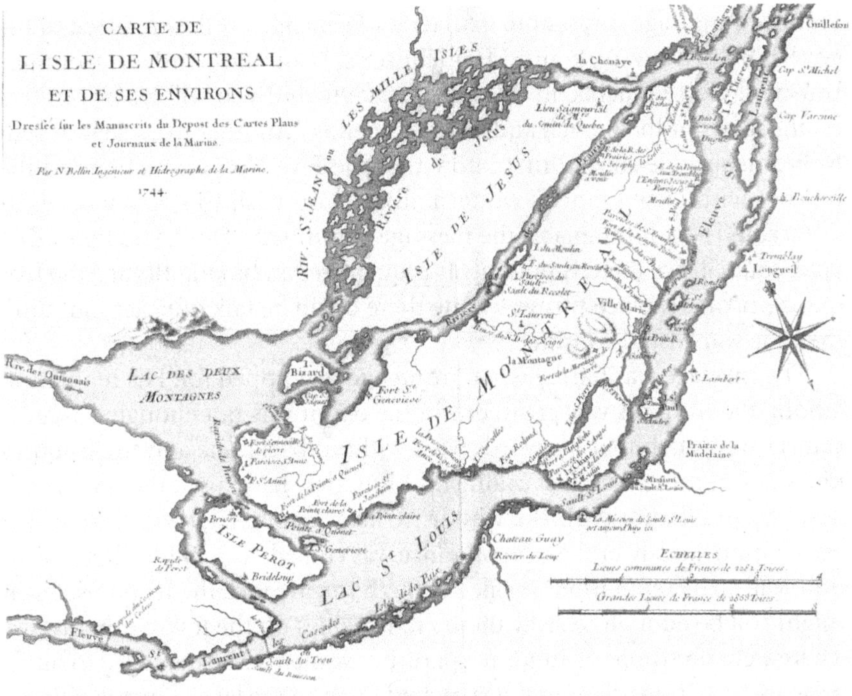

A 1744 map of the area around Montreal. (*National Archives of Canada*)

The Iroquois passed the message on to Albany and held a council at Onondaga to discuss the news. Frontenac sent a delegation to this assembly, which convened on January 22. The eighty chiefs and sachems listened as the French representative, an Iroquois named Cut Nose, rose to address the delegation. He presented his belts of wampum and advised the council to meet with Onontio or suffer his wrath. The Mohawk representative from Albany was next. He told all present to shut their ears to Onontio's call for a council, that Onontio's words were nothing but lies and his threats without force. A Seneca sachem was next. He called for an alliance with the western tribes against the French. He spoke for these tribes, who were disgusted with the French. They and the Iroquois would smoke the pipe of peace, and both should ignore the drunken words of Onontio. The Onondaga representative spoke next. He urged the chiefs to stand with their English brothers and treat Onontio as their enemy. There should be no more talk of a council at Fort Frontenac.

With this the delegates spoke among themselves for a time. Eventually they came to an agreement. There would be no negotiations with the

French. A message was sent to Corlaer and Kinshon, as they referred to the governors of New York and Massachusetts. "Courage, Corlaer! Courage, Kinshon! Go to Quebec in the spring; take it, and you will have your feet on the necks of the French and all their friends." Another message was sent to Frontenac. He should first know that the Five Nations had buried the hatchet with New France's western allies. "You wish to speak with us at Cataraqui [Fort Frontenac]," the message continued. "Don't you know that your council-fire there is put out? It is quenched in blood." Return the Iroquois prisoners. Once this was done there could be talk of peace, but until then the war would continue.[6]

The message was hardly what Frontenac had hoped for. His reputation among the Iroquois was great, but in the end it was not enough. Circumstances were such that his words were without backbone and the Iroquois knew it. But more than just calling his bluff, they had raised the stakes with news of an alliance with the western tribes. Frontenac realized that if it wasn't immediately broken, New France was ruined both militarily and economically. His reputation was not enough to convince the Iroquois, but it might still be enough to sway these French allies on the folly of their ways. There were no troops or funds to spare, but somehow he managed to outfit a force of 143 Canadians and dispatched them to the lake country with the first spring thaws. The detachment carried a haughty message from the governor. The old Onontio had returned and was astonished at what he had found. Did they think he would just stand by while his children disobeyed his wishes? Had they so quickly forgotten his power and his deeds? Were they so afraid of their enemies that they would now invite them into their wigwams? No. Their true father would not abandon them to the English rum that destroyed their senses and the Iroquois who would lure them into their kettles. They were to obey their father and take up the hatchet against their traditional enemies. "I am strong enough," the governor's message concluded, "to kill the English, destroy the Iroquois, and whip you if you fail in your duty to me."[7]

Frontenac realized that the message, and the gifts that accompanied it, might momentarily stave off a mass defection of his allies, but for it to take hold a display of force was needed. It was a perilous situation and a defining moment for New France. In the governor's mind an attack was the only alternative. It flew in the face of his standing orders and the advice of his council. He was warned that the dejected populace and wavering allies would crumble under news of another defeat. A chorus of voices agreed and stated that he would be better to stand on his defenses, but Frontenac scoffed at such talk. How better to restore the spirits of his troops and the allegiance of his allies than with a victory. Yes, a defeat would be devastating, but in the long run it would be no worse than standing by while their enemies devoured them a piece at a time. Better to die fighting in the field, he believed, than of hunger and fear behind a wooden palisade.

Resolved on an attack, the questions became where, when, and how. The governor summoned his commanders around him and spread a map upon his desk. If one attack was good, he informed them, then three would be more so. There were a few murmurs about the room, but the count quickly silenced them with a glance. He pointed to the map. The first war party would leave from Quebec and strike at the border settlements of Maine. He moved his finger over to Three Rivers. The second would leave from the town and attack the border settlements of New Hampshire. His finger moved again farther west. The last and largest detachment, he stated, would depart from Montreal. It would travel south by way of Lake Champlain and Lake George into the upper reaches of New York, where it would fall upon an unsuspecting and unprepared Albany.

There were a number of puzzled looks about the room. What about the Iroquois? Certainly a blow should be struck against them. Frontenac shook his head. The Iroquois were not to be attacked. The English were at the root of the Iroquois problem, and as such, it was they who would be the target. Any Iroquois encountered were to be left alone. The goal was to bring the Iroquois back into the French fold, not to push them further into English hands. After a moment of silence the question came forward: "When?" This winter, the governor replied, when the lakes had frozen over. Many remembered Courcelle's ill-fated campaign and hesitated at the timing, but Frontenac was insistent. First, the attack had to be soon so as to put teeth into the message being delivered to the western tribes. Second, although a state of war existed between France and England, the English colonies would not expect a winter campaign. It was true that the rigors of such a march would be difficult, but these were more than offset by the increased chances of success.

With the preparations in place, the expedition bound for Albany left Montreal in late January 1690. It consisted of 96 mission Indians and Algonquin and 114 Frenchmen. The majority of the Frenchmen were *coureurs de bois*, woodsmen, and bushfighters, all well versed in the forest arts and the tenets of Indian warfare. These skilled individualists made excellent partisans but, like their native brethren, were notoriously difficult to control. Fortunately for the detachment, the expedition was under the command of two experienced leaders, Le Moyne de St. Helene and D'Ailleboust de Mantet. Both men were well-known Canadian adventurers. Mantet had served for years in Great Lake posts and had recently been involved in the destruction of an Iroquois raiding party on the Lake of Two Mountains. St. Helene had made a name for himself during the capture of the English trading posts along Hudson Bay a few years before and was the son of the famous Charles Le Moyne, who had led his "Blue Coats" along the same path a generation before with Courcelle and Tracy.[8]

Several days out from Montreal, a council of war was held. Frontenac had left the choice of targets and the actual route to the discretion of St. Helene with the only proviso that the detachments not run any extraordinary risk in attempting to fulfill its mission. Up until now most of the French and Indians were unaware of the exact point of attack. St. Helene and Mantet informed all involved that it was their goal to attack Albany. Many of the natives were aghast at the announcement. The party appeared too small for such an undertaking. "Since when had the French become so desperate?" one of the natives inquired. St. Helene responded to the question by stating that it was their intention to restore the honor of French arms and that they would take Albany or die trying. The Indians, more familiar with the hardships that lay ahead, grunted at such talk. French honor or not, they were not interested in attacking Albany. Some time was spent trying to convince them otherwise but to no avail. For the moment the only thing agreed upon was to delay the decision.

For a little over a week the detachment navigated the frozen surfaces of Lake Champlain and Lake George, camping in the tree line at night. No fires were allowed, so the men huddled together in half-frozen clusters with a few blankets separating them from the clutches of winter. A few days out, a thaw turned the frozen landscape to a treacherous mix of broken ice, muddy water, and slush. When the path they were following diverged, the party turned right for Schenectady without uttering a word. Continuing on to Albany was out of the question. When they stopped to rest a few miles from Schenectady, it was not even clear whether they could continue on to that place. Frostbite and fatigue were taking their toll. Everyone was benumbed by the cold. It was late afternoon, and as the sun began to set, a series of windblown flurries filtered down from the dull gray skies. Strung out in small clumps along the barren crest of a ridge, most would have surrendered right then and there if an English patrol had appeared.

An hour later several scouts returned with news that they had captured a small wigwam not far away occupied by four women. The detachment moved forward to the Indian lodging. The men took turns warming themselves by the hut's fire while scouts were dispatched toward the village and the women interrogated. The leader of the mission Indians, a Mohawk chief known as the Great Mohawk, or Kryn, carried himself through the troops, calling upon his dejected comrades to ignore their hardships and shake off their fatigue. Now was the time to wash away the wrongs done to them in English blood, he called out. There were nods and murmurs of approval, and with their morale partially restored by the words and few minutes fireside, the force pushed forward. The scouts, led by a Canadian named Giguieres, rejoined the main body a few miles from the town. Giguieres informed St. Helene and Mantet that he and his party had been within a gunshot of the town and had seen no one. It was welcome news, and the detachment moved forward guided by the captured women. Around 11:00 p.m. the outline of Schenectady appeared through the swirling snow. The original plan was to wait until two o'clock before launching the attack, but the weather had turned so severe that it was deemed impossible to wait.

The village was enclosed by an oblong palisade with gates at its north and south ends. St. Helene sent his brother Iberville with a small force to secure the south or Albany gate, but amidst the darkened flurries and unfamiliar surroundings, it could not be located. Iberville returned to find that his brother and Mantet had discovered the northern gate, which, to the surprise of all, was wide open. The only sentries seen were a pair of snowmen that flanked the entrance, the real ones having apparently retired from the cold hours before. St. Helene and Mantet quickly formed their forces into two columns and quietly led them through the northern gate. Once through, St. Helene's column moved to the right while Mantet and his men circled left. The two columns strung themselves along the inner palisade walls until they joined hands at the south gate. With this, the town was completely encircled and its sleeping inhabitants doomed.

Two hundred and ten war whoops broke the silence as the French and their Indian allies burst upon the settlement. St. Helene led a detachment toward a blockhouse manned by a handful of Connecticut militia. Under the leadership of their lieutenant, these troops fired on their assailants from the loopholes cut in the walls but to little avail. The numbers were too great and the attack too sudden. At length the French broke down the blockhouse doors and put the tiny garrison to the sword before setting the entire structure ablaze. Within the town itself the massacre raged. Many of the inhabitants awoke only to see a glimpse of a falling tomahawk or the flash of a musket. Others were dragged from their homes and slain on the snow-covered streets that crisscrossed the village, and still others perished in the flames that began to take hold of the town. Occasionally a home resisted. The Marquis de Montigny attempted to enter one dwelling and was wounded by a spear-wielding inhabitant after his musket misfired. St. Helene was nearby and stormed the building with several men, killing all of the defenders as Montigny was dragged away to safety.

A few escaped through the Albany gate in the confusion, but most found themselves victims of the French and Indian wrath. The town minister Peter Tassemaker was to be spared in hopes that he might provide valuable information to the attackers, but the order was useless in the face of such a frenzy. Tassemaker was hacked down without a thought and his home set ablaze before anyone realized what had happened. The hardship of the march and the memories of La Chine and La Chesnaye fueled the attackers' efforts. For two full hours the carnage reigned. When it was finally spent, sixty villagers lay dead and, with the exception of a lucky handful, the remainder of the inhabitants, numbering almost one hundred, found themselves prisoners. Thirty Mohawk were discovered within the village. When they inquired as to their fate St. Helene informed them that it was the English with whom the French had a quarrel, not the Mohawk, and as such, they were free to do as they pleased.[9]

The remainder of the night was spent securing the village and tending to the handful of wounded. At daybreak a detachment under the command of Iberville and the Great Mohawk was sent across the river to the home of the town's chief magistrate, John Sanders Glen. Glen and his servants had fortified his home and were prepared to defend themselves to the end, but Iberville had specific orders that Glen, his family, and his property were not to be harmed. The magistrate had helped secure the release of several French prisoners in the past and thus had been singled out for special consideration. After some negotiations, Glen agreed to accompany Iberville back to the village to meet with St. Helene and Mantet. When he arrived, the French commander informed him that his property had not been harmed. He then led him before the captured mass and told him to identify his kin so they might be spared. Glen gazed upon the desperate faces before him and pointed to individual after individual until the natives that had accompanied St. Helene finally began to object, claiming that he was related to everyone.

With this task completed, St. Helene ordered all the dwellings within the village set to the torch. Only half a dozen homes were spared. One belonged to Glen and another held the French wounded. The remaining structures were spared by Glen's intervention. In all, some eighty homes were consumed. A blackened pall clutched the village as the French loaded their wounded and plunder onto sleds. Fifty horses were taken to haul the loot and provide food for the return trip. Of the prisoners, twenty-seven men and boys were selected to return to Canada. The rest, old men, women, and children, were spared at the insistence of Glen and the urging of the Mohawk who had begun taking up his cause.[10]

By noon the French were gone and Schenectady was in ashes. In many respects the attack was misplaced. The town was predominantly Dutch and had shown great sympathy toward French captives in the past. It was not a trading post like Albany, where the Iroquois received their weapons and encouragement to attack the French. It was a frontier hamlet struggling to survive against the hardships and perils of colonial life. But, then again, so were La Chine and La Chesnaye.

By five o'clock news of the attack had reached Albany, and the fort's cannon were fired to signal the alarm to the surrounding inhabitants. Letters were dispatched to Esopus and Kinderhook, and several Mohawk in Albany agreed to go warn the nearby Mohawk villages. The weather was so poor that it was hours, or even days, before the letters reached their destinations, and the Mohawk were so terrified after viewing the destruction at Schenectady that they refused to go any farther.[11]

On February 12, a makeshift force of Mohawk and English assembled outside of Schenectady and set out after the retreating French. Equipped with their captured horses and possessing a week's head start, it appeared the French would make good their escape. Around Crown Point the Englishmen abandoned the chase, but the Mohawk doggedly pressed on. Near Montreal they finally caught sight of their quarry. The French, exhausted from their trek and low on provisions, had separated into several detachments, each shuffling on toward Montreal at their best pace. A score of Mohawk fell upon a pair of straggling groups and, after a brief fight, killed or captured eighteen of their number.[12]

The last minute loss dampened the spirits of the French, but in all, the mission was treated as an unheralded success. The English had finally been chastised for their meddling with the Iroquois, and as for the latter, a clear message had been sent that there was no sanctuary to be found in their allies. New York mobilized and word began to spread through the colonies of the French and Indian depredations. In New England concern would turn to panic as the last two of Frontenac's war parties descended onto the Maine and New Hampshire frontier.

The second of Frontenac's three war parties was commanded by forty-seven-year-old Joseph-François Hertel de la Fresnière. A native of Three Rivers and a veteran of the Iroquois conflicts, Hertel served in the defense of his hometown on numerous occasions. In 1661 he was taken captive and spent two years among the Iroquois, learning their customs and their ways before escaping and returning to Three Rivers. He served in both Courcelle's and Tracy's expeditions against the Mohawk and later was entrusted with command of all of New France's native allies by both Governors La Barre and Denonville. A respected partisan leader, his exploits and tactics earned him the nickname "the Hero," from his contemporaries.

Hertel's force would consist of some fifty-two men, approximately half Canadians including his three eldest sons and his nephew. The rest were natives under the command of the Abenaki war chief Hopehood.[13] The plan was for this force to depart from Three Rivers and, after a trek of some 250 miles, fall upon the settlement of Salmon Falls (Rollinsford), Maine. Hertel departed Three Rivers in late January 1690, and after a grueling two-month march through the Vermont and New Hampshire wilderness during the height of winter, the detachment arrived outside Salmon Falls on the evening of March 27. Wasting no time the war party struck early the next morning. The surprise was near total. The town had failed to post a watch, and most of the inhabitants were still in bed when their attackers started breaking down doors. The town's fort was quickly seized, and before any organized defense could be mounted it was over. Forty-three of the town's inhabitants fell before the onslaught while another fifty-four were taken prisoner. With the town safely in his hands, Hertel ordered the fort and the surrounding homes to be put to the torch and the livestock killed.

With his prisoners in tow, Hertel moved off to the north. Around sunset scouts returned with news of a one-hundred-man English force in pursuit. Hertel crossed the Wooster (Worster) River and arranged his men in an ambush along the wooded north bank near a small bridge. When the English detachment, a hastily thrown together force from the militia of nearby towns, approached the bridge Hertel ordered his men to fire. With darkness descending a brief firefight commenced that "lasted as long as they could see friends from Enemies." Hertel departed not long after dark, and the English detachment, which had suffered a dozen casualties in the sharp encounter, showed no interest in pursuing.

Within a few days Hertel arrived at a friendly Eastern Abenaki village. Here he heard news that Frontenac's third war party, led by Rene Robinau de Portneuf, had just passed through the village a few days before. Although his mission had been accomplished Hertel sent his prisoners back to Quebec under a small escort and, with thirty-six volunteers, marched to join Portneuf.

Portneuf, who was a lieutenant stationed in Acadia, had the most difficult of the three tasks. Leaving from Quebec in late January his force of fifty Frenchmen and sixty Abenaki from the St. Francois Mission was to negotiate its way through the frozen wilds of northern Maine and, after ren-

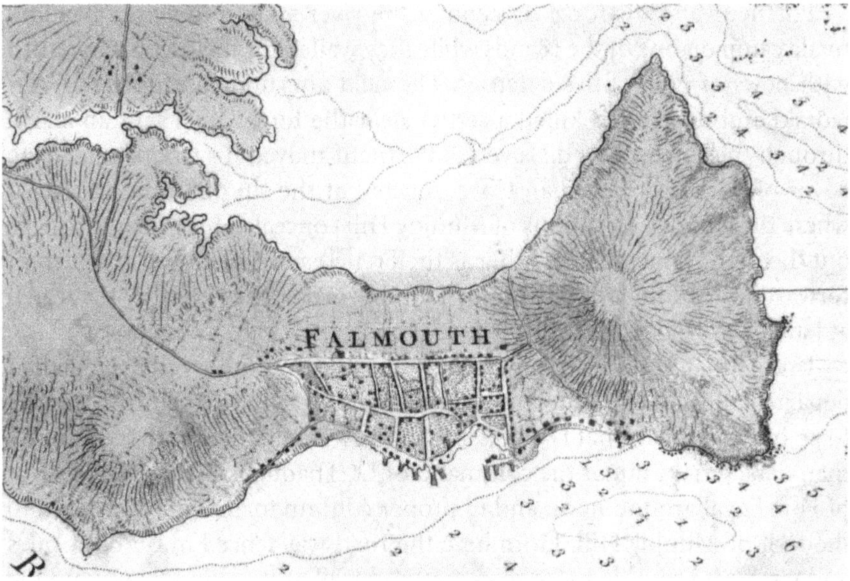

Falmouth Neck circa 1770. Fort Loyal was located at the head of the harbor. The cluster of buildings in the upper left hand corner of the map is where the Battle of Deering Oaks took place. (*Library of Congress*)

dezvousing with Wabanaki forces raised by Castin, attack Falmouth, Maine. On May 25, after a punishing three-and-a-half-month journey Portneuf's detachment arrived at a Wabanaki village a dozen miles from his intended target. Here he was delighted to meet Hertel and hear news of the partisan's successful attack on Salmon Falls. In addition, Castin and one hundred Wabanaki reinforcements were present as well, having descended the Kennebec River a few days before. The prospects for success looked good. In all, the entire force, after recruiting volunteers from the local tribes, was some four hundred in number and the garrison of Fort Loyal was known to be weak.

The defenses of Falmouth centered about Fort Loyal. Located upon a hill overlooking the harbor and the outlet of the Casco River into Casco Bay, the fort was a simple wooden palisade structure with loopholes cut in the walls for musketry and eight cannon mounted upon the four bastions that linked the curtain walls. The garrison consisted of a captain and sixty men, but this was augmented in the fall of 1689 by two companies under Captains Sylvanus Davis and Simon Willard, who occupied the stronghold with one hundred men. To supplement the fort there were four garrison houses in Falmouth, one of which, Lawrence's, was made of stone and located atop Munjoy Hill.

Portneuf and his force descended the river system to Casco Bay and made camp on one of the islands while they waited for their scouts to return with news of Falmouth's defenses. The next afternoon a number of Wabanaki ambushed and killed a settler near the fort, which sent an alarm through the town. Now discovered, Portneuf moved his troops under the cover of darkness to Indian Cove, located at the tip of Falmouth Neck, where the wooded elevations of Munjoy Hill concealed his forces throughout the night. The next morning as the French and Indian war party crept forward toward the top of Munjoy Hill they were discovered by the watch at Lawrence's blockhouse.

Unfortunately for Captain Davis, Willard and a number of his men had departed a few days before, but undaunted, the captain organized a sortie to go out and meet what Davis assumed was a small raiding party. A thirty-man detachment under the command of Lt. Thaddeus Clark marched out of Fort Loyal around noon and in proper column formation proceeded to the foot of Munjoy Hill. From here the road was fenced in on both sides and narrowed to little more than a wagon trail as it wound its way up the hill to Lawrence's garrison house. It was a perfect trap, and Clark, true to his orders, marched straight into it. About halfway up the hill the sounds of marching and rustling equipment was shattered by the crash of musketry, first from one side of the road and then the other. The shock collapsed the English column, and as the echoes of the last shots died out a thunderous war whoop came forth before the French and their allies charged with sword and tomahawk. It was not a matter of resistance for Clark's men but escape. In a running battle back to Fort Loyal only five of the original party made it safely through the stronghold's gates and all of these men were wounded. The retort of the fort's cannon dissuaded any thought the French might have of surprising the fort, and a pair of attackers fell victim to these guns when they advanced too far.

Portneuf moved forward to invest Lawrence's blockhouse while his advance guard scouted the town and the fort. The French commander pulled his forces back that evening, and the occupants of garrison houses in Falmouth used the opportunity to evacuate to Fort Loyal. By morning over two hundred inhabitants had found refuge behind the fort's wooden walls. Although safe for the moment, for Davis and his charges it was not good news. The enemy looked much stronger than first thought, perhaps several hundred in all, while within the walls of the fort the captain could call upon perhaps seventy fighting men. Davis's supplies were limited, both in munitions and foodstuffs, the latter of which would be quickly consumed with the numbers now within the fort. To make matters worse, there was little hope that a relief force could reach them in time. The French commander had summoned the fort to surrender, but Davis informed him "that they would defend themselves to the death."

With the element of surprise lost Portneuf cautiously moved forward the next day to invest Fort Loyal. If Davis's difficulties in defending the fort seemed daunting, so too were Portneuf's options at this point. Frontenac had directed him to avoid attacking fortifications for fear of excessive losses, but at the moment this was the only path open to him and in his estimation was a risk worth taking. The town was abandoned, and the raiders quickly occupied the houses close to the fort, sniping at its occupants while their comrades put the buildings to the torch. A black column of smoke rose from Falmouth Neck as Portneuf paused for the evening. The town was destroyed and the fort invested, but after skirmishing with its garrison during the day it was clear that it could not betaken by storm without suffering heavy casualties. As such it became a question of what to do next. It seems clear that Portneuf or one of the other partisan commanders understood the elements of siege craft. It was agreed to take advantage on a bluff some fifty paces from the fort that offered protection from cannon fire and musketry and open a trench toward the fort's waterside wall. Once at the wall they could burn the fort or blow a breach in the wall. While half his force probed and sniped at the fort's defenders, the rest of Portneuf's detachment made good progress on their siege trench using captured tools.

For Davis the advanced state of the enemy's siegeworks and his perilous position forced him to request a parley the evening of May 28. Portneuf informed the English officer that his terms required the English to surrender the fort, its guns, and its supplies in return for quarter. The English officer asked for six days to consider the terms, but Portneuf was not interested and gave him that evening. Both sides resumed a steady fire upon one another the next morning, but when the French finished their trench at the fort's wall and prepared an oxcart full of gunpowder, Davis ordered the flag to be lowered.

The terms of the surrender were broken almost at once. The French were to provide safe conduct for the prisoners, but to the horror of all, several were dispatched while the rest were broken off into lots. "The Indians retained the majority of them," one Frenchman's account noted. In terms of Davis and a few others, the French did honor the terms of the agreement and they were carried to Quebec. Portneuf spiked the cannon, set fire to the fort and the remaining homes in the area, and on June 1 set out for Quebec, arriving later that month.

As the last of his expeditions returned, Frontenac viewed the attacks as sorely needed successes. There had been some losses, but the governor put these aside in light of the larger gains. Canada had struck back. The English had been chastised and the Iroquois had been shown that Onontio still had teeth. And as he had hoped, the venture had restored the mood of the colony. "You cannot believe, Monseigneur," he wrote the French court, "the joy that this slight success has caused, and how much it contributes to raise the people from their dejection and terror."[14]

The loss of Falmouth was a crushing blow for New England and the Maine frontier. Towns from Saco to the outskirts of Boston braced for the raids that would soon follow. The militia was called out and sent to bolster the frontier posts, but at the moment little else could be done. "Unless the King help us speedily," a friend in Boston wrote future New Hampshire lieutenant governor John Usher, "we shall be ruined."[15]

CHAPTER ELEVEN

The Reduction of Canada

News of war in Europe did not reach the English colonies until the summer of 1689. Along the Maine and New Hampshire frontier this simply formalized the French-Wabanaki alliance and incorporated the current border conflict into what would become known as King William's War in North America. For New France a similar occurrence took place as the ongoing Iroquois conflict merged with a general conflict against the English and their allies. Although a state of war now existed between France and England, this did not necessarily translate into a direct conflict in the colonies. This was due in part to the sparse populations, the distances involved, and a general lack of funds. In addition both the English and the French were embroiled in wars along their frontiers, which stretched their resources and held the attention of both governments. For the English the matter was even worse. The change in administration that came with the Glorious Revolution had created confusion and disorder, particularly in the area of defense, as can be attested to by the fall of Pemaquid. At the moment the last thing the English colonies wanted was to broaden the scope of the conflict via a direct confrontation with New France.

Frontenac, however, had changed all this. By the spring of 1690 two of Frontenac's three raids had struck, leaving the New York and New England frontiers in shambles. Although collusion on both sides was apparent in the ongoing Wabanaki and Iroquois conflicts, Frontenac had raised the stakes by directly committing the resources of New France to organizing and executing these attacks. However, if the count had thought that New York and

New England would shrink from his challenge, he was badly mistaken. Alarms went out as far south as Virginia, but instead of adopting a purely defensive policy as he had hoped for, the English began speaking of retaliation, and soon this talk became centered around the conquest of Canada.

As rumors circulated, the initial English response was more measured. Several French prisoners informed the authorities in Albany that an invasion of New York was planned for the following summer. Fifteen hundred French would ascend the Lake Champlain–Lake George corridor and seize Albany before marching on the lower Hudson valley and New York City. The news caused a great stir. In the best of times the colony would have been hard pressed to counter such an effort, but these were not the best of times. The changes brought on by the Glorious Revolution had left the colony deeply divided. Questions of command, money, and loyalty paralyzed Governor Leisler's brief administration. Under such circumstances a French invasion would prove catastrophic.[1]

The magistrates of Albany appealed to New England for help, claiming that if the French attacked they would find little to oppose them. "Never poor people in the world was in a worse condition than we are at the present," they informed the council of Massachusetts. "No Governor, nor Command, no money to forward any expedition, and scarce men to maintain the city." They pleaded with New England to launch an attack against Quebec at the earliest possible moment. Such an effort would divert Canada's attention and, if successful, would end the problem with New France once and for all.[2]

Great hope was placed in their New England neighbors, but for the moment the leadership of Albany was forced to take more practical steps toward ensuring their security. In late March, a pair of detachments were dispatched onto the lakes. One, under the command of Captain Jacob de Warm, was stationed in the vicinity of Crown Point, while the second, under Captain Abraham Schuyler, was to advance toward Otter Creek along the eastern side of Lake Champlain. These twin sentinels, numbering a few dozen men in all, were to gather intelligence on French movements and interdict any war parties moving up the lake. Scouting parties were to be sent out daily, and volunteers were called upon to advance to the northern portion of the lake in search of prisoners and signs of the impending invasion.

The effort proved partially successful. Schuyler's detachment stationed itself on the east side of Lake Champlain at Chimney Point, where they constructed a small earth and stone redoubt. From there Ensign Ardent Schuyler led a handful of men down the lake to Fort Chambly. Lying in the woods about the fort, he surprised a woodcutting party, killing two of their number and taking a third captive. In the meantime, however, a French and Indian war party had penetrated the thin English screen and attacked the hamlet of Canastigaone, killing ten of its inhabitants and setting off a panic in Albany. The war party then retraced its steps back to Montreal, undetected by either de Warm or Schuyler.[3]

Sir William Phips. Adventurer, admiral, and administrator, Phips rose from humble beginnings on the Maine frontier to the highest levels of New England society. (*Salem State University*)

Massachusetts was sympathetic to Albany's appeal for help, but at the moment Governor Simon Bradstreet wrote back, "We are in no present capacity of granting, being Infested by the Enemy upon our Towns and Plantations Eastward and Northward And are setting forward a small Expedition against the French of Nova Scotia."[4] This latter venture was originally conceived in January 1689 after a pair of French warships operating out of Port Royal had seized seven English ships the previous fall. At the time there was no interest in fracturing the peace to see it through, but fears of French privateers operating out of Port Royal never subsided. Now, after the fall of Pemaquid and the sack of Dover, and with an official declaration of war in hand, there were more than enough reasons to push the plan forward. In mid-March a committee was assembled to map out the shipping, munitions, and provisional needs for the expedition.[5]

A few days later the task took on more meaning when news of the attack on Salmon Falls arrived. A new committee was formed on March 19 and given the powers to accelerate the campaign by impressment, and not long after the recruiting officers began beating their drums, Sir William Phips was appointed commander of the expedition. Phips, born on the Maine frontier, was a well-known ship's captain and adventurer, but with no military background to speak of he was an odd choice. He had married a wealthy widow and used this modest wealth to finance a series of treasure-hunting expeditions. After several dismal attempts, in 1686 Phips located and salvaged over £200,000 from a sunken Spanish treasure ship off the coast of Haiti. Not only was Phips now a rich man but the king's portion of the take was sufficient to earn him a knighthood and a colonial appointment as well.

It turned out there was no need for impressment. Over 700 men, 446 of whom were formed into a regiment under Captain William Johnson, volunteered for the venture, and seven vessels were gathered together, the largest of which was Phips's forty-two-gun *Six Friends* and the smallest being the two-gun *Mary Anne*. The fleet departed Boston April 28 and set course for the coast of Maine. Phips's first target was not Port Royal but Castin's fort at Penobscot. In this, the Massachusetts commander was fortunate. In the early morning hours of May 2, several scouts returned from a reconnaissance of the fort to report that Castin was not present and the stronghold was currently being held by two hundred natives. The news was enough to convince Phips to attack. The initial efforts, however, did not go well. The weather prevented Phips from landing his troops until the evening of May 4, and a few moments later the fort was found to be deserted. The next day was spent destroying the stronghold and welcoming a pair of colonial companies that arrived in two small vessels.[6]

From Penobscot Phips set sail for Passamaquoddy Bay, arriving before the French settlement the morning of May 6. Phips offered terms to several French homes in the area, and when they were refused, he landed troops. A sporadic firefight broke out, and before the French withdrew, they had wounded six of the English. Phips plundered and then burned the homes. Three days later his fleet dropped anchor in the Minas basin before Port Royal. Phips began landing men while, under a white flag, an envoy carried a summons for the fort to surrender.

Louis-Alexander de Menneval, the governor of Acadia, was in a difficult position. The fort's garrison of seventy-two men was short on powder and arms, and the fort itself was in such bad shape that an engineer had recently been dispatched to build a new one. To make matters worse, the stronghold's eighteen cannon, in anticipation of the new works, were not mounted, meaning that there was nothing he could do before the pair of forty-two- and twenty-gun English warships anchored not far away. With no hope of timely relief Menneval accepted the inevitable. The governor surrendered, as he claims, under honors of war, meaning he and his men were to keep their arms and be transported back to Quebec as part of the agreement. If this was the case, Phips did not live up to his end of the bargain, as Menneval, his garrison, and two French missionaries, Father Petit and Father Trouve, were immediately taken prisoner. Phips and his men then set themselves to ransacking the fort and the nearby buildings. The zeal for this task even found the fort's church a legitimate target, as by Phips's own admission, "we cut down the cross, rifled the Church, pulled down the high altar, and broke their images." When this was done the fort was demolished, its guns loaded aboard the fleet, and the inhabitants forced to swear an oath of allegiance to King William. The twenty-gun sloop *Porcupine* was dispatched to raid

French coastal settlements in Acadia, while Phips and the rest of the fleet took their prisoners and plunder back to Boston.[7]

Although the Port Royal expedition had struck back against the French, any excitement generated by the success soon faded into the background as news of a larger expedition spread across New England. The attack on Salmon Falls along with the other raids along the New York and New England frontier had not brought division as Frontenac hoped but instead a call for unity. In late March, Massachusetts governor Simon Bradstreet took the lead and invited representatives of the New England colonies New York, New Jersey, Maryland, and Virginia to meet in Rhode Island on the last Monday of April in order to discuss "Uniting and combining as one to withstand and Oppose the common Enemy." There was a great deal of interest, and by mutual agreement the agenda was shifted to New York City and the meeting delayed until May.

Before some of Bradstreet's invitations had even reached their colonial recipients, the governor was busy informing the king's secretary of state, the Earl of Shrewsbury, of his plans.

> We have stirred up the Maquas against the enemy and have resolved on an expedition by sea against Port Royal and other places, it being the general opinion of the country that the Indian war cannot be stopped, nor peace for the English secured without the removal of those ill neighbors the French. Their increase in Canada is judged utterly inconsistent with the interest of the crown of England, so success in the present attempt will greatly encourage an attack on Canada, if the King will assist us with shipping and a speedy supply of ammunition, of which we have hardly enough to furnish the present expedition. We asked His Majesty to order a supply of arms and ammunition for us, and we beg that the same vessel that bears this may be speedily sent back to us.[9]

Even though King William's new government was more concerned with matters at home, being currently embroiled in a Jacobite uprising in Ireland and a war with France, London could not wholly ignore the plight of its American colonies. If for no other reason than the Royal Navy drew its masts from the region of southern New Hampshire that was currently under siege, a response was necessary. The king dispatched five hundred muskets, two hundred barrels of powder, and twelve tons of lead to New England in late June aboard the merchantman *James*. In addition, to deal with the complaints coming from New York concerning Leisler's administration, Colonel Henry Sloughter was appointed royal governor and would sail shortly for the colony with two companies of regulars, which would further bolster the defenses along the New York frontier.[10]

As agreed upon, the colonial representatives met in New York City. The meeting was opened with a discussion of the state of affairs, which was quickly summarized with a retelling of the northern colonies' woes under the relentless assault of French and Indian war parties. The perilous nature of the Maine and New Hampshire frontier was reiterated, as was the need to secure Albany, which one Massachusetts representative had earlier referred to as "the Dam, which should it through neglect be broken down broken by ye weight of ye Enemy, we dread to think of the Inundation of Calamities that would quickly follow thereupon."[11]

With these matters attended to the negotiations quickly moved forward. It was agreed that the colonies, whether support arrived from England or not, would launch a coordinated attack on Canada. New England would raise an expedition to attack Quebec by sea while a second effort would be launched from Albany down Lake Champlain toward Montreal. Massachusetts and Connecticut pledged 355 men toward this last effort, and New York agreed to raise 400 men of its own. Added to this was the promise of the Iroquois to join the effort with up to 1,800 warriors. The twin attacks would overwhelm the forces of New France, leaving it in English hands by the end of the year. The meeting adjourned with a general plan of action but without the appointment of a commander for the land expedition. Colonial jealousies and agendas made the choice difficult—a theme that would surface more than once over the next eighty years.

With the agreement in place measures were set in motion in New England and New York to launch the largest military expedition ever seen in North America. The recruiters went out with the goal of three thousand men while committees assembled vessels and directed the conversion of merchant ships into warships. The number of troops to be raised was beyond anything ever attempted. On paper the militia of New England mustered 13,279 men, but many of the militia regiments were already busy on the frontier or were serving in key defensive positions. This made it difficult for colonial recruiters to raise such a large number of men in such a short period of time. As Bradstreet had predicted, Phips's success at Port Royal tempted some men with the prospect of plunder, which, according to the articles agreed upon by the colonies, would "be divided to officers and soldiers according to the custom of war." In another case, New York, short on men to fill its quota in the expedition, obtained permission to recruit a company in Connecticut. To further entice soldiers to enlist in this company each man returning from the expedition was guaranteed a thousand pounds of tobacco, while his commanding officer would receive ten thousand pounds for his service.[12]

By early July the expedition, command of which had been entrusted to Phips, had procured some thirty-two vessels. A handful of the larger vessels, such as the *Swan*, the *John and Thomas*, and the *American Merchant*, were busy being converted to carry cannon. They would serve alongside the *Six Friends* and a trio of gunships from New York as the primary escorts for the fleet. The rest of the vessels would carry the 2,300 soldiers raised by recruitment and drafts out of the militia regiments. It seemed that the fleet would be ready to sail by mid-July, but Phips delayed, waiting for supplies to arrive from England, particularly powder which he was desperately short on.

By early August it was clear that the expedition could wait no longer. With the season slipping away Phips ordered the troops and artillery aboard and put the fleet underway on the morning of August 10. Three squadrons of roughly equal size led by the converted warships traced their way along the coast of Nova Scotia without incident. A little over a week later, Phips dropped anchor near Cape Breton Island to allow the scattered elements of his force to catch up before proceeding. By late August the colonial armada was at the entrance to the St. Lawrence River, but as one participant recalled, "We went from Boston, thirty-two ships and other vessels with about 2,000 men, with four months provision and ammunition, little enough, but had not one man for a pilot." The lack of a pilot, and any map of use, was now a major problem. After conferring with his senior captains it was agreed that the fleet would push slowly up the great river. Navigation aside, the poor fall weather in the form of contrary winds on the St. Lawrence further complicated matters, such that when Phips finally arrived before Quebec on October 15, he found "the frost was already fallen in, and so sharp that it made two inches ice in a night."[13]

With news of the fall of Fort Loyal yet to reach him, Frontenac spent a busy summer dealing with the Iroquois. With the success of Schenectady still fresh, a war party of four French and a number of mission Indians under Kryn, the Great Mohawk, was organized. The expedition left Montreal on May 18 and by the end of the month was returning from a successful attack on an English village that had netted forty-two prisoners. In early June this detachment was camped at the outlet of Lake Champlain, busy making canoes for their return voyage, when they were mistakenly attacked by an Abenaki war party from Three Rivers. By the time the error was realized Kryn and a number of his party lay dead. "This is an irreparable loss," one French chronicler wrote, "which has drawn tears from the eyes of the entire country."[14]

In late May, Frontenac formed another expedition. A force of 143 French *voyageurs* and six Ottawa under the command of Captain Louis de Louvigny and Nicolas Perrot were dispatched to the Ottawa post of Michilimackinac, located along the Mackinaw Straits between Lake Michigan and Lake Huron. The governor was convinced that the size of this detachment, coupled with news of the French successes against the English, would prove more than enough to bring his wavering High Country allies back to the French fold. To ensure the success of this mission Frontenac ordered Captain d'Hosta to escort the convoy with an additional thirty men as far as the Ottawa River. On June 2, a few days out of Montreal, the combined detachments discovered a pair of Iroquois canoes on a point of land about a dozen miles above the Les Chatsportage on the Ottawa River. Louvigny and d'Hosta resolved to attack and agreed upon a plan. The latter, with a detachment of thirty men, would land on the point in three canoes while the former, with another sixty men, would attack the point from the land side.

The assault was a disaster from the start. Perrot would not allow Louvigny to march for fear of leaving the supplies and canoes vulnerable, which could jeopardize the governor's mission. D'Hosta's men continued on with their portion of the plan but found a rude welcome when they landed. The two canoes were bait. A much larger party of Iroquois had pulled their other eleven canoes into the tree line and were lying in wait. They greeted the French with a point-blank volley that either killed or wounded almost every person in the lead canoe. At a distinct disadvantage, and seeing no signs of the landward attack, d'Hosta quickly broke off the engagement and returned to camp with his wounded in tow.

Overcoming Perrot's objections, d'Hosta and Louvigny hastily organized a force of sixty men and advanced on the Iroquois position by land. When the party was close to its destination, Louvigny ordered a charge, the ferocity of which broke the Iroquois defenses. Soon the rout was on, and when all was said and done, only four of the original thirteen Iroquois canoes escaped the parting shots of the French; another thirty or so warriors of the longhouse lay dead or gravely wounded along the wooded point, while four were taken prisoner. D'Hosta and Louvigny parted ways shortly thereafter with Louvigny eventually reaching Michilimackinac without incident.[15]

The accidental death of the Great Mohawk at the hands of the Abenaki might have yielded more serious political ramifications had the Iroquois not threatened the colony once again. In June a large Iroquois war party was spotted in the St. Lawrence near Point-aux-Tembles on the Island of Montreal. At hearing the news a local officer by the name of Colembet recruited twenty-five settlers and laid an ambush for the attackers. The Iroquois uncovered the ambuscade and charged the French defenders. A sharp firefight soon devolved into a hand-to-hand struggle, and when Colembet fell, the French, already having lost half their numbers, quickly scattered. Thinking better of their attack, and worried that a stronger French force was in the area, the Iroquois abandoned their raid and returned home. More raiders appeared as well. Some sixteen settlers near Three Rivers were carried off by one Iroquois war party, while five or six children herding cattle near Sorel were carried off by another.

The governor sent out patrols along the St. Lawrence in an attempt to intercept future raids, but as was too often the case, it paid little in the way of dividends. Of more importance was intelligence reaching Frontenac that an English naval expedition had seized Port Royal and was in the process of reducing Acadia. Not long after an even more worrisome rumor reached him that preparations were underway in the English colonies for a far larger expedition. The news set the governor to work on the defenses of Quebec, and with these efforts well underway, he departed for Montreal on July 22 to oversee the fortifications being erected there.[16]

Although Phips had taken nine weeks to sail from Boston to Quebec, and in the process consumed much of his supplies, his timing had almost been perfect. After initial reports that an Anglo-Iroquois army was advancing down Lake Champlain toward Montreal failed to materialize, Frontenac, gauging the season too far advanced for an English attack, ordered the troops stationed there into winter quarters before setting out for Quebec in early October. The governor had traveled no farther than Sorel when an urgent dispatch reached him from the commander of Quebec, Major Francois Prevost. A letter from an Abenaki chieftain who had captured an English woman of means informed him that an English flotilla of thirty-four vessels was on its way to Quebec. Frontenac was skeptical but ordered his small boat to proceed directly for Quebec. Unfortunately, the craft developed a leak, which forced the governor to resume his journey by canoe. The next day a second letter arrived from a Canadian that seemed to confirm the earlier news. He stated that he had seen eight English ships, four being quite large, in the St. Lawrence above Tadoussac. The information was confirmed not long after by a trio of French mariners who, after escaping from Phips's fleet, warned that the English force was near Ile-aux-Coudres about forty miles from Quebec.[17]

Frontenac immediately sent word to Callières to forward all the troops in Montreal, save one company, to Quebec as quickly as possible. He was also to collect all the militia he could during his march. A similar order was issued at Three Rivers, which soon spread across the countryside. Two days later on October 14, the governor and three hundred men entered the colonial capital, much to the relief of the town's inhabitants. Prevost informed the count that scouting parties had been sent out to monitor the enemy and that the nearby settlements had been warned of the English threat.

The next day Frontenac bolstered the French scouting parties with a detachment of 150 marines under Vaudreuil, who was ordered to shadow the English fleet and, if possible, oppose any landing they might attempt. Next, the governor turned his attention to the defenses of Quebec. After a quick inspection he was impressed with the fortifications Prevost had erected during his absence. The town major had not only completed the works the governor had started in the spring but had finished several others as well.

Quebec, as it stood before the English invasion fleet, was two towns. The lower town, located along the waterfront on the east side of the peninsula, was inhabited by the poorer denizens of the capital as well as numerous storehouses, warehouses, and those structures associated with the town's maritime activities. From the lower town the terrain quickly rose to a plateau where the upper town was located. Here were the churches, seminaries, and homes of Quebec's well-to-do merchants as well as Fort St. Louis, the governor's place of residence, positioned such that it overlooked the lower town and the St. Lawrence. To the western edge of the town, which faced the mouth of the St. Charles River, was the Intendant's Palace. The stone structure was located below the ridgeline that closely traced the peninsula. From this point a wooden palisade ran along the shore from the Intendant's Palace, around the cliffs of *Sault au Matelot*, to encompass the lower part of the town on the east side. To protect the land side of the city, Frontenac had started a long fortified palisade, stiffened at regular intervals by stone blockhouses, from the edge of the St. Charles shoreline at the intendant's home, to the edge of the city's eastern shore, where it reconnected to the eastern shoreline wall. Thus, although the works could use perfecting, Quebec was an enclosed town at the time of Phips's arrival.

There were six batteries of guns within the town. Two, each consisting of three eighteen-pounders, were located in the lower town, while a pair of batteries were erected in the upper town at *Sault au Matelot* (three guns) and a recently started position of eight heavy guns on the heights just to the south of Fort St. Louis. Another battery of three guns was positioned at Windmill Hill near one of the town's two landward entrances, and work had started on another battery of three guns near what would be known as the Palace Gate on the St. Charles River. In terms of manpower the governor was fortunate. He had brought three hundred men into the town and expected that Callières would add at least twice that number to the garrison

A view of Quebec from Franquelin's 1688 map. (*Library of Congress*)

in a few days' time. When combined with the existing defenders and some 1,200 militia from the nearby towns, he had approximately 2,500 men at his disposal.[18]

At three o'clock the next morning Vaudreuil's detachment returned with news that the English were close behind. As dawn broke the next morning, Phips's fleet, some thirty-four sail in all, could be seen splayed out before the southwestern point of Ile d'Orleans. In the defender's estimation four of these vessels were the expedition's primary warships, four others were a lesser class of gunboats, and the rest were an assortment of smaller ketches, barks, and brigantines. At 10 a.m. a launch bearing a white flag on its bow made its way from the largest English warship toward the shore. It was met halfway by four canoes carrying a similar flag. Phips's envoy, Lt. Thomas Savage, was then blindfolded and placed in one of the French canoes. After marching the sightless herald through the streets of the town and past as many martial sounds as possible, he was eventually led to the governor's quarters.

When the blindfold was removed Savage found himself staring at Frontenac and a room full of his military and civilian advisors. After taking a moment to adjust himself to his surroundings, Savage announced his mission to the count and presented him a letter from Phips.

> To Count Frontenack or to him or them in Chief Authority at Present in Quebeck.
>
> The War between the two Crowns of England & France doth not only Sufficiently Warrant but the Destruction made by the French and Indians under your Command and Encouragement upon the

> Persons and Estates of their Majesty's Subjects of New England without provocation on their part hath put them under the Necessity of this Expedition for their owne Security and Satisfacton.
>
> And although the Cruelties and Barbarities used ag' them by the French and Indians might upon the present Opportunity prompt to a Severe Revenge yet being desirous to avoid all Inhumane and unchristian like Actions and to prevent Shedding of blood as much as may be I the afore sd Sir William Phips do hereby in the Name and on the behalf of their most Excellent Majesty William & Mary King & Queen of England Scotland France and Ireland Defenders of the Faith &c and by order of their said Majesties' government of the Massachusetts Colony in New England Demand a present Surrender of your forts and Castles undemolished and the Kings and other Stores unimbezeled with a Seasonable delivery of all Captives together with a Surrender of your Persons and Estates at my dispose Upon the doing whereof you may expect mercy from me as a Christian according to what shall be found for their Majesty's Service & the Subjects Security which if you refuse forthwith to doe I am come provided and am resolved by the help of God in whom I trust by force of Armies to revenge all wrongs & Injuries offered and bring you under Subjection to y" Crown of England And (when too late) to make you wish you had accepted of the favour tendered.
>
> Your Answer Positive in an houre Returned by your owne Trumpet with there turne of mine, is required upon the Peril that may ensue.[19]

Frontenac grunted as the letter was translated into French and read aloud. His fellow officers in the room were more vocal. When the letter was finished Savage produced a watch from his pocket and handed it to Frontenac. He informed the count that it was ten o'clock and that his answer was required at eleven o'clock. Frontenac closed the watch and handed it back to Savage. He did not need an hour or even a minute to respond to the English demand. "I will not keep you waiting so long," he informed Lt. Savage. "Tell your General, I do not recognize King William, and that the Prince of Orange is a Usurper who has violated the most sacred ties of blood in wishing to dethrone his father in law." The governor then pointed to the stern faces of his councilors. "Does your General imagine, even if he offered me better conditions, and that I were of a temper to accept them, that so many gallant gentlemen would consent to it, and advise me to place any confidence in the word of a man who has violated the Capitulation he had made with the Governor of Port Royal?"[20]

There was a pause as Savage looked about the room and considered his answer. Finally he asked if the governor would commit his statements to writing. "No," boomed Frontenac, in a display that was partly for the benefit of his officers. "The only answer I can give your General will be from the mouth of my cannon and musketry, that he may learn it is not in such a style that a person of my rank is summoned. Let him do his best as I will do mine!"[21]

Phips and his staff were not overly surprised by the news. Port Royal might fall with an easy threat, but it was highly unlikely that the capital of New France would not resist. The admiral called together a council of war onboard the *Six Friends* to discuss an attack. The plan, in its final form, called for the army to land the next morning along the northern shoreline between the St. Charles River and a tidal creek about two miles from the town. Once on shore the troops would advance as quickly as possible to the banks of the St. Charles River. At high tide, or the subsequent high tide, the small transport vessels would sail into the river and at this point ferry the troops to the other side. These ships would also carry munitions, provisions, and the field artillery. Once the army had successfully crossed the Charles River, Phips, along with the other major warships, would move forward to bombard Quebec. When the admiral saw that the English troops had ascended the heights to the west, he was to land two hundred men in the lower part of Quebec. Together these two forces would then storm the town.[22]

It was an optimistic proposal from the onset, and it got off to a bad start. Around 4 a.m. the next morning the New England troops took to their landing craft. The thought was to land under the cover of darkness and be at the St. Charles River in a few hours. It never progressed to the landing stage. A storm blew in that made it nearly impossible to row or make any headway toward the shore. Major General John Walley, who was in command of the army, had just called the operation off when Captain Ephraim Savage of Connecticut ran his captured French bark aground near the north shore.

The remainder of the day was consumed in rescuing Savage and his sixty-man crew. The tide soon went out, leaving the English vessel stuck fast in waist-deep water.

Savage attempted to lighten the ship but was soon interrupted by gunfire from the shore. The crew returned fire, and a smart skirmish quickly developed. Phips, seeing Savage's plight, maneuvered the *Six Friends* close to shore and fired upon the French with one of his cannon. A few smaller warships followed the admiral's lead and brought their guns to the support of the stranded vessel.

The additional firepower initially worked, and there was hope that the enemy could be held off long enough that high tide would free the ship. The French, however, soon regrouped, this time two hundred to three hundred strong. In addition they had brought one of the fort's cannon with them to help deal with Savage's vessel. A shift in the winds had forced several of the English warships away from the shore, and there was fear for a moment that Savage and his men would be lost, until one of Phips's smaller warships managed to work her way against the wind and chase the French away with several broadsides. It was a tense evening, but when the tide rose toward morning, the bark was freed and rejoined the fleet.[23]

Frontenac watched the skirmish for the stranded English boat for some time, but more important matters soon drew him away. It seemed likely that the English would attempt a landing between the town and Beauport. An effort farther south would entail scaling the heights of Cape Diamond up onto the plateau before the walls of the town or venturing far enough south that the French would have plenty of time to respond. A landing northeast of Beauport would run afoul of poor roads and a number of tidal streams that would delay any advance and offer perfect cover for the French and Indian war parties lying in ambush. Given this, it was clear where the English landing would be. This left the governor with the question of whether to leave the city and attack the English after they landed or to stay put behind his defenses.

The answer was dictated by the St. Charles River, which lay between the town and the likely English landing zone. Near the mouth of the river, the tidal nature of the waterway left the only practical way to cross at low tide, over mud flats, while at high tide small craft were required. Here Frontenac would stand, on the Quebec side of the river. If the English attempted a landing he would counterattack at high tide, leaving them with their backs against the river. If the attack were successful the governor would decimate the landing force. The English could always move farther upriver to cross, but Frontenac was free to shadow the enemy and oppose what would already be a difficult crossing. Of course, the nature of the river worked both ways. Although the count had dispatched several hundred Canadians across the St. Charles near where he suspected the English would land, he would not be in position to support them, at least not in force, for fear of being trapped on the wrong side of the waterway himself.[24]

"Yesterday's action mightily encouraged all our men," one member of Phips's expedition wrote of the skirmish for Savage's bark. This spirit was evident, as at daybreak on October 18 Phips once again gave the order for the army to take to its boats.[25] By early afternoon most of the troops had

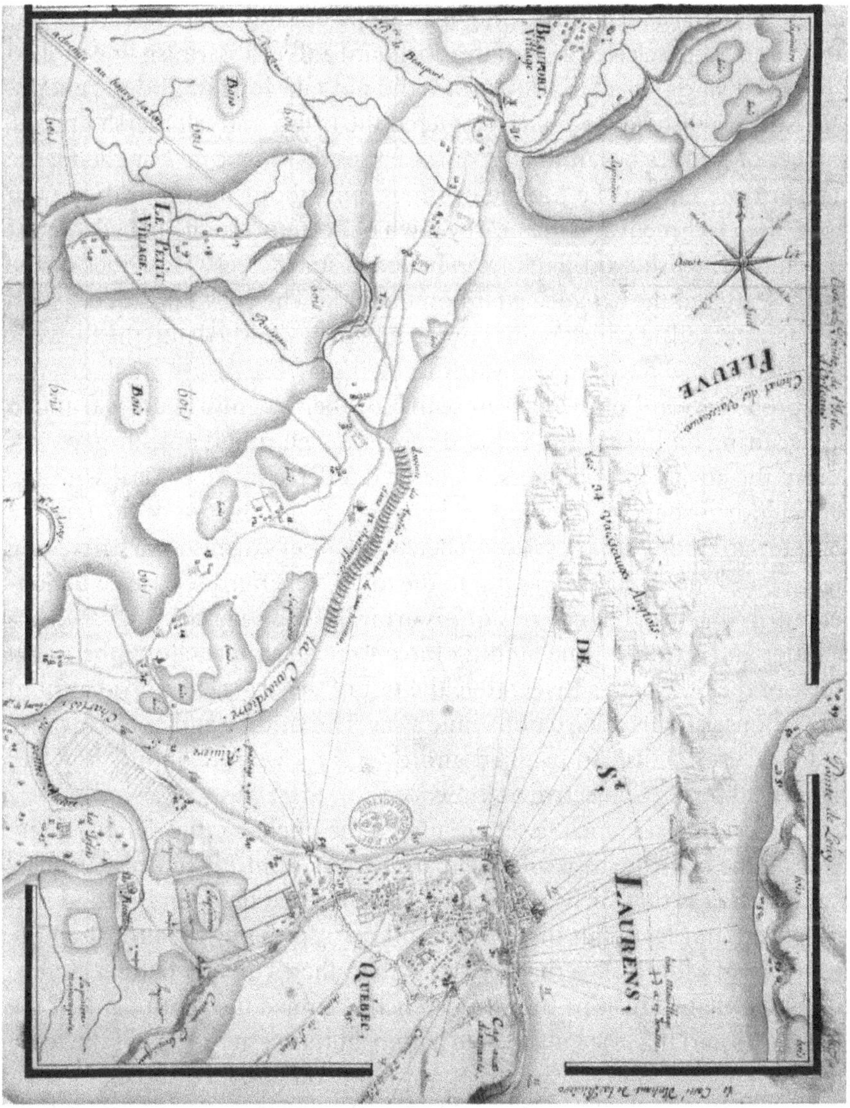

A French map of the siege of Quebec in 1690, showing the defensive works of the town and the English landing to the north of the Charles River. (*National Archives of Canada*)

made their way onto the whaleboats and small landing craft throughout the fleet. In all they numbered 1,300 men, most hailing from Boston and the towns about this city. "Considering how far many of our vessels were from the shoar, and the help we had, never more men were landed in less time," Walley wrote of the operations. The general met a few scattered shots but no real resistance in forming his troops upon the north shore. Four companies were selected as the advance guard and in a skirmish line probed a hundred yards ahead of the army. It did not take long to find the enemy. Once the English advance guard entered the brush and tall marsh grasses, patches of gunfire began to ring out. Charles Le Moyne de Longueuil, the eldest of the famous Le Moyne brothers, and about three hundred men from his detachment and the nearby town of Beauport soon opened a smart fire on the English right flank from behind a small creek. The shock of the attack scattered the advance guard on this side. The New Englanders soon counterattacked, at which point Longueuil's men vanished into the thickets, only to reform a few hundred yards to their rear, break into small groups, and probe forward once again in search of their enemy. There was much lighter firing on the English left and center as well, and it quickly gave way before the advancing numbers. Walley left a detachment to deal with the French skirmishers on the right and advanced with the rest of the landing force toward the St. Charles River. There was a brief skirmish at a barn along the way and the structure was put to the torch, which made clear to the observers in Quebec the progress of his army. By nightfall the English commander and a third of the landing force were encamped along the north shore of the St. Charles River while the rest of the army encamped around a farmhouse about a quarter of a mile away. The landing and quick advance had cost the English four killed and over sixty wounded, but they had achieved their first objective on time.[26]

That evening a French deserter entered the English camp. Under threat of death the Frenchman, a colonial marine from Montreal, informed Walley and his officers that six hundred men had disputed their landing and that there were not less than three thousand men in the town, almost all the troops from Montreal having arrived with Callières the day before. He also told them that some nine hundred French occupied the south bank of the St. Charles and that the Palace Gate battery at the western edge of the town had been increased to eight guns. It was not good news. With such opposition in place crossing the river would present a major challenge. Embarking operations and the small support vessels assisting in the operation would be subjected to a hail of gunfire and heavy cannon. For the moment Walley and his staff kept the deserter's report quiet so "that others might not be discouraged."[27]

Frontenac's guess as to the English landing was correct. As he watched the small boats form up around noon, he dispatched a sizable detachment of militia from Three Rivers and Montreal under St. Helene with orders to cross the St. Charles and aid the elder Le Moyne. These troops and Le

Moyne's men skirmished with Walley's army for several hours, until Le Moyne broke off the action on the English right and Frontenac ordered the Three Rivers and Montreal militia back to the south bank of the St. Charles. After sunset the French sentries watched Phips's four biggest vessels, the *Six Friends*, the *Swan*, the *John and Thomas*, and the *American Merchant*, unfurl their sails and take up a position before the lower town. The French gunners wasted no time and engaged the enemy as soon as they took station. Phips gave the order to return fire and the English ships began engaging the upper town's batteries and Fort St. Louis. Around eight o'clock both sides disengaged with little to show for the effort.[28]

Walley and his men waited for their support and landing vessels at high tide, but contrary winds had prevented their arrival. It was agreed in a council of war that the army would stand prepared to attempt the crossing at the next high tide. A few hours later the landing force watched the artillery duel between the English warships and the town. It was a spectacular sight. The flashes of cannon and the delayed boom created an effect as if a thunderstorm were on the horizon. The battle was only two hours long, and it was impossible to tell what exactly had transpired, but it left Walley and his men wondering why the admiral had engaged the town before the army was over the St. Charles.

The English army spent a wet, frost-filled evening on the banks of the St. Charles. Before daybreak, and without Walley's knowledge, six cannon were landed not far from the army. It made no sense to the English commander. Transporting these guns across the river and then hauling them up the heights on the opposite shore would accomplish nothing but slow the advance down. Why they were landed at all escaped him.[29]

At sunrise Phips returned to his bombardment. The French batteries opened fire as soon as the vessels were in range. At first the English were slow to respond, but it was not long before the engagement heated up. Captain Eldredge of the *American Merchant* took the lead and began a vigorous exchange with the *Sault au Matelot* batteries and the north-most battery in the lower town. The *Six Friends* followed, and together the two vessels closed to within a few hundred yards of the lower town. Phips and Eldredge soon realized their mistake as a volley of geysers straddled their vessels, indicating that the French had quickly found the range. The next volleys repeatedly struck both vessels, cutting away rigging and tearing through the hull, which sent reverberations down the length of the ships. Suddenly a cheer broke out from the city's ramparts when a cannonball cut the flagstaff on the *Six Friends*, sending the admiral's pennant fluttering into the St. Lawrence. Undaunted the pair of English vessels dueled with the French batteries, but what little success they might have achieved was more than outweighed by the damage they were taking. The *Six Friends*' main mast had been struck, and its rigging had become a tangled mess draped across parts of the ship. More than twenty cannonballs had pierced the hull, and there were half a dozen hits between wind and water to contend with. The smaller *American Merchant* was in serious condition as well, but it was not until Eldredge had nearly expended all of his ammunition that he broke off and withdrew downstream. Seeing the *American Merchant* departing, and fearing for his vessel, Phips ordered the anchor cable cut, and the *Six Friends* drifted out of range to the fading cheers of the defenders. The other two English warships, positioned farther east in the main channel, continued their long-range cannonade for the next few hours before they finally moved off around five o'clock.[30]

The English warships rejoined the fleet and licked their wounds. The *Six Friends* and the *American Merchant* required immediate attention, while the *Swan* and the twenty-six-gun *John and Thomas* had suffered only minor damage. Remarkably, casualties had been light, with a few killed and a few dozen wounded in the engagement, almost all of whom were on board Eldredge's or Phips's vessels. Courage was not lacking in the attack, but experience and common sense were. The damage could be repaired, but in their fury to neutralize Quebec's guns, Phips's warships had expended almost all of their powder, making a second effort out of the question. Nor had they succeeded in accomplishing much. One enemy gun had been dismounted and there was scattered structural damage to many of the buildings in the upper town, but ultimately they had failed to degrade the town's defenses or dissuade its defenders.

Walley and his officers watched Phips continue his attack on Quebec. There was little else they could do. Bad weather had once again delayed the supply and transport vessels from entering the St. Charles at high tide. After having skirmished with French detachments most of the previous day his men were short on ammunition. They were also short on provisions, as it had been agreed that the army would be resupplied by the vessels that would transport them over the river. Sporadic shots rang out throughout the day as English scouts sent out to guard the army's perimeter sparred with small Canadian detachments. Evening high tide came and went without the promised supply vessels, although half a barrel of powder and a small number of biscuits were landed, as were fifty men to handle the cannon that the general had not asked for.[31]

By now Walley had seen enough. The army's meager provisions were nearly exhausted, and his troops were ill-equipped to spend another freezing mid-October night along the banks of the St. Charles. He convened a council of war that evening to discuss the options. Almost all agreed that the weary and disheartened state of the troops, coupled with the news that Frontenac had marched three battalions of marines and erected an eight-gun battery on the north shore of the St. Charles, called any advance into question. Even if the army managed to force its way across the river, it still had to scale a steep and narrow passage to gain the heights before the town's walls. It would be impossible to transport the artillery over this route, without which a siege of the town would be meaningless, and if anything went wrong the army might well be trapped on the wrong side of the river. Taken together it was enough that the council requested that the general immediately meet with Phips and request that the troops be withdrawn and another landing site considered.

Walley met with Phips around noon on October 20. The admiral had still held out hope that the army might advance, but given the circumstances he agreed to re-embark the troops and promised to dispatch the needed boats that day. The meeting had no sooner ended than the sound of gunfire from shore caught the two men's attention. Early that day Frontenac had dispatched a detachment of Canadians and Indians to assist Longueil and St. Helene's forces, who still hovered around the English lines. Around midafternoon the Le Moyne brothers attacked a party of English scouts posted on the army's flank. The engagement, which began with a handful of shots, quickly drew reinforcements from both sides and soon turned into a smart skirmish. Taking advantage of the cover provided by the woods and tall grasses the Canadians and their native allies slowly pushed in the enemy pickets and roused the entire English army.[32]

The intense fire soon drew Frontenac's attention. Worried that Longueil and St. Helene's detachment might be forced to retreat across the St. Charles the governor ordered his troops along the south shore to form ranks and array themselves in order of battle. The sound of drums and trumpet calls from the direction of the river alarmed Major Thomas Savage, who was in command with Walley's absence. Believing that a major French counterattack was underway Savage ordered the army to fall back from their current position into more open terrain where, supported by their cannon, they would be in a better position to meet the enemy.

Along the south bank of the St. Charles Frontenac waited impatiently for news. An English warship had fired a few cannon at his formations, but this quickly stopped when the recently reinforced Palace Gate battery responded. Soon columns of smoke could be seen from the area around the English encampment. After a few hours it became clear that the numbers were too great for Longueil and St. Helene, and a retreat was ordered. Fortunately for the French, the English army was busy moving in the other direction. The French detachment, and their two wounded commanders, crossed the St. Charles under Frontenac's watchful eye without incident.[33]

Walley returned not long after the engagement had died down and informed his officers that the army was to withdraw. It was then suggested by several officers that the encampment should move to the shore to facilitate embarking the troops. The general agreed, and that night the English army quietly shifted its position. At dawn the landing craft appeared, which set off a chaotic rush for the beach among the beleaguered troops. Fearing a panic-driven disaster, Walley waved off the vessels and formed the army up into order of battle. The general then sent out three company-sized detachments to "beat up the swamps that were round us, and beat off these spies that we had reason to judge lay near us." These units skirmished with French detachments throughout the day, and at one point the Palace Gate battery even fired a few rounds at the English camp.

That night the landing vessels returned. Walley had informed the newly arrived master gunner Alexander Smart and his detachment that he wanted to embark three of the cannon before sending off the troops. The remaining cannon would stay with the rear guard to cover the operation. As waves of rain began to sweep the area the general ordered half the troops to the boats while the other half stood guard. What he got instead was most of the army milling about the landing zone.

> I ordered some souldiers to keep the rest from crowding down until those were gone off that were upon the flats; I called to them to be silent, but either of these were little regarded, for the crowd and the noise both increased; the seamen calling out for such souldiers as belonged to their vessels, and the souldiers for such boats as came from the vessels they belonged to, hundreds in the water up to the knees and higher, pressing into boats.[34]

Walley and some of his officers went from boat to boat attempting to restore order but with limited success. Fortunately, the weather deteriorated, masking the confused withdrawal from the French. After three hours all of the army had safely departed. Five of the cannon, however, were left ashore through a communications mix-up.[35]

Frontenac was surprised the next morning to find that the English had withdrawn. So great was their panic, the count concluded, that they had left five field pieces, along with their carriages, shot, and a hundred pounds of powder. The message was clear to the governor; the English were going to lift the siege. Fearing that the enemy might make an attempt on a smaller target before returning home, Frontenac sent a detachment to reinforce the settlements on the Ile of Orleans and ordered several others to reinforce Cape Torment farther downriver.[36]

The French governor was indeed correct: Phips and his men had seen enough. Although there had only been a few dozen casualties from enemy action, a smallpox epidemic had broken out within the fleet, striking far harder than French arms. Provisions were running low, there was very little powder, and the weather was growing worse by the day. Although there was talk of making another attempt, it was never seriously considered. A council of war a few days later made it official; the fleet would depart.

The expedition's return voyage proved far deadlier than the siege. Illness gnawed away at the army and the late fall weather brought a string of storms that scattered the fleet. Most of Phips's vessels arrived in Boston on November 19, but half a dozen others went missing. Captain Rainsford and the sixty-man crew of the brigantine *Mary* were driven ashore on Anticosti Island at the mouth of the St. Lawrence River. Rainsford and his men managed to get off the sinking ship with enough supplies to sustain them for several months before they were rescued. Several vessels were blown as far south as the Caribbean, while two were never heard from again.[37]

Coupled with the casualties before Quebec and those from smallpox, these additional losses cost Phips a fifth of his force. It seemed the adventurer turned admiral had not shown the same flair toward his new occupation as he had his old one. In fact, Phips committed several mistakes, but the most important one came before the expedition had even sailed. He simply waited far too long before departing for Quebec. It certainly should not have taken him anywhere near as long to reach the French capital as it did, but in this Phips met with two problems. The first was the lack of a pilot, which is somewhat puzzling given the length of time that transpired between the official start of the expedition and when it set sail. It was perhaps just a piece of bad luck that no pilot could be located, but if so, the second of Phips's problems, the prevailing winds from the southwest in the St. Lawrence valley, was truly a piece of misfortune.[38]

The delay in reaching Quebec placed the admiral before the town in mid-October, a precarious time of the year to be conducting a siege. An experienced military leader would have foreseen the risks posed by the season and would have called off the expedition, preserving his forces for another attempt. But Phips was an adventurer and not an experienced military leader. A siege was out of the question. The consumption of supplies from the long voyage, the shortage of powder, and the lateness of the year all but ruled out that option. Short of an immediate surrender like at Port Royal, the army would only be left with the option of storming the town. Such an operation, however, required precise timing and, more importantly, experienced coordination between the army and the navy. All of these were lacking.

Walley was criticized by some for his conduct, but it is difficult to see what other options he had once the supply vessels failed to arrive at the St. Charles over the course of a few days. By then the French were well prepared and it is perhaps fortunate that the English army did not attempt a crossing. With Frontenac occupying the opposite bank with a similarly sized force, backed by a battery of cannon, it is likely that the English would have paid an unacceptable price if the attempt had been made. When coupled with Phips's futile attack on the town's defenses, which not only went against the agreed-upon plan but also needlessly expended the fleet's scanty supply of powder, it all but ruled out any chance of success.

On the other side, once Frontenac received reports of the English fleet it is hard to criticize his conduct. He rallied the forces of New France to Quebec and stood behind the fortifications he had started earlier. He wisely dismissed the notion of engaging the English army in a pitched battle and instead harassed them with skirmishers while planning a trap along the banks of the St. Charles River. From here, poor English decision making and the weather did the rest. However, even with all the failings of the amateur New England army, Phips, the gambler, had almost arrived before Quebec when it was most vulnerable. Frontenac's insistence on stripping the capital of its men to reinforce Montreal had nearly been the colony's undoing. But the governor was lucky on two accounts. First, he was able to throw troops into Quebec a few days before Phips arrived, and second, the English advance down Lake Champlain had not gone as planned.

CHAPTER TWELVE

Winthrop's Folly

While Phips and his men crawled toward Quebec, the expedition against Montreal was moving forward in the west. Differences of opinion had delayed the appointment of a commander for this expedition, but after some debate, Fitz-John Winthrop of Connecticut was selected for the task. The product of a prominent Massachusetts family, Winthrop briefly attended Harvard but found that his interests lay elsewhere. In 1658 he accepted a lieutenancy in Read's Regiment, then stationed in Scotland. He was later promoted to captain and, along with the majority of the army, supported the restoration of Charles II. When his regiment was disbanded in 1660, Winthrop returned to New England, where, through his family's influence, he obtained the post of magistrate for the colony of Connecticut in 1664. His military experience led to his appointment as commander of the New London militia in 1672, and the next year he commanded a Connecticut contingent, which successfully repelled a Dutch attack on Southold. During King Philip's War, he was commissioned a major and was active throughout the conflict that raged across New England in the mid-1670s. At the conclusion of hostilities, Winthrop returned to politics, and upon the creation of the Dominion of New England, he was appointed Governor Andros's sole councilor from the colony of Connecticut. Although he supported the king's dominion plan and was a friend of Andros, neither association seems to have affected his popularity when the Glorious Revolution swept both away in 1689. Destined to become governor of Connecticut, Winthrop was somewhat self-indulgent, which was hardly an uncommon trait for a prominent man of the day, and although jovial with his friends, he was known to hold a grudge. By the time the Montreal campaign was over, the old grudges he held would seem minor when compared to his new ones.[1]

The basic plan for the campaign called for Winthrop and his New England troops to rendezvous with the New York and part of the Iroquois contingents at Albany in late June. From there the entire force would march to South Bay and embark via Wood Creek on canoes and small boats for Lake Champlain. The army would then negotiate its way down the length of the lake to the abandoned Fort La Motte. Here the remaining Iroquois elements would join the expedition. The force would then descend the Richelieu River until it reached Fort Chambly, where it would disembark. The French stronghold there would be seized and used as a staging point for the final march on Montreal a few miles away. It was a simple plan that, by using the South Bay and Wood Creek route, afforded the invaders an almost continuous water route to Montreal. It was true that the narrow confines of Wood Creek allowed for numerous ambuscades, but with over a thousand Iroquois warriors patrolling the flanks and van of the army, an enemy ambush along this route seemed unlikely. The only obstacle to be overcome along the march was Fort Chambly, but even this was not much of a hindrance. Designed primarily against small arms and Indian excursions, the wooden structure was untenable before a handful of cannon.

The venture faltered almost from the onset. The Massachusetts troops had started for Albany in early June, but about halfway to their destination an express reached them to order their return. News of the fall of Fort Loyal was to blame. With French raiders about, and so many men involved in the expedition to Quebec, the decision was made to recall the troops and deploy them along the frontier. Thus, before the campaign had even started, Winthrop found his colonial forces reduced by nearly a third. The slow recruitment of the Connecticut forces delayed Winthrop's departure from Hartford until mid-July, but by the twenty-first he and the remaining Connecticut troops had reached Albany. "Here," he wrote in his journal, "I found the design against Canada poorly contrived and little prosecuted, all things confused and no readiness or posture for marching the forces towards Canada." Upon surveying the muster rolls he found the New York detachment deficient by 250 men. Not that it got any better. Only a handful of Iroquois were to be seen, provisions were low, and the promised boats and canoes had not been constructed.[2]

It was a dismal beginning. Still, Winthrop held out hope. He was told that the Iroquois braves would meet him on the lake and that sufficient ca-

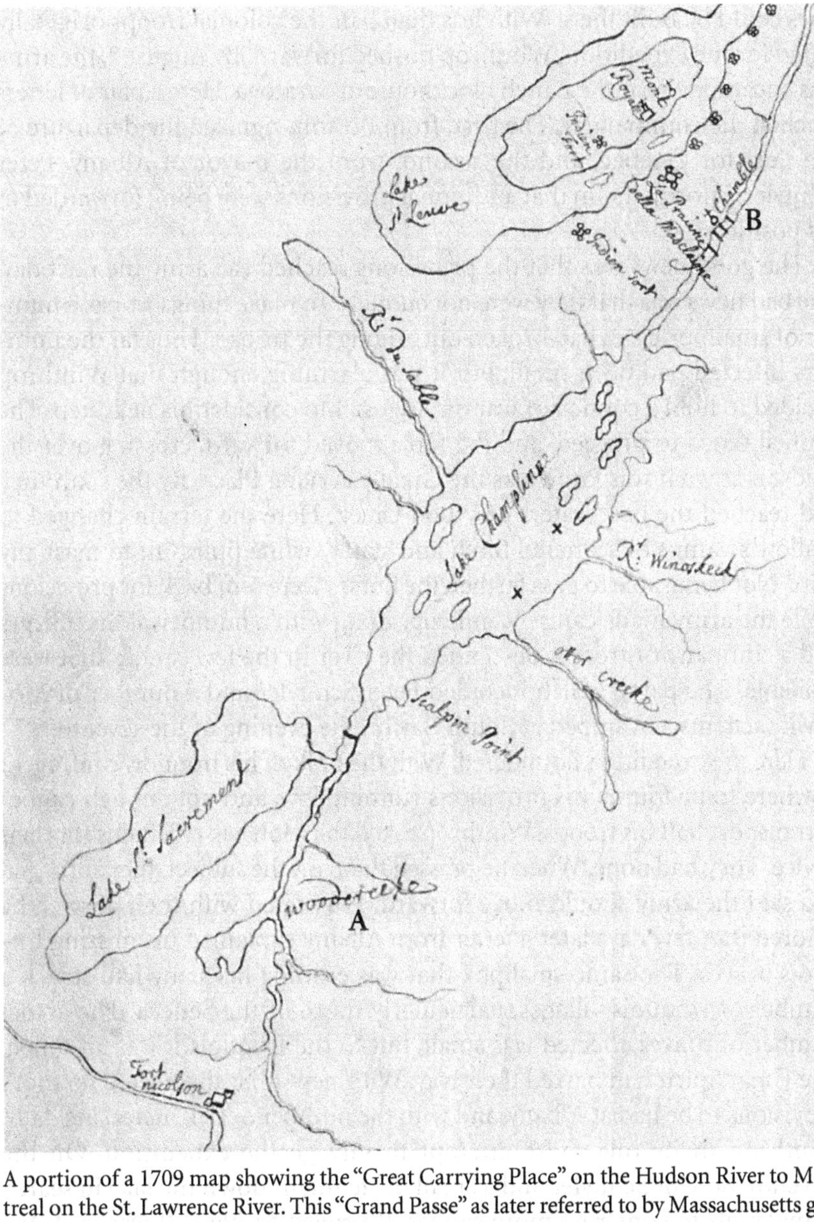

A portion of a 1709 map showing the "Great Carrying Place" on the Hudson River to Montreal on the St. Lawrence River. This "Grand Passe" as later referred to by Massachusetts governor Thomas Hutchinson, consisted of a nearly continuous water route. Leaving from Wood Creek (A), Winthrop's army would not have to leave their boats until they reached the rapids above Fort Chambly (B). From here the English army would be but a day's march from Montreal. (*The Crown Collection of Photographs of American Maps, Series I, 1907*)

noes could be built there. With less than half the colonial troops originally slated for the expedition, Winthrop pushed forward. By August 2, the army was encamped near the Dutch blockhouse at Saratoga. Here a pair of letters reached the commander. The first, from Boston, signaled the departure of the fleet for Quebec, and the second, from the mayor of Albany, Peter Schuyler, informed him that additional provisions were being forwarded to his position.

The good news was that the provisions reached the army the next day. The bad news was that they were not enough. To make things worse, a number of smallpox cases had broken out among the troops. Thus far the numbers infected had been small, but it was alarming enough that Winthrop decided to hold a council of war on August 4 to consider his next step. The council voted to proceed, and the force moved forward, crossing over the Hudson at what was known as the Great Carrying Place. By the sixth they had reached the headwaters of Wood Creek. Here the terrain changed to shallow swamps of scattered birch and stately white pines "fit to mast any ship." Not being able to pass farther, the horses were sent back for provisions while the army made camp. Winthrop, along with a number of his officers and a company of troops, descended the river in the few canoes that were available. The party, which included Peter Schuyler and a number of Mohawk sachems, encamped at South Bay on the evening of the seventh.[3]

Here the expedition floundered. With the bulk of his Iroquois contingent nowhere to be found, his provisions running low, and not enough canoes to transport half his troops, Winthrop asked the Mohawk chieftains for their advice. They had none. When he pressed them on the subject, they shrugged and said the army should move forward. Frustrated with their answer, he ignored it. A few days later a letter from Albany explained his missing Iroquois braves. The same smallpox that was eroding his army had struck a number of Iroquois villages, particularly those of the Seneca. The actual number of braves affected was small, but to the Iroquois it was an omen. The Great Spirit had barred their way. With news that there were no more provisions to be had at Albany, and with the number of sick increasing daily, Winthrop made one more attempt to salvage the expedition. On the eleventh, he sent Schuyler and a small detachment down the lake in search of materials to construct more canoes. It proved fruitless. It was mid-August, too late in the year to peel the required birch bark.

It was all Winthrop needed to hear. As far as he was concerned the campaign was over. On August 13, he suspended operations and ordered a return to Albany. With the army breaking camp, Captain Johannes Schuyler approached Winthrop with an offer to launch a raid against La Prairie. With little to show for their effort, the general agreed to the plan in hopes that it might divert enemy troops from the upcoming attack against Quebec. He gave Schuyler part of his provisions and ordered him to proceed down the lake against the enemy in whatever manner he thought fit.[4]

As Winthrop moved south, Schuyler and his band of 29 colonials and 120 Indians moved north. Near Ticonderoga they met up with a scouting detachment led by Captain Sanders Glen. Glen's party was on its way back to Albany, but Schuyler managed to convince eighteen of their number to join his cause. They moved up the lake, traveling at night to avoid detection. By August 21, the group had passed the ruins of Fort La Motte and lay a mile below Fort Chambly. Here they hid their canoes and proceeded by land along the trail to La Prairie.[5]

Frontenac had arrived in Montreal in late July to inspect its defenses. Throughout the spring and early summer months, teams of men had cut trees, dug ditches, and worked on erecting strong points. The governor had been in the town but a few days when news arrived that Lake St. Louis was covered with canoes. The alarm was sounded, but soon it was realized that the canoes, some 110 in number, were not Iroquois. They were manned by Ottawa, Huron, Cree, and Nipissing braves coming down from the lakes to trade their furs. The cries of alarm changed to cries of rejoicing. The five hundred visitors were met with complete fanfare. But the news was even better. A few days later, French traders brought in another fifty-five fur-laden canoes. It was one of the greatest fur convoys in the history of the colony, and the economy of Canada, so long paralyzed by the Iroquois siege, exploded. Frontenac smiled at the sight. His message, backed by the successful raids on the English frontier, had paid off. His allies were back in the fold.

A grand council was held the next day. The Huron took the lead and pledged themselves to Frontenac. They called upon him to fight not only the English but the Iroquois as well. "If this is not done," their orator bellowed out, "my father and I shall both perish; but, come what may, will perish together." This was followed by thunderous shrieks and calls of approval. Ever the Indian diplomat, Frontenac saw his moment. He seized a tomahawk and, swinging it over his head, began to chant the war song. It was the strange mark of the count. Here was a seventy-year-old man brandishing a hatchet and performing the war dance with the same ease that he socialized with royalty in the halls of Versailles. He was a man comfortable with the company of kings or woodland warriors. For in truth, he found elements of himself in both, a courtier of either court and master of both. Soon the mission Indians took up the dance. Then the Nipissing drew their tomahawks and joined in, followed by the rest of the native allies and the French officers a short time later. It was a frenzied pack of madmen hopping about, whooping, and hollering in a bond of allegiance that would last another seventy years.[6]

The ceremonies continued for the next several days until they were interrupted by the arrival of a scout from Lake Champlain. He had seen a large number of canoes on the lower portion of Lake Champlain making for Montreal. A second scout was sent out to verify the report and returned with news that the enemy was already upon the Richelieu River. Frontenac mustered his troops and, with his Indian allies, crossed over to the south bank of the St. Lawrence. At La Prairie he encamped with 1,200 men and awaited the English advance. After several days of inactivity, it became apparent that the reports were false. The western tribes were impatient to go home, and Frontenac saw no reason not to let them go. He gave them the customary gifts and sent them on their way, delighted in how events had unfolded. The next day he broke camp and returned to Montreal. The troops were redistributed back to their posts while a small detachment was left at La Prairie in case the English attack should actually materialize.[7]

Had Schuyler arrived a day earlier, it is doubtful whether he or any of his party would have escaped. But the Dutchman was fortunate. His party had heard a great deal of musketry the night before but had no idea that it was the departing troops firing a salute to the governor. As he and his men peered out of the dim morning woods about La Prairie they saw nothing unusual. The citizens of the town were leaving the fort to tend to their fields. They were escorted by a handful of troops, weary after the long alarms of the last several days. The plan had been to cut the French off from the fort, but a handful of eager braves and soldiers let lose a war cry and rushed forward before the trap was set. Schuyler was furious, but at this point there was nothing to do but order the entire detachment forward. It was over quickly. The escort was overwhelmed before it knew what happened. Six Frenchmen fell to musket balls and hatchet, and nineteen were captured, including four women. The remaining citizens and soldiers took flight and reached the safety of the fort before the attackers could reach them. Having missed a larger opportunity, the raiders took to killing livestock and burning the surrounding homes. Schuyler and several of his comrades wanted to attack the fort, but the natives, content with their plunder, would have none of it. With the countryside warned to their presence, the detachment leisurely retraced its steps. By the end of the day, they were back in their canoes and well on their way home before any pursuit was even contemplated.[8]

By the end of August, Schuyler and his men were back in Albany. His report was welcomed, but these were hardly the results envisioned when the project was first broached in May. Winthrop was here as well, explaining his reasons for calling off the expedition to Governor Leisler. Leisler, however, was not convinced of Winthrop's sincerity. The problem stemmed in part from Winthrop's association with Robert Livingston, a prominent local citizen, brother-in-law of Peter Schuyler, and leader of Leisler's political opposition. When Winthrop first arrived in Albany in July, he met with Livingston at his headquarters. There was nothing sinister about the meeting. Livingston was thoroughly acquainted with the logistics of the operation and the obstacles to be overcome. He offered his advice to Winthrop, and the general listened. Beyond this, the meeting was more a social call than anything else. Leisler's associates, however, had been looking for Livingston and possessed instructions to arrest him. They approached Winthrop's headquarters in an attempt to carry out their orders but found the general in no mood to comply. By the time the orders were verified and the issue resolved, Livingston had made good his escape.

This, coupled with Winthrop's former ties to Andros, painted a dark picture in the governor's mind. He pressed Winthrop for a detailed account of why he had not proceeded with the campaign. Winthrop stated that he had already made such an account both to Leisler and the government of Connecticut, but Leisler was looking for a scapegoat. He accused Winthrop of conspiring with his political enemies, of purposely mismanaging the affair, and of bribing the Iroquois not to join the expedition in order to discredit Leisler's government. It was, of course, absurd. The governor was giving his political adversaries far too much credit. The campaign was a dismal collection of miscues and misfortunes, nothing more. Unconvinced, he placed Winthrop under house arrest and confined him to Fort Albany until such time as he felt that his questions had been answered. It was a colossal political blunder. Winthrop was an extremely well-connected man both in New England and abroad. Nor had he done anything that might taint this reputation. The governments of Connecticut and Massachusetts were aghast at the news and demanded Winthrop's immediate release. As it turned out, this was not necessary. Livingston and Schuyler had already arranged to have a number of Mohawk smuggle the general out of the fort. By the end of September, Winthrop was back in Connecticut, and Leisler had made a new set of powerful enemies.[9]

So ended the first English campaign against Montreal. From the start it was ill organized and ill conceived. No one involved seemed to have understood the logistical requirements of the expedition and the political problems that might arise from an inter-colonial undertaking. There was a unified command but no unified logistic effort. Each colony was responsible for meeting its own supply needs, and as a result, items were missed and shortages resulted. It was true that misfortune played a large part in the failure. The smallpox that struck the army and held back the involvement of the Iroquois was an unfortunate stroke of bad luck, but the lack of adequate transportation was an unforgivable oversight. Even with Schuyler's success, the expedition failed to accomplish any of its goals. When Phips launched his attack on Quebec in mid-October, the French were free to shift several hundred troops from Montreal to help counter the threat. Alone, against the combined might of New France and the natural defenses of the city, the seaborne invasion never stood a chance. After a number of skirmishes and useless bombardments of the city, Phips gave up. By the end of the month, he set sail for home, having accomplished little more than Winthrop. "Thus, by an evident hand of heaven," Boston minister Cotton Mather wrote of the campaign, "as well-founded an enterprise, as perhaps was ever made by the New Englanders, most unhappily miscarried."[10]

CHAPTER THIRTEEN

The Battles of La Prairie

With Phips and Winthrop busy leading attacks against Quebec and Montreal, Massachusetts turned to its nearest and most immediate problem, the Maine-New Hampshire frontier. Governor Simon Bradstreet and his council quickly agreed to strike back at the Wabanaki Confederacy. Major Benjamin Church, who had recently led an expedition along the Maine coast and had an excellent reputation as an Indian fighter, was chosen to lead the expedition. After securing transport Church arrived in Portsmouth, New Hampshire, in early September 1690. Some three hundred militia and volunteers had rendezvoused here where Major Robert Pike, stationed at Fort Castle, was to issue the expedition additional transportation and supplies.

Church's orders were to seek out the enemies' villages and destroy them, and he was given a great deal of latitude in how to accomplish this task. Church decided to land at Casco Bay, march overland to the Androscoggin River, and ascend this waterway to Fort Pejepscot, which had been reported as captured. By mid-September Church and his men were standing before an abandoned Fort Pejepscot. With nothing to be found, the major ordered his troops farther up the river to a location referred to by the English as Amerascogin, where two Wabanaki villages were known to be located. A few days later Church ordered a halt when the expedition was within a mile of the Indian villages. Sixty of the "meanest men" were selected to guard the doctor and the detachment's supplies while the rest advanced with Church.

When they approached the village Church divided his men into two parties and attacked. There was no opposition, because the village was nearly deserted. A few of the fleeing natives where shot down and a handful captured. Better news was the liberation of five English captives, one of which soon informed the major that the warriors had all gone to the Saco River to help transfer supplies to natives from the Bay of Fundy who had taken up the hatchet against the English. Church was appalled by the prisoners' treatment, and although a few of the captured natives were spared either by request or hopes of them being used in a future exchange, "the rest," Church wrote, "were knock'd on the head." The expedition spent a day hacking down corn and destroying what they could before departing downriver.

Church and his men returned to their transports at Maquoit Bay. The plan was to set sail for Saco the next morning, and not long after sunrise lookouts reported smoke to the south. Church moved his forces to investigate and landed a small detachment of sixty men near the mouth of the Saco River. This party surprised a number of Wabanaki warriors, killing several and scattering the rest. An English captive, Thomas Baker, was rescued during the engagement. Baker informed Church that the natives had hidden a sizable cache of furs at Fort Pejepscot. The news caused the detachment to return to the fort where the furs were found and secured. The potential profits from this booty soon had several militia officers pressing for the expedition to return home. Church initially objected but later relented when a council of war overruled him.

The next morning the small fleet sailed across Casco Bay. It was a misty rainy day, impeding the fleet's progress such that it took shelter at Cape Elizabeth that evening. As the vessels were extremely crowded Church ordered three companies ashore. The troops found several deserted dwellings and passed the evening in uneventful fashion. That morning several of Church's native scouts lit a fire and began to cook breakfast.

Alarmed that they had given away the detachment's position, Church headed ashore in a small boat to deal with the breach of his orders. The major had no sooner climbed into his launch when gunfire erupted from along the shoreline.

Church was correct in fearing that the enemy lay nearby. A prisoner taken at Amerascogin had escaped during the detachment's march back to their transports. He soon spread word of the English detachment, and a war party was formed that had been shadowing the English for the last day. That morning, noting that the watch was not staying alert, the Wabanaki warriors burst upon the English encampment. The sudden bursts of gunfire and war whoops panicked Church's men, and the three companies retreated to the shoreline before they could be rallied by their officers.

Church soon arrived as the engagement settled down into an exchange of musketry. Reinforcements came with the major as well, but the position he found the detachment in was a precarious one. The entire force was now sheltered on the shore behind a sand bank. Pinned down there was only one option—a charge. Church informed his men that he would give three shouts and the entire army would go over the sand bank and charge upon the enemy. The first attempt did not fare so well. Church gave the third shout and climbed up the sand bank. As bullets kicked up the ground around him, he heard a call from one of his captains behind him that the army had not followed. Church scurried back down the sand bank and admonished his troops. This time the entire force moved forward with a yell, which set the outnumbered Wabanaki to flight.[1]

After licking his wounds, Church sent scouts out along the coast, but no sign of the enemy could be found. With little else to be accomplished the fleet set sail for Portsmouth, arriving September 26. Although the expedition had failed to secure its goals, the prisoners taken were eventually to prove of use.

In the end, Church's expedition, coupled with the failure of Winthrop and Phips's campaigns, had made 1690 a trying year for New England. With so much vested in these ventures, news that all had failed struck hard at Yankee morale. The scourge of smallpox returned with Phips's fleet and soon was at epidemic levels throughout Boston and the surrounding towns. Criticisms of Phips's expedition abounded and Sir William took affront when leading figures questioned his actions. "There are great complaints of neglect and want of proper provision and care," wrote Minister Samuel Myles of the expedition. "Those who are arrived at Boston or elsewhere die up and down like rotten sheep. The cost of the expedition is set down at £50,000, for which the people are rated, though already intolerably taxed. I fear there will be bloodshed as at New York. The French are making great preparations and we are utterly unable to defend ourselves."[2]

The financial loss crippled Massachusetts. The venture was financed in part with the assurance that the booty obtained would cover the costs. As there was no booty to speak of, the entire bill fell upon the colony. There was not enough money to pay Phips's men, which threatened to create another problem, as many of them hung around Boston in hopes of obtaining at least some of their pay. Paper money was issued for the first time in the colony in an attempt to alleviate the fiscal problems, but it proved nearly worthless.

The Massachusetts and New Hampshire frontiers were fortified with troops, but there was no way to pay them. Even if they all stayed at their posts despite this, it was not likely to make much difference. There was no way to know when or where a French and Indian war party might strike, and it was simply impossible to fortify and garrison the entire frontier. Even the seaports down the East Coast were in peril should a French fleet arrive in North American waters. Taken together with the colony's financial woes, the disrupted and slow leadership, and the smallpox epidemic, it set off a wave of despair. Fortunately Church's expedition had paid one dividend that lifted the colony's spirit. Although the expedition had failed to secure its goals, the prisoners taken were eventually exchanged for English captives and a temporary truce was agreed upon by both parties until May 1691.[3]

Along the New York frontier and the extent of the Iroquois homelands there was no truce. With Schenectady in ruins and Winthrop's withdrawal, Albany had become the northern frontier and a legitimate French target given its role in supplying the Iroquois. Unlike the ill-fated Schenectady, Albany was far better protected. The defenses of the town centered about Fort Albany. Constructed in the spring of 1676, the stronghold was placed on a hill to the northwest of the city. From this vantage point the fort's cannon could cover the town, its main approaches, and the river. High ground to the west called the position of the fort into question, but as it was unlikely that cannon could be dragged through the wilderness to take advantage of this weakness this point had little influence on the fort's construction.

The fort's main walls were constructed of fifteen-foot-tall pine trees anchored and lashed together in a typical stockade fashion. A second shorter and more widely spaced row of vertical logs backed the main walls and acted as supports for the platforms and walkways that circled the inner parameter. Bastions were added at each corner and planked over to allow for the mounting of five or six small cannon. The northwestern bastion was later rebuilt in stone and acted as the fort's magazine. Within the compound two long three-story buildings were constructed along the north and south curtain walls, both of which were tall enough that their second-story windows overlooked the main walls. A ditch backed by sharpened stakes circled the stronghold on three sides to provide protection against a surprise attack.[4]

Garrisoned by one hundred men and armed with twelve light cannon, Fort Albany was capable of defending itself against French and Indian marauders, but it failed to address the needs of the town to protect itself from these types of attack. To deal with this problem work turned toward enclosing the town within a stockade, which was supported at key points by log

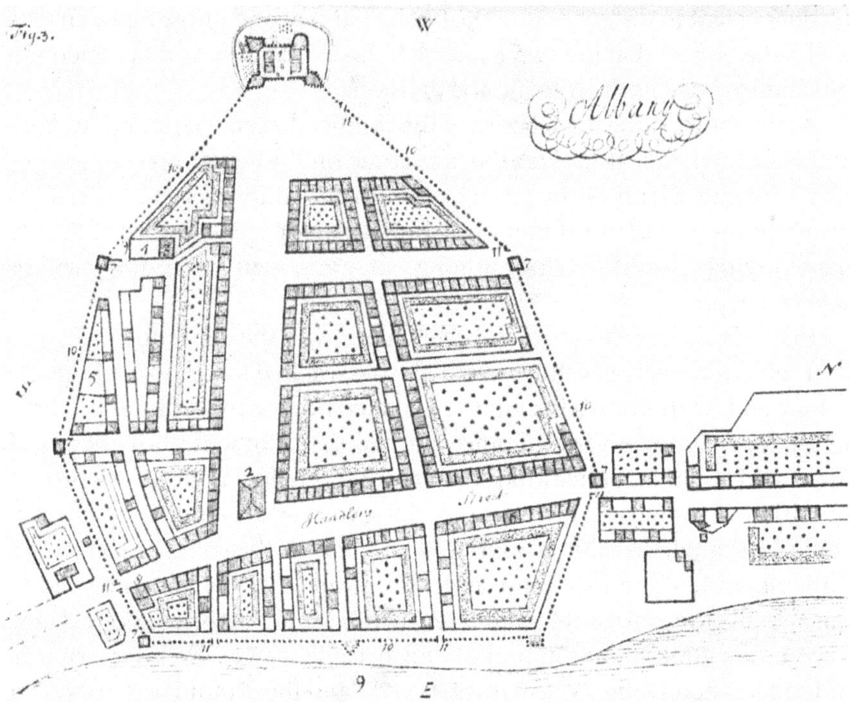

Albany, from John Miller's 1695 work entitled "New York Considered and Improved." The plan clearly shows the wooden palisades and block houses surrounding the town and Fort Albany situated on rising ground to the west, at top. The original legend reads, "1. The fort of Albany. 2. The Dutch Calvinist Church. 3. The Dutch Lutheran Church. 4. The burying place. 5. The Dutch Calvanist burying place. 7. The block houses. 8. The stadt-house. 9. A great gun to clear a gulley. 10. The stockade. 11. The gates of the city, six in all." (*New York Public Library*)

blockhouses. Benjamin Wadsworth, a Massachusetts representative who traveled to Albany in the early 1690s, left a description of this work.

> Ye town is incompass'd with a fortification, consisting of pine-logs, ye most of ym a foot thro, or more ; ye are hewed on two sides and set close together, standing about 8 or 10 foot above ground, sharpened at ye tops. There are 6 gates ; 2 of ye east to ye river, 3 north, one south ; ye are five block-houses ; 2 north, by two of ye forement,'d gates, and 3 south.[5]

Although the defenses of the town were bolstered with several hundred men and locations along the Hudson warned, the real threat to New York's defenses lay in the political division that had wracked the colony with

Leisler's assent to the governorship. Leisler's antics, and purge his of anyone under the pretext that they were Jacobites, had worn thin, and his detention of Winthrop did nothing to aid the division.

As the snows came the realities of the conflict descended upon New York and New England. "If no French ships come on the coast," one contemporary wrote his friend, "if no French and Indians come over the Lake, if the Five Nations prove true, if the young Indians of the East approve of the old men's sayings, and if we agree among ourselves, then the country will be safe and happy."

In Quebec there was relief and celebration with the departure of Phips's fleet. This, however, was short-lived. The harvest had failed throughout the colony and, with Phips's fleet in the St. Lawrence for most of the fall, little in the way of supplies from France reached the colony until the siege was lifted, and what did arrive amounted to no more than a month's worth of provisions. Frontenac had this cargo, along with whatever other stores that could be spared, distributed among the settlers as the colony braced for a difficult winter. The food shortages also meant that the governor had to quarter his troops with the populace. Winter set in and prices skyrocketed as common goods like wine and brandy became scarce. "Every description of food was acceptable," one witness noted, "and the ground was no sooner bare of snow than herbs, roots, and the trifling quantity of fish that could be caught, constituted the sustenance of a large number of families."[6]

Not only were there food shortages for the governor to contend with but powder and munitions of all types were in demand, as were reinforcements simply to replace those lost over the course of the year. When a band of Abenaki came to him asking for supplies to launch an attack on the English, Frontenac had little to give them, telling them that more would come once the first ships from France arrived. Until then, New France was too weak to attempt anything, and thus, "The entire Winter passed away without scarcely a single movement."[7]

It was clear to Frontenac and Governor Callières of Montreal that the solution to the colony's problems was to revive the old plan to attack New York by sea and land. Callières passed an updated copy of this proposal to the minister of the marine in Paris. In this letter he informed the minster that when Phips was before Quebec he "told our prisoners that they must subjugate us, or we must become their masters. This opinion," Callières concluded, "is sufficiently well founded, and it will be difficult for our Colony and theirs to exist except by the destruction and conquest of one or the other. The question is, then, either to place us in a position to resist the new efforts of the English, or to conquer them."

With the outbreak of hostilities more resources were needed than a few years before, but the plan was basically the same. A Canadian force of 1,500 would descend Lake Champlain and launch an attack on Albany. Once this post was secure, the force would sail down the Hudson to rendezvous with a French naval squadron of six frigates and 1,500 marines at New York City. The combined force would then seize New York, which would not only cut the Iroquois off from the English but would prove a haven for French privateers operating in North American waters. Frontenac supported Callières plan, but he questioned the feasibility of seizing Albany based primarily on logistics. On the other hand, the count pointed out that the assigned French squadron was more than capable of taking New York City by itself. At that point the rest of New York would fall in short order, accomplishing the same results. The French squadron could then be assigned to New York and perhaps even turn its attention to raiding Boston.

As spring came the colony's resources were being strained, as was the governor's patience with the Iroquois mission Indians, who, he maintained, carried on a "certain secret intercourse with the Mohawk." In March a Mohawk peace envoy arrived at Montreal. Given the condition of the colony, and even though the peace envoy he had sent under the Chevalier D'Eu to the Onondaga had been taken captive and half its members burned at the stake, Frontenac at least considered the ambassador's words. In the end he and Callières dismissed the peace overtures as a typical Iroquois tactic to distract the French while their comrades massed for another series of raids.

In this Frontenac was correct. In April a large band of Iroquois fell on the settlement of Point-aux-Trembles a few miles below Montreal. Some thirty dwellings were burned and a number of inhabitants were either taken or killed. Next was the mission at the Lake of the Mountain. An Iroquois contingent attacked the mission in broad daylight, capturing thirty-five converts almost under the gates of Montreal. To the west an attempt to surprise Fort Frontenac by three hundred to four hundred Iroquois warriors was thwarted when an alert sentry sounded the alarm, all while smaller groups of warriors prowled the deserted hamlets along the south bank of the St. Lawrence in search of anyone foolish enough to be outside the safety of the local fortifications. Things did not always go the Iroquois way, however. Later in the month a party of forty braves was set upon by a large detachment from Montreal. After a surprise attack that killed half the raiders, the French managed to corner the rest in a farmhouse near Repentigny. A brisk firefight ensued until a pair of soldiers managed to set the structure on fire. With no options before them, the Iroquois attempted to break through the French lines. One brave made good his escape, but the rest were either killed or captured in the melee. The captured warriors were turned over to the local citizens, who, in their fury, burned all of them at the stake.[8]

The Iroquois raids subsided after this initial onslaught. Bands of a few individuals still attacked isolated homesteads and searched for captives, but the large-scale raids ceased. With the improving weather the Iroquois now faced the same problem as the French—enemy raiders. The Miami and the Illinois to the west and the Ottawa and "high country" tribes of the Great Lakes sent out war parties against the Iroquois and in particular against the Seneca. To counter these attacks the Five Nations had been forced to keep more of their men at home.

The opening of July brought good news for the colony. A fleet of fourteen vessels along with the frigates *Soleil d'Afrique* and *Catherine* arrived from France. The famine was lifted. Powder, shot, replacements, and money to repair fortifications and build new ones arrived as well. As the citizens of Quebec rejoiced Frontenac read a letter that had arrived from the king. There would be no French naval squadron to support an attack on New York, as these assets were busy in Europe. The king left carrying through with the attack on Albany up to the governor but in general supported the colony taking on a more defensive role.

As the weather improved Frontenac's poorly coordinated enemies to the south braced for the upcoming campaign season. At least the issues of divided command in New York were settled when Colonel Henry Sloughter was sent to replace Leisler in the spring of 1691. Leisler had made too many enemies and he made one of Sloughter when he refused to turn Fort James over to the new lieutenant governor, Major Richard Ingoldsby, and his arriving troops. Leisler foolishly held out, claiming that Ingoldsby lacked the papers required for the governor to turn over the fort and colony. The issue degenerated into a military standoff with Ingoldsby threatening to storm the fort and Leisler with his supporters manning the stronghold's ramparts waiting for just such a moment. Sloughter, delayed by ship troubles, did not arrive until mid-March. When he did he presented his commission as governor and demanded Leisler immediately turn over the fort. Leisler initially refused, but by now the fort's garrison of some three hundred or so had seen enough. A powerful English warship rode quietly not far away, which could bring more and larger guns to bear than the old fort, and some five hundred troops lay outside the fort's walls prepared to attack on Sloughter's command. Leisler was finally convinced to surrender and found himself destined to meet the hangman on the charge of treason.

With the matter of Leisler closed Sloughter turned to the defenses of New York, and what he found alarmed him. To the north the colonies of

New England were in disarray operating under their old charters. Sloughter begged the king to revoke their charters and appoint him to establish royal rule before these colonies turned on each other in the face of the French. Closer to home the governor found that the division under Leisler had led to a fractured command and neglect of the colony's fortifications. "Albany has long expected a French attack, and the Maquas [Mohawk] are unsteady," he informed London. Sloughter immediately dispatched one of the companies of regulars that had come with him to Albany, and by June 1, he was meeting with the Iroquois to solidify the alliance.

Sloughter listened through a translator as a Mohawk sachem reminded him of the ruins the governor had just visited at Schenectady. The Mohawk had warned their brothers to fortify, the sachem pointed out, but the English refused, saying that "the French were a Christian Enemy and they would warn you, but you see how they have warned you by Schenectady." The sachem was grateful for the attention the governor took toward the alliance, as well as the supplies he had sent. He expressed the Iroquois commitment to the alliance but questioned the resolve of New England, Virginia, and Maryland.

The Iroquois had suffered a good number of losses pressing home their attacks on New France and repelling raids against their villages. Such losses were difficult but acceptable given their ultimate aims. Even so the Five Nations were beginning to feel the effects of constant warfare with the French and their allies. The Mohawk, for instance, could put no more than two or three hundred warriors in the field, a far cry from the thousands they boasted a half-century before. As the sachems of the longhouse took stock of their current situation, they began questioning the fidelity of their allies. Their English brothers urged them to attack the French at every turn, while they themselves watched from the safety of Albany, New York, and Boston. It seemed that they were carrying on the war alone. It was time the English took up the hatchet.[9]

For the government of New York, the message was too important to ignore. The loss or even wavering of Iroquois participation in the conflict would have disastrous consequences. It was quickly agreed that an English-led expedition should be formed to bolster the alliance. Major Peter Schuyler, the mayor of Albany and old friend of the Mohawk, was chosen to lead the effort. Schuyler recruited 120 English and Dutch settlers for his war party. Eighty Mohawk and sixty Mohegan braves joined the expedition at various points along the way, making the total force some 266 in number.[10]

Schuyler and his men set out from Albany on June 21, 1691, and, because of poor weather and a lack of canoes, were still descending the waters of

Wood Creek in early July. On the fifth, a number of Mohegan, in advance of the main force, fired upon a French Mohawk but failed to either kill or capture the brave. The news was coupled with the loss of two of Schuyler's men near Canastigaone. The first was killed and the second captured. The implications were clear, but at the moment Schuyler was more concerned with fashioning the needed canoes and collecting enough supplies to move forward. By mid month the expedition was ready. On July 17, the detachment reached Ticonderoga where it was joined by the Mohawk, who had elected to take the Lake George route to the rendezvous. At this point the weather deteriorated, and five days later they had only advanced as far as Crown Point, a little over ten miles away. While the rain pelted the encampment, a council of war was held, where it was agreed that the force would strike at La Prairie.

The downpour finally subsided, and the detachment moved forward. Late in the afternoon, scouts, who had advanced as far as Split Rock, reported seeing a number of campfires on the eastern shore of the lake. Schuyler detached another party to verify the news and anchored his little fleet at the mouth of Otter Creek. While they waited for the scout's report, the army busied itself preparing for an attack. A makeshift stone redoubt was constructed and pickets were placed about the camp. The men slept on their arms, but the night passed without incident. The next morning, the scouts returned with news that they had discovered a sizable enemy encampment but that it was now abandoned.

The threat removed, Schuyler ordered the army forward again, and the night of the twenty-sixth was spent encamped about the fractured remains of Fort La Motte. The next day, the force entered the Richelieu and by the twenty-eighth had pitched its tents along the eastern bank of the river, half a dozen miles below Fort Chambly. That evening, three of Schuyler's Mohawk scouts were wounded in a skirmish with a number of French Indians. The engagement brought forth the sound of cannon the next morning, which echoed back and forth between Fort Chambly and La Prairie, sounding the alarm. Schuyler dispatched fifty men to cut the path between Chambly and La Prairie and spent the remainder of the day securing his camp. Even though the element of surprise had been lost, there was no thought of abandoning the attack. The next morning, the army moved forward, leaving twenty of its number behind to guard the canoes and tend to the wounded Mohawk. The group stopped when it encountered the path between Chambly and La Prairie. Here there were clear signs that a large body of men had recently passed over the trail toward Fort Chambly. An impromptu council of war was held to determine whether or not the expedition should turn back. At length, it was decided to send seven men back to the canoes to warn the troops there, while the rest proceeded with the original plan. It was a decision that almost cost Schuyler and his men their lives.[11]

Thanks to the taking of an English captive near Canastigaone, Louis Hector de Callières, the governor of Montreal, knew of Schuyler's expedition from its infancy. Several war parties dispatched onto Lake Champlain to monitor English activity had made sporadic contact with this force, and a recent skirmish between one of these parties and a handful of French Mohawk on the evening of July 28 placed the enemy detachment somewhere below Fort Chambly. Surmising that the enemy would march on La Prairie Callières laid a trap. He dispatched a number of colonial troops, militia, and allied Indians to Fort Chambly on the night of July 29, under the command of a veteran officer named Valrenne.[12] Valrenne was to allow the enemy to pass the fort unmolested. Upon hearing the cannon at La Prairie, signifying that an attack was in progress, he was to sally out of the fort and place himself between the enemy and the Richelieu River. In the meantime, Callières would be waiting at La Prairie with seven hundred French and Indian troops. The English would be caught between two fires and, with their escape route cut off, annihilated.[13]

Keeping with the plan, Callières and his men crossed the St. Lawrence and encamped about Fort La Prairie. The wooden fort was no more than thirty paces from the south bank of the St. Lawrence. To the east ran a gently sloping field cut by a small streambed about three hundred yards from the fort. The militia and a number of Ottawa warriors were stationed here, between the fort and the stream. A nearby windmill served as a lookout post on the far left of this detachment. To the other side of the fort lay another field dominated by a small hill. Here Callières posted his colonial regulars. These were soldiers of the Free Companies of the Marine, so called because they were under the control of the department of the marine and not the department of war. The name, however, should not detract from what they were—regular soldiers with professional officers at their head. His trap set, Callières bowed out of the upcoming engagement, falling victim to a fever severe enough that it confined him to his bed for nearly a week. Command passed to Captain St. Cirque, who at this point had nothing to do but wait for the English attack.[14]

Schuyler and his men encamped in a marsh about a mile from the fort on the evening of July 31. At dawn the detachment moved forward through a cornfield until they encountered the small streambed about a quarter of a mile from the fort. From here they followed the depression until they came within gunshot of the windmill. A French sentry posted in the upper story of the windmill discerned some movement in the misty twilight. "*Qui vive*?" he called out. "*Qui vive*?" he questioned again. But this time he needed no answer, being able to discern the English and Indians arrayed before him. He fired at the column, killing one of Schuyler's Indians, whose comrades returned fire, leaving the sentry draped over the windowsill. Their presence betrayed, the English and their allies rushed forward, closing the gap before the Canadians and Ottawa braves could reach their arms. Behind a chorus of war whoops and wild yells, Schuyler's men rolled through the militia encampment. A few of the enemy stood their ground, but most, taken by surprise, broke for the safety of the fort.

On the other side of the encampment, the regulars were in much better order, having spent the night sleeping on their arms. St. Cirque, a veteran officer who had served as a battalion commander in Sicily, quickly organized a response. He dispatched one detachment along the beach behind the fort while he led another across the face of the post. The combined charge of 250 troops caught Schuyler and his men off guard. Outnumbered and on open ground, they quickly fell back to the streambed. The French pressed their charge, but now in possession of the streambed, the English loosed a volley into the packed formations, halting their advance. St. Cirque rallied his men and personally led them forward through the drifting pall of sulfur and morning mist. They marched to within a few rods of the ditch and fired a scattered volley at their half-hidden enemy. Schuyler and his men returned fire, breaking the French line once again. As the English and their allies feverishly reloaded, the French reformed for a third charge. This time the French threatened to outflank the English position, forcing Schuyler to abandon the streambed. On open ground the two sides exchanged short-range volleys. For the French it was too much. St. Cirque was mortally wounded, and his senior officers lay either dead or bleeding on the sodden ground. The French line faltered and then broke into headlong retreat when the English surged forward in a howling charge.[15]

Schuyler called off the advance when the fort's cannon began playing on the field. Thus far he had done quite well. He had routed two separate detachments and forced the French to fall back on their fort, all at the expense of two killed and a handful wounded. As the troops set about the task of burning the local structures and hacking down the green corn, Schuyler took a moment to interrogate a prisoner. The Dutchman questioned the captive on the numbers of French at La Prairie. Five hundred, the man replied. Forty were stationed with the governor inside the fort, and 420 were encamped outside. And what about the force that marched to Chambly the night before? How many were they? Three hundred French and forty Indians, the prisoner responded. The words nearly unnerved Schuyler. He was caught between two forces, each greater in number than his own. All thoughts of besieging the fort were cast aside. At this point the only option was to march to the canoes and, if need be, defeat the French force behind him before the troops at La Prairie recovered their wits.[16]

When he heard the distant gunfire Captain Valrenne executed his part of the plan and moved forward to cut the trail between Chambly and La Prairie. His forces were roughly equal to Schuyler's and he deployed them to his best advantage. Moving several miles toward La Prairie he selected a slightly elevated portion of the trail blocked by two fallen trees. Behind these he posted his soldiers in three ranks. The remainder of his troops, primarily Canadians and allied Indians, occupied the densely wooded ground to the left and right of the trailhead. These troops were thrown slightly forward, creating a half-moon formation about the natural redoubt. It was a strong position and one Valrenne felt confident that he could hold.[17]

By midmorning the two forces had come into contact. A handful of musket shots echoed through the forest as Valrenne's pickets sniped at the English vanguard. With the sound of gunfire Schuyler halted his column and ordered his men to drop their packs. He calmly moved up and down the length of the line as his men checked their weapons and muttered nervously amongst themselves. With a stern word, a sarcastic joke, and the occasional pat on the shoulder, he encouraged his troops. When the shuffling of packs and equipment was nearly complete he called out to them as a group. "Men," he shouted so all could hear. "The enemy stands between us and our canoes!" The column responded with war whoops and a "Huzza" and then launched itself at the center of the French lines.

When the English approached to within a pistol shot Valrenne gave the order to fire. A bluish-white cloud rolled forward from the French lines, engulfing the attackers, followed by another and then another, as the three ranks of soldiers fired in sequence. The English column staggered under the weight of the volleys and then broke for the rear, leaving a dozen of their numbers before the makeshift redoubt. Schuyler halted their flight and threw a line of skirmishers forward. The clatter of musketry and shouts of defiance traveled the border between the two sides. The English rallied and surged forward again. This time the French fire did not deter their advance, and soon the fighting about the trailhead became hand-to-hand. With tomahawks and knifes the two sides grappled with one another. Muskets flashed in the knotted mass of men burning the shirts and coats of those nearby. Thinking that the enemy was nearly broken an Algonquin chieftain named

Routine fell on the English flank with his warriors, sparking a second melee. With some effort the English broke the attack, sending Routine and his Algonquin's scurrying into the woods, but by now many of the Mohegan had seen enough as well and followed their lead. A number of the Canadians had similar thoughts and began to bolt, but their leader, Le Ber du Chesne, cursed their conduct and shoved them back into the fray with the butt of his musket. As the morning light filtered down through the canopy the two sides pushed at one another over fallen timbers and tangled brush. Finally the English attack ebbed and slid back into the surrounding forest.

Schuyler reformed his men once again and glanced to the rear. He was fighting two enemies: the French and time. The rear guard had yet to see signs of any pursuit, but one was certain to appear. They must be through the French position by then or all would be lost. With the determination of a cornered animal he led the English line forward against the French center, and once again the fighting became confused. Schuyler called on his men to fight for England and King William only to have his shouts returned by Valrenne. Sword in hand the French commander coolly paced his lines, encouraging his men and directing their efforts as the musket balls zipped past him in the haze. Next to him was Ourehaoue, the Mohawk chieftain who had returned from France with Frontenac. He had become a true convert to the French cause and, with tomahawk in hand, threw himself against the enemy with abandonment.

Valrenne had held the English at bay for almost an hour. With his casualties mounting he called to his officers for signs of the forces from La Prairie, but he received nothing but shrugs. There was no hint of them. He cursed to himself and peered through the smoke as his lines began to crumble under the fury of the English attack. Where were they? he asked. Where were they?

Where indeed. The failure of the forces at La Prairie to organize a pursuit is difficult to understand. Lack of leadership certainly played a part. Callières was out of the picture and his second-in-command, St. Cirque, was dead. A number of the senior captains had also been killed or disabled by their wounds, but this hardly explains why nearly five hundred men lay idle about the fort, especially when one considers that they knew a French force lay between the English and their escape route. The explanations were never forthcoming and the trap, so well set, was never sprung. Eventually several hundred of these troops did march to the sound of the distant gunfire but too late to play any role in the battle.

A little over an hour into the battle the English pierced the French center and, a short time later, seized control of the trail. His forces split, Valrenne had no choice but to fall back on his flanks and reform his troops along the original English lines. The two sides quickly exchanged facings and continued the battle anew but with nowhere near the same intensity. The musketry continued for a time but eventually abated into individual duels as the English slowly withdrew toward their boats. With the enemy past him, and his troops exhausted, Valrenne broke off the engagement around eleven o'clock to tend to his dead and wounded.[18]

The troops from La Prairie arrived that afternoon, as did sixty Iroquois from the Montreal missions. This should have provided more than enough men for an active pursuit, but neither party was all that interested. The Mohawk did set out after the English, but upon hearing firing back at La Prairie, which turned out to be part of the funeral procession for the fallen officers, they broke off the pursuit claiming that they thought that La Prairie was under attack again. It was clear to Valrenne that they wanted no part in actually overtaking Schuyler, which would have brought them into direct confrontation with their relatives. With no pursuit present Schuyler and his men marched unimpeded to their canoes. Here they waited several hours for stragglers before pushing out into the river. By August 2, they were back on Lake Champlain, and by the end of the week the lot of them had returned to Albany.[19]

In his correspondence Frontenac referred to the battle as the most stubborn and hotly contested ever seen in Canada. There was a great deal of truth to the statement. French casualties in the last engagement were estimated at twenty-five killed and twenty wounded. The losses at La Prairie were worse, with some forty killed and as many wounded. Schuyler reported twenty-one militia and twenty-two Indians killed in both engagements and twenty-five wounded, but he later amended the numbers when six colonists and Indians thought killed found their way back to Albany. The fact that almost all of Schuyler's losses occurred in the second engagement points to the ferocity of the struggle there. Both sides claimed victory and exaggerated their opponent's losses and numbers. In actuality neither could make such a boast. The French pointed to the captured English baggage and Schuyler's flag, which they proudly displayed at Montreal and Quebec as a symbol of their triumph. Valrenne was rightfully commended for his conduct, but claims of the extreme damage done to the English by his outnumbered corps were dubious at best. Valrenne and his troops fought well, but they were neither outnumbered nor did they inflict significantly more casualties than they suffered. The conduct of the troops and their officers at La Prairie was another matter, but this was brushed over in the rush to celebration. In Albany Schuyler was hailed as a hero, and his raid stamped an unparalleled success. It was true that he had brazenly overcome the odds and inflicted a number of losses on the enemy, but in doing so he had come perilously close to being annihilated. He realized his mistake too late and was forced into a desperate attack on Valrenne's position. Only the French failure to close the trap had saved him and his men. But like his brother Johannes, Peter had been lucky.[20]

CHAPTER FOURTEEN

A Shifting Tide

ALONG THE MAINE-NEW HAMPSHIRE FRONTIER New England townships braced for the end of the truce with the Wabanaki, but May passed and all remained quiet. It was not until June 9, 1691, that the hostilities resumed when Abenaki chieftain Moxus and two hundred warriors launched an attack on Wells, Maine. What was thought to be an easy conquest proved a bitter repulse, as the English had reinforced the town just hours before the assault. Moxus and his warriors had better luck in nearby York, where they ambushed a vessel being loaded by its crew. After a few isolated homesteads in the area were burned the war party lost interest and returned home.

Although Moxus's raid had accomplished little, it was clear to Massachusetts that it was just the beginning. In an attempt to be proactive, four companies were raised and placed under the command of Captain John March. March was given a number of vessels and directed to follow the route Church took last autumn; that is, sail to Maquoit Bay and ascend the Androscoggin River to Fort Pejepscot in search of the enemy. In July Captain March set sail and carried out his orders. After spending a short time at the abandoned fort and seeing no signs of the enemy, March ordered the detachment back to Maquoit Bay. As the English troops began boarding their vessels, which were aground waiting on the high tide to move off, a Wabanaki war party struck. It was strangely reminiscent of Church's expedition the year before. The English soon became pinned down along the shore, but this time there was no charge. Instead March ordered his men to board their vessels. From here the battle evolved into a duel of musketry, with the Wabanaki shifting positions along the shoreline and the English firing from the decks of their grounded vessels. The duel continued, at least in a sporadic fashion, well into the night until the rising tide made it clear how the engagement was going to end.

Roving bands of raiders struck at outlying targets near Exeter and Berwick, and surprised the inhabitants of Rye, New Hampshire, killing or carrying off twenty-one of their number. Small war parties, numbering but a few men, still lingered on the outskirts of the frontier towns, but overall the government of Massachusetts was relieved that no major attack had materialized. As for the current raids, given the colony's resources little more could be done.[1]

After Schuyler's raid on La Prairie, all fell quiet along the New York frontier as well. Taking advantage of the lull, Governor Sloughter placed detachments of militia north of Albany at Half Moon and among the ruins of Schenectady in hopes of thwarting a French attack. He then pleaded with the surrounding governments for reinforcements. "I need not relate unto you of how great import the preservation of this place (Albany) is," he wrote the various governors, and if "the French should assault and gain Albany how far your Government and all the English Colonys on both sides of us would be endangered, you can easily judge. For we have nothing but that place that keeps our Indians steady to us, and the loss of that must be the loss of them, and the loss of them must be the loss of all the King's interest on this Continent." Although compelling, the governor's pleas accomplished little. One after another, each of the colonies stated their pressing needs. Pennsylvania, Virginia, and Maryland could not afford the cost of raising men but did send a small amount of money. Rhode Island was afraid to release soldiers for fear of landing parties from French privateers that prowled the New England coast.

Connecticut claimed similar fears, while Massachusetts was in need of every man the colony could muster to stabilize the Maine-New Hampshire frontier.[2]

This proved to be one of the last acts attempted by Sloughter, who died suddenly on July 23, 1691, leaving Ingoldsby in charge of the New York government. Ingoldsby was eventually able to convince Pennsylvania to send 150 troops to help garrison the frontier forts during the winter, and Connecticut offered to let New York recruit a company from within its borders. Another company of New York troops was raised and dispatched to Albany while the fortifications there were repaired and expanded. When combined with the arriving Pennsylvania forces, a company of English regulars brought by Sloughter, and the troops raised by New York and local militia forces Albany, had well over six hundred men ready to answer for the town's defense. A bigger problem was the lack of supplies. Many troops did not have swords so hatchets were issued and spears made when these ran out. There was also a shortage of artillery supplies for the guns in the various blockhouses and in Fort Albany itself. "There are so many things wanting that we grieve to think of it," one officer wrote of the garrison's plight. It all seemed like too little with the rumors that a large French fleet had reached Quebec and that an all-out attack on Albany was to follow.[3]

If the war had stabilized for New York and New England, the same could not be said for their Iroquois allies. Repeated attacks by New France's allies had driven many of the Seneca out of their villages and forced the confederacy to hold off on any large-scale raids against the French. It was not until December that the Iroquois turned their attention back toward New France. A force of two hundred Onondaga and one hundred Cayuga were ordered to rendezvous near the headwaters of the St. Lawrence with the aim of falling upon Montreal and other targets downriver. Unfortunately for the Iroquois, a 325-man French and Indian war party headed for the high country surprised an early arriving detachment of fifty Iroquois not far from the rendezvous site. Caught unaware in their camp, the Iroquois crumbled before the sudden onslaught. Twenty-four Onondaga and Cayuga warriors were killed and another sixteen taken prisoner. Those that escaped soon spread word of the disaster and the presence of a large French and Indian force in the area, all of which was enough to convince the Iroquois to abandon their plans.

A second Iroquois force, consisting of twenty Mohawk and eleven Oneida chieftains, descended Lake Chaplain and, skirting around Fort Chambly, attacked a party of French mission Indians hunting near Mount St. Hilaire. The experienced Iroquois war party made quick work of their adversaries, killing five and capturing sixteen of their number, but three of the French Indians managed to escape and quickly sounded the alarm. A large French and Indian war party set out in pursuit of the Iroquois, who, slowed by their captives, were discovered five days later along the west bank of Lake Champlain. Having seen tracks the day before, the Mohawk and Oneida warriors knew that their pursuers were nearby, but it was not enough to prevent their destruction. Scores of musket barrels silently tracked the column as it snaked its way through the ice-draped pines and broken birch trees. When the van and main body of the column had entered the trap, a shot burst forth, followed in rapid succession by war whoops and the clatter of musketry. The Iroquois column collapsed upon itself as fire poured down upon it from all sides. The battle was decided at this point, but the Iroquois refused to yield. Crouched behind whatever cover they could find, they fired back at their assailants. When their powder ran out, they met their enemy's rush with tomahawks and knives. It was a valiant but futile stand. A few braves in the rear of the column managed to escape. As for the remainder, only three were captured, the rest having chosen to resist to the end.[4]

The two events, coupled with the losses from Schuyler's expedition and a wave of French and Indian attacks on the Five Nations villages, had undermined Iroquois morale and sapped its fighting strength. The loss of so many chieftains and leading men had rattled the Mohawk in particular. "The Mohawk are very loath to go out upon any occasion. This great loss of men hath struck such a terror in them that they are quite out of heart," the Albany council wrote the governor. Another New York officer agreed, saying, "All the principal captains of the Maquas and Oneida are dead, to the great grief of us all. We have not one leading man of their Castles now that we can depend on."[5]

Militarily the Iroquois were being ground down. The confederacy, led by the Seneca and Mohawk, had repeatedly criticized their English ally's disinterested conduct. Instead of gathering a powerful Anglo-Iroquois force to deal a major blow to the French, the English colonies either acted only upon their own concerns or seemed content to allow the Iroquois to bear the brunt of the French attacks. Despite this indifference the Iroquois had remained loyal to the cause, but it was not without consequence. French and Indian attacks on the western and most powerful member of the confederacy, the Seneca, had proven quite successful. New France's allies had driven this tribe back upon the Onondaga, where they found refuge. At a September 4 conference in Albany, the Seneca representative informed the English of the tribe's plight, saying, "we are a nation dispersed and scattered." The Mohawk had been hit hard as well. By the winter of 1691 the three primary Mohawk castles were only capable of fielding 130 warriors, while the Oneida, a smaller tribe, could only muster half as many.[6]

In England, Sir William Phips spent the early summer personally reporting the details of his failed campaign to the king and then pressing the monarch to allow him to lead a second effort against Quebec. Phips requested a ship-of-the-line to escort the New England fleet, a hundred cannon, powder, and two thousand small arms to see this task through. This time he would land on the Island of Orleans and set up cannon to completely block the St. Lawrence. From here the force would advance until it got close enough to erect batteries, at which point Quebec would be bombarded into submission. Phips specifically asked for "Four good mortars, with shells in proportion," pointing out that "there is a hill from which the enemy cannot hinder us, and this will so annoy them that the conquest will be easy."[7]

The king showed interest in the scheme and asked Phips for more information, but given the time of the year this request meant that it was unlikely that the expedition would go forward, even though Phips was soon able to secure a warship, the HMS *Dinant*, to act as escort. The prodding by the adventurer turned admiral did have some positive effects. Two hundred barrels of powder and ten siege guns were forwarded to Boston, and at Phips's urging, it was agreed to assign a frigate to patrol New England waters to counter the growing number of French privateers. Although a second expedition against the capital of New France was not to be, the Board of Trade and the Admiralty had taken notice of a memorandum Phips wrote concerning the ability of the New England colonies to provide all the major needs of the English navy. Timber abounded particularly in southern New Hampshire and Maine. Yardarms, masts, pitch—almost every naval need could be met by the colonies at typically half the cost that the Admiralty was currently paying in England. This statement was supported by a number of other witnesses including Sir Edmund Andros. Taken all together, when the new royal charter was completed for Massachusetts, Phips seemed the obvious choice and was appointed governor in late November 1691.[8]

After coming close to destroying Schuyler's force at La Prairie, Frontenac turned his attention toward Acadia and plans to strike back at the English. In September the frigate *Soleil d'Afrique* left Quebec bound for Acadia. On board was the colony's new governor, Joseph Robinau, the Chevalier de Villebon. The chevalier's appointment carried several directives. First, through encouragement, gifts, and supplies he was to keep the Wabanaki constantly engaged against the English. Second, he was to reestablish the colony and if possible secure and defend Port Royal. The journey to Port Royal was uneventful save for the capture and burning of a small English prize. The *Soleil d'Afrique* dropped anchor before the ruins of the fort in late September 1691. Villebon came ashore and met with the French sergeant that Phips had left in charge the year before. After meeting with a few of the French colonists in the area, and replacing the English flag flying over the fort with a French one, the governor quickly came to the conclusion that he could not defend the town. Hence, he left the French sergeant in charge and set sail for the St. John River.

Near the mouth of the river the *Soleil d'Afrique* surprised a pair of New England vessels. Both vessels surrendered after a short chase, and the larger of the two proved to be carrying an influential New England merchant and the recently appointed English governor of Port Royal, Colonel Edward Tyng. Villebon released the two crews and vessels under the agreement that they would return with a like number of French soldiers captured at the fall of Fort Royal the year before. Until then, he held Tyng and several of the more prominent captives in his new post on the Jemseg River, about fifty miles up the St. John. From here, with the help of Castin and Jesuit father Louis-Pierre Thury, Villebon began to focus on his primary task.[9]

At Quebec there were several plans put forth for major expeditions against the English. Most prevalent was the old plan to seize Manhattan and Albany. The scope of the plan would have to be changed, Frontenac informed the new minister of the marine, Louis Phelypeaux de Pontchartrain. Regardless of what had been considered in the past, the idea that a Canadian detachment could penetrate as far south as New York City was simply out of the question. It was more a matter of logistics and sheer distance to be traveled rather than English arms that called this task into question. Even an expedition against Albany, Frontenac added, would require reinforcements to prevent stripping the colony of its defenders. The best approach would be an attack on Albany coordinated with a French naval expedition against New York City. A small French fleet would engage Fort William Henry, as Fort James was now known, while French marines landed to attack the town from the landward side. The governor reiterated his support for this plan to the new minister of the marine, stating that "the capture of Manath and New-York," was the "most assured means of terminating this war and of utterly reducing the Iroquois."[10]

Frontenac was not alone in recognizing the potential benefits of a coordinated attack on New York. The intendant Champigny and the governor of Montreal, Callières, both wrote the king's ministers in support of such a plan, and the new French governor of Acadia, the Chevalier de Villebon, made it clear that such a move was the fastest way of terminating the Iroquois War, which would open the west to French dominion. "The expedition against Manatte would be the most advantageous for Canada," Villebon wrote the minister of the marine in October 1691. "It would render the King master of a fine Country, and put an end at once to the Iroquois war. The expense incurred for Canada during two years would be more than sufficient for this expedition."[11]

As enthusiasm for the project faded, the plan was altered to a more palatable form. Canada would launch an attack on Albany while a French fleet

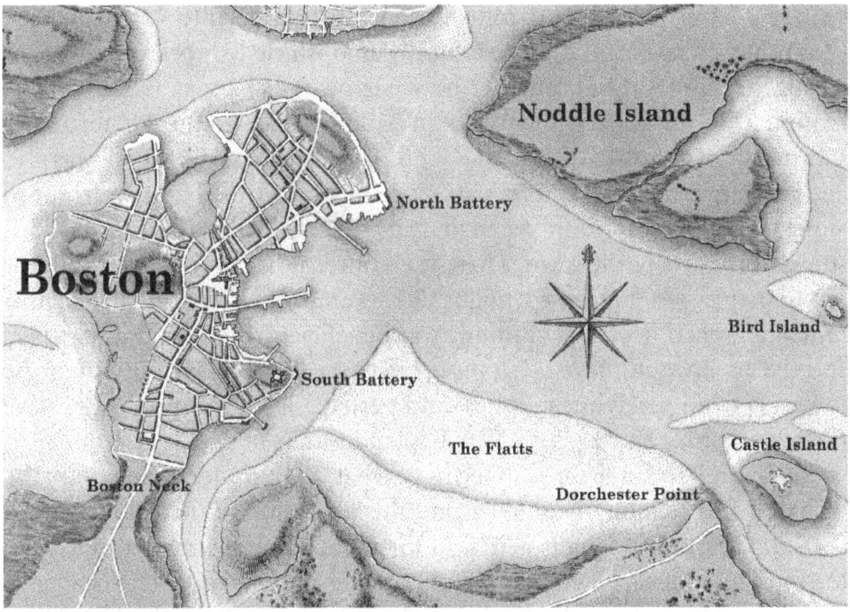

A map of Boston harbor circa 1705. The main channel into the harbor can be seen between Bird Island and Castle Island where a small stone fort stood. This fort would be rebuilt in the years after the war, and renamed Castle William. The fort would stand guard over the harbor until the evacuating British blew the structure up in 1776. (*Author*)

bombarded New York City and several other places along the coast as a diversion. Within the last element of this scheme, Boston was a particularly tempting target. Striking at New England's capital was attractive on several levels. First, it is where Phips's expedition had originated, and as such, an attack would send a political message while striking at the heart of New England morale. Second, it would have a crippling effect on the sea-based economy of New England. With Boston burned, as called for under the plan and a French squadron in the area, the New England cod fleet would be trapped in port for fear of capture. The Yankees, "loving their trade better than war," would be thrown into a panic, and perhaps would even seek peace terms, the pragmatic author of a memoir on the subject informed the French court. Such a peace treaty, "however indifferent it may be, would always be more beneficial to us than the greatest victories and advantages that we might gain over them, short of their utter annihilation which is very difficult to effect." Third, and perhaps most importantly, a successful naval attack against Boston was not out of the question. The town's defenses were suspect. Fort William, a small four-bastioned stone-faced structure, stood sentinel on Castle Island, guarding the narrow channel into Boston harbor. Mounting a dozen cannon, it was hardly an obstacle to block the efforts of frigate-sized warships, no matter how narrow the channel. Once into the main harbor there were only two gun batteries, located on the north and south edge of the town, to contend with. The New England capital was also an ideal target because of its construction. Wood-framed houses arranged along narrow streets would mean that any fire was likely to spread and consume large parts of the town. There was concern that the defenders, if they found themselves threatened, might sink several vessels in the main channel to halt a French fleet, but even this was beneficial from the attacker's perspective as it would have a crippling effect on the local economy, cut the town off from receiving supplies, and perhaps just as importantly, leave French warships free to roam New England waters in search of prey.[12]

The plan also made sense in terms of what was required to maintain the defenses of the colony. Frontenac and the leadership of the colony agreed that, at minimum, a squadron of four forty-gun frigates was needed to keep the mouth of the St. Lawrence free from English privateers and to challenge any future attempts by the English to launch an attack on Quebec. These vessels could cruise the Nova Scotia and New England coasts in search of prizes and even make up part of the squadron sent from France to undertake the attack on Boston or New York.

Attacking Boston or New York aside, there were more pressing matters for the French court to consider. It was imperative that supplies and reinforcements quickly reach Quebec. Two years of warfare had taken its toll on the colony's manpower. At the start of 1690 the thirty-two Free Companies of the Marine stationed in New France had numbered some 1,300 men. By the end of the 1691 campaign, Iroquois attacks and illness had cut their numbers by more than half, with some companies being left with a little over a dozen men in their ranks. In all, it was estimated that Canada had lost over two thousand militia and regulars over this period. If these men were not replaced and the attrition continued at the same rate, the colony would ultimately be lost. A thousand men were needed—nearly a full regiment by French army standards. Flour and foodstuffs were needed as was clothing and almost every manner of arms and munitions. Money was needed to pay the troops, to build a series of armed row galleys to patrol the lower St. Lawrence, and to build new fortifications, especially at Montreal, which was vulnerable to both English and Iroquois excursions.[13]

Although an attack on Boston or New York City never materialized, such an effort was hardly out of the realm of possibilities. Under the guidance of Colbert, the French navy, which in 1661 numbered only eight vessels, had been transformed into a fleet of sixty warships half a dozen years later. And to ensure the future of the kingdom's navy Colbert established armories at Brest, Rochefort, Toulon, Dunkerque, and Le Havre. Officers and men were recruited from France's growing merchant marine.

In 1690 France combined her Atlantic and Mediterranean flotillas and engaged an Anglo-Dutch fleet of some sixty ships near Beachy Head, England, not far from where William the Conqueror landed at Pevensey. Outnumbering his opponents, the French admiral, Anne-Hilarion de Cotentin, Count de Tourville, managed to bring his numerical superiority to bear by isolating the Dutch squadron at the head of the allied fleet. The English squadrons did not move forward to engage and the Dutch, after taking a severe pounding, broke off the engagement, which panicked and scattered the rest of the allied fleet. Several Dutch vessels were sunk or captured and for a brief period the French fleet controlled the English Channel.[14]

The Battle of Beachy Head demonstrated the usefulness and effectiveness of French naval power. More warships were on the stocks, and there appeared no reason why the fleet built and nurtured by Colbert and his son would not soon contest naval superiority in the Atlantic with the combined Anglo-Dutch fleets. It was in all practicality an opportune time to detach a small flotilla of French warships to contest American and Caribbean waters. English and Dutch commercial efforts would be damaged by such actions and their resources further stretched. Given the value placed on their American colonies, any territory seized by the French during such an effort would also prove a valuable trading tool at the peace table when the hostilities finally concluded.

With over one hundred warships in his arsenal, Louis XIV could have easily supported Frontenac's plans to strike at New York and New England, and given the state of the colonial coastal defenses, even a handful of warships could have wreaked havoc upon the Eastern Seaboard. The monarch's attention, however, was focused on his army and its campaigns in Europe. The money, the time, and the resources could not be diverted to support French naval aims. Instead, a policy of *guerre de course*, which focused on merchant raiding, was adopted. Privateers and cruisers, typically frigates, would strike at their enemy's commerce, causing damage out of proportion to the numbers employed and forcing their opponents to divert valuable resources to protect their trade. The approach was analogous to the policy of the *petite guerre* employed by New France. It was cheap and risked little in the way of resources to carry out. With such a transition taking place the king agreed to send several frigates to Canada to carry out privateering work along the northeastern coast, but no attack of any measure was to be conducted by the French navy against the ports of the English colonies. Little did Louis XIV know that his country would never again be in a better position to strike against the American colonies.

Part Three

Attrition

CHAPTER FIFTEEN

Disunity and Discord

On the northern New England frontier a heavy snowfall ushered in 1692. For the town of York, along the southern coast of Maine, January 25 was no different. It had snowed hard throughout the evening, leaving a thick white blanket draped across the landscape. Daylight brought relief from the snow, but it also brought something else. Three hundred Wabanaki warriors had arrived the previous evening and quietly slipped into position, their footfalls muffled by the fresh snow. As the first rays of sunlight filtered through the breaking flurries a shot rang out. A few townsfolk went to their windows to see where it had come from, but many had barely awoken when hundreds of war whoops rang out. Caught completely by surprise, most never had a chance to reach their arms before the door to their dwelling was kicked in and the inhabitants put to the tomahawk or carried away. A few individuals managed to make their way to one of the town's five garrison houses, and although badly outnumbered, from these strongholds they were able to fend off several half-hearted attacks. Most of the town, however, was not so fortunate. When the war party withdrew later that day, other than the garrison houses, not a single structure remained standing. Forty-eight of the town's inhabitants lay dead, many buried beneath the burning embers of their homes, and another seventy-three were led away as prisoners. Within the span of a few hours York had been reduced to a ghost town, a stark reminder of the price of vigilance on the frontier.[1]

Along the New York frontier the spring of 1692 brought much smaller enemy raids, which probed the colony's settlements in search of prisoners and information. Spring also brought an alarm that Frontenac was preparing to march on Albany with eight hundred men. Lt. Governor Ingoldsby called out the militia and rode to Albany to personally oversee the town's defenses. "By God's blessing Albany is still ours,"Ingoldsby wrote to the governor of Maryland in yet another attempt to solicit help in defending the frontier. "But in such a languishing condition that all the inhabitants are ready to retire to the waterside. Trade is extinguished and alarms of the enemy incessant. We have been obliged to forbid the people to leave the town, which the enemy would rejoice to hear of." The lieutenant governor oversaw small improvements to Albany's defenses, but by June nothing had materialized, so he released the militia and returned to New York City.

In May newly appointed Massachusetts governor William Phips arrived. After a long stay in England and a lengthy voyage across the Atlantic Phips was shocked upon his arrival to find he had to contend with spreading accusations of witchcraft that had spawned from an incident in Salem. What had started out as a single accusation had now become an epidemic. "No doubt you have heard of the wizards and witches," one gentleman wrote future governor Francis Nicholson. "There are now over a hundred of them in jail, but they betray each other so fast that they say there are seven hundred in all."[2]

The new governor was aghast by the circus the mania had created. In some cases the accused were being dragged from their homes and subjected to tests of fire and water, from which many, looking to spare themselves from further torment, confessed. Courts of inquiry had convicted a score of individuals on charges of witchcraft, and at the rate at which the accusations were being generated the courts would have to be expanded to keep up. Already engulfing several towns the matter was clearly escalating out of control. The mania was no doubt exacerbated by the anxiety of a frontier in shambles and the constant threat of instant annihilation lurking behind every tree, by political and economic woes brought on by the colony's poorly led government, and by the threat posed to the colony's maritime economy by French privateers operating off the coast.[3]

While the actions of the French and their allies were a more difficult problem to contend with, the governor at least had the power to stop the witch hunts. Phips, with the advice of his new council, intervened to head off the panic. "I have now forbidden the committal of any more accused persons," he wrote Whitehall, "and them that have been committed I would shelter from any proceedings wherein the innocent could possibly suffer wrong." The governor also put a stop to pamphlets that were being circulated that fanned the flames of the witch hunters and suspended the courts of inquiry until he received word from the king on how to proceed in "this perplexed affair."[4]

Meanwhile, to the north, with the arrival of spring Governor Villebon met with one hundred Kennebec warriors at his newly erected fort, named St. Joseph, near the junction of the Nashwaak and St. John Rivers.[5] At a large celebration the governor urged the Kennebec to carry through with their attacks against their mutual enemy. He then handed out gifts and, in a sign of solidarity, performed the war dance with his visitors. The next day the war party departed for Pentagoet, where Villebon had sent his brother, Lt. Rene Robinau de Portnuef, and twenty Canadians to help organize an expedition. By late May, three hundred Abenaki, Micmac, and Kennebec warriors had assembled at Pentagoet. Under the leadership of Castin, Father Baudoin, Portnuef, and their war chiefs, Modockawando and Moxus, the group agreed to attack Wells, the location Moxus had vowed to return to after his repulse last year.

The 320-man force had little to fear during its travels and arrived at Wells undetected on June 20. Before the expedition lay the town's five garrison houses, positioned in a string upon cleared ground near the shore. The numbers were overwhelmingly in favor of the French and Indians, but a pair of sloops and a small shallop anchored in a tidal creek near the garrison houses complicated the matter. These vessels, no doubt armed with swivel guns, would be free to pour fire upon any party attacking the strongholds. The Wabanaki seemed hesitant and turned to slaughtering the settlement's cattle, which gave away any element of surprise. Not interested in exposing themselves further they then opened a useless long-distance fusillade with the garrison and the nearby vessels throughout the day.[6]

It soon became clear to the attackers that the English vessels had to be dealt with. To offer some form of protection an abandoned oxcart was fitted with planks to act as a rolling shield for the attackers. At first the makeshift siege engine performed its task admirably as a handful of Canadians and Abenaki rolled the cart to within fifteen yards of one of the sloops. "This Chariot," one chronicler noted, "they pushed on, towards the sloops, till they were got, maybe, within fifteen yards of them." At this point one of the wheels struck a rock and the cart became stuck in the mud. Two Canadians were killed attempting to dislodge the cart and, under a concentrated fire from the vessels, the entire detachment broke in retreat, which led to a number of casualties as they scurried back to the safety of the wood line. The event was viewed as a bad omen by the Wabanaki, and interest in another attack quickly waned. Both Castin and Portnuef pushed on their allies to carry through with the plan but to no avail. The war party soon broke up, with each contingent returning to their respective villages.[7]

After attempting to squash the witch-hunting fervor through use of his royal authority Phips pursued one of his primary orders—that of rebuilding the fort at Pemaquid. A number of colonial leaders questioned the wisdom of his rebuilding the Maine outpost. Although a new fort could certainly be built at Pemaquid, its isolated location would make it difficult to support, as the only practical avenue to do so was by sea. Undeterred, the governor raised a force of 450 men, gathered together the necessary materials, and set sail for the Maine coast in early August 1692. The flotilla briefly stopped at Falmouth to inspect the ruins. The dead, still scattered about the town after its capture several years before, were buried, and the fort's great guns, which had been left behind by the victorious French and Indians, were recovered. As half of his force turned toward the task of constructing the new fort at Pemaquid, Phips detached Major Church with the rest of the troops to attack nearby enemy villages. Church accomplished little, but his efforts did seem to screen Phips's work at Pemaquid, as no attempt was made to disrupt it.[8]

In October the English flag was raised over Fort William Henry, as the structure was christened. Given the abundance of nearby rock, and the desire to build as secure of a fortification as possible, it was agreed to construct the fort of stone. Unfortunately, limestone was nowhere to be found in the vicinity. Instead, a mixture of clay and sand was used as a substitute. It was a mistake that weakened the structure and, in the estimation of Royal Engineer colonel Wolfgang Romer who visited the site after the conclusion of the war, led to the fort's early demise. The resulting structure was essentially a stone square, about 185 feet to a side. The seaside walls were six feet thick and twenty-two feet in height, with a three-story cylindrical bastion occupying the western corner. The walls facing the land side of the fort were slightly shorter, with a smaller bastion occupying the eastern corner of the structure. The interior of the fort was also bisected with 108-foot walls to create something of a keep. Twenty-eight gun ports were cut into the walls and bastions to allow the fort's fourteen cannon to be brought to bear, in particular the fort's largest guns, six eighteen-pounders, which were positioned to defend the seaside of the structure. With the weather soon deteriorating and little else to be accomplished Phips left Captain John March and sixty men to garrison the fort and departed with the rest for Boston.[9]

The year was to bring new leadership to New York as well. On April 28, 1692, a frigate carrying Governor Benjamin Fletcher dropped anchor in New York harbor. Little is known about Fletcher's past until in 1689 he becomes a major in Princess Anne's Danish Regiment of Foot. Princess Anne's Regiment, which would one day be known as the Queen's Regiment, had fought in several major engagements during William's Irish campaigns, including the Battle of the Boyne and both sieges of Limerick. It is perhaps here that William first encountered Fletcher. Whatever the case, by 1691 Fletcher had become the regiment's lieutenant colonel, and the following year, upon his appointment to the governorship of New York by the king, he was breveted to the rank of colonel of foot.

Fletcher's arrival did not start well. The two dispatch brigantines assigned to the governor were missing. One had been taken by a French privateer, while the other vessel had been lost at sea, and like his predecessors the new governor was soon forced to make a trip to Albany to meet with his Iroquois allies. Fletcher gave his condolences to the assembly of sachems and urged them to carry on the fight against the French. To help support the nearby Mohawk, the governor informed them that he intended to garrison several posts north of Albany, including Half Moon and Schenectady, and to answer the Five Nations' earlier calls for help from the other colonies, Fletcher informed them that Virginia was sending help as they spoke. Unfortunately, the governor also scolded the Five Nations for their failure to launch an attack on Montreal last year while Schuyler approached the French town from the south.

The Iroquois, who had conducted most of the fighting against the French and their allies along the New York frontier, took offense at the governor's statements. Corlaer, as they referred to the governor of New York, was ignoring the mounting Iroquois losses. Thus far the Five Nations were the losers in this conflict. They then reminded the governor that they continued "the war for your sakes and for your interests and avoid the making of a peace, which we could do very advantageously." These tense moments for the alliance were quickly passed over as the Iroquois informed the English delegation that they were committed to continuing the fight against the French no matter what.[10]

Fletcher considered himself fortunate in that beyond a few small raiding parties the frontier remained quiet for the remainder of the year. The colony was still in turmoil after the political divide brought on by Leisler and his revolutionary council, and it was deeply in debt and short on revenue. Rumors abounded that fourteen French ships had landed at Quebec and disembarked two thousand troops destined to march on Albany. Fletcher had dispatched three hundred men to man the frontier posts over the winter but could do little more. "It appears to me," he informed Whitehall, "utterly impossible for this single Province to support the war another Year."[11]

For New France the spring of 1692 brought the return of two seasonal constants to the colony: planting and Iroquois raids. In late May, a ninety-man French and Indian trading party was ambushed at the Long Sault. The convoy was busy pulling their canoes ashore to carry them around the rapids when an Iroquois war party, under the Onondaga war chief Black Kettle, attacked. A surprise volley and a sudden rush scattered the French and Indian covering force. Those near the canoes immediately tried to embark, but in the confusion a number of canoes were upset either by the enemy fire or by their occupants' haste. Once in the water the only good thing that could be said for the freezing current was that it carried these individuals away from the Iroquois. When it was done, seven French and Indians lay dead, while another fifteen were taken prisoner, including the French commander and two of his officers.

It was not the last to be heard from Black Kettle. On July 15, his war party struck first near Fort Roland and then La Chesnaye, capturing a dozen French farmers. Governor Callières of Montreal immediately organized a pursuit and sent eighty men under Captains Duplessis and Merville to intercept the Onondaga war chief. The French officers tracked the Iroquois to a tree line and, fearing a trap, held their position. A second larger force of 150 men under Major Vaudreuil arrived the next day, but by then Black Kettle and his warriors were gone. There was some good news, however, as a French officer named Vildenay, who had been a prisoner of the Iroquois for three years and was brought along by his captives, managed to escape. Upon his return to Montreal Vildenay informed Callières and Vaudreuil as to the identity of the attackers and that they had left two canoes full of fur above the Long Sault. Upon hearing the news the governor reinforced Vaudreuil's detachment with local troops and 120 volunteers from the mission Indians at Sault St. Louis and the mountain. He then ordered the major to set an ambush at the reported location of the canoes.[12]

Vaudreuil's party ascended the Ottawa River and had ported around the Long Sault when they came across an Iroquois canoe in the river before them. Believing that his forces had been discovered the French commander ordered a landing. One hundred men were left to guard the canoes while the rest quickly set off with Vaudreuil along the shore in search of an Iroquois encampment. Around nightfall the advanced guard of the French and Indian column, following the sound of wood being chopped, surprised a party of Iroquois. The Iroquois sounded the alarm and the nearby encampment rushed for its arms. Not wanting to give his opponents the time to organize Vaudreuil ordered a charge with the advance guard. War whoops and bursts of musket fire rang out as the French moved to press the advantage. At first Black Kettle and his men resisted, but when the French main column came into sight a few minutes later, the Iroquois broke and disappeared into the woods, leaving everything behind. The French had struck a serious blow. Twenty-eight Iroquois were either killed or were now French prisoners. In addition, all of the French captives were rescued, but it had come at a price. Vaudreuil had lost eleven men in the engagement, including three of his seasoned officers, "the best qualified for war in this country."[13]

There were smaller encounters through the summer, but in all it was far less than previous years. As fall approached Frontenac assembled a detachment of two hundred militia and fifty mission Indians to help cover the harvest in the Montreal district. On his way to Montreal at the head of this force the governor encountered a French canoe, the occupants of which informed him that a four-hundred-man French and Indian detachment had arrived at Montreal from Michilimackinac. Frontenac was delighted to see the Ottawa, Huron, and Illinois warriors, as well as the French *coureurs de bois* from the high country. The detachment had not come to trade furs but in response to the threat posed by Black Kettle. The governor was also delighted to hear news of continued attacks on the Iroquois by his high country allies.

Although no expedition was launched against the English due to a disagreement with the Ottawa, good news arrived not long after. A supply convoy had arrived from France. It brought provisions and munitions but none of the reinforcements the colony desperately needed to man its frontier posts. Fortunately, the Iroquois incursions had faded to a trickle, and as to what remained Frontenac informed the French court, "It is impossible to prevent these sorts of surprisals however prudent we be, or to overtake these people after they have struck a blow, because they disperse through the woods, and are no longer to be found in the places where they are expected to be; and herein consists the great difficulty in waging war in this country."[14]

The harvest of 1692 was brought in without serious interruption, but it proved less bountiful than hoped due to the ravages of caterpillars, and only the late arrival of supply ships from France averted widespread shortages. With the threat of famine removed and news of French and Indian victories from the high country to the coast of Maine, confidence began to soar within New France. The net effect was to shift the governor's thinking over to the offensive. Frontenac had detained a pair of frigates, the thirty-eight-gun *Poli* and the thirty-four-gun *Envieux*, at Quebec. Under the command of Pierre LeMoyne d'Iberville these two vessels were to rendezvous with two more and a number of troops from the *Compagnie du Nord* and together launch an expedition against Fort Nelson in Hudson Bay. Iberville, however, was delayed in getting the expedition out of France, as the *Poli* and *Envieux* were directed to act as escort for a supply convoy destined for the colony. As such, Iberville did not arrive at Quebec until the end of late August, far too late in the year for an expedition into Hudson Bay. With the availability of Iberville's vessels and crews Frontenac proposed an expedition against the new English fort at Pemaquid. The venture was agreed upon, and by mid-October Iberville was meeting with Governor Villebon near the mouth of the St. John River. Here the two leaders agreed that a large Wabanaki force would besiege the fort from the land side while Iberville's frigates attacked from the sea side.

The two parties advanced the next day, and as the Wabanaki watched from the tree line near Fort William Henry the two French frigates came into sight, loitered about for a bit, and then sailed off without having attempted anything. Disgusted with the conduct of the French warships, nothing Villebon could have said would have held together the Wabanaki war party, which broke up and returned home later that day. Iberville blamed the weather and the lack of a good pilot who knew the shoreline, but it seems more likely that, having had a closer look at the stone fortress and seeing an English vessel lying under the guns of the fort, he chose not to risk the vessels he planned to use against Hudson Bay next spring. With the venture aborted, Iberville and his frigates cruised New England waters for the next few weeks, eventually taking three prizes before setting course for France in mid-November.[15]

Frontenac was frustrated by the missed opportunity at Pemaquid but relieved that the late fall weather all but ensured that any English attack on Quebec would have to wait until the spring. The governor had dealt with rumors of an attack on Quebec since Phips had arrived as the new governor of Massachusetts, and although they concerned him given the state of the colony's defenses, nothing had materialized. What the count did not know was that a second expedition against Quebec, although considered, had been put off for another year.

In the meantime a threat did come to one of the most remote parts of the colony—Placentia, Newfoundland. The French fishing village was located on the west side of the Avalon Peninsula, which makes up Newfoundland's southwest point. Numbering a few hundred at most, the outpost served as a port for the seasonal fishing fleets that arrived out of France. In mid-September, as this fleet was preparing to return to Europe, one vessel informed the town's governor, Jacques-Francois de Brouillan, that an English fleet was anchored not far away at Cape St. Mary. The news spurred

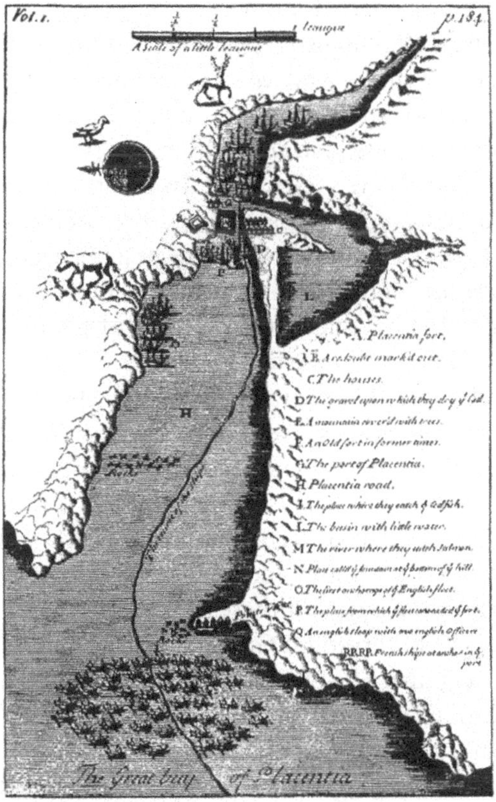

Commodore Thomas Gillam's attempt on Placentia, September 1692. (*D. W. Prowse, A History of Newfoundland, 1896*)

Brouillan to sound the alarm, which proved a wise move, as the next morning five English warships, the smallest of which mounted twenty-eight guns, were seen positioned in the harbor just out of cannon range. Fearing a landing the governor assembled a company of sixty men under the command of Baron La Hontan with orders to oppose an English landing near the fort. It was a brave but likely meaningless maneuver. Any one of the English ships had a crew larger than the fort's garrison of fifty men. Nor was the fort itself much in the way of a defensive obstacle. Brouillan had worked at improving the defenses of the town. He built the wooden frame of Fort St. Louis, which was positioned to the north of the old earthen fort to better protect the nearby town, and planned to face this fort in stone next year. A supporting four-gun battery at nearby Point du Goulet and cables hung across the channel to bar vessels from passing the town were also added, but against such a force it did not seem sufficient.[16]

The English commander, Commodore Thomas Gillam, soon sent a boat bearing a white flag. The English officer envoy in the boat was blindfolded and, after being led about for a bit, was brought before Brouillan. The envoy informed the governor that Commodore Gillam had dispatched him to summon the fort's surrender and all French possessions in the bay. The English commander had also requested that Brouillan send an officer to meet with Gillam so the latter could explain the purpose of his visit. As requested, Brouillan dispatched La Hontan and an officer name Pastour to speak with Gillam, but little came of the meeting. It seemed the commodore was more interested in showing his guests the strength of his fleet firsthand than speaking to any matters of importance.

If Gillam had hopes that showing his overwhelming firepower might force a French surrender, these were dashed when Brouillan officially refused. With the preliminaries attended to Brouillan opened fire on the English fleet on the morning of September 19. The English vessels were quick to take up the challenge that lasted off and on for nearly six hours. Brouillan had been reinforced at the last moment by 120 French sailors from the fishing fleet trapped in the bay, and these men helped serve his batteries. A number of hits were observed on Gillam's flagship, and not long after she fell out of the firing line. The French commander, however, had to use his limited ammunition sparingly, but even so, by the time the English fleet broke off their attack, Fort St. Louis was down to its last barrel of powder. The fort itself, although subjected to a heavy bombardment, had done well, and there had only been a few casualties, but without powder none of this would matter. To Brouillan's relief, the English fleet moved off the next morning, stopping only to burn a few cabins before setting sail for England.[17]

CHAPTER SIXTEEN

The Mohawk Expedition

As 1692 FADED FRONTENAC FELT STRONG ENOUGH to switch to the offensive. Where to attack was not a difficult choice. With the onset of winter the Mohawk would return to their castles, offering an excellent opportunity to bring the war to their doorstep. A strike against this tribe was important for several reasons. Although they were not the strongest or most numerous of the Iroquois nations, they were at the head of the war effort against the French. The campaign would also help secure the allegiance of the mission Indians, most of whom were Mohawk, and damage the credibility of the English as well. For if it were successful, the mission Indians would realize the strength of the French cause, and the Mohawk would realize what little security their alliance with the English offered.

Preparations for the expedition started in Montreal in early November. Provisions, snowshoes, ammunition, sleds, blankets—all the accoutrements necessary to sustain 625 men in the field for a month—were routed to the island. The troops were the last element to reach the town. Huron, Abenaki, Algonquin, and a sizable number of mission Indians had been enticed to join the undertaking. They numbered two hundred in all and made their way into the town in small groups. Added to these numbers were one hundred soldiers, each picked for his ability to endure the hardships of the march ahead. The core of the expedition, however, was to be made up of Canadians, 325 in all, selected from the best-qualified militia in each of the parishes. At their head were three seasoned leaders, each of whom was selected based on his experience and the respect he commanded from the natives. Lieutenant Mantet, a veteran of the Schenectady raid and countless encounters with the Iroquois, commanded the troops from Three Rivers. Lieutenant Courtemanche, who had served as second-in-command in the capture of Fort Loyal, commanded the detachment from Quebec. And Lieutenant La Noue, a leader of several small raids into the region, led the contingent from Montreal.[1]

The expedition left Montreal on January 25, 1693, and ascended the frozen core of Lake Champlain, dragging their provisions behind them on small sleds. The route was becoming a familiar one to many involved. The army spent the nights encamped by detachments in the woods along the lake's edge. They cleared away the snow and built small covered fires to warm themselves, around which they spread fir branches to lie upon. Here they slept until dawn brought forth another day's march. By the evening of February 16, they had arrived within sight of the first Mohawk castle. Remarkably, they had accomplished their trek undetected. As night set in it was agreed that the detachment would divide in two. The first division, under La Noue, would attack the nearby castle while the second, under Mantet and Courtemanche, would march on a larger Mohawk castle a mile away. Neither party encountered any resistance to their attack. La Noue found only five men and a few women in the first castle, and Mantet found even fewer occupants upon seizing the second. At daybreak La Noue burned the smaller village, gathered together his prisoners, and joined forces with the other two commanders.

It was agreed that Courtemanche would hold the second village while Mantet and La Noue marched on a third some twenty miles away. Pushing through the snow, they reached their objective on the night of the eighteenth. As they crept forward, they were surprised to hear whooping and singing coming from within the palisades. The troops stood fast as the commanders discussed their options in whispered tones. Several Mohawk had escaped from the attack on the first two castles. Had they warned their brethren? If so, the expedition could be walking into a trap. No, the pair decided. Something else must be afoot. The troops were ordered to hold their positions. The men rubbed their arms and blew into their hands to warm themselves as the frozen hours passed. Finally, when all was quiet, Mantet ordered the troops to stand to and sent a native scout to investigate. The scout moved unseen to the palisades, paused, and then scaled the wall. Seeing no activity within, he motioned for his comrades and then lowered himself to unbar the gates. Within moments the French and their allies had fanned out across the compound. The doors to the longhouses were splintered before the onslaught. Most were killed or captured before they rose from their slumber or fell victim as they reached for their weapons. There were a few shots fired in resistance, but the surprise was near total. Within the span of a dozen minutes, thirty Mohawk warriors lay dead and almost three hundred men, women, and children were taken prisoner. It was a stunning success. The entire castle and its contents lay in French hands. The army spent the evening within the palisades. When morning arrived everything that could not be carried off along with the village was set ablaze, and the long line of prisoners was led back to the second village.

Thus far the expedition had exceeded its expectations, but things soon began to go awry. Before leaving Montreal, the mission Indians had made a pledge to Frontenac that they would slay any Mohawk captive capable of bearing arms. It was now time for them to fulfill this pledge, but when reminded on the point, they refused. The French pressed their allies, but they remained firm in their conviction. Frustrated, the three commanders briefly deliberated on attacking Albany but decided against it. Their allies were not interested, complaining that there were too many prisoners to guard. There was also troubling news that a Dutchman captured in the Schenectady raid, and foolishly brought along by the mission Indians, had escaped on the night of the eighteenth. By now he had certainly warned the English. With no other option before them, the last of the villages was torched on the morning of the twenty-second and the expedition began its long trek back to Montreal.[2]

News of the French advance reached Albany on the afternoon of February 19,when a patrol near Schenectady brought in a half-frozen Jan van Eps. Van Eps, the Dutchman who had escaped from the French war party, informed his rescuers that 350 French and 200 Indians were preparing to fall upon the upper two Mohawk castles. The militia of Schenectady and Albany was called out and the news relayed to Governor Fletcher in New York City. A number of scouting parties moved forward and a few days later confirmed the report, having heard firing from the upper two Mohawk castles. By the time a relief force had been assembled, news arrived that the lower Mohawk castle had fallen as well. With reports filtering in that the French had burned all three villages and begun their march home, Major Peter Schuyler ordered his 273-man detachment forward. He had neither the provisions nor ammunition needed for a forced march or fight, but with his Indians threatening to desert, there was little choice. Couriers were dispatched to Schenectady and Albany for supplies while the detachment made its way over the Mohawk River on the afternoon of the twenty-fourth. The next evening Schuyler was joined by 290 Mohawk braves, many unarmed. The combined force pressed on, passing the old French encampments one by one. By the evening of February 27, scouts reported that the enemy had stopped to build a palisade, which lay no more than a mile away. It was a lucky break for Schuyler. Low on provisions, and with the French several days ahead of him, it seemed that his hasty pursuit would be for naught. But for some reason the French had chosen to stand and fight, and he planned to make the most of the opportunity.[3]

Having left the second Mohawk castle on the morning of the twenty-second, the French had no reason for concern. They had a several day head start over any pursuit, and even with the large number of prisoners in the column, it seemed unlikely that they would encounter any interference before crossing the Hudson and reaching the lakes. A few days out, a Mohawk brave hailed the column from a distance. The war was over, he claimed. A peace treaty had been signed in Europe. A large body of English was a few days' march from them, but they had come to parley, not to fight. Mantet and his fellow commanders scoffed at the news, but their allies viewed it as genuine. They refused to continue the march and insisted that the column stop to speak with the English. It was a ruse to allow the English to overtake them, the French argued. They were still on the wrong side of the Hudson River, without supplies, and burdened with three hundred prisoners. To stop now would be to invite disaster. But their allies refused to budge. Just as with their promise to Frontenac they would judge what was best for them. Infuriated, the French commanders spent the day attempting to break their allies' resolve but to no avail. Finally they agreed to wait but insisted that a palisade be constructed just in case the enemy was not intent on negotiating. With at least this much the Indians agreed, and the next several days were spent hacking a rude wooden fortification out of the forest.[4]

Early on the morning of the twenty-eighth, Schuyler moved toward the French position, his flanks and van covered by a cloud of skirmishers. He feared that the French had only stopped to arrange an ambush, but when he came within sight of their defenses it became clear that this was not the case. The woods rang with shouts and hurrahs as the two sides eyed each other through the broken winter foliage. Having seen the French fortifications and uncertain of their true numbers, Schuyler began work on a palisade of his own a few musket shots from the French position. Mantet angrily pointed to the sight of the English entrenching themselves as proof of their intentions. His allies relented and admitted that they had been deceived. But the time for arguing had passed, and now there was but one choice—to fight. Bands of French Indians sallied out of their breastworks toward the English. Their French comrades and the remaining Indians soon followed them, leaving only enough men behind to guard the prisoners.

Whooping and shouting, they darted from tree to tree, unleashing sporadic fire upon the English. The fire proved too heavy for Schuyler's men, and they fell back into the forest only to rally and surge forward to reclaim their position. The French fell back and the English resumed work on their fortifications with such haste that several men were nearly crushed by falling trees. But it was short-lived. The French returned moments later, and once again the English were forced from their works, and once again the English counterattacked, pushing the French back. A third French attack followed and was beaten back in a similar manner. As the snow began to fall, the two sides contented themselves with sniping at each other as they tended to their wounded. Casualties had been relatively light on both sides, given the numbers involved. The English reported eight killed and fourteen wounded, and the French claimed seven killed and fifteen wounded, one of whom was La Noue. Given the terrain and their comparable numbers, neither side was in a position to force the other from their fortifications. As the weather deteriorated, both sides eyed each other from their breastworks, the quiet stalemate broken only by the occasional musket shot or unnerving shout.

For Schuyler the battle was something of a victory. Expecting reinforcements and supplies, he could afford to wait. The French were in sight and still on the west side of the Hudson. If sizable reinforcements arrived soon, he could cut off the enemy's retreat and destroy their entire force. What bothered him was the lack of provisions and ammunition. Many of the men had been without food for two days, and the supply of ammunition, scarce at the start of the march, had fallen to the point where most men had only a few rounds left in their cartridge boxes. If the French attacked again, he might not be able to hold his position. His Mohawk allies, however, had found provisions of their own. As Schuyler surveyed his lines, he was invited to join a number of Mohawk who were preparing midday's meal of broth. Not having eaten in several days, the major initially accepted but made his apologies and passed on the opportunity after a Mohawk withdrew a severed hand from the boiling kettle.

For Mantet, Courtemanche, and the wounded La Noue the situation was much worse. They could not afford to delay any longer. Provisions were running low, and the Hudson River with its questionable crossing still lay before them. With each day the English would get stronger and they weaker. There was little choice in the matter but to march on. For once they managed to convince their allies, and it was agreed to abandon the fort the next morning and strike out for the Hudson. The weather proved an ally. The next morning was so snowy that it made it difficult for Schuyler's scouts to get a good look at the French position, and when they approached close enough, a handful of French sentries left behind to cover the retreat popped away at the scouts, giving the impression that the main force was still present.

By noon, however, the scouts were convinced that the French had abandoned their fortifications. Having no more than a few hours' head start and encumbered by three hundred prisoners, Schuyler was certain that he could overtake them or even cut them off from the Hudson. The problem was that most of his men refused to march. They were low on ammunition, were poorly clothed, and had not eaten for days. Until his supplies reached him, the best he could do was dispatch a force of sixty men to follow the enemy's movements. The next morning supplies and eighty reinforcements finally reached the English camp. Schuyler urged his men forward. There was still a chance to overtake the French, but this time the Mohawk refused to join him. The French had released several prisoners with word that they would kill all their captives if the English pursued them. Whether true or not, it was a risk the Mohawk were not willing to take.[5]

As it turned out, it made no difference. Upon reaching the Hudson a panic befell the French and their allies. The ice on the river had broken, leaving a dark ribbon of freezing water between them and their escape route. But once again luck visited the war party. A fractured ice jam, secure enough to cross, was found nearby. The detachment negotiated the makeshift bridge just in time, for Schuyler's scouts arrived the following day and found the river impassable. This news, coupled with the urging of his Mohawk allies, forced Schuyler to call off the pursuit.

With the English gone, the French now faced a greater enemy—the elements. Just as it had on the Hudson, the ice on Lake George and Lake Champlain had broken, forcing the column to take the more arduous land route along the shore of the lakes. To make matters worse, the thaw had spoiled the provisions hidden on Lake George. With their food supply almost gone, a number of wounded to tend to, and many of the Indians striking their own route home, it became impossible to secure the nearly three hundred prisoners. Many just walked away, others left with the departing allies, and a large number were simply told to go home. In the end only fifty continued on to Montreal.

On March 11 the tattered detachment stopped at the Chazy River. Most could not go on for want of food or clothing. Many had thrown away their arms, not having the strength to carry them. Several had already perished from hunger, and many more would be lost if assistance was not forthcoming. A small party was sent forward to Montreal for provisions and aid. Callières responded immediately, dispatching 150 men and a large supply of provisions. Somewhat restored by the effort, what was left of the army shambled into Montreal on March 18 half-naked, without blankets, and "so wasted by the fatigue of the march and by hunger, that those alone who saw them could conceive their condition."[6]

The campaign, which appeared to have held every measure of success, had collapsed into a tattered shuffling of broken men through the gates of Montreal. If blame need be placed for the failure of the expedition, one need look no further than the French mission Indians. Their insistence on stopping to parley with the English had snatched defeat from the jaws of victory. Nor had their failure to carry through with their promise to Frontenac done anything to enhance their position in the French eyes. They were fickle allies that the French dared not abandon for fear that they would change loyalties, and because of that they paid the price. All told, the French were fortunate. Their losses were not large, with some eighty dead from all causes and half as many wounded. These numbers, however, needed to be tempered by the fact that many of the men who returned were so shattered by the experience that they would never fight again. Nevertheless, had the English not called off their pursuit and caught up with the expedition on Lake Champlain, not a single Frenchman would have returned.

Although the campaign had failed to secure the loyalty of the mission Indians and had lost many of its prisoners along the way, it did send a quiver down the spine of the Mohawk and the rest of the Iroquois Confederacy. It was clear that the English could not protect their Iroquois allies any more than the French could protect theirs. The tide was beginning to turn. The French allies sensed it, the Iroquois felt it, and the French knew it. By failing to destroy the French, the Iroquois had made the mistake of becoming their greatest teachers. A generation of Canadians, having survived the perils and terrors of the Iroquois, had reared a generation of men who knew nothing else. While the Iroquois suffered losses that were difficult to replace, New France grew stronger. No longer were they and their allies content with the idea of defense. More and more they sought out their enemy, striking in large numbers into English territory, and it was the Iroquois, not the English, who were becoming their primary targets. Exhausted from nearly a century of constant warfare with the French, and unable to rely upon the English for protection, the confederacy was entering perilous days.

CHAPTER SEVENTEEN

Missed Opportunities

With the spring of 1693 there was hope in New England. Along the Maine-New Hampshire frontier there were a few isolated attacks, but in general all remained quiet. Being proactive Massachusetts had dispatched a force of nearly five hundred men under Major Converse to scour the coast from Portsmouth to Pemaquid in search of the enemy, although they ended up with little to show for their efforts. Phips used the lull to send a work party under Major Francis Hooke and Captain John Hill to build a new fort at Saco Falls. Finished in July, the resulting stone structure stood on high ground along the western bank of the Saco River a short distance below the falls, which were so loud that one visitor remarked "that one can scarce hear ones selfe speak." The odd-shaped stone structure was dominated by a three-story five-sided tower, which faced the landward approach to the fort. Firing ports were cut along the ramparts to bring cannon to bear, and by all appearances the new position seemed formidable, but like Fort William Henry at Pemaquid, the architects of Fort Saco used clay and sand as a substitute when limestone could not be found, thus calling into question the real strength of the fortification.[1]

A number of tribes within the Wabanaki Confederacy, the Kennebec and the Penobscot in particular, were being worn down by the constant war parties and the lack of supplies from their French allies. Signs that the English, who had been dispelled from the Maine coast a few years before, were returning in strength, coupled with a desire for a prisoner exchange, led to a proposed truce by the tribes during a conference at Fort William Henry in

May. The suggestion found a receptive audience in Massachusetts. With the political strife imposed by a new royal charter and a witch-hunt hysteria threatening to engulf the colony, Governor Phips was quick to press for a more lasting peace treaty. To his satisfaction thirteen Wabanaki chieftains arrived at Pemaquid on August 11, 1693, and signed just such a document. Phips was high on the accomplishment, which he informed London would now allow Massachusetts to divert some of its resources to aid New York.

This latter cause had proved a major point of contention among the English colonies, and had Frontenac known how divided the English were before him he would have rested much easier throughout the summer. In late 1692 and again in early 1693 the English court had sent a circular out to the colonial governors addressing the concerns for the New York frontier and the need for the other colonies to assist in this mutual defense matter. New England and colonies as far south as Virginia were to send men and money to New York after deciding among themselves on a quota that each colony should provide for this task.

It was not that simple, as Governor Fletcher soon found out. Phips, who was busy fighting his own war against the French and the Wabanaki, dealing with witch trials, and trying to plan a second attack on Quebec, was not interested in helping. Neither were the other colonies. Soon personal spats broke out between the various governors. Phips argued with Fletcher over his authority and over the fate of Leisler and his cause. The exchanges between the two men and the perceived insults escalated to the point that witnesses thought it was to be settled by a duel. Both sides complained to England, but it would not be until fall, when express orders from Whitehall arrived, that these matters would be addressed. Phips also sparred with Lt. Governor John Usher of New Hampshire and with the assembly of Rhode Island as well. Nor were the members of the Royal Navy in Boston immune to Phips's temper as Captain Richard Short found when the governor beat him senseless with a cane and had him thrown in jail for a questionable defect in his conduct.[2]

News of the setbacks on the New York frontier soon faded into the background as a plan hatched in England the previous fall took hold. To protect English interests in the Caribbean Rear Admiral Francis Wheler, with eleven warships and a number of merchant vessels carrying two regular regiments, would sail for Barbados, where they would join with a pair of militia regiments raised by Governor James Kendall. After seeing to matters in the Lesser Antilles, Wheler was to depart for Boston no later than May. Here he would rendezvous with a New England force, and together they would launch a combined attack on Quebec. Letters were sent to the various colonial governors informing them of the plan and ordering them to make preparations for the expedition against the French capital.

By the end of February 1693, Wheler's fleet had dropped anchor in Carlisle Bay before the colonial capital of Bridgetown. Joined by several warships on station and augmented by a contingent of eight hundred militia, Wheler now had a force of some 2,300 soldiers and marines at his disposal and a fleet strong enough to carry it anywhere it wished to go in the Caribbean. After consulting with Governor Kendall it took little time for the admiral to decide upon Martinique as the expedition's first target. Wheler sent a sloop to Governor Christopher Codrington of the Leeward Islands, informing the latter of his intentions to attack Martinique and his desire that Codrington rendezvous with his forces at the French-held island.[3]

With all the arrangements in place, and his fleet supplemented by colonial transport and supply vessels, Wheler set sail for Martinique. On the morning of April 1,the English fleet dropped anchor at Cul de Sac Marin along the southwest coast of the island. It was agreed in a council of war that until Codrington arrived the fleet would avoid Fort Royal and instead would attack the French settlements along the coast. The army was landed the next day, and by the following evening the French plantations and homesteads at Cul de Sac Marin were in ruins. The fleet re-embarked the next day and for a week ravaged the west coast of the island from Pointe Diamant to Fort St. Pierre.

On April 9, Codrington arrived with five hundred regulars and eight hundred colonial troops. With the combined strength of the two forces Wheler turned his attention to the key French post of Fort St. Pierre. On the morning of the seventeenth, the admiral landed his entire army near the fort and within a short period of time had driven the French into the stronghold. The problem was that the army was not in a position to conduct a siege, and within three days over eight hundred troops had fallen ill during this rainy time of year. Wheler held a council of war on April 20 to determine the expedition's next steps. The admiral favored a siege and a few of his senior officers concurred, but most, including the expedition's engineer, Captain Christian Lilly, were for retiring. "The fort is unassailable without heavy guns, which we can only land under fire of the enemy's batteries," the royal engineer reported to the council of war. "Then, owing to the steepness of the country, cannot move to a suitable position. Even if the fort be breached, an assault will be very hazardous, the enemy being as strong as we." The report convinced all to abandon the effort. An attack on Guadaloupe was briefly considered, but the illness that now ravaged the English fleet ruled out the venture.[4]

Wheler took the fleet to St. Christopher's while the Barbados troops and Codrington's men returned home. Wheler stayed at the island for nearly a month, refitting his vessels and tending to his sick. Since leaving England his fleet had lost 668 sailors and marines, and the two regiments of regulars had suffered heavily under the veil of the epidemic, as had their senior officers. Although the expedition had thus far proven a disaster, there was still an opportunity to strike a serious blow against the French. In mid-May the admiral set sail north for Boston, with the intention of joining with the colonial forces for an effort against Quebec.[5]

Sir William Phips had pushed for a second attempt on Quebec for over two and a half years, but now as the opportunity presented itself he could only stare in surprise at Wheler's vessels. The letter from London informing him of the admiral's plans to rendezvous with New England forces for another effort against Quebec had not reached him, and the first time the governor learned of the plan in writing was secondhand via a letter from the governor of Virginia in late July, after the fleet had been at Boston for over a month.[6]

First, under the advice of Wheler and his council, Phips quarantined the fleet and isolated the sick onboard. Next, he explained to Wheler that, having no advance notice of his intentions, nothing had been prepared for an expedition. A few weeks later Wheler pressed Phips upon the possibility of still attacking Quebec. He found Phips against the idea. Although the naval force was more than sufficient the governor claimed that four thousand men would be needed to siege the French colonial capital. Right now the two regiments from England numbered only 650, and without warning it would be impossible to recruit the required colonial troops in less than three months. This in turn placed the timing of the attack out of the question.

It was an odd response for a man who was pressing New York in February as to what their contribution to an attack on Canada would be. Wheler's force brought 462 cannon to bear, likely more than contained in all of New France. In addition, his fleet had sailed with a bomb ship, a shallow draft vessel designed to carry mortars to bombard targets on shore. Provisions, munitions, and supplies were not an issue, and a royal engineer accompanied the admiral who would see to the siege. In all it begs the question as to whether or not Phips could have raised a force of at least 1,500 men in two months, which would have placed the departure of the fleet in mid-August. Although Phips had taken nine weeks to reach Quebec it is likely that Wheler could make the journey in a third of the time. Would such a land force, below the numbers pointed to by the governor, have been sufficient when backed by such overwhelming firepower? And would not a descent upon the St. Lawrence by such a powerful force make every settlement from Gaspe to Montreal vulnerable to bombardment? Although not a perfect opportunity, it was a better one than the previous attempt, and as such, it is surprising to see the normally fiery Phips so cool to the idea.[7]

For his part Wheler was ready to make the attack by himself, but when Phips dissuaded him from the idea he asked if there were other targets that his fleet might attack. The governor pointed to Placentia in Newfoundland as one opportunity, but when Wheler asked for four hundred troops to assist in the operation Phips shrugged and said that he had no authority to raise the troops without the consent of the legislature and they had just adjourned.[8]

Even without New England's help Wheler decided to attack Placentia. In August the fleet set sail for the French colony, but after exchanging a few long-range volleys with the defenses of the town the French position was judged too strong and Wheler set course for England. The entire expedition was a disaster and cost England over a thousand lives. Delays, disease, and faulty communications unraveled a plan that might well have secured the Caribbean for England and ended the war in North America. "I regret greatly that the affair should have been disappointing," Phips wrote the secretary of state for the Northern Department, the Earl of Nottingham, understanding quite well that the failure of Wheler's expedition likely meant an end to the idea of seizing Quebec.[9]

To the north Frontenac spent the better part of 1693 worrying about reports of an impending English attack on Quebec. The rumors first started after the attack on the Mohawk villages. Prisoners taken along the New York and New England frontier were speaking of plans for a colonial army to rendezvous in Boston with a Royal Navy fleet from the West Indies in early summer. The combined force was then to launch an assault on Quebec while another colonial army descended Lake Champlain with the aim of seizing Montreal. The count had heard these types of rumors before, but this time the reports appeared credible enough that they deserved a response. There was little choice. "Our city which, without difficulty, had sustained the attack of thirty miserable craft," one witness noted, "was not in a condition to resist a more considerable force."[10]

The previous fall Frontenac had assigned the Chevalier Dubois-Bertelot deBeaucours, a reduced captain at Quebec, chief engineer and tasked him with a major improvement in Quebec's defenses. Some of the initial layout work was accomplished before winter set in, but most of the effort was set into motion by legitimate fears of an English expedition during the spring and summer of 1693. Calling upon *corvee* labor from within fifty miles of

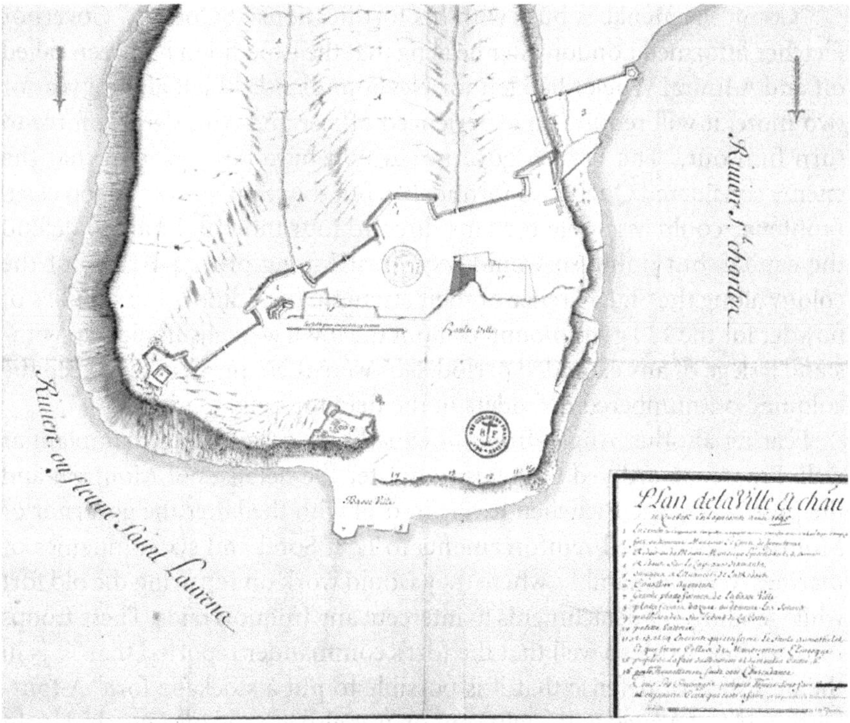

A plan of the fortifications of Quebec in 1695. The new earth wall and bastions can be seen along the land approach to the city, while the stone redoubt at Cape Diamond at the southeast end of the wall and the stone fort built towards the lower town are also present on the plan. (*National Archives of Canada*)

the town to work on the project, Beaucours directed that the old wooden palisades on the land side of the city be replaced with earthen walls. The eighteen-foot-high thick earth walls were constructed by bracing parallel wooden walls and filling them in with dirt from the ditch in front of the wall. The tops of the ramparts were sodded, and platforms were fashioned to allow a large number of men to fire from behind a sloped parapet. A pair of redans, designed to mount heavy guns, jutted out at equal intervals from the thirty-foot-tall walls, while the ends were covered by half-redans, and at the southeast end of the structure, on the heights of Cape Diamond, a stone redoubt was erected to hold a battery of cannon. In addition, a small stone fort armed with sixteen guns was constructed farther north on Cape Diamond at a point that commanded the lower town. By fall, even though there remained a number of items still left to finish, the conversation had already started about facing the new wall in stone.[11]

"Count Frontenac is busy with his fortifications at Quebec," Governor Fletcher informed London after hearing that the expedition had been called off and Admiral Wheler had left for Newfoundland. "If left alone a year or two more, it will require an experienced officer and considerable force to turn him out." The French governor would have been pleased that the enemy considered Quebec so formidable, but the realities were all too clear. Frontenac could assemble perhaps three-to four thousand men to defend the capital, but doing so would require stripping other portions of the colony along the St. Lawrence of their strength. In addition, the supplies of powder for the 130 guns mounted about the town were insufficient to withstand a siege of any extended period. Nor were there provisions to keep the colonies' outnumbered defenders in the field for long.

Fearing another Anglo-Iroquois expedition down Lake Champlain as well, Frontenac ordered Callières to bolster the defenses of Montreal and the posts along the Richelieu River. To deal with the latter the governor of Montreal dispatched reinforcements to Fort Sorel and six companies of marines to Fort Chambly, where they would work on repairing the old fort while sending out detachments to intercept any Iroquois raids. These troops took to their work so well that the fort's commander reported that "it is in the best state of defense that it is possible to put a stockade fort." A four-bastioned fort armed with eight cannon was also erected on a nearby height that dominated Montreal, and what holes that could be found in the palisade that circled the town were repaired, but there was time and resources for little else.

In June several more prisoners were brought before Frontenac and his council. One, a Frenchman who had been captured several years before, and had recently been repatriated by a French and Indian War party, assured the count that preparations for an English expedition against both Montreal and Quebec were underway. The other prisoners gave similar stories. This news, however, was quickly supplanted by the arrival at Quebec of an Oneida chieftain named Tareha. Tareha returned a prisoner to Frontenac as a sign of his good faith and informed the governor that, although he could not speak for the other tribes, the leading cabins of the Oneida desired peace.

Frontenac responded to the simple overture by acting like an angry father, berating the Onondaga and the Iroquois for their conduct but in the end pointing to his love for his children as overcoming his anger. If the Seneca, Onondaga, Cayuga, and Oneida wished to discuss peace they should send two representatives each to the governor and he would listen to their words. The count then issued a warning to Tareha.

"It is for them to consider the resolution they are to adopt," the count informed Tareha, waiting for the delay imposed by the interpreter. "Because if they refuse to enter promptly at the door the Oneida have begun to open for them, Onontio is determined to close his ears, to listen no longer to any proposition of arrangement, and to pursue them until they be wholly exterminated." In reality, had the governor the means, he would have struck the Onondaga at the soonest moment, being convinced that it was "absolutely necessary to go and attack them in their villages."[12]

In July reports arrived that the English fleet had sailed for Quebec, and information from an escaped French captive claimed that eight hundred Iroquois would descend the St. Lawrence to attack the settlers bringing in the harvest. The reports filled the colony with an air of anxiety. On the evening of July 13, the alarm was sounded, as a vessel could be seen entering the roadstead before the town. Sentries struggled to make out the vessel's flag and then, with a sigh of relief, announced that it was French. For the next few weeks vessels from a French relief convoy led by Iberville anchored before the town. The ships were carrying food, munitions, and, most importantly, over four hundred recruits for the companies of the marine. The reinforcements were welcomed, and soon 150 of them were dispatched along with five companies under Major Vaudreuil to help deal with a large Iroquois war party above Montreal.

The threat proved to be nothing, and as summer slipped into fall it became clear that an English attack on Quebec was to become nothing as well. The mood of the colony began to shift, and the arrival of fur convoys at Montreal from New France's allies helped with this. A trade fair was held at Montreal, and Frontenac used the occasion to meet with chieftains from each of the nations present. It was also an opportunity to address a number of issues on the western frontier. Foremost among these was word that the Miami had accepted gifts from the English-allied Mohegan. Fearing a possible breach in the alliance the governor dispatched a force of Canadians under experienced frontiersmen Manteth and Courtemanche to look into the matter.[13]

News of the Abenaki peace treaty with New England came to the governor's attention later in the fall, but it was not of great concern to him. French influence over the tribes in question needed to be doubled and the supplies being requested delivered to their allies, but in the end the long discord between the English and the Wabanaki would do the rest. It was the discord brewing within the Iroquois Confederacy that interested Frontenac more. In meeting with the numerous tribes at Montreal the governor got a better sense of the efforts being made by his allies against the Five Nations. Hundreds of Iroquois had been slain or captured, which, combined with the success of the Mohawk expedition earlier in the year, had begun to crack the resolve of the confederacy. The English could not protect them, and elements of the Five Nations began to understand this. A major effort now against the Onondaga would push the confederacy into a separate peace treaty with the French—precisely what Frontenac needed. Unfortunately the count did not have the resources available for such a campaign even though he was convinced that such an action was inevitable.

After meeting with the Five Nations at Albany Governor Fletcher saw the shift in the confederacy's attitude as well. He also realized the dire consequences that came with it, informing the Board of Trade,

> That if our Canton Indians, who seem to stagger and are enclined to make peace with the French of Canada, through want of those usual supplys and presents which this poor Province cannot longer support itself under, and they should be induced to makeup a separate peace, the ruin of the whole country would unavoidably ensue; and that if the frontiers of Albany should happen to be pushed by the enemy, the neighboring governments cannot hope to escape; for if we lose our Indians, who are our cheifest &cheapest bulwarks against the French, we cannot keep less than 1,000 men in garrison at the frontiers.[14]

CHAPTER EIGHTEEN

Stalemate in the East

Although Governor Fletcher was able to convince the Iroquois to hold peace talks with the French in Albany, which he was certain Frontenac would refuse, it was becoming clear that the Five Nations were reaching their limits. After accepting a large shipment of muskets and powder from Fletcher the various chieftains pledged their loyalty "to the last drop of our blood & altho wee are tossed to & fro' We will remain stedfast to the last man." Such fidelity, however, did not come without criticism. The disorganized English war effort baffled and concerned the Iroquois, who could not understand why their allies did not present a more unified front against the French. The arrival of Wheler's fleet and talk of a coordinated attack on New France "was extream' joyfull News to us," the Iroquois spokesman informed the governor. "We were glad to end the war at one push to facilitate the fleet's success in subdueing that place to remove all our troubles & make an end of this blood-shed, but to or great sorrow now Wee hear of no such designe."[1]

Fletcher certainly had his own questions and criticisms regarding colonial unity, and protest as he might, to both the nearby colonies and Whitehall, little came from the effort. It was not until the fall of 1694 that it looked like the New York governor might finally receive some satisfaction in the matter. A number of directives arrived from England looking to assist Fletcher while also providing some order in the area of colonial defense. First, the militia of Connecticut was transferred from Governor Phips's command to Governor Fletcher's command. This move alone would provide New York with the men it needed to guard the frontier. Second, the colonies were to send representatives to a conference that would establish troop quotas among each for the common defense, and third, the colonies were ordered to assist in the defense of the New York frontier.

As promising as it might have first seemed, nothing came of this. Connecticut resisted Fletcher's authority, several of the colonies made excuses for not sending representatives to the quota meeting, and those representatives who did appear refused to do anything unless all the representatives were present. Nor was any significant aid coming to New York. In a repeat of his previous attempts Fletcher found that all that could be secured was a small amount of money from Virginia and Maryland and a handful of troops. In search of men the governor even visited Pennsylvania, whose militia his commission gave him command of, but it was a wasted journey. "They have neither arms nor ammunition," he wrote the Board of Trade, "nor would they suffer the few men fit for it to be trained."[2]

In the end Fletcher found himself once again writing London with his complaints. "This Province cannot hold it thus longer, their Majesty's large Territories upon this Main are so divided in Government and circumstance from one another they drive private interest, and though we be a numerous People, yet weak exposed to the Enemy and fit for no design." In a plea for royal intervention Fletcher asked for funds to build a stone fort at Albany and for four companies of grenadiers to be sent out from England to help with the colony's defenses. He also asked for funds to recruit the two current regular companies on station back up to their full strength of one hundred men each, for two hundred muskets, and for cannon to help guard the numerous seaways and rivers in the province. Weary and facing a seemingly impossible task, Fletcher agreed with the Iroquois and confided to the Board of Trade that, "I heartily wish for another Squadron of Ships with Land Forces to put an End to the matter next Summer."[3]

The summer of 1694 was to bring just the opposite. Along the Maine-frontier the peace treaty signed the previous summer appeared to be holding, but for those who actually thought that both sides had seen enough it proved to be wishful thinking. The French distributing presents and supplies through Villebon and Castin called upon the tribes that had signed the treaty to take up arms again. Combined with the efforts of Father Thury and a number of leading chieftains, success was never truly in doubt.

Durham, , was the unfortunate target of this renewed cause among the French and the Wabanaki. Durham was a scattered set of farmsteads along both sides of the Oyster River with a small concentration of buildings near the falls where a sawmill had been erected. It was a town of a few hundred souls at most and one that had seen the peace hold for the better part of a year. On the evening of July 17 no one suspected an attack, and as such, most of the inhabitants slept in their homes rather than one of the dozen garrison houses.

Hidden in the shadows below the falls were three hundred Wabanaki and twenty French, led by their familiar war chiefs as well as Marine captain de Villieu and Father Thury. Around 3 a.m. Villieu's scouts returned from Durham. They had arrived at this location undetected, they informed him. A brief war council was held to discuss how to attack, and within short order it was agreed that one detachment would move up the north bank of the river while the other moved up along the south bank. Both would attack at daybreak.

Villieu's war party had ample time to fan out across the community, but one band had a chance encounter with the owner of the mill and fired on him as he came out of the structure. The shots warned a few in the town, but in general it signaled a start to the carnage. War whoops and more shots followed as the attackers broke into the homes along both banks of the river. Soon flames began to appear as the pillaged homes and their slain occupants were put to the torch.[4]

The war party had particularly targeted several of the garrison houses. The first was Stephen Jones's house, but Jones, uneasy about a barking dog, was in one of the flankers when a shot was fired at him. A few more followed, including one from Jones toward his adversaries. Seeing that the English were on guard the Wabanaki moved on to easier targets. Nearby Charles Adams's garrison house was not so fortunate. It was quickly overrun and its fourteen inhabitants slain. Four other garrison houses were taken in a similar manner. The remaining garrison houses, however, put up an active defense—enough at least to convince the war party that they were not worth attacking. At Robert Burnham's garrison house the outer gate was left open, but a toothache awoke one of the house's inhabitants who shut and barred the gate as half a dozen Wabanaki warriors approached after the opening shots. In another case, a single inhabitant, Thomas Bickford, reportedly held off the attackers by frequently changing his hat and jacket and firing from different points in the garrison house, all while shouting out fictitious orders to give the illusion of a stronger force.

For most of Durham it was havoc and destruction. When Villieu's war party moved off later that morning they carried with them twenty-seven prisoners and left another 104 dead, scattered about the burning ruins of the town. The main body of the war party returned to their homes, but several war chiefs, Moxus included, were not happy with the plunder from

Durham and headed south in small bands in search of more profitable targets. "They mean," Villieu later reported, "to divide into bands of four or five, and knock people in the head by surprise, which cannot fail to produce a good effect."[5]

After attacking a small farmstead, Moxus and several small bands launched a surprise attack on Groton, Massachusetts. Caught unaware, twenty-two of the town's inhabitants fell before the attackers, while another thirteen were led away as prisoners. Only a stout defense at one of the garrison houses prevented the attack from being worse. All in all, the citizens of Groton put up far more of a fight than those of Durham. Moxus had two nephews killed at his side and his clothes torn by musket balls in half-a-dozen places. It was enough to convince the war chief to return home.[6]

When news of the attack on Durham reached Governor Usher of he called out the militia and asked Massachusetts for two hundred troops to help pursue and destroy the enemy. To Usher's amazement Phips balked at the request, saying that he could not impress men to serve outside the colony without the assembly's consent.

For many, such an action was the last straw, but in reality it had passed that point. Governor Phips's behavior had become more erratic and his personal interests more dominant over the last few years, and it was beginning to catch up with him. He had been accused of overstepping his authority on numerous occasions, confiscating French naval prizes for his own gain, arguing with and failing to support nearby governors in the war effort, and a fair number of other infractions. A long series of charges were laid down against the governor, and although liked by King William for his adventurous spirit, it was agreed that Phips had proven problematic as a governor and his recall was issued. A few months after it was received Phips passed the governorship over to Lt. Governor William Stoughton and departed for England to face the charges leveled against him. Not long after reaching London Phips fell ill and died a few days later on February 18, 1695, at the age of forty-four, having never made his case before the king.[7]

For most there were two William Phipses: the adventurer and risk taker and the frustrated man out of his element as a colonial governor. The former Phips was greatly admired for his traits, and often-disconcerting elements of his behavior were thrown into the shadows by these bright and daring qualities. He was a man that many would say would rather be ruined by praise than saved by criticism. Few would ever call Phips's bravery into question, but many questioned his leadership abilities after the campaign against Quebec in 1690. In his defense there is no question that Phips made a number of mistakes in this expedition, but he was hardly alone. Blame was easily placed within the amateur army after the disaster without addressing the fact that just as much of the failure behind the expedition lay in the sluggish colonial bureaucracy and inefficient logistics which, coupled with weather, placed the New England fleet in front of the French capital too late in the year. To his credit Phips was one of the first to advocate the idea of seizing Quebec as the speediest way of ending the war—a theme that would resurface many times over the Anglo-French conflicts in North America—and after a disastrous attempt on Quebec by the English navy in 1711 it could be said that amateur Admiral Phips did not look quite so bad.[8]

If Phips's credentials as admiral are problematic his tenure as governor of Massachusetts is more so. The daring spirit that made Phips so likable was poor preparation for the world of politics or a witch-hunt epidemic, as the new governor found when he landed in Boston. The latter problem Phips handled as well as anyone given the circumstances, but with other matters of state he was not so fortunate. He fought with the assembly regarding the new royal charter and argued with other governors to the point of turning these disputes into personal matters. He abused his authority, bullied those about him, and delved into illegal trade to enrich himself. There was a good deal of merit to many of the charges placed against him, and in the end one is left to conclude that he was a poor choice for governor.

Although tensions were relieved upon Phips's departure it did not immediately translate into more cooperation between the colonies. Governor Stoughton was much easier to get along with, but by the time the Massachusetts assembly dealt with the matter, it was far too late to be of help. Although a handful of attacks struck the Maine-New Hampshire frontier during the late summer, there was more calm than expected. In late November 1694, a number of prominent Abenaki leaders entered Fort Pemaquid under a flag of truce. The Abenaki were looking to trade, but when several were recognized as having participated in the attack on Durham, the safety granted by their white flag was considered null and void by the fort's commander, Captain John March. Three of the Abenaki were seized, thrown in chains, and sent to Boston where they were held as negotiating pieces. The other four in the party were sent to Saco where they were executed by the garrison.

The Abenaki were furious over the deception and threatened to burn down the New England frontier. For his part Stoughton chastised the Abenaki over their conduct and threatened retribution on the hostages. The governor then attempted to defuse the situation by considering it a criminal act and demanding that the Wabanaki hand over the ringleaders of the attack. In a gesture of goodwill and a display that Massachusetts was willing to negotiate a hostage exchange, Stoughton released one of his Abenaki prisoners to carry his message.

Both sides were cautious not to let the matter slip out of hand. Stoughton was facing a serious financial crisis, a disenchanted populace, and a shortage of troops to man the frontier. The Abenaki also had good reasons not to aggravate the situation. The English held a number of their relatives in Boston and would certainly hang them if there were a major attack. To make matters worse the supplies promised by the French had failed to materialize. Given the circumstances, something of an unofficial truce took hold along the frontier. The handful of French officers in the area tried to incite the Wabanaki back to the warpath, but without presents and munitions to supply them their words fell on deaf ears.[9]

Fall turned to winter and winter to spring without a major incident along the Maine-New Hampshire frontier. In June 1695, Villebon summoned the representatives from the various Wabanaki tribes to meet with him and Father Thury. The intent was to encourage their efforts against the English, but this was not the message the governor received from his guests. "It was our need for many things, and our distress at seeing our families destitute, which drove us to make overtures to the English," the spokesman from the Kennebec tribe informed Villebon when questioned on the matter. "But it only depends on thee that we do not in the future," he followed in a clear indictment of the French failure to support their allies. At the conclusion of the talks it was clear that the Wabanaki were still in the French camp, but it was also clear that without material support they would do little to forward the conflict.[10]

Looking for an avenue to open peace talks Stoughton arranged a small prisoner exchange in the summer of 1695. The effort yielded the desired results, and a larger conference and prisoner exchange was agreed upon at Fort Pemaquid in August. Hope was quickly dashed, however, when the English failed to produce the Wabanaki taken at the fort under a white flag the previous fall. From here talks quickly broke down, much to the delight of the French.

The failure brought forth an immediate concern for the frontier, and troops were dispatched to bolster the defenses of the towns and posts likely to be attacked. There were a few sporadic attacks, the worst falling upon Tewksbury, New Hampshire, where ten were killed and several carried away. In Newbury the attackers carried off nine inhabitants only to slay all but one when a pursuing party of English militia got too close. These incidents were alarming, but in general, most had expected much worse. The same could not be said for the garrison of Fort Pemaquid. Being located in the midst of hostile territory any foray out of the fort bore a certain risk and level of caution. A woodcutting party of twenty-four men forgot this dictum and was ambushed in September, leaving four dead and half a dozen wounded. From that point on the garrison stayed on a constant state of alert.[11]

The lack of Wabanaki activity during this time was also the result of an active English naval presence along the coast of Maine and Acadia, as well as their establishment of Fort William Henry at Pemaquid. The latter location was a problem, as the Abenaki had often sought negotiations with the English garrison to obtain the items the French couldn't supply. This collusion became Governor Villebon's focus not long after the attack on Durham. In making a case to the minister of the marine for an expedition against the stronghold, Villebon saluted the foresight of his English adversaries. "They judged very correctly that in building Pemaquid, they were depriving our Indians of the power of going freely coastwise on their expeditions; embarrassing them in an extraordinary degree in hunting Deer which were very abundant thereabout, and that the Indians, finding themselves thus straitened, would be obliged to enter into negotiations, as has in fact been the case." Seizing Pemaquid would not only recement the Wabanaki-French alliance, but it would also remove the strongest English position along the Maine coast, opening up a large stretch of the coastline with its excellent harbors for French use. To accomplish the task the governor called for three ships—a pair of frigates and a flyboat—to land troops. A force of one hundred soldiers along with a like number of sailors from the fleet would be joined by Villebon and two hundred Abenaki once they landed. With a force this size it would take little to invest the fort, and from here the governor estimated that a battery of four eighteen-pounders and a pair of mortars would be sufficient to reduce the stone fortress, especially when supported by the cannon on board the frigates.[12]

A more pressing problem was the English naval activity, but there was little Villebon could do in that regard. A pair of frigates had routinely fitted out in Boston each year to cruise the Maine-Acadia coast in search of prizes. The warships, coupled with a number of privateers, had a devastating effect on the Acadian fishing fleet and often intercepted French supply vessels. It appeared to the Wabanaki that the English ruled the seas, and that was why the French could not supply them, which was in part true, but it did not account for logistical failures and errors wholly within French hands.

At the beginning of 1695, the French sought to assert some control over the coastal waterways. A privateer named Pierre Maisonnat Baptiste outfitted a forty-five-ton corvette named the *Le Bonne* with a handful of cannon and took to sea. In mid-January Baptiste's efforts proved successful when he captured a sixty-ton schooner loaded with molasses and sugar from the West Indies, but the corsair was not finished. After taking on provisions he set out from the St. John River on April 21 in search of more prey. By mid-May the *Le Bonne* had returned with a twenty-five-ton English prize in tow. Villebon then sent Baptiste to Spanish Bay with orders to wait for the anticipated French supply fleet and warned him of reports that a thirty-six-gun English frigate and another twenty-two-gun vessel were being outfitted in Boston along with a large row galley.

The orders proved unfortunate for the *Le Bonne*. While sailing to Spanish Bay the vessel was damaged in a gale and set into a small harbor to make repairs. The next morning as Baptiste sailed out of the bay, he encountered the thirty-six-gun New England frigate *Sorling*. Although badly outgunned, Baptiste put up a running fight for the better part of the day, but the disparity in firepower eventually caught up with the *Le Bonne*. The vessel's pilot and eight of its crew had been killed, and after being repeatedly hit, the ship was taking on water. The shattered rigging left few options, as it was nearly impossible to maneuver, so bowing to the inevitable Baptiste ran the vessel aground, which allowed him and the crew to escape. The *Sorling* sent a boarding party over to the *Le Bonne* and at high tide refloated the French corvette, but she proved too damaged and sank shortly thereafter.[13]

The loss of the *Le Bonne* had brought more New England fishing vessels to the area which, coupled with the *Sorling*'s activities, only seemed to reinforce the Wabanaki position. On July 8, this changed when Captain Bonaventure arrived at St. John in the frigate *Envieux*. Bonaventure informed Villebon that he had arrived at Pentagout on June 19, where he had been informed by Father Thury that a forty-gun English frigate had been seen at St. John. After taking on provisions he sought out the enemy warship and around three o'clock on the afternoon of July 5 he found his quarry. The thirty-six-gun *Sorling* was an even match for the Frenchman. The two vessels dueled for five hours, exchanging broadsides and trying to maneuver to rake the other from stem to stern. Bonaventure had severed the *Sorling*'s main topmast, and part of the Englishman's mizzenmast had splintered upon a direct hit and fallen on the aft deck. The *Envieux* was struck hard as well, but Bonaventure believed that if the last enemy broadside hadn't cut a number of his lines and damaged his mainmast he would have taken the enemy vessel. Bonaventure unloaded his supplies and made repairs before setting sail for Quebec on July 21. The timing proved fortunate, as not long after the *Sorling* and the twenty-four-gun frigate *Newport* arrived at the St. John River looking for the French warship.[14]

The French supplies seemed to have had the desired effect on the Wabanaki, and Bonaventure's actions certainly questioned any perceptions they had regarding English naval dominance, but this did not translate into what Governor Villebon had hoped. Small bands of Wabanaki did strike at isolated targets along the frontier but not in the numbers needed to alarm the English. Soon the season for such things slipped away, and the conflict sputtered out. It almost seemed as if both sides were resting for what was to be a tumultuous year to come.

CHAPTER NINETEEN

The Peace Offensive

Although the peace overtures made by the Iroquois during the summer and fall of 1693 failed to materialize, a new opportunity presented itself in the spring of 1694 when three Mohawk representatives arrived at Montreal wishing to speak with the Christianized Mohawk of the Mountain and Sault missions. After questioning these three men Callières sent them to Quebec to speak with Frontenac. Here the envoys laid three wampum belts before the governor to symbolize each of their three propositions. The first two dealt with the Christianized Mohawk, calling for them to lay down their hatchets and return home, while the third called for the French to open negotiations with the Five Nations at Albany.

As Governor Fletcher suspected, Frontenac gave an angry response. The count kicked the belts aside and railed at the Mohawk representatives for thinking that they could try to seduce or frighten away the mission Indians. "You deceive yourselves," the count growled at them. "They are submissive and obedient to me, as true Children ought to be to their fathers." Sensing an opportunity Frontenac made a counterproposal. The envoys had requested a forty-five-day truce, in part to allow the mission Indians to travel to the Mohawk villages if they wished. Frontenac agreed to this truce under the condition that an Iroquois delegation consisting of two chiefs of every nation come to Quebec during that period. If this did not happen, the governor warned the delegates, "I will no longer listen to your voice, and should you return to submit to me any new proposition, I protest and declare to you, that I will commit to the kettle those who shall be so rash as to dare to undertake such an embassy."[1]

Whether the governor was bluffing or not, his tone seemed to yield results. In June the Iroquois delegates arrived at Montreal and from there traveled to Quebec. Frontenac was delighted by the news and arranged a formal welcome for the ambassadors. When the negotiations opened on May 24, the Iroquois were quick to state their desire for peace. "You have devoured all our chief men and scarce any more are left," the Five Nations spokesman informed the governor. They wished to bury the hatchet with the French and their allies. To show their good faith the delegation returned three French prisoners and only asked that Frontenac consider releasing some of his own in return.

The count did indeed release several Mohawk prisoners, and as a sign of sincerity on the part of the Iroquois he called for them to return to Montreal in eighty days with all of the French and Indian prisoners in their possession. In return the governor would send representatives to his high country allies to convince them to suspend hostilities and meet with the Iroquois at the end of the eighty-day period. Frontenac then informed the envoys that they should reconsider the English influence over their actions. "My war with them has nothing to do with my war against you," he pointed out. "They are two things entirely different." It would not be the last time the count uttered such words to the Five Nations.[2]

In a stroke of good luck a number of Huron and Ottawa chieftains arrived at Montreal before the Iroquois delegates had departed. On their way to Montreal this group had encountered one of the governor's parties heading west with news of the negotiations. Frontenac used the opportunity to reconvene the conference and present the Iroquois proposals to his allies. After hearing from the Iroquois, the Huron and Ottawa chieftains were convinced and agreed to spread the news and return to Montreal in eighty days to conclude a more lasting peace treaty with the Five Nations.

On September 22, a handful of the Iroquois and most of the high country representatives gathered for a conference at Montreal. The Iroquois brought thirteen prisoners as a sign of goodwill, but they needed more time to collect the others, and this was why the other delegates had not arrived. Frontenac was skeptical but granted the time, in part because he required it as much as the Iroquois. Earlier in the year the French court had informed the governor that it was their opinion that the Iroquois were not serious about the negotiations and were just using the time to gather strength while they waited for another English effort, such as a second attack on Quebec. It seemed to the court that only a major expedition against the Five Nations would convince them to carry through with a lasting peace treaty. In this sense the truce benefited the governor as much as the Iroquois in allowing him to collect the necessary supplies and munitions for a campaign. True to the governor's initial instincts the promised Iroquois delegates did not arrive that fall, and with the onset of winter there was no expectation of them until spring. Thus the year passed with little accomplished in the way of a lasting peace treaty.[3]

On the surface it would seem Frontenac's reluctance to discard the peace negotiations was based on his objectives and motivated by a misunderstanding of the state of the Five Nations. The end game for the count did not include the extreme condition—that being the destruction of the Iroquois. In fact such a conclusion would prove catastrophic for New France, as the high country tribes, without the Iroquois blocking their access to Albany, would quickly succumb to the lure of cheaper English trade goods, ultimately forcing New France to either give up much of the west or fight a costly war that it was not likely to win. On the other hand, the Iroquois could not be allowed to remain strong enough to threaten New France's native allies and their commerce, but at the same time they had to be strong enough to bar the high country nations access to Albany and strong enough to prevent English merchants from trading directly with the Canadian tribes. Lastly, it was imperative that the Iroquois be politically separated from the English so as to prevent the latter from inciting the Five Nations against New France in the future.

It does not take much to realize that the solution set containing the governor's peace terms was small and, just as importantly, difficult to judge. Much of the answer depended on an accurate assessment of the strength and will of the Five Nations. By the summer of 1694, the Iroquois were a fraction of their former strength. They had lost nearly a thousand men to the French and their allies since the fighting had started—close to two thirds of their fighting strength. But matters were far worse than losses to the enemy. Although the Iroquois incorporated a large number of captives into their tribes during this time, disease and epidemic far surpassed what musket and hatchet could accomplish.[4]

There was also the admission of their weakened state to both the English and French to consider. This only seemed to confirm that the toll from the conflict had driven the Five Nations further away from the English, and there was little doubt in anyone's mind that the Iroquois had borne the brunt of the conflict against the French. For Frontenac it seemed obvious that the inactivity and lack of commitment on the part of the English, coupled with the Five Nations mounting losses, had brought them to this point.

After all, they had sent representatives seeking a treaty. Certainly the English did not approve, nor would the English be so foolish as to use the conference as a ploy for fear that their wavering allies might actually secure a peace with the French.

To the count it seemed that the conditions were almost right to accomplish his objectives. A push or two in the right direction might secure his goals without a major campaign, and in this sense exploration of a peaceful settlement was difficult to argue with. As the months passed, however, many, Callières and Champigny among them, questioned the Iroquois motives and the governor's patient response. It was almost as if Frontenac had not remembered the Iroquois tactics of the past or foolishly expected that his reputation among the Five Nations was so great that it would carry the day.

In March 1695, two chiefs from the Mountain and Sault missions returned from the Mohawk villages with an Iroquois spokesman. Stopping at Montreal, the trio was interviewed by Callières. After a number of long conversations the governor became convinced that the Mohawk had a sincere desire for peace, having told the English that "Onontio had conquered them without the English affording them any assistance." The remaining elements of the Five Nations, however, were wholly in the English camp. Frontenac did speak with the Mohawk ambassador, and little came of the effort. He too believed that the Mohawk wanted peace, but news from the west was that the other members of the Five Nations were launching attacks on New France's allies—hardly the type of conduct one would expect from those professing a desire for peace.[5]

With the improving weather came the return of the yearly rumors of an English attack on the French capital. Work on the fortifications of Quebec restarted as did preparations to repair Fort Frontenac. By early July Frontenac was in Montreal completing his final arrangements for an expedition to repair his old fort. It was an impressive array of power. One hundred and ten militia from Three Rivers and Quebec accompanied the governor to the island, where he raised another one hundred and fifty troops. Two hundred Marines and a like number of mission Indians had filled out the count's ranks. Numbering some seven hundred in all, with thirty-six officers under the command of the Chevalier de Crisasy, many wondered what was preventing the count from striking a blow against the Iroquois with this force as the expedition pushed out into the St. Lawrence.[6]

A few days before the expedition departed Frontenac had received orders from France not to undertake the restoration of Fort Frontenac this year, given that the expense incurred and the supplies used would be of more service in a general campaign against the Iroquois homelands. In the end the governor ignored the order and sent Crisasy on with his mission. This latter move brought the governor in direct conflict with the intendant Champigny, who reminded him of the court's wishes to no avail. "I believed that he would change his design, as he might easily have done," Champigny wrote the minister of the marine Count Pontchartrain on August 11, 1695. "For this purpose I suggested endless reasons, but all in vain, except in that he sent orders to reduce the garrison by twenty men." The intendant was not alone in questioning why a large-scale expedition had not been launched against the Onondaga if for no other reason than to secure the allegiance of the French high country nations allied against them.[7]

Although the governor's past dealings with the fort had raised an eyebrow when he sought to restore it, in a letter to Pontchartrain he explained his actions. First, the governor agreed that a show of force was necessary to keep the French allies true to the cause. Had he cancelled the planned operation, which was only days away from departing Montreal, he would have sent quite the opposite message. Second, although many about him wanted to assemble a grand army and descend upon the Onondaga, such talk was foolish. He had neither the troops to accomplish this task, nor was it likely to amount to anything, as the Iroquois had shown time and again that when faced with a superior threat they would simply abandon their villages and disappear into the forest. Thus, the money and time invested in such a venture would be wasted for little in return. Third, the reestablishment of Fort Frontenac would provide the least expensive and most probable path toward convincing the Five Nations to seek peace by acting as a supply depot for the high country tribes and a launching pad for raids into Iroquois territory. Locked in a war of attrition that they could not possibly win the Iroquois would return to Montreal sincere in their desire to end the conflict.[8]

At least there were no criticisms when it came to the task of repairing the old fort. Crisasy took only twenty-six days to accomplish his task. At first it was thought that simple wooden palisades would be erected to cover the holes blown in the fort's walls when the garrison abandoned the fort several years before, but Crisasy's men were able to use a nearby mixture of fine clay to fill in and repair the breaches in the stone. Firewood for the winter was cut and barracks built within the stronghold's interior for the forty-eight men who would garrison the post. By mid-August Crisasy and the detachment were back at Montreal having accomplished their goals without the loss of a single man.[9]

The onset of summer also brought a rise in Iroquois raids, not only in the French settlements but in their allies' villages as well. None of the raids were what one might deem large scale, but the general tone of the summer drifted from peace back toward war. The raids escalated into rumors and sightings of a large—seven-to eight-hundred-man—Iroquois war party descending the St. Lawrence. By mid-August the information had become concerning enough that Frontenac deployed several hundred troops to Isle Perrot in Lake St. Louis to intercept the invaders, but nothing came of the incident.

To the west Marine captain Antoine de la Mothe Cadillac, in command of the French post at Michilimackinac, had convinced a number of Ottawa to launch an attack on the Iroquois. The venture proved successful and elicited an unexpected response from the Iroquois to the Miami to either declare war against the French or be driven off their land by the Five Nations. To enact the plan a large Iroquois war party moved against a major Miami village on the St. Joseph River, but in the process they were ambushed and defeated by a French-Miami force under Marine lieutenant Augustin de Courtemanche. This is not to say that the Iroquois had not made inroads into the French alliance in the region. There were enough near defections and secret negotiations between the Iroquois and the Huron alone to keep Cadillac busy all summer trying to undo the damage.[10]

With the onset of harvest season there was no lack of targets for Iroquois war parties and a number succeeded in carrying away a handful of captives in scattered attacks. One of the larger Iroquois expeditions, however, was not so fortunate. In late September news reached the governor that a large Iroquois war party had been sighted on Lake Champlain. Fearing an attack on Longueuil, Boucherville, or another settlement in the area Frontenac dispatched a force of thirty or so Canadians, soldiers, and mission Indians under Sieur de La Durantaye to intercept this force. The detachment immediately set out by canoe from Quebec and, upon reaching the Richelieu River, ascended the waterway to within sight of Fort Chambly. Here Durantaye pulled his canoes ashore and set off to the west. French scouts soon found signs that a large Iroquois war party had recently passed by. Armed with this information and their movements masked by rain and dark weather Durantaye's force moved toward Boucherville where they found the Iroquois war party encamped at the edge of a woods before the town. Never surrendering the element of surprise the French and Indian detachment burst upon the Iroquois encampment, setting the majority of the raiders to flight without their arms or supplies. A brief firefight broke out in the woods that felled two of Durantaye's men, but the Iroquois were completely shattered by the attack. A second war party of Sault mission Indians attacked the fleeing remains of the Iroquois a few days later on the Richelieu River, further scattering what was left of the attackers.[11]

With the harvest brought in and the season advancing Frontenac's fears regarding an English attack on Quebec slowly subsided. Reports of a New England frigate and a brigantine cruising the mouth of the St. Lawrence caused some concern for the relief fleet daily expected from France, but on the last day of September even this apprehension vanished as the news quickly spread of the arrival of eight vessels from France loaded with supplies and munitions. "What pleasure, what joy, what consolation for people in want of everything!" one chronicler wrote of the occasion, perhaps capturing not only the feelings surrounding the appearance of the flotilla but the general relief of having survived another summer under a constant threat of invasion.

The leadership of New York viewed the fall of 1695 in a similar light. For Governor Fletcher in particular, the last two years had been something of a confirmation of his previous warnings to Whitehall. The population of the colony had dropped by 40 percent, to the point that one out of every ten men in the colony was on military duty at any given time. It was not surprising. With too small of a population to defend itself, and a crushing tax burden to support the troop levels needed to defend the province, many people had simply left. The colony's fortifications were badly in need of repairs, and cannon, powder, and muskets were in short supply. Added to this was the strain from the frequent militia call-ups, and frontier garrison duty was starting to be reflected in the colony's declining agricultural output.

To make matters worse, the Iroquois, who to a large degree the colony depended upon to guard the frontier, were stretched to the breaking point and had entered into peace negotiations with the French. "Though always our friends," the governor confided to a colleague, "they are much wasted by the war and too sensible of the weakness of this province when they find the neighbouring Colonies give us no assistance. Without losing their affection for the English they have struck up a treaty with the French for themselves, wherein I am obliged to acquiesce for want of force." On several occasions Fletcher had done his best to discourage these negotiations, or at least direct their intentions, but he had little to show for the effort in the way of results.[12]

At least there appeared to be some relief for the colony. Orders arrived in late 1694 laying out Fletcher's powers to call upon 120 of the Connecticut militia in time of war. In late fall even better news arrived concerning the colonial quotas. Since the colonies could not agree upon such numbers themselves the king specified the following troop commitments: Connecticut, 120; Rhode Island, 48; Massachusetts, 350; Maryland, 160; Virginia, 240; New York, 200; and Pennsylvania, 80. Governor Fletcher was appointed commander-in-chief of this colonial force and, as he already occupied the governorship of New York, no quota was specified for Connecticut, New York, and New Jersey. It was hardly an end to the inter-colonial problems. Several colonies chose to send money or supplies in lieu of men. There were questions as to who paid for and equipped the troops and fears that constant false alarms would tax the militia and lead to escalating costs. Together these points and a number of others undermined the effort to raise a colonial army for the defense of the frontier. In October 1695, an exasperated Fletcher informed Whitehall that he could not "procure one man of the 1,198 appointed." The crown's attempt to put some form of unified colonial command in place had failed miserably. Fletcher was a commander in name only.[13]

Like his adversary to the north Fletcher dealt with constant rumors of French intentions toward the Iroquois and New York. Rumors of a planned attack on Albany, Kingston, or the Mohawk villages in the fall of 1694 occupied much of the governor's time, but nothing came of the alarm. Spring brought new whispers concerning an impending attack on the Onondaga. The reports appeared substantial enough that Fletcher immediately dispatched powder and shot to his allies as well as called out three hundred New York militia to march to their aid. The matter proved to be yet another false alarm, and although Fletcher was concerned that he did not have enough troops to guard the frontier, he need not have been. Albany was an enclosed town supported by some three hundred troops and the town's militia. It would take a sizable French and Indian force to truly threaten the town, and without cannon, which would prove incredibly difficult for a French and Indian force to transport to the town, there was really little chance of Albany falling. Many of the smaller posts north of the town were garrisoned as well, but they protected little these days. The perils of war on the frontier had chased away most of the settlers and left their villages a fraction of their prewar numbers. Small-scale raids still dotted the landscape throughout the summer and fall of 1695, but it was impossible to stop these even if the governor had three times as many troops under his command. In some sense the citizens of New York were fortunate in that little else would occur on the frontier during the war to upset the status quo. There would be scares and rumors in the coming years, but the Hudson and Champlain valleys were soon to take a back seat while King William's War reignited to the north, east, and west during its final full year.[14]

CHAPTER TWENTY

Frontenac and the Onondaga

By the fall of 1695 any English threat to Quebec had passed, but for Frontenac matters concerning the Iroquois and his native allies had already become a priority. Dealings with both had deteriorated into a crisis. What the French court had warned the governor about had become a reality; the Five Nations were not serious about a peace treaty and had only sought time to regain their strength. Renewed attacks on the colony made this clear. What was far worse was that the truce in place over the last year had allowed the Iroquois to open direct negotiations with the Ottawa, Huron, and several other high country tribes. The Iroquois aim was a commercial arrangement that would break the ring of French trade and political alliances in the west, and the timing of the Five Nations' proposals could not have been better. The high country tribes had seen little in the way of effort on the part of the French to strike at the Iroquois, and lingering on-again, off-again peace negotiations had left them open to the arrangement. There was also the matter of several French traders who had begun bypassing the Ottawa and trading with the Sioux at the southwestern edge of Lake Superior. Arming the traditional and powerful enemies of the high country tribes had led to conversations concerning a military alliance with the Five Nations in exchange for commercial considerations.

The Iroquois move had created nothing short of a calamity within the Franco-native alliance. It appeared the high country tribes were on the verge of agreeing to a separate peace with the Iroquois—one which would undoubtedly bring them into contact with the English in a short order of time.

Such an event would be nothing short of a disaster. Although the governor had sought to weaken and bring the Iroquois to a sincere peace through a *petite de guerre*, or a conflict of raids and attrition, the current situation required immediate action. Frontenac had expressed his doubts about whether a major expedition against the Five Nations would accomplish anything, but now such a large-scale operation was needed to secure the commitment of the Ottawa and other allied tribes in the war against the Iroquois. Callières, Champigny, and even the French court were pleased to see the count's change of heart.[1]

Fortunately for New France the resourceful Cadillac, who had taken command at Michilimackinac, was able to rally a number of principle chiefs against the Iroquois. One of these, a prominent Potawatomi chieftain named Onaske, soon raised a war party and in October attacked a large Iroquois contingent that had been hunting near the Ottawa River. In a running engagement Onaske and his men managed to pin the Iroquois force against the river and slowly decimate its numbers until many in desperation drowned braving the frigid river. Some forty Iroquois warriors were killed, thirty scalps taken, and another thirty-two Iroquois brought back as prisoners. The war party also captured nearly five hundred beaver skins worth a sizable amount of money and English supplies that had been given to the Iroquois. Iroquois losses aside, the attack accomplished what Cadillac had hoped in derailing the Iroquois peace talks and buying Frontenac the time he needed to organize a response.[2]

Resolved on a major campaign there were no questions as to where to attack. Frontenac and his council had agreed earlier that the blow should fall upon the Onondaga, who were now leading the Five Nations' efforts against the French and their allies. The question was more when and with what forces. Serious consideration was given to a winter attack on the Onondaga villages primarily because the season made it more likely that a significant number of the tribe would be present. If the villages and the Onondaga's supplies harbored within them were destroyed during the winter, it would inflict the maximum amount of damage even if the Onondaga chose to flee and not fight. The approach was sound and borne out by the winter raid on the Mohawk villages in 1693. It was also wholly unrealistic. The logistics were simply too immense. A war party large enough to face the combined might of the Iroquois would have to travel over 450 miles from Montreal over brutal country during the most inhospitable time of year. Even by Canadian standards this seemed a stretch. A record snowfall earlier in the season soon put any thoughts of a winter expedition out of the question.

Frontenac considered another attack on the Mohawk during the winter, but instead he dispatched a handpicked force of three hundred men under Louvigny to fall upon the Iroquois who had wintered near the Ottawa River. Although the detachment was ready to leave Montreal at the end of January a two-week blizzard halted their plans. The war party would eventually make its way toward Fort Frontenac, but exhausted by navigating seven-foot-deep snow drifts their task appeared to be in vain. Luck was on their side, however, and they surprised a party of eleven Iroquois, killing three of their number before the rest were led back to Montreal in chains.[3]

Preparations for the upcoming campaign continued, and by May 1696 the governor was meeting with Callières and his senior officers in Quebec to discuss the final details. On June 22, Frontenac, along with the detachments of colonial marines assigned to the operation and the militia contingents from Quebec and Three Rivers, arrived at Montreal. The army encamped at La Chine and on July 4 were joined by five hundred Huron, Abenaki, and Iroquois from the various local missions. The native warriors combined with the eight hundred troops of the marine and some 1,200 militia made Frontenac's army an impressive sight.

On July 6, the army moved to Ilse Perrot. From here the six hundred boats and canoes carrying the expedition departed in stages. Callières, commanding the vanguard of five hundred natives and two battalions of marines, took the lead. This was followed by a contingent of Canadians and two large bateaux, which carried a pair of small cannon and a number of small mortars that would be used to demolish the Onondaga's palisade villages. The provision vessels along with Frontenac and his staff came next, followed by the four battalions of militia from Quebec, Three Rivers, and Montreal. A pair of marine battalions and a detachment of natives under the command of Vaudreuil brought up the rear. One witness recorded the slow precession of Canada's military might as it threaded its way up the St. Lawrence.

As nearly thirty leagues of rapids were to be surmounted, progress was very slow, and it is inconceivable how many difficulties were encountered in making the portages, as the men were frequently obliged to unload the bateaux several times a day of the greater portion of their freight. Those unacquainted with the country cannot understand what we call *Cascades* and *Saults.* Falls are often met seven to eight feet high, over which fifty men have plenty to do to drag a bateaux; and in the least difficult places, it is necessary to go into the water up to, and sometimes beyond, the waist, it being impossible to stem the current even with the lightest canoes by the aid of poles and paddles.[4]

After a journey of 150 miles the lead elements of the army arrived at Fort Frontenac on July 19. As the rest of his troops filtered into Fort Frontenac over the next several days the governor put his forces to work securing the stronghold. Enough firewood for the winter was cut, and Sieur Levasseur, acting as the expedition's chief engineer, saw to masonry repairs and the construction of a number of wood buildings for the garrison. The surplus in manpower was also turned toward the bay where three small vessels, scuttled when the fort was abandoned in 1689, were raised a few feet out of the water. The best of the three vessels was then hauled ashore to be repaired.

Here the governor waited a week for the four hundred Ottawa warriors that Cadillac had promised would rendezvous with the army. These forces, in part due to the recent Iroquois negotiations and in part due to the influence of the Jesuits, had refused to join the expedition. With no sign that the Ottawa were coming Frontenac ordered the boats to be readied, and after leaving Captain Du Luth and forty men to garrison the fort, he set sail on July 26.

Two days later the flotilla appeared off the mouth of the Oswego River. Detachments were landed to occupy both banks as the flotilla entered the narrow waterway and crept forward another five miles before stopping for the evening. The next day the army divided into two columns and marched forward along the banks of the river as the vessels slowly made their way upstream. On the thirtieth they halted at Oswego Falls (Fulton, New York). The twelve-foot waterfall required that all the expedition's vessels and supplies be ported around the obstacle. In their exuberance the mission Indians told the seventy-year-old Frontenac to remain in his canoe, and fifty warriors "singing and shouting with joy" carried the vessel around the falls with the count in it.[5]

By August 2, the French and Indian force had sailed up the length of Lake Onondaga and started work on a small palisade fort along its southern shore. Scouts returned that evening with news of fresh tracks from the main Onondaga village toward the Oneida and Cayuga villages. It seemed likely that the women and children had fled toward their allies, but of more concern was that the tracks could just as easily imply that large reinforcements had arrived from the other cantons. A yellow glow in the direction of the village spotted after sunset seemed to answer the question, and most agreed that the Onondaga had put their village to the torch.

The fort was completed the next morning, and after leaving 140 troops under Captain Crisasy to garrison the stronghold and protect the boats, the army advanced in line, with Callières commanding the left, Vaudreuil the right, and Frontenac being carried in an armchair behind the artillery, stationed in the center. After encamping for an uneventful evening the army returned to its march the next morning. As in the day before it was a cautious march over difficult terrain where almost every part of the forest before them seemed ideal for an ambush. There was little to fear, however. The army arrived before the smoldering remains of the Onondaga village late that afternoon. The double palisade walls and four bastions at the corners belied English influence in the town's construction, but ultimately the strength of these works was not enough and the Onondaga had chosen to abandon their village as opposed to risking a direct engagement with the French.[6]

A few prisoners, mostly elderly and women, were rounded up and soon confirmed that the tribe had burned their homes and fled. As the army moved forward to destroy the Onondaga's crops and secure the ashes of their village, Frontenac dispatched Vaudreuil with seven hundred men to the Oneida villages with orders to burn them, destroy all the surrounding crops, and seize whatever influential chieftains he could get his hands on. To the governor's delight Vaudreuil accomplished his task in less than three days, returning with thirty-five Oneida, including several of the principal chieftains. Vaudreuil also brought news from several prisoners, including a liberated French girl, that three hundred English were on their way from Albany to reinforce the Oneida.

A council of war was held that evening. With the destruction of the Onondaga and Oneida villages as well as their crops there was little left to accomplish. Talk turned toward attacking the Cayuga in the same manner and erecting forts in all three cantons to prevent the towns from being reestablished. It was an old idea first proposed by Tracy in the 1660s, and it found an audience with Frontenac and his council. Callières even volunteered to stay and command, but the resources were not in place to carry through with this plan, and the idea, along with an attack on the Cayuga, was soon set aside. With no more suggestions before them all agreed that nothing more was to be done and that the army would return to its boats the next day. After burning their newly constructed fort Frontenac's troops made their way back to the lake without incident and by August 15 had successfully returned to Fort Frontenac having lost only a handful of stragglers. The expedition's cannon and a good deal of its supplies were left at the fort to help secure the western stronghold before a long procession of boats and canoes pushed on for Montreal, reaching the town five days later.[7]

Accolades were quick to be heaped upon the expedition, some far out of proportion with what had actually been achieved. Although initially against a large campaign Frontenac was one of the first to praise his army's success. "The blessings which heaven has been accustomed to shower upon your Majesty's arms," the count wrote the king, "have extended even to this New World, and we have ocular proofs thereof in the expedition I have just terminated against the Onondaga, the chief and principal of the Iroquois Nations." The Onondaga and Oneida villages were now ashes, and although the enemy had fled, the loss of their crops and possessions "will cause more of them to perish of hunger than we could have destroyed by fire and sword." The Iroquois had been taught the force of French arms and, just as importantly, that the English could not protect them. The Ottawa and Huron who had refused to join the expedition were also convinced of French power, and soon any thoughts of a peace treaty between them and the Iroquois were replaced by strings of war parties headed south to attack their ancient enemy. Lastly, Frontenac took pleasure in highlighting the crucial role Fort Frontenac played in the success of the expedition. The arguments against the fort, the governor pointed out, were fine for those who had never visited the place or possessed true understanding of what warfare in North America entailed but did not stand before the realities of the situation. Without this post it would have been impossible to conduct an operation some 450 miles from Montreal, and without a place of retreat a small incident could place the entire army at risk. Now the fort stood as a sentinel in the west, proof of French power and commitment to her allies—a secure launching pad and supply depot for further attacks against the Five Nations.[8]

Frontenac had been fortunate. After reports that a number of tribes had reached peace terms with the Iroquois, the governor needed a one-sided victory to bring back his high country allies. Politically he found what he was looking for, but militarily the triumph was exactly what he had expected. The Iroquois ran and left their villages to be burned. This scenario had played out in the past, and the campaign of 1696 against the Onondaga and Oneida took a similar course. In this sense little was accomplished, but the affair, and a noticeable lack of English assistance, had sent a clear message to the Iroquois, which would once again cause them to question the validity of their alliance. The campaign also brought an additional benefit. Although a handful of enemy raiders were spotted along the shores of the St. Lawrence, for the most part the harvest and the remainder of the year passed without a serious threat posed by the Five Nations.

For the Onondaga and Oneida there were few choices. Rumors of a French expedition against the Mohawk in the spring had escalated to the point that Governor Fletcher had forwarded ammunition to his allies and called out the militia. It proved yet another false alarm, although it is interesting to note that Frontenac had considered just such an operation. Fletcher wrote the colonial governors for their agreed-upon troop quotas and then argued with each in turn when the designated men did not materialize. Better news was that the two additional independent companies of English regulars, those originally dispatched over a year before, arrived in May. Once they had secured their equipment, Fletcher forwarded them on to Albany to bolster the frontier defenses. A few weeks later the governor was complaining to the Board of Trade about the quality of recruits sent. Not long after their arrival, there had been a large-scale desertion in one of the independent companies stationed at Schenectady. A few of the deserters were shot when the party was caught and a brief firefight ensued. The entire lot had been sentenced to death, although this was later commuted for all but one man.[9]

In early July far more alarming news reached Fletcher. A Frenchman taken prisoner near Albany had reported that the Canadian militia was being called out for an expedition that summer against the Onondaga. A large number of French mission Indians and the Ottawa were to join this force. Meeting with his council at Fort William Henry, the governor suggested that four hundred men be sent to reinforce the Onondaga. There was unanimous agreement with the idea but no money in the colony's coffers to execute the plan. The matter appeared again later in the month when two new French prisoners confirmed that three thousand French and Indians had marched on the Onondaga. This news was supplemented by credible reports that a French army had departed Montreal twelve days prior. Fletcher asked once more for men to support their allies, but his council pleaded poverty and instead suggested "that a letter be wrote to the Indians to give them encouragement and to acquaint them the King of England has sent them some presents & desires them to be watchfull."[10]

By early August Fletcher had obtained several private donations and had raised a number of troops that he would personally lead to Albany. It was far too late. By the time the New York forces arrived at the northern post the Onondaga and Oneida villages were in ashes and their inhabitants seeking asylum elsewhere. Fletcher met with the Five Nations on September 29 to console them on their losses and pledged to supply both the Onondaga and the Oneida with corn throughout the winter. For their part the Iroquois thanked the governor for the kettles and food he had provided. The spokesman then informed him that "We come to desire you to acquaint the Great King that the enemy has brought us to a very low Condition and have destroyed five of our Castles; one is now left, and if that be destroyed we know not what to do; we know not what shall become of us next; pray let the Great King know this." They then pleaded for the colonies to unite and for the "Great King" over the seas to send men and ships to conquer Canada. "And if he will not send forces to destroy Canada," the spokesman continued, "then to send us word thereof that we may make peace for ourselves, forever, or for some time."[11]

For Fletcher, whose days as governor were numbered, it was simple logic. The Iroquois had been worn down and exasperated by their English allies. Although the English colonies badly outnumbered the French, for the sake of self-interest they had left the Five Nations to do the majority of the fighting, and now, even as the cantons reached the breaking point, the English urged them on. They promised to take up the cause and strike at the French, but few within the Iroquois camp saw this as anything more than hollow words. With the English faltering and the French growing stronger, a lasting peace treaty, one that did not include the English, became one of the few options left to the Five Nations.

Part Four

Uncertain Peace

CHAPTER TWENTY-ONE

The Fall of Pemaquid

The narrator of the "Most Remarkable Occurrences in Canada for 1696," the official colonial journal delivered to the French court, opened his account with, "It will not be difficult to fill this Relation with facts of importance. . . . For never has a year, since M. de Frontenac's return to this country, been so fully occupied, nor the war waged with greater vigor." Given the events with the Onondaga alone it would be difficult to argue with the narrator, but a French offensive in the east was to be launched as well—one that would prove as successful as the campaign in the west.[1]

The plan had been submitted by Governor Villebon a few years before and called for the capture of Fort William Henry at Pemaquid. If France could provide a pair of frigates to rendezvous with a French and Indian force at St. John, the combined detachments could besiege the fort. The ships would provide the cannon, and their crews would man the guns as well as help with the siege. Once this task was complete the warships would then be free to raid the New England coast.

For the French court there seemed little choice but to act in the direction of Acadia. Should the Wabanaki Confederacy collapse or agree to a long-term peace treaty the region would prove vulnerable to the New England colonies. This would mean the possible loss of the Acadia fishing industries and likely the extensive fishing interests in Newfoundland as well. Given the circumstances and consequences there was general agreement among the king's ministers to go forward with Governor Villebon's plan. This consensus was aided in part by inserting the plan to attack Pemaquid into a larger scheme that called for seizing all of Newfoundland and then expelling the English from Hudson Bay.[2]

Execution of this broader plan was given to Pierre Le Moyne de Iberville. Iberville was one of eleven brothers, sons of the Montreal legend Charles Le Moyne. Like his older brothers St. Helene and Maricourt, Pierre learned his woodland skills from his father during the latter's many fur trading expeditions, and like his father, he would have a long connection with the *Compagnie du Nord*. It seems that Iberville had decided on a naval career early on for he frequently sailed on his father's trading vessel on the St. Lawrence and as a young man had visited France. His first official opportunity to serve New France came in 1686 when, alongside his older brothers, he was appointed a lieutenant in Troyes's expedition to James Bay. His woodlands knowledge and abilities were instrumental in navigating the eighty-five-day voyage north from Montreal to the Hudson Bay Company posts. After serving with distinction on this front for several years, Iberville returned to Quebec in time to participate as second-in-command in St. Helene's attack on Schenectady in 1690. After this he returned to his interest in seeing Hudson Bay secured for the French cause, of which we shall have more to say about later.[3]

Iberville was given a pair of thirty-four-gun frigates, the *Envieux* and the *Profond*, along with the transport vessel *Wesp*. His orders directed him to set sail for Spanish Bay, Cape Breton, and from there sail to St. John and rendezvous with Governor Villebon's forces. Here he would offload supplies and munitions needed by the governor to reestablish a fort at the mouth of the St. John River. Once this was complete the combined forces would lay siege to Fort William Henry at Pemaquid. Upon the capture of the English fort Iberville was to set sail for Placentia, Newfoundland, and there join forces with Governor Brouillan for a descent upon the English-held eastern coast of the island. Brouillan was to command the naval element of the expedition while Iberville, accompanied by his Canadians and some sixty Micmac volunteers, would command the land forces. With this task complete and the English settlements on this island destroyed, if time permitted the young mariner was to set sail for Hudson Bay and attack the English trading post on the Nelson River. To assist in these plans the court had sent letters to Villebon, Frontenac, and the governor of Placentia, Brouillan, informing them of the project. Frontenac in particular was to raise a company of eighty Canadians who would accompany Iberville on his mission to Newfoundland, while Villebon and Brouillan were to organize their forces so as to be ready to cooperate with Iberville's detachment.

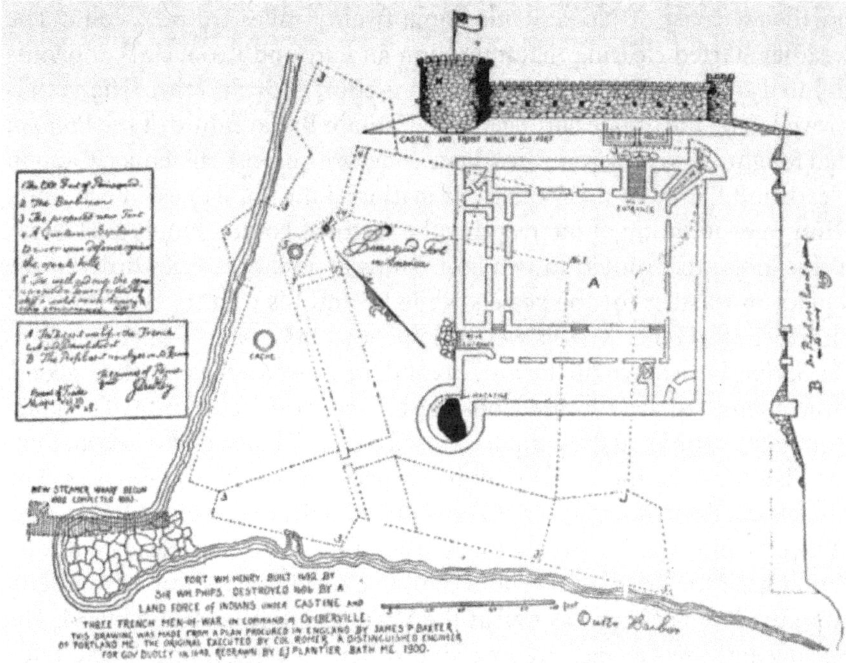

Fort William Henry at Pemaquid constructed by Governor William Phips in 1692. (*The Crown Collection of Photographs of American Maps, Series III, 1915*)

It was an ambitious plan that required four separate parties, three of them in the New World, to meet their timetable, and it was riddled with questions concerning command and the responsibilities of the various elements involved. The problems started almost at once. Iberville's squadron, which was loaded with provisions, gifts, and artillery for the new fort at St. John, was late getting out of La Rochelle. The tender *Wesp* was sent on to Quebec to collect the company of Canadians who were to rendezvous with the expedition at Placentia, while the *Envieux* and *Profond* steered a course for Cape Breton and dropped anchor at Spanish Bay on June 26, 1696. Letters from Governor Villebon awaited the vessels. Three English warships were patrolling the mouth of the St. John River and had effectively blockaded the intended landing area. Iberville stayed at Spanish Bay only long enough to make minor repairs, replenish the crew's provisions, and take on a number of Micmac and Abenaki recruits. On July 4, everything having been seen to, he set sail in search of the English warships.[4]

The poor weather slowed Iberville's approach, and on the morning of the fourteenth the fog was dense enough that he dropped anchor off the northwest coast of Nova Scotia some twenty miles from St. John. The weather started clearing that afternoon and around two o'clock lookouts pointed to three English warships on a course for St. John. The vessels proved to be the frigate *Sorling*, which Captain Bonaventure of the *Profond* had fought the year before, the frigate *Newport*, and a small tender. Captain Fleetwood Eames of the *Sorling* had stationed his flotilla near the St. John River in expectation of intercepting the seasonal French supply fleet. Now, as his lookouts pointed to two large ships at anchor, Eames ordered the squadron to steer for the vessels while he and his officers eyed the craft closely. Both French vessels weighed anchor, and a pair of duels began as the *Sorling* bore down on the *Envieux* and the *Newport* targeted the *Profond*. In an attempt to make himself look like an unarmed merchantman, Captain Bonaventure ordered the gunports closed on the *Profond* and raised an English flag to make the vessel look like a prize in tow by the *Envieux*. The French warships, however, could only carry on the masquerade for so long. When the ploy was discovered the *Newport* unleashed a broadside but soon found itself the target of far more cannon and a huge volume of musketry from the *Profond*'s crew as well as the Micmac and Abenaki on board. The *Sorling* and the *Envieux* fired passing volleys at one another and circled about in a twisting affair of passing fire for the next several hours, repeatedly scoring hits upon one another.

Seeing that he was outgunned by the pair of French frigates, Eames ordered the squadron to make sail to the southwest. The decision to retreat came too late for the *Newport*. Iberville and Bonaventure, keeping the weather gauge in their favor, exchanged broadsides with the English frigate. Badly outgunned it was only a matter of time for the *Newport*. It had been hit several times between wind and water and there was five feet of water in the hold. Iberville's ship scored the decisive blow when a broadside from the *Envieux* cut the *Newport*'s main mast. The warship, out of control, turned into the wind and slowed to a crawl before the two enemy frigates. Helpless, Captain Paxton wisely struck the vessel's colors. Not happy with just the *Newport*, Iberville ordered a prize crew onto the captured vessel and then, along with Bonaventure in the *Profond*, set out after the fleeing English squadron. The *Sorling* and the tender were fortunate, as fog banks and misty rains rolled in masking their escape.[5]

While the *Envieux* and *Profond* chased the retreating English their new prize, under the command of local pilot and corsair Jean Baptiste, made sail for St. John. Unfortunately the tides and poor weather, coupled with the ship's impaired performance, resulted in Baptiste running her up onto the rocks at the mouth of the St. John River. At length the *Newport* was freed, and soon all three French vessels dropped anchor at St. John. The supplies destined for Villebon were unloaded over the next few days, including an impressive array of artillery for the new fort. Attention was also turned toward repairs on the *Newport* and a crew for the prize. With these matters seen to, some fifty Abenaki were taken on board and the three vessels set off for Pentagoet. Here Iberville finished the repairs on the *Newport* while he waited several weeks for Castin's native allies to appear. By the end of the first week of August Castin had assembled 240 Abenaki and 25 colonial marines. When added to the one hundred or so Micmac already on board, and a complement of the vessels crews to man the artillery, it put Iberville's numbers close to five hundred men or about five times that of the English garrison of Fort William Henry.[6]

The force departed in two detachments, with Castin and his native warriors traveling to Pemaquid by canoes while the rest of the expedition sailed aboard Iberville's warships. The fleet anchored about a league from the English fort a few hours before sunrise on August 15. Iberville summoned the stronghold's commander, Captain Pasco Chubb, to surrender, but the latter replied that he would not yield even "if the sea were covered with French vessels and the land with Indians." The French commander had expected as much, and while the opening formalities of the siege were being enacted his men had been busy landing cannon and marking out trenches to approach the fort.

The French pressed their siege trenches forward throughout the morning to the flash of musketry or thunder of cannon as the fort's defenders attempted to repulse their efforts. By afternoon a firing battery of two large mortars and two twelve-pounders had been erected a few hundred yards from the fort. A little before two o'clock a call rang out and one of the mortars let out a hollow thump as its bomb arced through the air, clearing the fort and exploding behind it. The next shot was long as well, but after that the crew found the range and several rounds fell within the confines of the fort. The point being made, Castin ordered the guns to stop firing and sent a surrender demand to Chubb. The French envoy met with Chubb and a few of his officers outside the fort and informed the English commander that if the fort was not surrendered by the time the next mortar was fired "he did not know whether there would be man, woman, or child saved; for the Indians would come in upon us if our walls were breached, and would give no quarter."[7]

Given the garrison's past conduct toward the Abenaki the threat resonated with the English, but to convince Chubb of the futility of resisting he was invited to send an envoy to the French camp. The English commander agreed and sent a sergeant from the garrison. The man returned an hour later to report about the French battery. Six more cannon had just been landed and would be in position within a day or two. The enemy appeared to be six hundred strong, five hundred Abenaki and one hundred French, and this did not include the crews on the warships, which numbered several hundred.

Chubb, latter claimed by many to be a marginal officer, was in a predicament. It is true that he had a new stone and earth fort to stand behind, with over a dozen guns mounted on its ramparts and a garrison of ninety-two men, forty of whom had just arrived from Massachusetts. They were well provisioned and sufficient in number to guard the walls of the structure. If determined there was little doubt that the English garrison could seriously contest the French siege, but part of the problem was the enemy had attacked in a direction where only one cannon could be brought to bear against them, and after firing this gun a few times the ramparts beneath it began to crumble. To make matters worse the enemy had cut them off from their water supply, and with news that the French warships had beaten off a New Englander fleet in the area there was little hope of timely relief.

In the end Chubb surrendered the fort on the condition that the garrison would be allowed to keep their personal possessions and would be carried back to Boston where they would be exchanged for French and Indian prisoners being held there. Iberville agreed to the terms and marched the garrison out as prisoners of war. The gates were opened and the fort ransacked. A half-dead Abenaki was found in the fort's jail, which set off a furor among Castin's allies. Fortunately Iberville had been wise enough to immediately ship the garrison off to a small island in the bay where he could keep a close guard over them. When everything of value had been taken efforts turned toward destroying the fort by pulling down its walls and putting everything that would burn to the torch.[8]

News of Fort William Henry traveled the length of New England like a shock wave. The fort, reputed to be one of the strongest in North America, had fallen in less than twenty-four hours. Captain Chubb, who along with the rest of the garrison was returned when Iberville held up his end of the surrender, was accused of treason and thrown in jail. The militia was called out, and there was fear that Iberville's next target would be Portsmouth, but at least in this regard Governor Stoughton of Massachusetts was fortunate. The frigates HMS *Arundel* and HMS *Orford* had just arrived at Boston with a number of merchantmen in tow. Stoughton contracted a large merchant ship fitted out with thirty-six guns and, along with the *Sorling* and the *Province* galley, sent the two Royal Navy warships out in pursuit of Iberville.

The hastily constructed English fleet nearly accomplished their task. They surprised the French who were lying at anchor with the captured *Newport* at Mount Desert Island. Had the wind not suddenly died off, Iberville might have had a serious dilemma on his hands, but instead he used the cover of darkness to slip away. He was briefly sighted the next morning, but foggy weather ended any hopes of a pursuit. The English, however, were not to return empty-handed. As the *Orford* was returning from this chase it captured a French shallop, which held Captain Villeau and twenty-three marines bound for St. John.[9]

The New England response to the fall of Fort William Henry came quicker than anticipated. This was in part because earlier in the year the Massachusetts assembly had sanctioned another eastern expedition under Major Church. This was to be Church's fourth expedition of the war, and this time he approached the matter differently. Throughout the spring and earlier summer Church traveled from New Hampshire to Connecticut recruiting men for the venture. He also recruited a large number of Bay Indians to man the whaleboats he had constructed for his force. In the past the major had been frustrated by his enemy discovering his movements before he was in a position to strike. By employing the whaleboats he could have the major vessels carrying the expedition anchor out of sight while his forces moved forward undetected. The boats would also give his war party the ability to navigate the inland waterways in search of his quarry, which would not only make his movements faster but offer the opportunity to strike with the element of surprise.

Church was in Boston seeing to the final details of his campaign when reports arrived about Fort William Henry. The news only added more urgency to the preparations, and a few days later the major and a part of his force set sail for the rendezvous point at Portsmouth. Church and his men waited a week at Portsmouth while the remaining troops arrived. His presence brought relief to those who feared a French attack on the seaport, and during this time Church sent out detachments of his men to scout the frontier and guard the settlements. By August 22, close to four hundred men had arrived—enough to convince Church to move forward. A part of the army was loaded aboard three brigantines and dispatched to Winter Harbor. Their orders were to secure the area and send out scouts in search of the enemy. Church and the rest of his forces, traveling by whaleboat, would follow a few days later.[10]

At Winter Harbor Church found no sign of the enemy. Fearing that he might be too late, and that the French and Indian army that had besieged Fort William Henry had scattered, Church advanced up the coast toward

Penobscot Bay, a known French and Indian rendezvous point. The major was cautious to mask his approach and sat in ambush at this location for several days without observing anything. There was no sign of the enemy. Acting on information from one of his men who had been a prisoner in the region the detachment ascended the Penobscot River to the Great Falls in search of an Abenaki village. No village was found, but an Abenaki canoe ambushed by some of Church's men contained a letter from one of the Jesuit fathers in the region that spoke about the construction of a French fort at the mouth of the St. John River and the artillery recently delivered by Iberville that would be mounted in this structure.[11]

With the new information, Church was for returning to the brigantines and descending on St. John. The enemy was clearly alerted to the expedition's presence, meaning that there was nothing else to be accomplished here. The ship's captains, however, were not so keen on the idea. They might well find a French warship or a privateer at St. John, and none of the English ships were heavily armed, being fitted out primarily as transports. Instead a compromise was struck and the detachment set sail for Chignecto in Acadia. Here they burned and plundered several French villages and skirmished with a handful of French settlers.[12]

With their task in Chignecto complete, the expedition seemed to have a change of heart and set sail for St. John. The ships hid at a nearby island while Church and some of his men landed on the west bank of the St. John River. Fanning out into the woods the detachment advanced until they were opposite the old French fort on the east bank. From their vantage point they saw a dozen men at work erecting new fortifications. After monitoring the enemy's activities for a while Church withdrew. The next morning his entire force, including the transports, moved forward at sunrise and seized the partially fashioned fort. The surprise was near total and most of the work crew scattered into the woods, leaving Church with a single wounded prisoner. After being treated for his wounds the French corporal proved of help by showing Church where the fort's heavy cannon were buried. There was some discussion of moving upstream and attacking Governor Villebon's Fort St. Joseph, but this was dismissed when it was revealed that the water level in the river was currently too low for the boats. Satisfied with his take of twelve French cannon and a number of other stores, Church spent the next few days loading everything onto the boats for a return trip to Boston, and after a false start when the winds shifted, he set to sea.

A few hours later one of the lookouts gave a cry and pointed to three sails on the horizon. With the distinct possibility that the vessels were French the fleet prepared for action. It soon proved unnecessary, as the ships were

Major Benjamin Church, left, and Massachusetts governor William Stoughton. Considered the first American Ranger, Church would lead expeditions against French and Indian targets in King William's War and Queen Anne's War. (*New York Public Library/Harvard University*)

seen flying English colors. They turned out to be the Royal Navy frigate *Arundel*, the *Province* galley, and a small sloop. Onboard were one hundred men under the command of Lt. Colonel John Hathorne. Hathorne had orders from the governor placing Church and his men under his command for an attempt on the new fortifications at St. John and Fort St. Joseph farther upriver. Church was less than delighted by the orders and was further aggravated after he informed Hathorne of his recent actions. The latter listened but still elected to pursue an attack on Villebon's headquarters. Church argued that there was little more to accomplish, but Hathorne ended the conversation by informing the major "that he must attend to his orders."[13]

For Governor Villebon all had been relatively quiet after the capture and destruction of Fort William Henry. That is until Church attacked the fort being built at the mouth of the St. John River. Within a few days matters turned far worse. On October 9, Villebon dispatched an officer and seven men to the site of Fort St. John with provisions for the detachment there. A dozen miles from Fort St. Joseph this party encountered a soldier from the detachment constructing the new fort. The man was exhausted from his trek but informed them that two frigates and four other transports had entered the harbor and landed two hundred English and Indians before the partially built fort. Taken completely by surprise the detachment of fifty men was scattered after a few shots. He knew that one Frenchman had been killed and another one taken but had no idea what had become of his commander and the rest of the detachment.[14]

The detachment returned to Fort St. Joseph with the news. The information was enough for Villebon to write Father Simon, a missionary in the area, urging him to come to Fort St. Joseph as quickly as possible with all the Abenaki he could muster. A number of other messengers were sent out as well with simple instructions to convince the natives they came across to march to Villebon's aid. As reinforcements trickled into the fort and were set to work bolstering its defenses, the governor sent an officer named Neuvillette and three men downriver to look for the English. Neuvillette did not have to look hard. On October 16, the scouting party returned informing Villebon that they had encountered the enemy a few miles below Jemseg. Although the morning mists had allowed them to approach within a pistol shot, it was too difficult to make out anything more then several small vessels in the river.

Taken with the other information it was enough to convince Villebon that the English were serious about making an attempt on Fort St. Joseph. He ordered a house near the fort torn down and the fort's munitions to be distributed among his garrison. The cannon were checked and supplied with additional powder and buckets of water positioned throughout the fort to deal with any threat of fire. On October 17, twelve French settlers entered the fort, raising the governor's numbers to around one hundred men. After assembling the garrison and giving a rousing speech, which ended with three cheers of "Vive le roi," there was little left to do but wait.

It did not turn out to be much of a wait. The sound of barking dogs all night convinced the garrison that the enemy was near, and not long after daybreak the sight of a whaleboat full of men moving upriver confirmed what everyone expected. Two more vessels appeared behind the first one, and when they approached to within half a cannon shot Villebon gave the order to fire. A series of commands echoed out, and one by one a string of cannon mounted along the fort's ramparts shattered the quiet landscape. The French failed to hit their targets but succeeded in forcing the three English ships to disembark along the eastern shore.

For the next hour the English and French traded shouts of "Viva le roi," and "God save the king." As Church's men crept closer to the south bank of the Nashwaak River they came within musket range of the fort. With the thirty-yard-wide ribbon of water between the two parties a brisk exchange commenced, with the French side occasionally punctuating their effort with one of the fort's cannon, which sent grapeshot tearing through the woods like a cloud of angry hornets. The fort's fire, quite intense at times, still did not prevent the English from erecting a redoubt, and by nightfall a battery of three three-pound guns had been raised on the south bank of the river.[15]

It was an uneasy night for the attackers, as Villebon prevented them from lighting fires by directing volleys of grapeshot toward any sign of light. At daybreak the firing began again. Around eight o'clock the English brought their new battery into play, adding to the cacophony. One of the enemy guns proved too exposed and its crew was quickly chased away by musket fire. The other two guns required a more concerted effort on the part of the defenders, but within a few hours one English gun had been dismounted and the other abandoned under the focused bombardment. The firing remained steady from both sides until nightfall. Shortly after sunset the English lit a large portion of the shore on fire. Villebon immediately suspected that the English were covering their retreat and ordered all the garrison's guns to open fire. The governor was correct and no doubt the French fire sped the New England forces on their way.

By October 21 it was over. Hathorne's troops had returned to their vessels and the fleet had put back out to sea for Boston. Fort St. Joseph had proven too difficult of a nut to crack. The problem was as Church had stated; the water level was unusually low for this time of year. This limited the approach toward the fort, particularly from the logistics side, but more importantly it limited what artillery could be brought before the structure. Had it been possible to carry a battery of twelve-pounders upriver, the siege of Fort St. Joseph likely would have ended much differently. As it was the attack had cost the French one killed and several wounded—a small price given the circumstances.

English losses in the attack on Fort St. Joseph are not mentioned in any of the journals and documents of the time. Given the more exposed nature of the attackers the numbers are probably twice that of the French—still a small number given the resources committed. What is certain is that the St. John campaign and Church's earlier expedition had accomplished little. It was true that they had the French cannon destined for the fort at St. John in their hands, as well as a good number of artillery supplies, but overall they failed to achieve their goals. Coupled with the loss of Pemaquid, a vulnerable frontier, rumors of French warships prowling off the coast, and a failed harvest, it proved too much for the bay colony.[16]

In late September Governor Stoughton and the Massachusetts council directly appealed to the king for his help. "The French interest is greatly advanced and your Majesty's interest is languishing," Governor Stoughton wrote, after recounting the disastrous year for the colony.

> The places from which you have been supplied with naval stores are in danger to be seized, and our trade both north and south is

> greatly decayed. The charge of war has lain heavy on this province, Connecticut having contributed little and Rhode Island and New Hampshire nothing at all to the support of your interest, but having drawn a considerable charge on us for their defence. We therefore implore your royal aid.[17]

With a bankrupt colony, short on men, and exposed on all sides there seemed only one solution to Stoughton and his advisors, "that you will take into consideration the reduction of Canada, the unhappy fountain from which issue all our miseries." The question now was whether the king would listen.

CHAPTER TWENTY-TWO

Iberville

BY THE FALL OF 1696 the French outpost of Placentia was struggling to survive. A remote village of some forty buildings clustered along the water's edge, Placentia was the key to the French cod fisheries on the Great Banks. It was a seasonal town whose population fluctuated wildly with the arrival of the fishing fleets from France in the spring and their departure under escort of the French navy in the fall. Governor Brouillan, who had tended to the colony for over half a dozen years, did what he could to protect this far-flung and isolated outpost. He had expanded the colony's defenses, reinforced the principal forts, particularly Fort St. Louis with a stone magazine, and erected several batteries to help secure the entrance to the harbor, but in the end it was not determination, know-how, or vision that limited Brouillan's efforts but resources.[1]

Although the governor had fended off two major English expeditions and a number of smaller raids, which had proven just as difficult, his pleas for assistance were largely ignored. The town's garrison of a hundred men a few years before had been whittled down by desertion and illness, and without replacements it was now less than half of its former state. To aggravate matters, the supply ship did not come in 1694, and what arrived the following year was barely enough for the few hundred or so inhabitants to subsist on. Thus, when the letter from France arrived outlining a campaign to secure all of Newfoundland Brouillan was finally convinced that his stars had aligned.

As mapped out in the orders sent by the French court, Iberville's mission to St. John and the capture of Pemaquid was but the first step in the assault on the English. While Iberville executed his step the French frigate *Pelican* accompanied by six privateers from St. Malo, France, and supported by a number of smaller vessels arrived at Placentia. The plan called for the governor to join forces with Iberville, and together with the reinforcements sent from France they would seize the English towns along the western side of the island. The English settlers would be sent back to England while the booty would be returned to France to help offset the cost of the expedition. With a sizable force assembled, Brouillan waited until the end of August for Iberville to join him. When Iberville didn't appear, the governor waited until September 9 and then set sail for St. John's with his fleet.[2]

Brouillan's attack on St. John's was doomed almost from the onset. After dealing with a storm that scattered his vessels the governor attempted a surprise descent on the harbor. Contrary currents, as well as questionable sailing, however, placed the French fleet "a whole day at the entrance to the harbor, within range of a 4-pound cannon, with a wind off the land." The maneuver had netted one positive result. A shallop came out of the harbor to inspect the intruders and now found itself in French hands. One of the individuals on board, Captain Ites of the frigate *Soldadoes*, claimed there were forty ships in St. John's harbor, a number of which were armed with eighteen to thirty-two guns. The information did not deter Brouillan. In the morning he would land his troops and seize the gun batteries at the entrance to the harbor. Once this was accomplished he could turn these batteries on the town as well as sail into the harbor and support an attack with his warships.

Despite the effort of the crews, this plan unraveled when the tide and current carried the French fleet twenty miles south overnight. In their new position the English post at Bay Bulls lay not far away. Reports had reached Brouillan a few days before that two merchantmen and an English frigate, the thirty-two-gun *Sapphire*, were in the harbor as well as a number of fishing vessels waiting to be convoyed back to England. The governor had detached two of his vessels to make an attack on the English colony here two days before, but contrary winds had prevented the ships from entering the harbor. Now, with a light breeze at his back, Brouillan's entire force advanced on the harbor. Two landing parties were formed. The first, under the command of the governor's nephew Captain St. Ovide, was tasked with taking the English batteries and redoubts at the south entrance to the bay while the second detachment under the commandant of the Placentia garrison, L'Hermite, would land and seize the enemy posts on the north side.

Both commanders quickly accomplished their tasks, which allowed the French fleet to approach the town unmolested. A brief firefight broke out between the anchored *Sapphire* and Brouillan's warships, but Captain Thomas Cleasby quickly realized that he would not last long before the French force. After a few volleys he ordered the *Sapphire* set ablaze and withdrew to shore with his crew. With the English frigate engulfed in flames and the harbor's defenses captured the town fell quickly. Most of the inhabitants had fled into the woods, but one hundred of the *Sapphire*'s crew had been captured, the rest, including Cleasby, having made good their escape. Brouillan and his men sacked the village, pausing only as the powder magazine went off on the English frigate sending what was left of it to the bottom of the bay in a hissing fashion. With the pillaging complete the governor ordered the town burned and put back out to sea. Ferryland was the squadron's next target, and after some stiff resistance the town fell on September 21. Like Bay Bulls the governor and his men looted the town, put it to the torch, and sent the inhabitants back to England in several small ships they had captured. Brouillan looked in on several smaller ports but found them deserted. Satisfied with his take of twenty-nine vessels, and finding no support from the St. Malo captains for another attempt on St. John's, the governor set sail for Placentia, arriving on October 17.[3]

Here he found Iberville and his men. Although the latter had been at Placentia for several weeks he could not sail to the aid of Brouillan for lack of supplies. The Pemaquid operation had taken longer than expected and exhausted the detachment's supplies. Iberville asked for supplies from the town's garrison, but there were none to be had. With no other options the detachment waited for a pair of vessels from Quebec carrying the men Frontenac had raised for the expedition and a quantity of much-needed supplies. In early October the *Wesp* and *Postillon* arrived from Quebec. Reinforced and resupplied Iberville was about to set out for an attack on Carbonear, the northernmost English post on the island, when Brouillan entered port.

The two men began to disagree almost from the moment they met. The governor was not interested in Carbonear and ordered Iberville to call off his attack. Instead he pushed for a second naval assault on St. John's with the combined forces. Iberville was wholly against the idea, pointing out that St. John's was now warned and would expect just such an action. The difference in opinion was magnified by a confused command structure. Brouillan was in command of the naval forces, but Iberville had been given an independent command over his Canadians who were to conduct land operations. The argument reached an impasse and Brouillan threatened to use his rank as governor to take command of Iberville's men. At this point

Iberville came close to abandoning the operation and returning to France with his grievances, but it did not prove necessary.

Brouillan had seriously underestimated the Le Moyne name. When his Canadian troops heard that the governor was to bypass Iberville's command they threatened to leave. They had signed on to serve with Iberville, they had orders from Count Frontenac appointing Iberville their commander, and if this were not to be the case then they would march back to Quebec and ask why.[4]

Brouillan was taken aback by the display and quickly moved away from any such decision, knowing that the Canadians were likely to carry through with their threat. The two men soon found a compromise. Part of the problem was that Iberville and his investors were funding his portion of the expedition, which meant that the task at hand was as much about booty as it was seizing the island in the name of the king. The St. Malo privateers were thinking in a similar fashion and, the governor realized, were just as likely to leave as the Canadians. Brouillan attempted to diffuse the situation by stating that he only desired the honor of taking St. John's in the name of the king. To address this matter an agreement was reached where Iberville would take the lion's share of any captured loot. In return, Brouillan would be nominally in command and would attack the English settlements by sea while Iberville attacked by land.

With an understanding in place both men agreed that St. John's was the prize, but their orders were to reduce the English settlements along the coast as well. To address this, the plan called for Brouillan to set out with the fleet for Renews Harbor while Iberville and his men marched across the frozen island to the town. The latter proposition must have seemed like madness to the governor, but he agreed and sailed out with the remainder of the troops. On November 1, 1696, Iberville and 125 men began a grueling sixty-mile trek that essentially bisected the island. "We marched nine days," one participant noted, "sometimes in woods so thick we could scarcely pass, sometimes in these lands of moss, through rivers and lakes, quite frequently up to our waist in water."[5]

On November 10, Iberville arrived at a deserted Ferryland. The next day while arrangements were being made to contact Brouillan, who was anchored a few miles south, a small detachment under an officer named Rancogne arrived. Iberville was at first annoyed to find out that Brouillan had sent a detachment toward St. John's and then dismayed when Rancogne informed him that his party had captured an Englishman from St. John's and then allowed him to escape after they were ambushed by an English patrol.

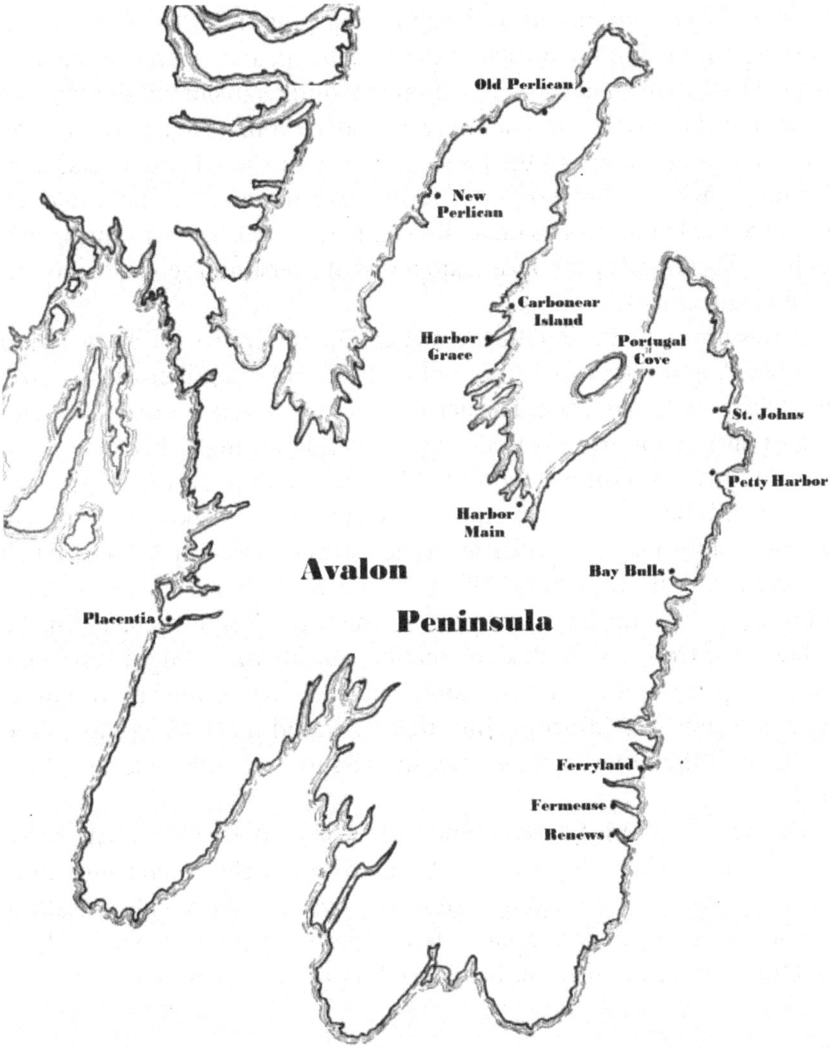

A map of the Avalon Peninsula showing key locations in Iberville and Brouillan's Newfoundland campaign. Brouillan returned to Placentia after the surrender of St. John's while Iberville proceeded against the English settlements in Conception and Trinity Bay. Together they devastated the English colony, invoking a major response on the part of England. (*Author*)

Iberville met with Brouillan on the twelfth and expressed his concern regarding Rancogne's scouting expedition, but before the conversation proceeded any further the old arguments resurfaced. The governor once again asserted his authority over Iberville and disavowed any agreement between the men concerning claims to the spoils taken at St. John's or elsewhere. Iberville objected to the breach in the agreement, and when Brouillan informed him that there had never been any other agreement, Iberville left without further discussion. Back at Ferryland the young French commander penned an angry letter to the king's secretary of state, Pontchartrain, informing him of the proceedings with the governor and how he would not release control of the troops under his command to such a man. Fortunately for Iberville, the governor once again reversed course and agreed to the previous arrangement.

It was not to be the end of the matter. On November 22, the governor sent the *Profond* back to France with letters and a number of prisoners Iberville's scouts had taken. The departure of the frigate seems to have created a political opportunity in Brouillan's mind, causing him once again to return to his old position. He moved his troops up to Ferryland and laid his demands before Iberville. Apparently the honor of taking St. John's in the name of the king was no longer sufficient, and Brouillan demanded half the booty from the expedition. When Brouillan attempted to exercise command over the Canadians and news of the broken agreement reached a gathering of troops on both sides, matters quickly turned ugly. Perceiving the consequences of the divided command Iberville relented to the governor's demands and informed him that he would make his complaint at court. Until then there were greater matters to deal with in terms of the English.

On the twenty-third the combined forces, loaded onto longboats, sailed into Bay Bulls. There they found a hundred-ton English merchantman in the harbor and seized it along with its crew. A number of colonists, busy rebuilding after Brouillan's attack a few weeks before, were also taken. Now established at the bay Iberville began sending scouting parties north toward

Opposite: A portion of a map showing the defenses and layout of St. John's harbor in 1799. While several new fortifications have been added after King William's War many of the fortifications are simply repaired and reworked versions of the original fortifications from the late 1600s. As can be seen on the map, a pair of batteries were arranged to the north of the entrance to the harbor near Cuckolds Cove and at South Head. These were then backed by a second set of gun batteries at the narrows of the entrance. These batteries covered a boom or chain that was strung across the channel to block passage. Backed by Fort William which dominated the bay, St. John would be a difficult target to take from the sea. Unfortunately for the English defenders, Iberville exploited the lack of defenses on the landside of the settlement and forced the commander of Fort William to surrender the town after a brief siege. Key: B: Fort William C: Wallaces Battery D: Signal Hill Blockhouse E: South battery F: Queen's Battery G: Chain Rock I: North Point Battery L: Frederick's Battery M: South Head (*National Archives of Canada*)

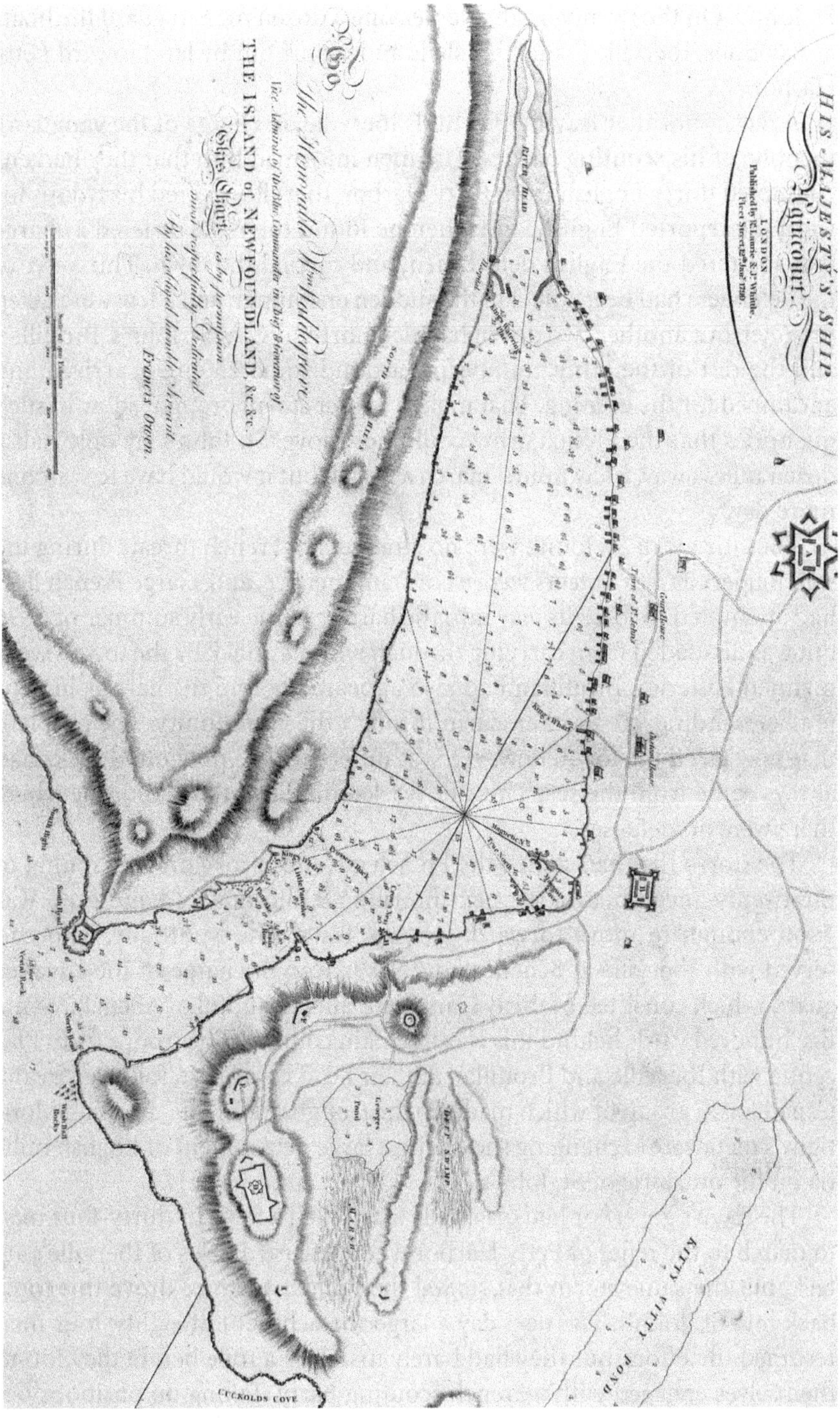
HIS MAJESTY'S SHIP
Agincourt
LONDON
THE ISLAND of NEWFOUNDLAND, &c.&c.
This Chart
Francis Owen.
RIVER HEAD
SOUTH HILLS
DEEP SWAMP
KITTY VITTY POND
CUCKOLDS COVE

St. John's. On the twenty-sixth after leaving a dozen men to guard the boats at Bay Bulls, Iberville loaded his sleds and struck out by land toward Petty Harbor.

A few hours after leaving Bay Bulls Iberville, in charge of the vanguard, met one of his scouting parties. The men informed him that they had encountered thirty English from Petty Harbor. Iberville steered his troops toward the reported English, and when he found them, he ordered a charge that shattered the English detachment and carried the town. Thirty-six of the defenders had been killed in the sudden encounter, and a few were taken prisoner, but another two dozen had fled north toward St. John's. Brouillan and the rest of the army, numbering around some 250 men, arrived and encamped for the evening. That night a winter storm brought snow in such quantities that the French army could not move. St. John's lay only half a dozen miles away, a few hours' march at most, but it would have to wait one more day.[6]

The citizens of St. John's were no strangers to French threats during the war. Raiders and privateers were a constant menace, and a large French fleet had attempted to force its way into the harbor in the early summer of 1696 but was dissuaded from carrying through with its attack by the town's well-manned batteries. Brouillan had also appeared before the harbor in September, sending yet another alarm through the community. The problem that now faced the town, however, was different. The previous attacks had always come from the sea. This one was coming from the land side where there were no defenses.

The storm that had stalled the French advance broke on the evening of the twenty-seventh, and the next morning, although cold and grey, was good enough to move forward. Jacques Testard de Montigny, who had served with Iberville at Schenectady, was placed in charge of the advance guard, which consisted of thirty Canadians and a handful of Abenaki. Some five hundred yards behind this was the main column. The troops from Placentia with Iberville and Brouillan at their head came first, followed by the Canadians, a group of which made up the rear guard. By late morning Montigny's men were exchanging shots with a large detachment of English militia on the outskirts of St. John's.

The town's governor had originally assembled a force of thirty-four men to march to the relief of Petty Harbor when he heard news of Iberville's attack, but the same storm that stalled the French advance drove this force back into St. John's. The next day a larger detachment of eighty-four men resumed the effort, but they had barely marched a mile before they found themselves engaged with a French scouting party. Taking up positions behind a rocky crest the English detachment exchanged shots with Montigny, still unaware of how large a French war party they had stumbled upon.

Pierre Le Moyne de Iberville. His daring and guerilla tactics crippled the English positions in Newfoundland and Hudson Bay, while at the same time earning him a reputation as an individual capable of accomplishing the impossible. (*National Archives of Canada*)

Upon hearing the gunfire in front of them Iberville and Brouillan agreed on a plan. The governor would lead the Placentia men forward and reinforce Montigny while Iberville took the Canadians and circled around the English right. For over a half hour the St. John's militia, by virtue of their defensive position, held off the steadily increasing fire coming from before them. Suddenly, Iberville was upon their flank, threatening to cut them off from St. John's. Caught between two fires, the militia panicked and broke for St. John's. Iberville followed the retreating English into the town and, using the confusion generated, quickly seized two small forts. The panic was such that he might well have carried Fort William, where over two hundred people had taken refuge, but at this point the risk was unnecessary.

Fort William was a neglected, poorly supplied structure in want of food and ammunition. It was now filled with most of the town's inhabitants. With the French in control of the town itself, and Brouillan's fleet not far down the coast, it was not if but only when the fort surrendered. Iberville sent a detachment back to Bay Bulls to bring up some mortars while the remainder of the army set themselves to the task of pillaging the town. The next evening the first steps toward reducing the fort were undertaken when the homes near the stronghold were put to the torch. The act yielded the desired results when the following morning,

> A man came from the fort with a white flag, to speak of surrender. Afterwards the Governour with four of the principal citizens came for an interview. They would not allow us to enter the fort, lest we should see the miserable plight to which they were reduced. It was agreed they should surrender on condition of being allowed to depart for England. The capitulation was brought in writing to the fort, and approved of by the principal citizens and signed by the Governour and M. de Brouillan.[7]

St. John's had fallen. A few settlers had escaped by ship when the attack first began, but most of the town's men, women, and children had been captured. Another fifty-five were estimated killed and perhaps as many wounded. In addition 125 fishing vessels were captured as well as a third of the English fishing production on the island.[8]

After the prisoners were placed on a handful of vessels and sent back to England another argument broke out between Brouillan and Iberville. The governor wanted to garrison the port. A French fleet was expected in the spring and the location would be a perfect anchorage for them. Iberville objected. His orders were to expel the English from Newfoundland and there were still a number of locations to the north to be dealt with. He could not afford to leave men behind if he was to take these posts. Brouillan realized that he already had several incidents to explain to the minister of the marine regarding his conduct but as of yet none that could be construed as outright preventing Iberville from carrying through with his orders. Thinking the better of pursuing the matter the governor dropped the idea, and St. John's was burned to the ground and its guns thrown into the harbor.

Brouillan returned to Placentia while Iberville gathered his men and marched toward Conception Bay. On January 13, a vanguard of ten men under the command of de Montigny broke a path with their snowshoes to Portugal Cove. By January 17, Iberville and the main party, numbering 114 in all, had joined Montigny on their march to the base of Conception Bay. It was treacherous winter terrain. Rocks buried under the snow broke snowshoes, and fallen timber covered in white provided plenty of trip hazards, so much so that it became something of a joke when someone was caught by one and fell headlong into the snow.

On January 19, the war party arrived at the bottom of Conception Bay. Here they encountered eleven Englishmen busy sawing planks, which no doubt made surprising them much easier. All were captured without a struggle, but more importantly, their fishing vessel was captured. Iberville dispatched Montigny in the seized shallop to Harbor Main half a dozen miles away on the west side of the bay. The surprise was near total, and by the time Iberville arrived by foot with the main column, Montigny and his men had taken sixteen prisoners, two shallops, and a skiff.

Now equipped with enough vessels to carry his entire detachment Iberville set sail for Port de Grave. Here, nestled within a cove midway along a thin spit of land that jutted into the bay, was a hamlet of seventeen homes and a number of warehouses. "This place is very beautiful," Father Baudoin noted in his journal, struck by the shingled rock beaches that the homes sat up against. The 116 men and 26 women and children that occupied this town never realized what was happening until Iberville and his men were inside the town. There were no shots fired, and the entire village surrendered without a struggle.

Carbonear, a dozen miles to the north, was Iberville's next target. The village was the primary fishing post on Conception Bay and by now had likely been warned of the French raiders. On January 23, Montigny and a detachment of fifty men sailed to Musket Cove (Bristol's Hope). The following day Iberville sailed to within sight of Carbonear. When he approached Carbonear Island, which sat at the mouth of the bay, he realized that he was too late. The inhabitants of this town had long since eyed the island as a possible place of refuge. Some 2,200 feet long and half as wide Carbonear Island was essentially a grass-covered rock, but the cliffs along its circumference and the limited number of landing points made it a natural fortress. As the little fleet sailed past the island Iberville's men noted the large number of English defenders along the heights, and a few puffs of smoke announced that they had cannon, which would make seizing one of the few possible landing sites a costly proposition. Iberville was not interested in attacking and set sail north where he surprised and sacked Old Pelican and Bay de Verde on February 4 and 6. He then moved down the east shore of Trinity Bay and seized three more towns before returning to Carbonear on February 11. Iberville sought a negotiated solution, but the English refused. Frustrated by the impasse Iberville turned to burning Carbonear. Every building was put to the torch, including a number of homes owned by wealthy merchants, considered by one witness to be "some of the finest in Newfoundland."[9]

Although portions of his detachment continued to operate in the north, by the end of March Iberville was back at Placentia. When the losses to the English colony and the fishing industry in Newfoundland were tallied, Iberville's campaign was nothing short of an astounding success. Combined with Brouillan's efforts, the pair had captured and destroyed thirty-six English settlements. Only Bonavista and the settlers entrenched on Carbonear Island remained on the Avalon Peninsula. Estimates are that a little over 100 English settlers were killed and another 791 captured. Most of those taken prisoner were placed on a few of the 435 captured fishing vessels and sent back to England. A portion of the captured vessels were used to haul enormous amounts of cod, seized at the various settlements, back to France and Placentia. The rest of the fishing fleet was burned, as was everything that stood at each of the settlements. For all practical purposes the English had been ejected from the Avalon Peninsula and the English fishing industry in Newfoundland destroyed.[10]

Militarily Iberville's campaign showed the potential of the *petite guerre.* A handful of Canadians and colonial marines had struck from where no one expected, wreaking havoc on an entire colony in the dead of winter when communications were at their worst. The entire campaign took little in the way of resources and played upon the strength of the colony's skills in adapting native tactics to strike at their larger enemy. It was a campaign that even Robert Rogers and the later French partisans would never accomplish and one which begs the question of what might have occurred if Frontenac had put Iberville at the head of 1,500 Canadians and native warriors and let him loose on the New York and New England frontier.

The attacks were carried out with a ruthless efficiency; destroy everything, send the occupants of the settlement away, and collect the booty. As Iberville stood to profit from this venture one gets a mercenary or buccaneer feeling from the campaign, but there should be little doubt that the French commander believed that his work would strengthen the colony he called home. There were no massacres, although English rumors claimed otherwise, and almost all of the English who fell did so fighting. Fortunately, most of the communities simply surrendered, which was far easier on the exhausted detachment and minimized the bloodshed on both sides.

When combined with the capture of Pemaquid, the failed siege of Fort St. Joseph, and Frontenac's campaign against the Onondaga it had been a terrible year for the northern English colonies. And now with reports that Iberville might be planning a descent upon the New England or New York seaboard, things only seemed to be getting worse. Every colony's trade had been hit hard by French privateers, and the economic impact of the war was showing not only in New York and New England but farther south where the tobacco crops of Maryland and Virginia sat in warehouses waiting for escorts and ships to be transported to England. Maryland had been one of the few colonies to actually contribute to the defense of the New York frontier with monetary donations, but now with trade dwindling from maritime threats they now asked to be exempted from making this contribution.

A number of prominent colonists made the plight of the king's North American colonies clear in a letter to the Board of Trade. "We are under deep apprehension from the late attempts of the French, wherein we have in a manner lost our fishing, furs, mast, timber and peltry-trade alike in Newfoundland, New England and New York, so that unless the further progress of the enemy be checked it will end in the subversion of the Colonies."[11]

CHAPTER TWENTY-THREE

The War at the Top of the World

WHILE THE ENGLISH PUSHED FORWARD a plan to retake their conquered Newfoundland settlements, Iberville waited at Placentia for orders from France. Small detachments of his men harassed what was left of the English on the peninsula, while each morning he hoped for his brother Serigny and the fleet promised from France, which would allow him to finish his work in Newfoundland. Finally on May 18, 1697, the flotilla he had been waiting for dropped anchor at Placentia. As soon as he was ashore Serigny handed his brother a set of orders from France. They were not what Iberville had expected, but on the other hand, they did not come as a total surprise. He was to leave the remaining operations in Brouillan's hands and set sail for Hudson Bay as soon as possible to capture Fort Nelson and secure the area for France.[1]

The destination was a familiar place to both Iberville and his brother. After demonstrating his abilities during the taking of the English forts on James Bay, Iberville was left in charge of these posts when Troyes's detachment returned to Quebec on August 19, 1686. The twenty-five-year-old commander did not experience any difficulties with the English at Fort Nelson, which was helpful, as failing food supplies proved enough of an adversary for his forty-man detachment. The next summer Iberville returned to France to solicit aid from the *Compagnie du Nord*, not only in the way of men and supplies but also in terms of providing trade merchandise that would help lure the local tribes away from Fort Nelson. To his credit

Iberville was successful in both areas. He was also able to secure the twenty-eight-gun frigate *Soleil d'Afrique*, in which he returned to James Bay during the spring of 1688, just in time to capture the English supply ship *Churchill*, which had spent the winter trapped in the ice at Charlton Island.[2]

A few months later three English vessels entered Hudson Bay. Looking to seize an opportunity and reverse their losses a pair of vessels anchored at the mouth of the Albany River, effectively blockading the *Soleil d'Afrique*. The English demanded the fort's surrender and Iberville promptly refused. A brief exchange of arms took place before the situation devolved into a stalemate. Within a few weeks all three vessels were locked in the ice. The winter treated the intruders poorly and Iberville refused to allow the English a pass to hunt game. The English outnumbered his garrison five-to-one and he was not going to do anything to help them. When the English, who had encamped on a small island in the river, did attempt to venture out Iberville organized ambuscades that sent them scurrying back to their encampment. It did not take long after that. Disease and exposure had killed a third of the ships' crews before they surrendered under terms that Iberville would send them back to England in one of their vessels when the ice broke.[3]

In early June Iberville's brother St. Helene arrived with orders for Iberville to return to Quebec. On September 12, the *Soleil d'Afrique*, with the larger of the English prizes in tow, set out for the colonial capital. To his surprise Iberville fell in with an English ship near the Hudson Straits. The enemy vessel was too powerful to attack so he raised an English flag and managed to convince the English captain that he was a friend. The trio of vessels navigated the straits together and then went their separate ways.

Iberville arrived at Quebec on October 28, 1689. His return coincided with Frontenac's plans to attack the New York and New England frontier. He soon joined the expedition led by his brother St. Helene, which destroyed the town of Schenectady in February 1690. By summer, however, Iberville was anxious to return to Hudson Bay. In July, he set sail from Quebec with three small vessels: the *St. Anne*, the *St. Francis*, and a tender. His force amounted to some eighty men and thirty guns. It was nowhere near what he would have liked, but the northern sailing season dictated his departure, leaving him with little choice other than to abandon the project.[4]

By August Iberville was approaching Fort Nelson. His fears had come to fruition. The English were on their guard, but more importantly a thirty-six-gun enemy frigate forced the French commander to flee toward Fort St. Anne. Along the way he planned to attack the English position at New Severn, but with little in the way of defenses the commander of this post had it put to the torch and marched the garrison to Fort Nelson.

A French map published in 1703 of Hudson Bay, James Bay, and the Hudson Straits showing the principal posts on Hudson and James Bays during King William's War. (*Library of Congress*)

Matters would not improve for Iberville for several years. He returned to Quebec the following year and accepted command of another expedition against Fort Nelson, but it fell through, as did planned campaigns in 1692 and 1693. In 1694 Iberville would have more success. In mid-August he left Quebec with three hundred men in the frigates *Poli* and *Salamander*. It was by far the most powerful French expedition yet to be launched against the English Hudson Bay stronghold. After a harrowing passage through the gale and iceberg-strewn Hudson Straits, Iberville's force dropped anchor before Fort Nelson on September 24.

Fort Nelson appeared impressive. The fort sat on a peninsula formed by the conjunction of the Nelson and Hayes Rivers. Located on a high spot along the north bank of the Hayes River the four-bastioned wooden structure was surrounded by a *cheval-de-frise* and supported by a battery of six guns, which were positioned in a redoubt on the river side of the fort. When combined with the other outworks and the guns within the stronghold, there were over eighty cannon available with which to repel an attacker, making Fort Nelson, on paper at least, one of the more heavily defended posts in colonial North America. The problem was that the garrison of fifty-three men were not soldiers. They were traders, merchants, and trappers and all ill prepared to handle any kind of an assault.

The French moved upriver past the fort and skirmished with the garrison for a few days while siege batteries were being raised. On October 13 the cannon were in place and ready to fire. Iberville summoned the fort's commander to surrender, and to his delight, the garrison hauled down the English flag. Captured along with the fort was a remarkable haul of artillery, trade stores, and a warehouse full of furs, all of which was now claimed by the victors. It was too late in the season to depart, so the entire force along with their fifty-three English prisoners remained at Fort Nelson for the winter. When the ice cleared in early summer Iberville placed his warships in the river and waited to pounce upon the yearly English supply fleet. By September he had seen nothing and, with the window of opportunity to leave closing, he assigned a garrison to the fort under Lt. La Forest and departed for Quebec.[5]

Fort Nelson, or Fort Bourbon as it was now called, would not remain in French hands very long. In late August 1696, an English squadron of five vessels cleared the Hudson Straits and steered for Fort Bourbon. Captain William Allen, in command of the forty-gun *Bonaventure* along with the frigates *Seaford* and *Dering* and two smaller vessels, had been given express orders to take Fort Bourbon and reestablish the Hudson Bay Company's presence in the area. Lt. La Forest, who Iberville had left along with a garrison of sixty-seven men, did his best to resist. He ambushed the initial English landing, forcing the attackers back into their boats, but this only bought a short amount of time. Allen maneuvered the fleet closer to the fort and began a bombardment. The English commander had brought a bomb ketch as part of his force, and after twenty-two mortar rounds exploded within the fort La Forest became convinced that it was senseless to resist. When Allen halted the firing to demand the fort's surrender, La Forest agreed under the conditions that he and his men march out under honors of war and be transported, along with two pieces of artillery and the furs they had accumulated, to Placentia on an English vessel. The terms were agreed to and the French flag lowered. To La Forest's dismay, instead of being returned to Placentia, he soon found himself in England answering charges about how he and Iberville had treated the English prisoners from the capture of Fort Nelson in 1694.[6]

Now, as Iberville read over the orders his brother Serigny had presented him, it seemed clear that he was not finished with Hudson Bay. Once again the king had ordered him to the frozen waters of the north to seize Fort Nelson. At least this time he had a sizable force at his disposal. His flagship would be the fifty-gun *Pelican*, while his brother Serigny would command the forty-gun *Palmier*. The frigate *Profond* was stripped down to twenty-six guns so it could take on more supplies, and the smaller *Wesp* along with the supply ship *Esquimeau*, carrying another two-dozen guns between them, rounded out the squadron. Together the five vessels carried close to 500 men and could bring 140 cannon to bear, making it more than twice as strong as the force Iberville had used to capture Fort Nelson a few years before.

After over a month of refitting and preparation at Placentia, Iberville's squadron put out to sea on July 8. By late July the force arrived at the entrance to the Hudson Straits. Here they faced their first enemy—ice. Shifting frozen mountains and their fractured remnants littered the passage. Coupled with the currents it made for treacherous going, often forcing the crews to grapple with the ice to keep it away from their ships. Amidst such circumstances disaster could strike quickly, as the crew of the *Esquimeau* discovered when two shifting bergs crushed their vessel in a horrifying cacophony of cracking wood and splintering ice. The twelve-man crew clung to their frozen attackers before being rescued, but their ship and a good portion of the expedition's supplies had gone to the bottom.

A few days later on July 24, a gale blew through the straits, scattering Iberville's fleet and covering everything in several inches of ice. Iberville, ahead in the *Pelican*, cleared the straits and waited for the rest of the fleet. After a few days, however, the French commander became convinced that the fleet must have passed him and he set sail for Fort Nelson. In fact Iberville's fleet was far behind him and on August 25 they encountered a second enemy—the English.[7]

To secure Fort Nelson the Admiralty had assigned Captain John Fletcher of the frigate *Hampshire* to escort three Hudson Bay Company ships to the Hayes River. Led by Fletcher's fifty-two-gun warship, the *Dering*, the *Royal Hudson's Bay* and the fireship *Owner's Love* arrived at the entrance to the Hudson Straits a few days behind Iberville's fleet. As with the French the common enemy claimed another victim when the *Owner's Love* was crushed in the ice flows and lost with all hands.[8]

On August 25, the remaining elements of the English fleet awoke to find the *Profond* not far away to the south. The French frigate had become separated from the rest of the fleet and stumbled upon Fletcher's convoy. In a running battle that lasted throughout the day the four vessels fired upon one another when the ice flows permitted.

The outnumbered *Profond* was hit a number of times and badly damaged but managed to fend off the enemy until the sight of the *Wesp* and *Palmier* convinced the English to move on with their mission.

The *Pelican* had dropped anchor near Fort Nelson on September 4. Even though his fleet had yet to arrive, Iberville wasted no time in launching into operations and sent twenty-five men ashore to scout the approaches to the fort and to select a site to land the artillery. At six the next morning a shout came from the lookout on the *Pelican*. Three ships, about ten miles away, were approaching. The French commander shouted at the gun crews to fire the prearranged signals. A pattern of cannon shots rang out. Iberville and his crew listened for an answer and when none came he ordered his crew to clear for action. With the men left ashore and the sick on board Iberville was down close to one hundred men, but it did not dissuade his decision. To the hoarse shouts of the ship's officers the sails on the *Pelican* dropped and caught the wind. Without hesitation the French commander turned the warship in a wide arc and steered directly at the oncoming English.

Iberville soon saw the three vessels before him: a Royal Navy frigate about the *Pelican*'s size and two smaller converted merchant ships, each carrying about thirty guns. This placed the French commander at a distinct disadvantage, but he suspected that the armed merchantmen would not put up much of a fight, and with the wind in his favor he set his sights on the *Hampshire*.[9]

Iberville swung past the *Hampshire* firing his port batteries against the frigate that quickly replied, sending plumes of water up about the warship and a burst of wooden splinters and flying debris when the rounds found their mark. The French commander then wheeled his ship to port and unleashed his starboard guns on the trailing *Royal Hudson's Bay*. Soon it became a circling game of passing exchanges and rolling clouds of blue-white smoke. For several hours the four vessels weaved their way before the wind and fired away at each other until Iberville focused on the *Hampshire* and brought his ship alongside Fletcher's. Yardarm to yardarm the two frigates exchanged broadsides. The move to close on the English warship had worked in the sense that the *Dering* and *Royal Hudson's Bay* had checked their fire for fear of striking their countrymen. The odds were even now.

Legend has it that over the din of guns and shouting men Fletcher called upon Iberville to surrender, and when the fiery Frenchman refused Fletcher raised a glass of wine to toast him. Whether the case or not, the short-range duel between the two warships was not destined to last long. Iberville had only fired a few broadsides when one caused the *Hampshire* to lurch and knife into the frigid waters of the bay. "I fired my broadside and sank her immediately," Iberville reported, "the vessel not passing onward three lengths." Another French witness recalled that "we ran alongside of her [the *Hampshire*], yard-arm to yard-arm. As we were so close to each other, I ordered a volley of musketry to be fired at her forecastle, where there were many sailors who called out for us to leap aboard. They immediately returned our volley with a discharge of grape which cut nearly all our rigging in pieces and wounded many of our men. As they ran along by our ship, we fired our batteries which were so well aimed that they proved most effective, for we were no sooner separated from one another than the Hampshire immediately foundered under sail." Although Iberville's guns may have been well aimed it was a shoal and not his cannon that tore the bottom out of the vessel and sent it to the bottom with its entire crew.[10]

With the sudden shift in fortunes the *Pelican* steered for the *Royal Hudson's Bay*, but the latter ship had seen enough and immediately lowered its flag. Iberville wrestled with his damaged rigging and set out in pursuit of the fleeing *Dering*, but taking on water and his rigging badly in need of repairs he returned and put twenty-five men aboard his newly acquired prize. The two vessels then dropped anchor southwest of Fort Nelson. On the night of September 7 the common enemy, the north wind, accomplished what the French and English had struggled to do the day before. A gale out of the north drove both the *Pelican* and the *Royal Hudson Bay* onto the rocks, sinking both of them in shallow water and drowning twenty-three of their crew in the process.

The loss was offset by the arrival of the French fleet the next day. The sight of the wrecked vessels did not dishearten the arriving forces and proved nothing more than a background to their work. The mortars onboard the *Profond* were brought ashore and the next few days were spent building firing platforms about two hundred yards from Fort Nelson. On September 12, these batteries opened fire and began a methodic bombardment of the fort. As Iberville suspected it did not take long for the fort's commander, Henry Bailey, to beat a parley out on the drums. Both sides realized it was senseless to resist, and Bailey surrendered the fort and its fifty-two-man garrison the next day.[11]

For Iberville it was an improbable victory while at the same time a testimony to his leadership and daring. He received the thanks of the court, and although the profit involved was diminished by the loss of several vessels, his name became associated with bold ventures and synonymous with success against the odds. For the English the loss of Fort Nelson was unfortunate and ill timed. Ill timed because by occupying a post on Hudson Bay the French had another bargaining piece at the peace negotiations and a position to better back their claims to the region. For the Hudson Bay Company there was one small silver lining. The advanced season had prevented Iberville from attacking Fort Albany (Fort St. Anne), which had been retaken by the English several years earlier.

With Fort Nelson once again Fort Bourbon, Iberville departed for La Rochelle with the *Profond* and *Wesp* on September 24, 1697. As he cleared the straits and plied the rough northern waters he no doubt wondered if he would be back the next year to accomplish the same task. He left his brother Serigny and fifty others behind to garrison the fort and see to the *Palmier*, whose rudder had been so damaged in the September 7 gale that the ship was not fit to go to sea. After a long and sickly voyage Iberville arrived at the French seaport on November 23. Once ashore he found an answer to his earlier question. The war was over.[12]

CHAPTER TWENTY-FOUR

The Treaty of Ryswick

THE FALL OF 1696 and the early months of 1697 brought forth a series of plans calling for both the English and French navies to take on a more active role in the waters of North America. The English were first, spurred on by reports from banished settlers of Newfoundland as they arrived in Bristol, Dartmouth, and other ports along the English coast. There was shock and then outrage and then the realization that the economies of whole villages in England had been devastated. This economic blow quickly reached the owners of the companies that chartered fishing rights to the Grand Banks, and soon their anger was added to the chorus. All of this reached the Board of Trade, who packaged it in the appropriate form, and passed it on to the king. The Board's recommendation was that six frigates be assigned not only to convoy the fishing and salt fleets but to cruise the waters about the island, and as "the French have already so fortified themselves in the Island, and seem so intent on the improvement of their interests there that the planters cannot suffice to protect our part," it seemed necessary to send out an engineer from England to build new fortifications and several companies of troops to man these defenses.

A few weeks later news concerning the scale of the French attacks in Newfoundland arrived, spurring a more urgent petition to the king.

> They [the French] are now masters of the Island, depriving us of the trade, and must continue so unless a sufficient land and sea force be sent out. We recommend therefore that four more ships of war

> and land-forces be added to those already desired for the end of February, to visit the coast of Newfoundland lately possessed by the English, secure them during the preparations for the fishery, and if possible attack and capture Placentia. For these purposes we think that a regiment of not fewer than 700 soldiers would suffice, of which, at the close of the season, two companies should be left at St. John['s], and one each at Ferryland and Fermouse, to secure them from attack during the winter. For this purpose the regiment should be provided with tents, ammunition and provisions, not only for the summer but for the winter. Further instructions in accordance herewith should be given to the commanders of the sea and land-forces; and some of the ships if possible should be employed in cruising upon the Bank of Newfoundland and on the coast, to disturb the French fishery. Lastly, the whole enterprise should be carried on with the greatest despatch and at the times mentioned, lest the French by earlier preparations prevent us.[1]

The message came to the king through other channels as well. Many of his prominent merchants and noblemen, who not only politically supported him but helped to finance his war, had been struck in the pocketbook by Iberville's campaign. Something would have to be done to rectify the situation, and given the circumstances, there was really only one response. In late January, William ordered the Admiralty to assign escorts to the fishing and salt fleets as well as launch an expedition to retake Newfoundland, including the French-held post at Placentia.

Coordination of the logistics between the Admiralty, War Office, Board of Trade, master of the ordnance, and the king's secretary of state took some time and was not without the normal level of confusion. Although available, the warships needed to escort the fishing convoys to Newfoundland lacked provisions and needed to fill out their crews. In mid-March the delays began to worry the fishing fleets. The season for departing was already late, and when they arrived they faced building new docks, warehouses, and living quarters before they went to sea. As difficult as this might be, what would be worse would be a French fleet arriving before them. It might prove costly to dislodge them, if not impossible, meaning the entire fishing season would be lost.

It would not be until April 6 that a fleet of warships was assembled at Portsmouth. They consisted of two ships of the line, the *Monck* and the *Lion*, two fifty-gun warships, and six frigates. Two bomb ships, which would be required for the attack on Placentia, and a fireship rounded out the squadron, which was placed under the command of Commodore John Norris. Dispersed among the thirteen craft were 760 soldiers and their artillery under the command of Colonel John Gibson. Gibson and his men would not only be involved in taking Placentia but would also help rebuild the colony's defenses and garrison them throughout the winter.[2]

By late April, Norris's warships and most of the fishing fleets had departed for Newfoundland, and under heavy escort the supply convoy departed not long after. On June 7, 1697, the commodore's squadron arrived before St. John's. There were no French troops or ships to be found, and the town had been razed. Everything that could be torn down was torn down and what could burn was now ashes. Scout ships dispatched down the coast and into Conception and Trinity Bays told similar stories, and survivors from Iberville's onslaught soon appeared at St. John's with their accounts. As the reports filtered in Colonel Gibson was struck by the ferocity of the attacks. "There is not a living soul left, yea not at Ferryland," he informed the Board of Trade, "which was always looked upon (as I am told) as the best harbour and the pleasantest place in the whole Island." It soon became even more depressing as the news from the other settlements painted a similar picture.[3]

The English fleet occupied its main Newfoundland outpost with little effort, and with the arrival of the supply convoy on June 27, it was now time to rebuild. "We began to fortify the harbour's mouth by a battery on each side, and by erecting a fort on a hill on the north side," Gibson wrote of his regiment's activities. There was good reason to proceed with haste. A French prize taken by one of Norris's ships informed the commodore that French admiral Nesmond was in the area with a large squadron under orders to secure the Newfoundland coast.

On July 22, Norris's squadron had just returned from a nine-day cruise with a prize that was part of a convoy bound for Quebec when five enemy ships were reported to the southwest of St. John's. The squadron appeared off of the harbor the next day, but heavy fog obscured any operations. The enemy fleet had barely moved off when it was discovered from one of the French prisoners that the warships were not part of Nesmond's forces but elements of a fleet arriving from the West Indies. Reports of more vessels arrived and with fear that the two French fleets were to unite before St. John's a debate broke out as to whether the English fleet should sail out to meet them. Gibson was against the idea of dividing the English land and sea forces, and after a long argument with Norris, the final consensus was for the fleet to stay in the harbor.[4]

The successful campaign of 1696 had also created a need and an opportunity for the French navy to play a prominent role in North America. First, it was necessary for a French squadron to be dispatched to Newfoundland, not only for the safety of Placentia but to prevent the English from reestablishing their outposts on the Avalon Peninsula. Second, the time was right to employ this fleet not only in securing Newfoundland but in attacking Boston. The idea of attacking the New England capital was not new and had been discussed as early as the opening year of the war, but the necessity of a French fleet at Placentia, and the weakened state of the New England colonies after the previous year's campaign, had presented New France with one of the few credible threats that it would ever pose to the city.

The king approved of the expedition and placed the Marquis de Nesmond in command. Nesmond had proven himself a capable naval commander in several major engagements during the war. He also had a flair for capturing enemy prizes, two of which, loaded merchant ships from India, earned him and the king a sizable payday. The Marquis was given ten warships, a galley, and a pair of fireships and ordered to sail as soon as possible for Placentia. If he found the English there he was to attack them, whether they had secured the town or not. If the enemy fleet was not to be found at this location he was to sail to St. John's in search of it, and once he found it he was to engage and destroy it. To assist the marquis in this critical task a fleet under the Baron de Pointis would be diverted from the West Indies.

Should Nesmond defeat the English in Newfoundland, he was to set sail immediately for Pentagoet (Castin), where he would rendezvous with 1,500 men sent from Quebec by Frontenac and all the Wabanaki warriors that could be raised by Castin, Father Thury, and Villebon. From here most of the nine hundred Canadians and colonial marines would be put aboard the warships while their native allies took to their canoes and paddled down the coast. The troops would land on either side of Boston harbor while the warships bombarded the town. If Nesmond was successful in destroying Boston, and time permitted, he was then to proceed down the coast and likewise put New York City to the torch.

Even with Pointis's vessels and the resources of Placentia at his disposal, Nesmond's force was further augmented by several more warships in a clear indication of the importance of his mission. With a force of almost twice that which Commodore Norris commanded at St. John's, Nesmond departed Brest in mid-April. As speed was necessary to relieve Placentia, the fleet sailed in two detachments. Nesmond and the bulk of the warships departed first, followed by a supply convoy escorted by several warships under Admiral Magnon.[5]

The marquis dropped anchor at Placentia on July 24, and his supply convoy arrived not long after. With the outpost secured and no sign of an English threat in the vicinity, Nesmond pursued his orders and set sail for St. John's. On August 29, his fleet of sixteen vessels, some of which had scouted Conception and Trinity Bay, rendezvoused in sight of St. John's. Reports had already reached the French admiral that an English relief fleet lay in the harbor and that troops from England were busy refortifying the location. Scouts had confirmed a pair of gun positions on both sides of the harbor's entrance, and two vessels that approached closer noted not only cables strung across the channel but that the English warships within the anchorage were arranged so as to contest an attacker attempting to enter.[6]

Although the English were convinced that two French fleets had converged before them, in fact, Pointis was still busy besieging Santo Domingo in the Caribbean. Even without Pointis Nesmond held a decided advantage over his English counterpart, at least in an open engagement, but it was clear from what he saw that there would be no sea fight. The English would stand on their defenses, which they were well aware would exact a high price should the French attack from the sea. "I think that if they had attacked the harbour they would have met with a very hot reception; indeed, I looked upon it as impracticable, with the land and sea-forces thus joined," Colonel Gibson later wrote of the situation. A French council of war essentially agreed, and any thought of attacking St. John's was unanimously rejected.[7]

With the season too far advanced to carry through with an attack on Boston and with little else to be accomplished Nesmond ordered the squadron to set sail for France. There would be no naval battle to contest Newfoundland, nor any attack on the Eastern Seaboard, which might well have collapsed New England and New York resistance. Nesmond failed to accomplish any of his goals, in part because his orders and goals were unrealistic from the onset. Norris did little better. He reestablished St. John's but failed to threaten Placentia even though he arrived in Newfoundland five weeks before Nesmond. Nor did he sail out to challenge Nesmond when he had the opportunity. Instead, both Nesmond and Norris, the latter of whom was harshly criticized for his inactivity and handling of the fleet, returned home to the news that the war was over.[8]

In New York, Governor Fletcher had a much simpler time than in the past seeing to the defenses of the frontier. Orders had arrived directly from the king assigning each colony its quota of troops to be placed at his disposal. There were to be no excuses and no exceptions to this rule, with Connecticut being specifically pointed out given its past reluctance to abide by earlier directives. The manpower was useful, but after the scare from Nesmond's fleet there were no serious threats posed against New York. Skirmishing and small war parties still occurred, but most of the fighting had shifted west toward the Iroquois homelands as the French and their allies slowly ground the Five Nations down.

For New England the spring of 1697 began with a powerful Abenaki raid on Haverhill, Massachusetts. A frontier town of some thirty homes along the Merrimack River, Haverhill was completely unprepared for what was to befall them. On the bleak windswept morning of March 15, Thomas Dunston was up early to look over his fields in anticipation of spring planting. A simple morning ride suddenly took a horrifying turn as he eyed several dozen Abenaki warriors moving toward the town. Random shots flew in his direction as he whirled his horse and rode at breakneck speed to warn his sick wife and eight children.

When he arrived he hurriedly sent his children, ranging from two to seventeen years old, running toward the three blockhouses in the center of the village. Dunston turned next to his wife, but it was already too late, as the Abenaki were knocking down the door to the house. Faced with an agonizing decision Dunston rode off to catch up with his children, who were running for their lives. By occasionally turning on their pursuers and leveling his musket toward them he would bring the pursuit to a momentary halt. Dunston would then ride on and execute the same maneuver, in each instance buying a few precious moments for his fleeing offspring. After a few minutes of this game, and seeing the children about to enter one of the blockhouses, the Abenaki gave up and turned their attention toward easier targets.[9]

When the attack was over twenty-seven of Haverhill's citizens lay dead and another thirteen were led away as captives. Among those taken captive were Thomas Dunston's wife, Hannah, her infant son, and her nurse, Mrs. Neff. Their captives pushed the prisoners forward through the snow-patched forest, and when one was displeased by a cry from Hannah's infant, he tore it from the nurse's arms and dashed it against a tree. A few of the older prisoners who could not keep up were dispatched with a quick blow by a tomahawk as the war party slowly distanced itself from any pursuit. Within a few days the party had traveled nearly sixty miles to the confluence of the Merrimac and Contoocook Rivers where they pitched camp on a small island formed by the two waterways.

The captives were informed that the party would stay here until they were ready to depart for Canada. Talk of what was in store for them and opportunity spurred Hannah into action. For now the party was on the Merrimac River, and from here all Hannah and her nurse needed to do was follow the river home, but once they departed for Canada, even if the women could possibly escape, they would be hopelessly lost and inevitably doomed. They had to act now if there was to be any chance. Fortunately, the two women did not pose much of a threat to the war party and as such were not closely guarded. Hannah, Mrs. Neff, and an English boy named Samuel Leonardson, who had been held captive for a year and a half and had gained the trust of the Abenaki, agreed upon a plan that called for dispatching their captors while they slept. There could be no pursuit if the three were to gain their freedom. The appointed time arrived in the wee hours of the morning. The three figures selected their targets one by one and killed all of their captors except a small boy and a woman who ran off badly wounded. With the grisly task done, the three gathered together supplies, destroyed all the canoes but one, and set off for freedom down the Merrimac River.[10]

Haverhill was to be but the start of a long year for New England. As in the previous years Massachusetts had organized a detachment of several hundred men under Major March to patrol the frontier and intercept enemy war parties, but it was an impossible task. Small groups of Abenaki soon struck at Exeter, and finding their old nemesis Major John Frost returning home one day, they ambushed his wagon, killing the major and his companions. Small bands of raiders struck Saco, York, and several other towns along the New Hampshire and Maine frontier. On September 9, March's diligence finally paid off, as he was able to ambush a war party as they grounded their canoes along the bank of the Damariscotta River. A sudden volley followed by a charge from the soldiers posted in the tree line routed the war party and left two dozen of their number dead along the shoreline. Two days later the last major effort on the part of the Wabanaki fell upon Lancaster, Massachusetts, where twenty-one of the inhabitants were slain and six carried away after a surprise morning attack on the town.[11]

It had indeed been a difficult year on the New England frontier. Almost a dozen raids had killed, wounded, or captured over one hundred colonists and, with the exception of March's actions at Damariscotta, the enemy had suffered little in the way of losses. When coupled with the panic set off by rumors of Nesmond's fleet and its plans to burn Boston, it had been an unsettling time for New England. Fortunately on December 10 good news arrived. A peace treaty had been signed at Ryswick. The war was over.

News of the Treaty of Ryswick reached New York and the rest of the Eastern Seaboard not long after and was met with similar celebration wherever it came. Drums were played, church bells rung, and cannon fired, echoed by calls of "God save the king!" The colonial militias were released and any costs associated with defenses quickly slashed. Connecticut, which had drawn specific comment from the king in regard to her quota obligations, had no sooner heard news of the treaty then were writing the English court that, "The happy return of peace has rendered the quota needless, but we shall not neglect, in times of peace, to take such care of our forces as the King has directed."[12]

In fact the war was only over between the French and the English, and while "the people have very sensibly tasted the direful effects of war and are glad to be freed from the heavy taxes, laid upon them," Governor Stoughton noted, "they will enjoy great ease if the barbarous Indian rebels can be reduced to obedience." This last issue proved more difficult than first hoped. Small numbers of Abenaki returned to the warpath in the spring of 1698, striking at Andover, Haverhill, Spruce Creek, and York. By midsummer a temporary truce was agreed upon, and that fall the two sides formally met at Penobscot. Given that both sides were worn down by the conflict and sincerely wanted peace, the conference went well. A prisoner exchange was worked out, and it was agreed to meet again at Casco in January 1699, where a more permanent peace treaty was signed, bringing an end to the Wabanaki War.[13]

The Anglo-Wabanaki conflict had cost hundreds of lives on both sides, with dozens of villages destroyed and countless lives ruined. In one sense the Wabanaki had accomplished their goal in keeping the English encroachments on their land in check. They had required French help to see this through, but the French had proven worthy allies in their cause. Unfortunately, for all their success, the simple truth was that the English were far more numerous than the Wabanaki and were slowly grinding the confederacy down with or without the help of the French. With peace between France and England now at hand it seemed likely that French support would wane as well, perhaps leaving the Wabanaki in a worse position if they continued the conflict. To most in the confederacy peace was the logical course to be pursued.

For New England, the Wabanaki War was a disaster. Militarily the colonies of Massachusetts, Connecticut, Rhode Island, and New Hampshire could not defeat a severely outnumbered force at their doorstep. In fact, for a good part of the conflict New England was on the defensive, and what campaigns that were launched against the Wabanaki or their French allies seldom arrived upon the desired results. The Wabanaki had launched at least fifty-nine raids on the Maine, New Hampshire, and Massachusetts frontiers from June 28, 1689, to the summer of 1698, and even this number likely does not account for many of the smaller incursions. The result was over seven hundred New Englanders killed, wounded, or captured and the destruction of hundreds of homesteads. Commerce suffered, agriculture suffered, and the cost of garrisons and troops for the frontier further deepened a recession that raged through the colonies. Fear of death lurking in every shadow or behind every tree gripped the communities of New England and no doubt played a prominent role in the witch hunt epidemic that haunted the bay colony for a good portion of the conflict. "For the present then the Indians have done murdering," Reverend Cotton Mather wrote of the subject. "They'll do so no more until next time." The long tragedy was over.[14]

As it turned out, peace was foremost on the minds of all the belligerents. In May 1698, Johannes Schuyler and a delegation from Albany arrived at Quebec with copies of a peace treaty signed at Ryswick. The war was over. The kings of France and England had agreed to set up a commission to settle any boundary disputes in North America, but until then, the Albany delegation had brought with them twenty French captives with the purpose of beginning the prisoner exchange as provided for under the terms of the treaty.

Although Frontenac had yet to receive official word of the treaty, rumors of such had reached him, and he agreed to release all English prisoners. As it turned out, for various reasons most did not wish to return. As for the English prisoners in the hands of his native allies, Schuyler was surprised to learn that the count was having difficulty in obtaining the release of these captives. The governor dismissed the issue as reluctance on the part of his allies to release their captives while the English still held several of their warriors. He was even more dismayed when he learned that an Abenaki war party had just raided the New England frontier, but again the governor dismissed the issue, saying that he had issued orders to the contrary and that the entire matter was the result of miscommunications.[15]

Schuyler also presented Frontenac with a letter from the new governor of New York, the Earl of Bellomont. Couched as an official greeting announcing the Treaty of Ryswick, the letter informed Frontenac that in addition to the prisoners traveling with Schuyler he had directed the Iroquois to release all of their captives, and in return he expected that Frontenac would order his native allies to do the same. Although a reasonable request on the surface, it created a serious problem for the count, for it raised one of the questions that still remained unresolved, that being the status of the Iroquois under the newly signed treaty. By agreeing to Bellomont's demand, the count would validate his enemy's claim that the Iroquois were English citizens. The consequences of this arrangement could easily spiral out of control, leading to the forfeiture of vast tracts of the western frontier and making any lasting peace treaty with the Iroquois contingent upon English interests. There was also another important matter to consider along these lines. At the moment, the Iroquois prevented the tribes of Canada from trading directly with the better-supplied merchants at Albany. Should the English, however, assert their claim over the Iroquois and somehow convince the Five Nations to allow these tribes to pass unmolested to this post, the entire fur trade, and hence the economic core of New France, would be compromised. Such a situation would be nothing short of a disaster. Within a short period of time, New France's western allies would become economically dependent on this trade and, not long after, politically attached to the English cause. With the west lost, the colony would either be forced to accept a contracted position along the banks of the St. Lawrence or fight a war they could not possibly win to recover this trade.[16]

It was not a path Frontenac was interested in taking, and although Schuyler pressed him on the matter, the governor refused to release his Iroquois captives. A few days later he clarified his position in a letter to Bellomont. The English and Dutch he had in his hands would be immediately turned over, but as for the Iroquois, they had already approached him with peace envoys, therefore "it would be needless for you to give yourself the trouble to interfere in the matter, inasmuch as these are children disobedient to their father, who have uninterruptedly been subject to the king's dominion, even before the English took New-York from the Dutch."[17]

The matter would further heighten tensions between the French and English colonies when Frontenac, taking advantage of the failure of the treaty to mention the Iroquois as English subjects, continued to unleash his native allies on the confederacy and even threatened direct French intervention. The count knew there was little Bellomont could do to oppose him given the orders arriving from the French and English courts to maintain the peace between the colonies. Suffering under the relentless blows of Frontenac's allies and fearful of a major French attack the Five Nations appealed to the English for help, but as Frontenac had surmised, beyond a handful of guns, a few barrels of gunpowder, and several threatening letters, little came of the effort. Isolated and on the verge of being overrun, the Five Nations had no choice but to ignore the pleas of their English allies and dispatch emissaries to Montreal to negotiate a peace treaty.[18]

Conclusion

King William's War and the Future of North America

In all there would be four conflicts between the French and the English to determine the destiny of North America: King William's War, Queen Anne's War, King George's War, and the French and Indian War, which concluded with the English conquest of Canada. Of these, King William's War was not only the first but the only conflict that can be said to have been won by the French.

The margin of French victory may not have been large, but given the realistic aims and possible outcomes, it was significant. First, New France had survived. Upon considering the strength of her adversaries, the American colonies, the Iroquois, and the occasional foray on the part of Old England, it was a remarkable feat. Second, the Iroquois had been detached from the English cause and a few years after the war would be forced to sign a separate peace treaty with the French and their allies. With Iroquois neutrality in place, the confederacy was no longer a major military threat but still acted as a barrier against the French tribes who might wish to trade at Albany. This was no simple feat, but through the sometimes rocky efforts of Frontenac and Callières, New France had accomplished this strategic aim. Third, the French made territorial gains in Hudson Bay and by treaty had Port Royal restored to them. Fourth, the Wabanaki Confederacy, although it wavered on occasion, had held and stifled English expansion into Acadia. Lastly, and most importantly, with the Five Nations removed the West now fell under French influence and claim.

The first question to be asked is how this was possible when one considers that the relative populations of the English and French colonies were on the order of twenty to one in favor of the English. In fact, New England alone could muster thirteen thousand men to that of three thousand for all of New France. To make matters even more questionable, New France was not self-sufficient and depended on the seasonal fleets from France for its survival. This was not true of the English colonies. Lastly, although French naval power at the time was on par with the combined Dutch and English fleets, it was predominantly occupied with the West Indies and European theaters. This left local control of North American waters to the English navy and, more importantly, to the numerically superior colonial naval forces. Under such circumstances how could the French colony have won the war?[1]

There were a number of factors that contributed to French success but none more than the fractured colonial political system and the failure on the part of England to correct this flaw. The immediate cause of much of the failure of the English settlements to fully cooperate can be traced to the Glorious Revolution and the political chaos that ensued with the provisional colonial governments. The combined militias of the English colonies during the conflict were close to twenty-five thousand men, and the vessels plying the merchant trade in the ports of New England alone dwarfed the maritime resources of New France, but disunity and the lack of a commander in chief for the colonies for part of the conflict undermined any advantage this strength might have brought. Even when Governor Fletcher of New York was appointed commander in chief of the English colonial forces, any benefits derived from this move were short circuited by a lack of intercolonial cooperation and the policy of placing local concerns over that of strategic concerns.

Another important element in the English defeat was the role of the English navy. It should be understood that the English navy of this day was not the Britannia that would rule the Spanish Main. It would still be some fifty years before one could say such things. As such, support from the Royal Navy was limited to patrols and escort duties, and because of this throughout the conflict there was genuine fear of a concerted French expedition against one of the major colonial seaports. Even when the Royal Navy appeared in force under Admiral Wheler, poor communications and a lack of coordination between England and New England resulted in a wasted opportunity. The lack of a major English naval presence in North America also meant that the more powerful French navy could consistently deliver supplies to New France and, as Iberville aptly demonstrated, assert local superiority with daring cruiser operations.

Lastly, a lack of will on the part of the English contributed to their failures. To be fair this spirit was not present at the opening of the conflict after Frontenac's raids on the New York and New England frontiers. The English response to these attacks, that being an attack on Quebec, was indeed the correct response, even if poorly executed. While the *ad hoc* effort failed, setting off an economic and psychological backlash, the failure was easily attributed to a lack of military supplies from England that delayed the expedition from the onset, poor logistics, poor intelligence in terms of navigating the St. Lawrence, and the limited military experience within the colonial ranks. Lack of effort on the part of the Yankees, however, was not to be counted among the causes of the defeat, and it can easily be said that under better circumstances these troops would have captured Quebec. Even as it was, if Phips had arrived a week earlier the French capital would have fallen and likely New France with it.

While the failed expedition shattered English will, Phips was correct in his assessment that, with support from the Royal Navy, colonial forces could seize the French capital the next year and end the war. The plan, however, received a cool reception, and although it was attempted a few years later with Admiral Wheler's squadron, even here we see a lack of spirit at work. With a little effort, at least five hundred to one thousand men could have been raised to assist the admiral, but there was little taste for the sudden venture in New England. Nor did Wheler himself show an abundance of enthusiasm for the expedition. While he possessed a fleet powerful enough to wreak havoc along both banks of the St. Lawrence and launch a sustained bombardment of the French capital, he quickly accepted Phips's advice and sailed away, having accomplished nothing for his efforts.

For the English the counter to French policies was clear from the beginning. The Iroquois had pointed to it time and again: "Unite and cut the head off the serpent." Others saw it, Phips perhaps foremost among them. The response was correct, but Quebec was far too difficult of a military task for the amateur colonial army. When the Royal Navy did make a serious commitment to the taking of the French capital, miscommunications and hesitation on the part of Phips undermined the effort. Thus, although the solution to the problem was well understood, it would not be for twenty-one years before the English tried their luck again at Quebec (with disastrous results).

While division undermined the English colonies, a more unified command system directed the resources of New France. When coupled with an active and reliable French naval effort that not only ensured that aid reached the colony but conducted attacks against English commerce and fortifications, this yielded an approach that, when pitted against a fractured English response, proved vital in a French victory against what seemed like overwhelming odds.

In furtherance of the French cause there is little question that Frontenac's war of terror on the colonial frontiers coupled with a *guerre de course* naval policy yielded results. Both approaches strained the English and left them scrambling for an immediate response when there was none. To the satisfaction of the French both paths were cheap, never risked a large number of resources, and occupied far more of the enemy's resources to counter. Perhaps one of the best examples of this approach in action would be Iberville's campaign against Pemaquid in 1696 and Newfoundland shortly thereafter. French naval commitments enabled both of these successful ventures while Iberville, with a handful of men, employed Native American tactics to essentially expel the English from the Maine frontier and the Avalon Peninsula.

The French were also successful in using their *petite guerre* in coercing the English into a defensive-minded policy, which further stretched colonial resources across the frontier. This allowed the French and Indian war parties the freedom of movement—to mass, select a target, and essentially command the terms of the engagement. With the English stretched thin the French became masters of using their enemy's paralysis to seize an opportunity to switch over to the offensive in the form of a major operation, which in turn instilled more panic, leading to more resources committed to a failed defensive policy.

While successful in their actions the leadership and citizens of New France drew a wrong conclusion from the results of the conflict. The French underestimated the scope of English disunity. This in turn magnified the outnumbered colony's victories and led to a sense of overconfidence, which then manifested itself into a false belief that Canada was a match for its larger English neighbors and, more importantly, that it was capable of defending itself without any extraordinary efforts to strengthen the colony. The author of a 1701 memorandum on the threat posed by the English colonies reflected this attitude in his opening remarks regarding New England.

> That country, 'tis true, is twice more populous than New France, but its people are cowardly to an astonishing degree, absolutely undisciplined and without any experience in War; the smallest party of Indians has always got the better of them; in fine, they have no Regular troops there. This is not the case with Canada. There are 28 Infantry Companies of detachments from the Marine, there; the Canadians are brave, well disciplined and indefatigable on the

> march. Two thousand of them will always beat, on any ground, the subjects of New England.[2]

After all, had not the Five Nations been laid low? Was not the West now open to the colony and the number of French-allied tribes increased? Had not the French reestablished themselves in Hudson Bay and with their Wabanaki allies fought New England and New York to a standstill? Had not English Newfoundland been destroyed by Iberville and a handful of men, ruining the enemy's commerce by devastating their fishing industry and coastal economies?

Among the leadership of New France the feeling was even greater that the English colonists were no match. The French had adapted Native American tactics into a successful policy that leveraged their allies and their population's natural skills into an operational model that pinned down large numbers of their adversaries. This feeling of superiority on the battlefield was supplemented by a psychological element as well. The inhabitants of New France had been mentally toughened by their long conflicts with the Iroquois to endure the hardships of war. Their English adversaries on the other hand, "loving their trade better than war," would always be at a disadvantage facing such a determined foe. As it was, this false sense of security would soon haunt New France when the War of Spanish Succession arrived upon the shores of North America in 1702.[3]

While justifiably declaring themselves the victors, the defenders of Canada and the court of France also drew the wrong conclusions from two policies: the French navy's shift toward *guerre de course* and the war of terror on the English colonial frontier. Both of these approaches yielded surprising results at little cost and effort, but both would eventually doom New France. The decision to shift resources away from France's well-equipped and large navy would not only fail to influence the outcome of any of Louis's European struggles, but it would make Canada's lifeline to the mother country vulnerable and would one day call it into question. The raiding of the English frontier by Frontenac also set in motion a similar policy that would be followed until the last days of New France and, like the *guerre de course*, would yield results at little risk. One of the issues, however, is that Frontenac found an important ally in the form of English disunity that, as we have seen, played into the hands of the French. This too would prove to be a common theme that the French would exploit throughout the subsequent conflicts. Ultimately, however, such an approach was a losing effort on the part of New France. It was clear from King William's War that the best Canada could hope for in a conflict was a draw or at best a minor victory. Even at this point in time the English colonies were simply too large and too populated to think otherwise. This meant the survival of the French colony would likely rest in a negotiated settlement—an honorable treaty that restored the colony or lost parts of it back to France at the end of any conflict. The problem here was that the French underestimated the generational hatred that would come from seventy years of raiding the English frontier. One day, calls of "*Carthago delenda est*" ("Carthage must be destroyed") would ring out throughout the English colonies, and with unity imposed by Old England, the resources and manpower of these colonies along with that of the mother country would become focused on the conquest of Canada. When this was complete the decision was made that Canada was not to be returned; the French colony could not be trusted.

What is clear from King William's War is that the French and English colonies had far too many issues to expect a peaceful coexistence under any treaty. The basic contentions, claims, and ambitions on both sides would simply make this an impossible proposition. By late 1696 official requests that the crown "take into consideration the reduction of Canada, the unhappy fountain from which issue all our miseries," began arriving at the highest levels of English government while representatives of the crown in New York arrived at a similar conclusion. "We offer the following suggestions for the securing of New York and the English dominions on the main land of America," they wrote to the Board of Trade in late 1696.[4]

> The best and surest means would be the dispossessing the French of Canada and settling an English Colony there. Hereby all future expense of garrisons would cease; the whole of the fur-trade will be secured ; the Indians will be deprived of all power of doing mischief to the English, but will be wholly at their command, there being no other nation from whom they could obtain the goods which long trade with Europeans has made necessary to them ; and the inland parts of the country, which are reported to be full of minerals, could be more easily explored.[5]

To the north similar sentiments were being expressed. Governor Callières, after interrogating a number of prisoners from the siege of Quebec in 1690, learned that the English general had informed his troops "that we must subject them, or they must become our masters." "This opinion is sufficiently well founded," Callières wrote the minister of the marine, "and it will be difficult for our colony and theirs to exist except by the destruction and conquest of one or the other."[6]

Neither side would have to wait long to test their theories.

Notes

ABBREVIATIONS

DCB (*Dictionary of Canadian Biography*)
NY Col. Doc. (O'Callaghan, *Documents Relative to the Colonial History of the State of New York*)
DHSNY (O'Callaghan, *Documentary History of the State of New York*)
RAPQ (*Rapport de l'Archiviste de la Province de Quebec*)
NAC (National Archives of Canada, Ottawa)
NEHGR (*New England Historical and Genealogical Register*)
NYHSC (*New York Historical Society Collections*)
MHSC (*Massachusetts Historical Society Collections*)
JR (*Jesuit Relations and Allied Documents*)
Cal. A&WI (*Calendar American & West Indies Papers*)
RAPQ (*Rapport de L'Archiviste de la Quebec*)

CHAPTER 1: THE BEAVER WARS

1. O'Callaghan, *History of the New Netherlands, Vol. I*, 47–48, 76–78. The trading house at the fort's center measured thirty-six feet by twenty-six feet. About this was a fifty-foot square stockade covered by an eighteen-foot-wide moat. The fort's first commander was Jacob Jacobz Elkens, who remained in this post for four years. (O'Callaghan, *History of the New Netherlands, Vol. I*, 76.) The rebuilt fort was located a few miles below Castle Island at Norman's Kill.
2. Trigger, "The Mohawk-Mahican War (1624–1628)," *CHR*, Sept. 1971, 278–279; Hunt, *The Wars of the Iroquois*, 32–33.
3. The fivefold increase in the value of the Dutch fur trade can be clearly seen in the table below (Brandao, *Your Fire Shall Burn No More*, 86).

Year	Pelts Value (Guilders)	Year	Pelts Value (Guilders)
1624	4,700 27,125	1629	6,594 62,185
1625	5,758 35,825	1630	7,126 68,012

1626	8,115	45,050	1632	15,174	143,125
1627	7,890	12,730	1633	10,183	91,375
1628	7,685	61,075	1635	16,304	134,925

4. Hunt, *The Wars of the Iroquois,* 33–35.
5. "Journal of the New Netherland," *NY Col. Doc.*, I, 179–182.
6. Steele, *Warpaths,* 115; *Narratives of the New Netherlands, 160–164*; 274; *NY Col. Doc. I,* 150; *Jesuit Relations, Vol. XXII,* 35–37. For Kieft's commission, see *NY Col. Doc.*, I, 104.
7. Hunt, *The Wars of the Iroquois,* 74–75, 169–170; Steele, *Warpaths,* 115. *NY Col. Doc.*, I, 150–151, 182. One observer noted that "not only the Colonists, but also the free traders proceeding from this country, sold for furs in consequence of the great profit, fire-arms to the Mohawk for full four hundred men, with powder and lead." (Ibid., 150).
8. O'Callaghan, *History of the New Netherlands, Vol. I,* 355–356; *NY Col. Doc.* XIII, 18.
9. JR, 24, 287–288, 295.
10. JR, 27, 63–65. Lalemant blamed much of the Iroquois problem on the advantage the Iroquois possessed over the native allies of New France, "through the arquebuses that they obtain from certain Europeans," in clear reference to the Dutch. (Ibid., 71).
11. *NY Col. Doc.*, I, 311–312, 392, 495–502, XIII, 35–36; Goodwin, *The Dutch and English on the Hudson,* 67; *Narratives of the New Netherlands, 1609–1664,* 370–372, For Stuyvesant's appointment and commission, see *NY Col. Doc.*, I, 175–178. Legend has it that Stuyvesant's ghost can still be heard thumping about the aisles of St. Mark's Cathedral, now located near his final resting place (Goodwin, *The Dutch and English on the Hudson,* 67).
12. JR, 40, 49–51.

CHAPTER 2: NEW FRANCE AND NEW HOLLAND

1. JR, 40, 89. The Jesuit recorder of this event was amazed by how the Onondaga, after all the treachery that had occurred between the French and the Iroquois, arrived unarmed and felt secure, satisfied with the mere word that had been given them for their sole defense. Ibid., 91.
2. JR, 40, note losses and events in August.
3. JR, 40, 157. The Seneca and Cayuga did not officially conclude a peace treaty with the French until 1655 although they were represented by the other tribes present.
4. *NY Col. Doc.*, I, 541–549; Birch, *A Collection of the State Papers of John Thurloe*, I, 721–722, II, 418–419, 425. The controversial document entitled, "The Second Part of the Amboyna Tragedy; or a True Account of a Bloody, Treacherous, and Cruel Plot of the Dutch in America," can be found in Appendix G of *History of the New Netherlands,* II.
5. O'Callaghan, *History of the New Netherlands,* II, 261–265; Fernow, *The Records of New Amsterdam from 1653 to 1674,* I, 208–223.
6. JR, 27, 221.
7. *History of the New Netherlands,* II, 482–483; *NY Col. Doc.*, XIII, 245–251, 256–257. A later document dated June 17 states that forty-six Dutch were being held prisoner. (*NY Col. Doc.*, XIII, 252).
8. Brodhead, *The History of New York, Vol. II,* 32.

9. *Narratives of the New Netherlands, 1609–1664*, 414–415, 451–452, 460–465; *NY Col. Doc.*, II, 248–253, 469. In Holland Stuyvesant was unfairly criticized for giving up New Amsterdam without a fight. Given the state of the city's defenses, the militia's refusal to fight, and the strength of the English the governor rightly concluded that any resistance would have been senseless.
10. *NY Col. Doc.*, III, 67, 71, 73–74; *Cal. A &WI* , V, 236–237.

CHAPTER 3: THE KING'S HAND

1. Tracy entered the service as a captain of light horse in 1632. He fought in Germany throughout the Thirty Years' War, eventually commanding a regiment before being appointed commissary general for the French armies in Germany. He fought for a time in the ranks of the Fronde but later returned to the king's service. He was created lieutenant general in 1652 and served briefly in Guiana before being appointed "Lieutenant General throughout the length and breadth of the continental countries under our authority situated in South and North America." Although the official title of viceroy in the Americas belonged to Comte d'Estrades, Tracy held and exercised all the powers of this office and acted unimpeded in this role. (Prouville de Tracy, Alexandre de, 1596–1670, *DCB*, I).
2. Verney, *The Good Regiment*, 13–17. As well as being the finance officer or accountant for the colony, the intendant, who was second only to the governor, was also responsible for the judicial system and the police.
3. *Jesuit Relations*, Vol. 50, 127–131; Verney, *The Good Regiment*, 38–41.
4. This lake was called Lac St. Sacrement by the French. To avoid confusion I have elected to refer to it by its more modern name throughout the text.
5. *Jesuit Relations*, Vol. 50, 133–135, 181.
6. Lotbiniere, *Le Bulletin des recherches historiques*, 33, #5, 264–282; *Jesuit Relations*, Vol. 50, 135, 181–183. Schenectady was also known by its Dutch name of Corlac.
7. Verney, *The Good Regiment*, 67–68; The King to Tracy, 24 March 1666, Ministere des Affaires entrangeres, Correspondence politique, vol. 88.
8. *Jesuit Relations*, Vol. 50, 141; Marshall, *Word from New France*, 321–322.
9. Ibid., 322–323; *Jesuit Relations*, Vol. 50, 143–145.
10. Marshall, *Word from New France*, 324–325; *Jesuit Relations*, Vol. 50, 145.
11. Marshall, *Word from New France*, 325. There may have been fear on the part of the Mohawk sachems that such a campaign would have weakened the Mohawk fighting force to such a point that they would have been vulnerable to the various Canadian and New England tribes which they were at war with or had been at war with in the past.
12. *DHSNY*, I, 77–78; *Jesuit Relations*, Vol. 50, 145.
13. Ibid.,147, 201–203.
14. Ibid.,145.
15. Marshall, *Word from New France*, 327; *Jesuit Relations*, Vol. 50, 237. Cadwaller Colden in Volume I of his *History of the Five Nations* (1727) makes no reference to any hardships suffered by the Mohawk in the proceeding winter nor are there any references to be found among the correspondence of the various New York officials of the period.
16. Colden, *History of the Five Nations*, Vol. I, 17–18; *Jesuit Relations*, Vol. 50, 209–211. The treaty concluded Tracy's and the Carignan-Salières Regiment's task in Canada, but given the previous dealings with the Mohawk it was deemed unwise to call for their

immediate return to France. Tracy and the two La Colonel companies departed for France in late 1667, but the bulk of the regiment and the Marquis de Salières were to remain in Canada manning and consolidating the defensive works along the Richelieu River for another year. When the regiment finally did embark for France in 1668 over four hundred officers and men chose to accept the king's offer of land and money and decided to stay in Canada. (Verney, *The Good Regiment*, 116–117).

CHAPTER 4: THE FRENCH AND THE FIVE NATIONS

1. JR, 51, 171.
2. *Royal Fort Frontenac*, 108–114; *NY Col. Doc.*, IX, 85–90, 117–118.
3. *NY Col. Doc.*, IX, 114–116.
4. Ibid., 126.
5. Charlevoix, III, 194–196; *NY Col. Doc.*, 128–149.
6. J. Stockdale, *A Collection of Treaties Between Great Britain and Other Powers*, Vol. I, 133–150. Under the Treaty of Breda the New Netherlands was exchanged for the West Indies sugar colony of Surinam. *NY Col. Doc.*, III, 85–144, 163–166, contain a number of Nicolls's letters pertaining to this period. These are supplemented by excerpts and corrections in the *Calendar American & West Indies Papers, Vol 5 (1661– 1668).* "Tis not easily to be imagined what pains I have taken," Nicolls wrote the Earl of Clarendon in regard to his approach toward the conquered colony. (*Clarendon Papers, NYHSC for 1869*, 119.) *NY Col. Doc.*, IX, 95–114; Eccles, *Canada Under Louis XIV, 1663–1701*, 103; Colden, *The History of the Five Nations*, 18–19.
7. Whitmore, *Memoir of Sir Edmund Andros*, xvii–xviii; *NY Col. Doc.*, III, 214–220, 227, 233, 260–265, 283, 302–308; Brodhead, *History of New York*, II, 287–296. See Church, *History of King Philip's War*, and Lincoln, *Narratives of the Indian War, 1675–1699* for contemporary accounts of King Philip's War and the First Abenaki War.
8. Kingford, *Hist. of Canada*, I, 455–467, 475–478; Charlevoix, III, 211–212; *Tonty Relation*, 35–45. The number of Illinois captured varies widely. Frontenac put the number at six hundred to seven hundred.
9. *La Salle Relation*, 249–265; Westover, 49–54; Charlevoix, III, 212–213.
10. Charlevoix, III, 218–219; Eccles, *Frontenac*, 110–111.
11. *NY Col. Doc.*, IX, 147–148.
12. Eccles, *Frontenac*, 111–118; *Royal Fort Frontenac*, 142–144.
13. *NY Col. Doc.*, IX 167–168; La Barre, *DCB*, I.
14. *NY Col. Doc.*, IX, 194–195.
15. Ibid.
16. Charlevoix, III, 224–226; *NY Col. Doc.*, IX, 194–198.
17. Ibid., IX, 222–223.
18. Charlevoix, III, 244–247; *Tonty Relation*, 115; Lanctot, *History of Canada*, II, 87–88; *DHSNY*, I, 99–103.
19. Ibid., 100–101.
20. *Cal.A&WI*, XI, 740; *NY Col. Doc.*, III, 417–418; Charlevoix, III, 251.
21. *NY Col Doc.*, IX, 239–242; Eccles, *Canada Under Louis XIV*, 132–134; Charlevoix, III, 245–250; *Royal Fort Frontenac*, 149–151. La Barre's army at Fort Frontenac consisted of: King's Troops (Free Companies of the Marine) 137, Vanguard 206, Rear Guard 215, Reserves 228, Fort's garrison and misc. 35, for a total of 821. (*NY Col. Doc.*, IX, 234–236.)

22. *NY Col. Doc.*, IX, 241–242, 252–258; Eccles, *Frontenac*, 167–169; Charlevoix, III, 249, 252–254.
23. *NY Col. Doc.*, IX, 236–239.
24. Charlevoix, III, 253–256; Colden, *History of the Five Nations*, 49–57; *NY Col. Doc.* IX, 243-248. Meulles also claimed that La Barre had arrived at his decision without consulting a single officer or official with him. He then departed in such a hurry that he appeared to have "lost his wits, caring little what became of the army." Given how ill La Barre was during the negotiations, the latter statement might go far in explaining La Barre's state of mind and his actions during the conference. (Ibid., 245–249.)

CHAPTER 5: RIVALS TO THE NORTH

1. *NY Col. Doc.*, IX, 269; Denonville, *DCB*, I.
2. *NY Col. Doc.*, IX, 271–272.
3. Ibid., IX, 280–287; Denonville, *DCB*, I.
4. *NY Col. Doc.*, IX, 271–287; Eccles, *Canada Under Louis XIV*, 141–147. Denonville noted that although the English colony of Virginia had problems with the Iroquois "the gain of the merchant of Orange and Manatte is paramount to every public interest." (*NY Col. Doc.*, IX, 281).
5. *Battle for James Bay*, 21–23, 93–96.
6. Willson, *The Great Company* , 39–41; Kellogg, *Early Narratives of the North West*, 27–66; Bryce, *History of the Hudson Bay Co.*, 1–8.
7. Willson, *The Great Company*, 33–35, 38, 41–48; Bryce, *History of the Hudson Bay Co.*, 8–17; *Report from Committee on Boundaries of Ontario*, 55–63. Although the French would reject the English water basin claim to Hudson Bay, they employed similar types of claims to the south.
8. *NY Col. Doc.*, IX, 72–73; *Boundaries of Ontario*, 131–132; Bryce, *History of the Hudson Bay Co.*, 110–111. Albanel's journal of his expedition can be found in *JR*, LVI, 148–217.
9. Albanel, *DCB*, I; Frontenac to Colbert, 13 Nov. 1673, NAC, MG8-A1 serie 2.
10. *Battle for James Bay*, 8–9; *Boundaries of Ontario*, 132–133; "Radisson Relation," *RCA* 1895, 3–7; *NY Col. Doc.*, IX, 796–798.
11. Radisson Relation, *RCA 1895*, 9–49; *Boundaries of Ontario*, 133–135; *Cal.A&WI* , XI, 565.
12. State Papers-Hudson Bay, *RCA* 1895, 1–3; *NY Col. Doc.*, IX, 800.
13. *Battle for James Bay,* 40–41, 66–76; *Boundaries of Ontario*, 139. The French detachment's astonishing march is detailed in Troyes's Journal in *Battle for James Bay,* 40–66.
14. *Battle for James Bay,* 76–88, 102–111. See *Cal. A&WI* , XII, 369, 388–390, 404–406, 412, 426, 468, for French and English territorial claims over Hudson Bay and the financials losses claimed by the Hudson Bay Company.

CHAPTER 6: DENONVILLE'S EXPEDITION

1. *NY Col. Doc.*, III, 455–463, IX, 271–273, 280–292; Lahontan, *New Voyages to North America*, I, 97–98.
2. *NY Col. Doc.*, III, 388–389, 428, 504–505, IX, 319–332; Lahontan, *New Voyages to North America*, I, 119–120; Colden, *The History of the Five Nations*, 61.
3. Lamberville was not aware of the plan.
4. *The Windsor Border Region*, 10–11; *NY Col. Doc.*, IX, 362–363; Lahontan, *New Voyages to North America*, I, 121–124.

5. Charlevoix, III, 284–285; Lahontan, *New Voyages to North America*, I, 125–126; *NY Col. Doc.*, IX, 363. Denonville dealt severely with a French guide who led one of the English parties. He treated him as a deserter and had him shot. (Charlvoix, III, 286.)
6 *NY Col. Doc.*, IX, 363–365; Charlevoix, III, 285–289; *DHSNY*, I, 237–238, 246–250; Lahontan, *New Voyages to North America*, I, 128–129; French sources give 800, while Iroquois sources claim 400 to 450. Given that many of the warriors were gone at the time the latter number seems more likely.
7. *NY Col. Doc.*, IX, 365; *DHSNY*, I, 237. French casualties reported by Denonville were one regular, five militia, and five Indians killed (among the latter was a Mohawk chieftain of the Sault St. Louis Mission), five regulars and six militia wounded. Denonville does not specify the wounded among his allies, which given the nature of the fight was probably a dozen or so. The casualties among the regulars are interesting given that they were not engaged and likely reflect friendly fire (Charlevoix, III, 286–289).
8. *NY Col. Doc.*, III, 431–436, IX, 332–344, 368–369; Colden, *The History of the Five Nations*, 63–65.
9. *NY Col. Doc.*, III, 436–444, 466–479, 512–519; *Cal. A&WI* XII, 432–438. Dongan was unquestionably in favor of English intervention on the side of their allies, writing England that, "the French are encroaching as fast as they can and a little thing now may prevent great expense of blood and money hereafter." (Ibid., 432–433.)
10. Ibid., 457–458; *NY Col. Doc.*, III, 537–550, 569–571, IX, 369–393; Charlevoix, III, 304–308, IV, 14–15.
11. *NY Col. Doc.*, IX, 375–377, 395.
12. Ibid., 401–408.
13. Ibid., 416–418.

CHAPTER 7: ACADIA AND NEW ENGLAND

1. Murdoch, *History of Nova Scotia*, I, 36–37, 45–49, 55–59, 64; Calnek, *History of Annapolis*, 13–16.
2. Charlevoix, III, 128–129; Calnek, *History of Annapolis*, 16–19; *Cal. A&WI*, I, 132, 152.
3. Calnek, *History of Annapolis*, 19–29; Charlevoix, III, 129–132; Charles de St. Etienne de la Tour, *DCB*, I.
4. Hutchinson, *History of Massachusetts*, I, 168–169; Murdoch, *History of Nova Scotia*, I, 126–127; Calnek, *History of Annapolis*, 13–16.
5. Chalmers, *Collection of Treaties*, I, 133–150 (Treaty of Beda). Under the treaty English interest in Nova Scotia was exchanged for the return of a portion of St. Christopher's Island.
6. *Cal. A&WI*, VII, 2–3, 7–11, 35–36, 153–154. See Lincoln, *Narratives of the Indian Wars*, Drake, *A History of King Philips War*, and "Soldiers in King Philip's War," NEHGR, XXXVII (1883), 61–76, 170–189, 278–285, 362–375 for New England accounts of this conflict.
7. Baron Jean-Vincent de St. Castin, *DCB*, II; Charlevoix, III, 294–295. The Wabanaki Confederacy consisted of the Abenaki, the Mi'kmaq, the Maliseet, the Passamaquoddy, and the Penobscot. The confederacy was a traditional enemy of the Iroquois.
8. Whitmore, *Memoir of Sir Edmund Andros*, xvii-xix; *NY Col. Doc.*, III, 248–249, 254–257.

9. *NH Prov. Papers*, II, 46–47; Charlevoix, IV, 15–16; Hutchinson Papers, *MHSC*, 3rd ser., I, 85–87.
10. Drake, *Border Wars of New England*, 10–11; *Doc. Hist. Maine*, VI, 429–430.

CHAPTER 8: THE GLORIOUS REVOLUTION

1. Hall, *The Glorious Revolution in America*, 3–5; For the immediate causes of the Glorious Revolution in England, see Jones, *Convergent Forces.*
2. Neal, *History of New England*, II, 428–429; *NY Col. Doc.*, III, 536–550.
3. Hutchinson, *History of Massachusetts*, 316–324, 332–341; Hall, *The Glorious Revolution in America*, 30–36, 39–48; *Andros Tracts*, I, 149–173. Complaints as to Andros's conduct had previously reached England to the extent that the Board of Trade recommended recalling Andros. (*NY Col. Doc.*, III, 573.)
4. *Cal. A&WI*, XIII, 71, 101–102. The judges appointed by Andros as well as the custom agents and tax collectors were also seized as part of the revolutionary zeal creating havoc with basic government functions.
5. *Cal. A&WI*, XIII, 109–110.
6. *Ibid.*, 80–81; *NY Col. Doc.*, III, 277–278. Lt. Governor Nicholson wrote to the Board of Trade, "It has been very fatal to this city and province to be annexed to Boston; indeed, if continued it would have been our ruin." *Cal.A&WI*, XIII, 35, 38–39.
7. *NY Col. Doc.*, III, 574–576.
8. *Cal. A&WI*, XIII, 64–65; *NY Col. Doc.*, III, 594. Stephen Van Cortlandt of the New York Council wrote that after arguing with Cuyler's captain, Abram De Peyster, the two men stormed out of the fort and alarmed the town, greatly magnifying Nicholson's comments. (*NY Col. Doc.*, III, 593–594.)
9. Purple, Edwin, *Geneological Notes Relating to Lt. Governor Jacob Leisler*, Private Printing, New York: 1877, 7–8.
10. Hall, *The Glorious Revolution in America*, 102–114; *NY Col. Doc.*, III, 738–739.
11. Ibid., 102–114; *Cal.A&WI*, XIII, 80–81. Leisler commandeered the £773 that had been raised for the relief of Albany and used it to repair Fort James. (Ibid.)

CHAPTER 9: THE WABANAKI AND THE IROQUOIS

1. *N.H. Prov. Papers*, I, 357–358; Drake, *Border Wars of New England*, 15–19.
2. *Ibid.*, 19–20; *N.H. Prov. Papers*, II, 47–50.
3. Lincoln, *Narratives of the Indian Wars*, 186–187, 195–196; Drake, *Border Wars of New England*, 20–22; *N.H. Prov. Papers*, 50–55.
4. Johnston, *History of Bristol and Bremen*, 163–170; Charlevoix, IV, 39–42; *Collection de Manuscrits. . . Relatifs Nouvelle-France*, I, 477–481. Of the 156 men assigned to the fort, desertion and recalls had reduced their numbers to a little over 30 at the time of Castin's attack. (Johnston, *History of Bristol and Bremen*,163.)
5. *Cal. A&WI*, XIII, 114–115; *Ten Years at Pemaquid*, 144–153; Charlevoix, IV, 42–44.
6. *Doc. Hist Maine*, IX, 66; *Giles Memorial*, 108–111.
7. *Cal. A&WI*, XIII, 111, 120.
8. *Doc. Hist. Maine*, IX, 54–56; Drake, *Border Wars of New England*, 36–37.
9. Belknap, *History of N.H.*, I, 131; *Cal. A&WI*, XIII, 157, 166.
10. Church, *King Philip's War*, 93–104; *Siege of Falmouth*, 38–39; *New Plymouth*, 75–78.

11. Church, *King Philip's War*, 103–104.
12. *NY Col. Doc.*, IX, 431, 434–435.
13. Girouard, *Lake St. Louis, Old and New*, 124–135; *Collection de Manuscrits... Relatifs Nouvelle-France*, I, 567–571; Colden, *The History of the Five Nations*, 72; Lahontan, *New Voyages to North America*, I, 224–225.

CHAPTER 10: THREE WARS, ONE NAME

1. *NY Col. Doc.*, IX, 422–428; Parkman, *Count Frontenac and New France*, 195.
2. Lahontan, *New Voyages to North America*, I, 150, 152; *NY Col. Doc.*, IX, 431.
3. Frontenac to Minister, Nov. 15, 1689, MG1-C11A, vol. 10, fol. 217–224; *NY Col. Doc.*, IX, 435–438.
4. Frontenac to Minister, Nov. 15, & Nov. 17, 1689, MG1-C11A, vol. 10, fol. 217–224, 343–344; *NY Col. Doc.*, IX, 435.
5. Parkman, *Count Frontenac and New France*, 205; Lanctot, *History of Canada*, II, 116–117.
6. Colden, *The History of the Five Nations*, 93–100.
7. *NY Col. Doc.*, IX, 448–451.
8. *DHNY*, I, 186.
9. Ibid., 186–188; Charlevoix, *The History of New France*, IV, 121–125; *Andros Tracts*, III, 114–116. The compiled casualty list and those carried away as prisoners are printed in *DHNY*, I, 190–191.
10. *DHNY*, I, 187; *Andros Tracts*, III, 117; *Cal. A &WI*, XIII, 247–249.
11. *DHNY*, I, 188–189; *Cal.A&WI*, XIII, 247–249.
12. *DHNY*, I, 188, II, 87–88; *Cal. A&WI*, XIII, 247–249. The French reported twenty-one lost, four natives and seventeen Frenchmen. (*King William's War in America*, 8.)
13. Also known as Wohawa. Hopehood was already known across the frontier for his raids during King Philip's War (Drake, 116).
14. Frontenac to Minister, April 30, 1690, MG1-C11A, vol 11, fol. 83–85. Frontenac's strategy was not without its critics. The intendant, Champigny, pointed out that the three attacks should have been concentrated on Albany. "If this blow had been struck against Albany we would have seen the Iroquois greatly humbled, being out of reach of Manhatten and Boston, particularly during the winter." (*Memoire de ce qui s'est passé en Canada . . . durant l'annee 1690*, F3, Moreau de St. Mery. Cited in Eccles, *Frontenac.*)
15. *Cal. A&WI* , XIII, 272.

CHAPTER 11: THE REDUCTION OF CANADA

1. *Cal. A&WI*, XIII, 17–27; Clarendon Papers, 172–176. For accounts of Andros's capture and imprisonment, see *Andros Tracts*, III, 95–102. An accounting of original documents pertaining to the political crisis can be found in Hall, *The Glorious Revolution in America*.
2. *Andros Tracts*, III, 119. The Iroquois also pressed the governments of Massachusetts and New York to undertake an invasion of Canada (Colden, *The History of the Five Nations*, 93–100).
3. *DHNY*, II, 113; Brandow, *Old Saratoga and Schuylerville*, 17; *NY Col. Doc.*, III, 700–701, 716–717, 727; Munsell, *The Annals of Albany*, II, 210–211, 213–215.
4. *Doc. Hist. Maine*, V, 68.

5. Ibid., V, 59–63. Fears of a French fleet operating out of Port Royal would escalate to a point that one Bostonian wrote his colleague, "We are in great danger, if four or five French ships should attack us sharply we should probably be reduced under another Government." (*Cal A&WI*, XIII, 213.)
6. Phips, Sir William, DCB, III. Phips lists his squadron as: *Six Friends* (forty-two guns), *Porcupine* (sixteen), *Mary* (eight), *Union* (four), *Mary Anne* (two), and a pair of ketches, the *Lark* and the *Bachelor*. Total compliment: 286 (*A Journal of the Proceedings of the Late Expedition to Port Royal*, 15).
7. *Cal. A &WI*, XIII, 275–276. *NY Col. Doc.*, IX, 474–475, 921. Captain Southack of the *Porcupine* claimed that there were eighty-four French prisoners in all (*Doc. Hist. Maine*, V, 127). The French engineer, de Saccardy, that was dispatched to erect a new fort at Port Royal was taken prisoner by New England privateers in the Bay of Fundy not long after Phips's departure. Fortunately for him, a French privateer overtook his New England captives and freed him a few days later. (*NY Col. Doc.*, IX, 474–475; *Villebon Memoirs*, 22–24). One of Southack's crew on this voyage was none other than future privateer Captain William Kidd.
8. *Doc. Hist. Maine*, V, 65–66. In a petition to Massachusetts concerning an attack on Quebec, New York questioned the wisdom of attacking Port Royal, as it would only warn the French of English intentions. (*NY Col. Doc.*, III, 695–698.)
9. *Cal. A&WI*, XIII, 240.
10. *NY Col. Doc.*, II, 263–269; *Cal A&WI*, XIII, 273, 283.
11. *Doc. Hist. Maine*, V, 64
12. Ibid., V, 93–94; *NY Col. Doc.*, III, 700–705, 731–732; *Cal. A&WI*, XIII, 255–256, 261. Maryland also promised to raise a hundred men to support the expedition.
13. "Phips's Account," *Phips Devant Quebec, 1690*, 35; "Savage's Account," ibid., 49; *Cal. A&WI*, XIII, 213, 376; *The Expedition to Canada*, 1690, 29. One account of the expedition claimed that there was only seventy barrels of powder for the entire fleet. (*Cal. A&WI*, XIII, 376.)
14. *NY Col. Doc.*, IX, 473–474.
15. Ibid., 470–471; *Wisconsin Hist. Coll.*, V, 65–67.
16. Charlevoix, IV, 142; *NY Col. Doc.*, IX, 474–478. French losses were reported to be a dozen with claims of twice as many Iroquois casualties. (Charlevoix, IV, 142.)
17. Prevost was originally an officer in the Carigan-Salières Regiment. By Royal Commission he was appointed town major of Quebec in 1668 and would hold this post for more than thirty years (Prevost, DCB, II). Charlevoix, IV, 152–153; "Relation de Janclot," *Phips Devant Quebec, 1690*, 74; *NY Col. Doc.*, IX, 482–483; Frontenac to Minister, Nov. 12, 1690 MG1-C11A, vol. 10, 121–122.
18. "Relation de Janclot," *Phips Devant Quebec, 1690*, 74–75; *NY Col. Doc.*, IX, 459, 483–485; Charlevoix, IV,168–169; "Plan de Quebec. . . ". At this point none of the gates into the city had doors. Frontenac had them barricaded, particularly the palace gate near the intendant's home. (*NY Col. Doc.*, IX, 484–485.)
19. *Cal. A&WI*, XIII, 376–377; "Relation de Janclot," *Phips Devant Quebec, 1690*, 75–76; *NY Col. Doc.*, IX, 485–486.
20. *NY Col. Doc.*, IX, 485–487.
21. Ibid.
22. "Walley's Journal," *The Expedition to Canada*, 10; "Savage's Account," *Phips Devant*

Quebec, 1690, 49; Cal. *A&WI*, XIII, 376–377. In addition, several large vessels were sent up the St. Lawrence to give the illusion that another English force was landing south of the town. ("Walley's Journal," ibid.)

23. *Two Narratives*, 9, 36–37; *NY Col. Doc.*, IX, 487; "Walley's Journal," *The Expedition to Canada*, 10–11.

24. Frontenac to Minister, Nov. 12, 1690, MG1-C11A. To the delight of the defenders Callières entered the town that evening with eight hundred men. ("Relation de Janclot," *Phips Devant Quebec, 1690*, 76.)

25. For simplicities sake I have attempted to use Gregorian calendar dates. The French had already adopted this current calendar style, while the English still used the Julian calendar, which was ten days behind the Gregorian calendar.

26. *Two Narratives*, 37–38; "Walley's Journal," *The Expedition to Canada*, 11–12; *NY Col. Doc.*, IX, 487.

27. "Walley's Journal," *The Expedition to Canada*, 13.

28. *NY Col. Doc.*, IX, 487–488; Charlevoix, IV, 176–177. French casualties were reported as five killed and a dozen wounded. (*NY Col. Doc.*, IX, 487.)

29. "Savage's Account," *Phips Devant Quebec, 1690*, 50; "Walley's Journal," *The Expedition to Canada*,13–14.

30. *NY Col. Doc.*, IX, 488; *Two Narratives*, 38; Charlevoix, IV, 179.

31. "Walley's Journal," *The Expedition to Canada*, 13–14; "Savage's Account," *Phips Devant Quebec, 1690*, 50–51.

32. "Walley's Journal," *The Expedition to Canada*, 16–17.

33. *NY Col. Doc.*, IX, 488; "Relation La Potherie," *Phips Devant Quebec*, 1690, 65–66; Charlevoix, IV, 179–181. There were less than half a dozen French casualties, but among them were the two Le Moyne brothers. (Ibid.)

34. "Walley's Journal," *The Expedition to Canada*, 16–19.

35. Ibid.; *Two Narratives*, 23–25. Rev. John Wise, who left a biting narrative of the campaign, placed the blame for the loss of the cannon and many other things on Walley. Savage, in his account, defended Walley, saying that it was more likely the fault of the captain in charge of the guns. (*Two Narratives*, 5–18; "Savage's Account," *Phips Devant Quebec, 1690*, 51.)

36. Frontenac to Minister, Nov. 12, 1690 MG1-C11A; *NY Col. Doc.*, IX, 489.

37. *History Of New England*, 465; "Savage's Account," *Phips Devant Quebec, 1690*, 51; *Cal. A&WI*, XIII, 376–377.

38. The wind channeling from the southwest (downriver) or from the northwest (upriver) is a common occurrence in this area triggered by low-pressure systems tracking north or south of the St. Lawrence valley. (*The Weather of Atlantic Canada and Eastern Quebec*, 97–99.)

CHAPTER 12: WINTHROP'S FOLLY

1. *Winthrop Papers*, MHSC 6th Series, III, 3, 508–510; *Cal. A &WI*, XIII, 280–281.

2. Ibid.; *DHNY*, IV, 193–194; *Winthrop Correspondence*, MHSC 5th Series, VIII, 308–310. In his July 29th report to the governor and council of Connecticut, Winthrop confided that the situation ".leaves me in great distress about his Majesty's service and your interest. I find very truly that your designs and those of York have very different intentions and they have led you too cunningly into an association, just to serve their extremity. . . ."

3. *DHNY*, IV, 194–195.
4. Ibid., 194–196, II, 160; *Winthrop Correspondence*, 318–322; *Winthrop Papers*, 12–13.
5. *DHNY*, II, 160–161.
6. *NY Col. Doc*, IX, 478–479; Charlevoix, *The History of New France*, IV, 142–145; Parkman, *Count Frontenac and New France*, 265; La Potherie, *Historie de l'Amerique Septentrionale*, III, 94–95.
7. *NY Col. Doc.*, IX, 479–480; La Hontan, *New Voyages to North America*, I, 158–159; Charlevoix, *The History of New France*, IV, 145–149.
8. Ibid.; *DHNY*, II, 161–162. The two sources disagree only on English losses, which Schuyler listed as one Iroquois brave.
9. Ibid., 162–163; *NY Col. Doc.*, III, 751–754; *Cal. A&WI*, XIII, 339–341; *Winthrop Correspondence*, 322–324. A London merchant, James Lloyd, claimed in a letter on the matter that the Iroquois "at once released Winthrop, threating to make a Jesuit of Leisler" (that is scalp him). (*Cal. A&WI*, XIII, 376.)
10. Myrand, *Sir William Phips Devant Quebec 1690*, 111; Additional documents detailing and pertaining to Phips's siege of Quebec, and the campaign of 1690 in general, can be found in this text.

CHAPTER 13: THE BATTLES OF LA PRAIRIE

1. Drake, 68–69. Church, 119–121. Church recorded seven killed and twenty-four wounded in the engagement.
2. *Cal. A&WI*, XIII, 368–369. The minister is referring to the attack on Schenectady, NY.
3. Belknap, 134–135.
4. John R. Brodhead (ed.), *Documents Relative to the Colonial History of the State of New York* (Albany: Weed, Parsons & Co., 1853), III, 255, 260. (Hereafter *NY Col. Doc.*).
5. "Wadsworth's Journal," *Massachusetts Historical Society Collections*, series 4, #1 (1852), 105–106.
6. *NY Col. Doc.*, IX, 513. The intendant claimed that of the ten or eleven vessels sent out from France in 1690 only three arrived. (*NY Col. Doc.*, IX, 497).
7. Ibid.
8. *NY Col. Doc.*, IX, 516–518; Charlevoix, *The History of New France*, IV, 193–195; JR, 64, 67–71.
9. *NY Col. Doc.*, III, 776–780.
10. Ibid., 778–785, 802.
11. Ibid., 800–805.
12. Clement du Vault de Valrenne, Philippe, c. 1644–1707, *DCB*, Vol. II. Commissioned ensign in the De Pagny Regiment in 1662, lieutenant in 1665, and captain in 1672. He served in various field battalions receiving several wounds in the 23 years before being made a captain of the marines in Canada in 1685. A descendent of the first four field marshals of France, he had a reputation for being a brave soldier, a good officer, and a master of his calling.
13. *NY Col. Doc.*, IX, 520–521.
14. Ibid.; Charlevoix, *The History of New France*, IV, 202–204; La Hontan, *New Voyages to North America*, I, 173.

15. *NY Col. Doc.*, III, 803–804, IX, 521; La Potherie, *Historie de l'Amerique Septentrionale*, III, 138–141.
16. *NY Col. Doc.*, III, 804.
17. Ibid., IX, 522.
18. Ibid., 522–523; La Potherie, *Historie de l'Amerique Septentrionale*, III, 141–142; *NY Col. Doc.*, III, 804; Charlevoix, *The History of New France*, IV, 206–208.
19. *NY Col. Doc.*, III, 804–805, IX, 523
20. Frontenac to Minister, Oct. 20, 1691 (two letters), MG1-C11A, vol 11, fol. 230–232, 233–247; *NY Col. Doc.*, III, 805.

CHAPTER 14: A SHIFTING TIDE

1. Drake, *Border Wars of New England*, 70–72; *Cal. A &WI*, XIV, 475–477.
2. *NY Col. Doc.*, III, 784–789.
3. Ibid., III, 791–793, 814–816; *Cal. A &WI*, XIII, 526, 562–563.
4. *NY Col. Doc.*, IX, 534, III, 815, 817. The French claim to have taken fourteen of the Iroquois prisoners.
5. *Cal. A&WI*, XIII, 580–581. *NY Col. Doc.*, III, 815.
6. *Ibid.*, III, 805–806, 815–816; Colden, *History of the Five Nations*, II, 125–126.
7. *Cal. A&WI*, XIII, 178.
8. *Ibid.*, XIII, 529–530, 546, 550, 572–575.
9. *Villebon Journal*, 32–33.
10. *NY Col. Doc.*, IX, 505–506.
11. Ibid., 492–493, 506–507.
12. Ibid., 404–408, 510–511. No doubt prompted by rumors of French expeditions, in late 1692 the Massachusetts council passed an act entitled, "An Act for Building in Stone or Brick in the town of Boston and Preventing Fire," which called for all future buildings within the town to be constructed of stone or brick with slate or tile roofs. (*Mass. Acts and Resolves*, I, 42–43.)
13. *NY Col. Doc.*, IX, 497–503, 508–510. Matters had become so bad that Intendant Champigny wrote the French court, "I am reduced to the necessity of having the leaden gutters and weights melted in order to be made into bullets." (Ibid., 503.)
14. Clowes, *History of the Royal Navy*, II, 334–344; Guerin, *Histoire Maritime de France*, III, 451–463.

CHAPTER 15: DISUNITY AND DISCORD

1. Lincoln, *Narratives of the Indian Wars*, 230–231; *N.H. Prov. Papers*, II, 56; Rawlyk, *Nova Scotia's Massachusetts*, 76. Villebon states in his journal that the Abenaki had burned over 60 homes and had taken or killed 187 of York's inhabitants. (*Villebon Journal*, 36).
2. *Cal. A&WI*, XIII, 627–628, 653; *NY Col. Doc.*, III, 833–835.
3. *Cal. A&WI*, XIII, 653, 720.
4. Ibid., 720–721.
5. Modern-day Fredericton, New Brunswick.
6. Williamson, *History Of Maine*, I, 631–633; *Villebon Journal*, 36–38; *NY Col. Doc.*, IX, 537.
7. *Villebon Journal*, 41–42; *Narratives of the Indian Wars*, 233–237; Williamson, *History Of Maine*, I, 632-634. Villebon wrote of the Wabanaki decision that, "It has, so far, been

impossible to overcome the superstition that, if they receive such a reverse when they set out on the warpath, they must stop at once, no matter how large the party may be, or how insignificant the action." (*Villebon Journal*, 42.)

8. Church, *King Philip's War*, 173–182; *Cal. A &WI*, XIII, 700, 721. Fear that supporting Fort William Henry might prove difficult was born out in late November 1692 when a twenty-ton supply vessel was captured by a Kennebec war party in sight of the fort. (*Villebon Journal*, 46).

9. *Ancient Pemaquid*, 150–151; *Doc. Hist. Maine*, X, 47–48. After his examination of the fort Romer concluded that the structure had "been extremely ill built and not defensible . . . there was no order or proportion observed in building it, and its Walls were made of clay mixed with Sand brought from the Seashore instead of Lime." (Ibid., 47.) Governor Villebon gave another opinion saying of the fort "that within it they are quite safe from the Indians, unless they be taken by surprise." (*Villebon Journal*, 67.)

10. *NY Col. Doc.*, III, 827–833, 840–844.

11. Ibid., 847–848.

12. Charlevoix, IV, 219–220; Lahontan, *New Voyages to North America*, I, 270.

13. Charlevoix, IV, 219–220; *NY Col Doc.*, IX, 535–536.

14. *NY Col. Doc.*, IX, 538.

15. *Villebon Journal*, 43–44; *Collection de Manuscrits . . . Relatifs Nouvelle-France*, II, 80–81; Charlevoix, IV, 227–228 *NY Col. Doc.*, IX, 531–532, 538, 544; Lanctot, *History of Canada*, II, 175. This English vessel appears to be a sloop outfitted in Boston by Phips to keep the fort supplied throughout the winter. Had Iberville been a little earlier he would have encountered two English warships, the HMS *Nonsuch* and the HMS *Conception*. (*Cal. A&WI*, XIV, 24–25.)

16. La Hontan, *New Voyages to North America*, I, 273–275; *DCB*, II, Monbeton de Brouillan, Jacques-Francois.

17. Charlevoix, IV, 222–226; La Hontan, *New Voyages to North America*, I, 275–278.

CHAPTER 16: THE MOHAWK EXPEDITION

1. *NY Col. Doc.*, IX, 550, 557.

2. Ibid., 550–551, 558–559.

3. *A Journal of the Late Actions of the French at Canada* (1693), 4–7. Note that the English dates are old style. To align them with the French new style dates eleven days have been added.

4. *NY Col. Doc.*, IX, 551, 559.

5. *A Journal of the Late Actions of the French at Canada*, 7–10; *NY Col. Doc.*, IX, 551–552, 559–560; Colden, *The History of the Five Nations*, 127–133; Frontenac to Minister, Oct. 25, 1693, MG1-C11A, vol.12, fol. 225–238; Governor Fletcher of New York also penned a journal of his actions during this period which can be found in *A Journal of the Late Actions of the French at Canada*, 1–4.

6. *NY Col. Doc.*, IX, 552, 560–561.

CHAPTER 17: MISSED OPPORTUNITIES

1. *Old Times in Saco*, 40–41; *Doc. Hist. Maine*, X, 50.

2. *Cal. A &WI*, XIV, xi–xvi, 9–10, 124, 133, 156–157; *Ancient Pemaquid*, 151–152; *Doc. Hist. Maine*, X, 7–11; Hutchinson, *History of Massachusetts*, II, 73–74.

3. *Cal. A &WI*, XIV, 13, 31, 39–41; Clowes, *History of the British Navy*, II, 469–470. Wheler's fleet consisted of the *Resolution* (60), *Dunkirk* (52), *Ruby* (42), *Tiger* (42), *Advice* (42), *Chester* (42), *Dragon* (40), *Falcon* (36), *Experiment* (32), *Mermaid* (32), *Pembroke* (32), *Quaker* (10), a bomb ship, three fireships, and a pair of merchant ships carrying Godwin's and Foulk's regiments. This force also had available on station the *Diamond* (48), *Mordaunt* (46), *Guernsey* (28), and the *Henry Prize* (24), along with a number of converted merchantmen. (Ibid.) When combined with Governor Codrington's forces Wheler had some five thousand men under his command.

4. Clowes, *History of the British Navy*, II, 469–471; *Cal. A &WI*, XIV, 87–88, 99–102.

5. Ibid., XIV, 100–103. Codrington claimed that the fleet caught "an infection or a plague from a merchant ship in harbour at Barbados." (Ibid., 103.)

6. Ibid., XIV, 118–119, 165–166. The letter from Whitehall along with several other directives from the crown did not arrive until September 24. (Ibid., 165–166.)

7. Hutchinson, *History of Massachusetts*, II, 70–72; *Cal. A &WI*, XIV, 28, 124, 128–129.

8. *Cal. A&WI*, XIV, 133.

9. Ibid., XIV, 165–166.

10. *NY Col. Doc.*, IX, 561.

11. *Cal. A&WI*, XIV, 714; *N.Y. Col. Doc.*, IX, 530, 553, 561–562.

12. Eccles, *Frontenac*, 256–257; *N.Y. Col. Doc.*, IX, 530, 553, 561–562, 565–566.

13. Charlevoix, IV, 240–241; *N.Y. Col. Doc.*, IX, 567–569.

14. *NY Col. Doc.*, IV, 33.

CHAPTER 18: STALEMATE IN THE EAST

1. *NY Col. Doc.*, IV, 41–43.

2. *Cal. A&WI*, XIV, 115, 171–173.

3. Ibid., 171–172. Fletcher's letter to the Board of Trade also included a quota plan to provide six hundred men and officers for the annual defense of Albany. The plan seen in the table below is an interesting estimate of the English colonies' fighting strength as of December 1693.

Colony	Strength	Albany	Quota Cost (£)
Virginia	6,000	120	4,200
Maryland	4,000	80	2,800
Pennsylvania	2,000	43	1,400
Connecticut	3,000	60	2,100
Massachusetts/N.H.	9,500	176	6,160
Rhode Island	1,200	24	840
New York	3,000	100	3,300
Totals	28,700	603	20,800

4. *Villebon Journal*, 63–65; Belknap, *History of N.H.* I, 138–139.

5. *Adventures of Baptiste*, 355.

6. Belknap, *History of N.H.*, I, 139–141; Charlevoix, IV, 256–257; *Narratives of the Indian Wars*, 252–254; *N.H. Prov. Papers*, II, 124–129.

7. *Cal. A &WI*, XIV, 234–235, 246, 250, 347, 398, 498; Hutchinson, *History of Massachusetts*, II, 76–79.

8. For a narrative of the English navy's disastrous attempt on the French capital in 1711 see Walker, *A Full Account of the Late Expedition to Canada*.

9. Drake, *Border Wars of New England*, 104–105; Hutchinson, *History of Massachusetts*, II, 83–84; *NY Col. Doc.*, IX, 613–616.
10. *Villebon Journal*, 78.
11. *Ancient Pemaquid*, 155–157; Drake, *Border Wars of New England*, 104–107.
12. *NY Col. Doc.*, IX, 574–576.
13. *Villebon Journal*, 75–80, 160–161; *NY Col. Doc.*, IX, 617; "The Adventures of Baptiste," *Proceedings Pocumtuck Memorial Assoc.*, IV (1905), 342–360.
14. *Collection de Manuscrits . . . Relatifs Nouvelle-France*, II, 200; *Villebon Journal*, 81; Bonaventure after speaking with an English prisoner claimed that the *Sorling* lost three killed and thirty wounded in the engagement.

CHAPTER 19: THE PEACE OFFENSIVE

1. *NY Col. Doc.*, IX, 577–578.
2. Ibid., IX, 580–582.
3. *NY Col. Doc.*, IX, 588–590.
4. *Your Fire Shall Burn No More*, 72–76; *NY Col. Doc.*, IV, 337–338.
5. Ibid., IX, 599.
6. *Royal Fort Frontenac*, 189–190; Charlevoix, IV, 265–266.
7. *Royal Fort Frontenac*, 188; Charlevoix, IV, 266. De Mothe de Cadillac, who was in command at Michilimackinac, claimed that the French would lose all of the tribes if a grand expedition was not launched against the Iroquois. (Charlevoix, IV, 266.)
8. *Royal Fort Frontenac*, 188–194. Although there were many critics of Frontenac's move to reestablish Fort Frontenac, Cadwaller Colden, the author of the *History of the Five Nations* presented the Iroquois reaction to the reestablishment of Fort Frontenac saying, "the French gained a great Advantage, by possessing this Place, as it is of great Security to their Traders, in their passing between Montreal and Missilimakinak. It served likewise as a Place of Stores, and Retreat in all their Enterprises against the Five Nations." (Colden, *Five Nations*, II, 163.)
9. *NY Col. Doc.*, IX, 618.
10. Charlevoix, IV, 266–270.
11. *NY Col. Doc.*, IX, 628–629.
12. *Cal. A&WI*, XIV, 361. "It is very unreasonable that the burden of this war should fall wholly on New York, but it cannot be remedied until the provinces are governed by one Assembly and one law," Fletcher would write in regard to his lack of resources to prosecute the conflict. (Ibid., 403.)
13. *Cal. A&WI*, XIV, 315, 335–336, 597. In a letter to the governor of Connecticut Fletcher made clear that the king had appointed him to command the quota troops from the several colonies, amounting to 1,198 men. (*Cal. A &WI*, XIV, 588.)
14. *NY Col. Doc.*, IV, 113, 118–119.

CHAPTER 20: FRONTENAC AND THE ONONDAGA

1. *NY Col. Doc.*, IX, 590–591, 633–641; Eccles, *Frontenac*, 260–265; Charlevoix, V, 9–10.
2. *NY Col. Doc.*, IX, 646; Charlevoix, IV, 269, 277–278. Cadillac wrote of New France's shaky allies "that we are going to lose them all unless we remedy it, by forming a grand expedition against the Iroquois, and convincing our allies that we really intend to destroy that nation." (Ibid., 266.)

3. Eccles, *Frontenac*, 263–265; *NY Col. Doc.*, IX, 641–642.
4. *NY Col. Doc.*, IX, 649–650.
5. Ibid., IX, 649–650; Charlevoix, V, 12–14; *RAPQ*, 1928–29, 320; *Royal Fort Frontenac*, 195–196.
6. Charlevoix, V, 15–16; *Papers Relating to Count Frontenac's Expedition*, 329–331.
7. Eccles, *Frontenac*, 265–267; *NY Col. Doc., IX*, 654–656; *RAPQ*, 1928–29, 320.
8. *Royal Fort Frontenac*, 195; *NY Col. Doc., IX*, 639–640; Colden, *Five Nations*, II, 167–172.
9. *NY Col. Doc.*, IV, 160–164.
10. Ibid., IV, 171–176.
11. *Papers Relating to Count Frontenac's Expedition*, 349–350; *NY Col. Doc.*, IV, 171–176.

CHAPTER 21: THE FALL OF PEMAQUID

1. *History of King William's War*, 115.
2. *NY Col. Doc.*, IX, 574–576, 590; *Villebon's Journal*, 83–85.
3. Pierre Le Moyne D'Iberville, DCB, II.
4. *Collection de Manuscrits . . . Relatifs Nouvelle-France*, II, 216–218; *Father Baudoin's War*, 15; Charlevoix, V, 22–24.
5. *Father Baudoin' s War*, 17; *Cal. A&WI*, XV, 132, 224. An account by Lt. Roger Wright estimated Iberville's flagship at forty-eight guns and the *Profond* at forty guns. Wright also claimed that the *Sorling* did not disengage until after the *Newport* had surrendered at which point Captain Paxton drove the frigate ashore to prevent it from sinking. (Ibid.)
6. *Father Baudoin' s War*, 17–20; *N.Y. Col. Doc.*, IX, 658.
7. Charlevoix, V, 24–26; *Cal. A &WI*, XV, 70–71, 142–144.
8. *Cal. A&WI*, XV, 144; *Ancient Pemaquid*, 157–160. *Father Baudoin' s War*, 21. Credit Iberville and the other French leaders for preventing a massacre
9. Charlevoix, V, 27–28; Hutchinson, II, 94; *Cal. A &WI*, XV, 132.
10. Church, 138–141.
11. Church, 141–144; *Cal. A &WI*, XV, 184. The Great Falls are at Orono, Maine.
12. Church, 148–150. Church noted that after plundering and burning down the inhabitant's homes "The French being sensible of the Major's kindness to them, kiss'd his hand, & were very thankful to him for his favour to them in saving their lives." (Ibid., 150.)
13. Church, 151–156; *Cal. A &WI*, XV, 4, 93, 132.
14. *Villebon's Journal*, 90.
15. Ibid., 90–92; Hutchinson, II, 98–99. Fort St. Joseph was a four-bastioned wooden palisade structure running almost 115 feet to a side. Also known as Fort Nashwaak or Fort Naxoat the location would be abandoned after King William's War.
16. *Villebon's Journal*, 92–94; *Cal. A &WI*, XV, 132, 218.
17. Ibid., 245–246.

CHAPTER 22: IBERVILLE

1. Charlevoix, V, 33–34; One visitor to Placentia noted that "the richest of our settlers was not more comfortably lodged than one is on shipboard." (Ibid., 34.)

2. Prowse, *History of Newfoundland*, 214–216; Pontchartrain to Brouillan, 21 April 1697, *Report on Canadian Archives 1889*, 94.
3. *Journal de l'expedition D'Iberville*, 82–83; Charlevoix, V, 35–37.
4. *Journal de l'expedition D'Iberville*, 79–86; *Father Baudoin's War*, 34–35; *NY Col. Doc.*, IX, 657–658.
5. *Father Baudoin's War*, 39; Charlevoix, V, 37–39.
6. Ibid., 39–42.
7. *Cal. A&WI*, XV, 305–307; Prowse, *History of Newfoundland*, 216–217, 230–232.
8. *Father Baudoin' s War*, 50.
9. Charlevoix, V, 42–47; *Father Baudoin's War*, 41–49; *Journal de l'expedition D'Iberville*, 51–61.
10. Ibid., 68–69.
11. *Cal. A&WI*, XV, 339. The letter called for the king to appoint one of his governors as commander in chief with powers over all of the colonies as the only means of effectively dealing with the French.

CHAPTER 23: THE WAR AT THE TOP OF THE WORLD

1. Reed, *Iberville*, 63. Pontchartrain to Brouillan, Pontchartrain to D'Iberville, Instructions for D'Iberville, 9 March 1697, *Report on Canadian Archives 1889*, 322. Iberville's brother Serigny was directed to carry out the operation if he could not locate Iberville before the season, which made any attempt on Fort Nelson impractical. (Minister to Serigny, Ibid.)
2. *Report on the Boundaries of the Province of Ontario*, 142; Pierre Le Moyne D'Iberville, DCB, II.
3. *The French Regime in the Upper Country*, 271–274; Charlevoix, IV, 37–39; *The Great Company*, 138–139, 143–144; *The Battle for James Bay*, 37.
4. *The French Regime in the Upper Country*, 271–274; *The Great Company*, 144; Charlevoix, IV, 39,
5. *Twenty Years of York Factory: Jeremie's Account of Hudson Strait and Bay*, 26; Eccles, *Canada Under Louis XIV*, 196–197; *Report on the Boundaries of the Province of Ontario*, 142.
6. *Jeremie's Account*, 27–28; *London Gazette*, Oct. 29, 1696; *Cal. A&WI*, XV, 239-240. A series of complaints laid down by English prisoners in 1694, and testimony that Iberville had fairly treated the surrendered garrison by other Englishmen, led to a confused case against both Iberville and La Forest. (Ibid., 267–268, 291–301.) Iberville's brother Lt. Serigny arrived at Fort Bourbon with two vessels not long after the appearance of Allen's fleet. Judging the odds too great, Serigny ordered the ships back to France. One of these, the *Hardi*, was lost in a storm along the Labrador coast during the return voyage. (Charlevoix, V, 52–53.)
7. *Doc. Early Hist. Hudson Bay*, 151–157, 184, 188–192, 202–203; Charlevoix, V, 54–55. Among othersailing hazards in the vicinity of the Hudson Straits is that the ship's compass is useless this close to the magnetic north pole.
8. *The Great Company*, 199–200. Both the *Dering* and the *Royal Hudson's Bay* were armed merchantmen. The *Dering* carried thirty guns and the *Royal Hudson's Bay* thirty-two.
9. *Doc. Early Hist. Hudson Bay*, 202–203, 206; *Jeremie's Account*, 27–28.

10. Charlevoix, V, 54–55; *Jeremie's Account*, 27–29; *Doc. Early Hist. Hudson Bay*, 206–208; *Iberville*, 113–119.
11. Ibid., 210–218; *The Great Company*, 201–208; Kingsford, *History of Canada*, III, 36–37. During the storm that wrecked the *Pelican* and *Royal Hudson's Bay* seventeen men from the *Royal Hudson's Bay* including the ship's captain used the confusion to escape to Fort Nelson.
12. Charlevoix, V, 58–59.

CHAPTER 24: THE TREATY OF RYSWICK

1. *Cal. A&WI*, XV, 315.
2. Prowse, *History of Newfoundland*, 222–223; *The Life of Captain Stephen Martin*, 27–29.
3. *Cal. A&WI*, XV, 522–524.
4. Ibid., XVI, 39–42; *The Life of Captain Stephen Martin*, 29–31.
5. *NY Col. Doc.*, IX, 659–662; *Collection de Manuscrits . . . Relatifs Nouvelle-France*, II, 260–274; Charlevoix, V, 70–72; *Hist. Maritime France*, IV, 69–70.
6. Charlevoix, V, 70–72.
7. *Cal. A&WI*, XVI, 39–42; *Father Baudoin's War*, 91–93; *The Life of Captain Stephen Martin*, 31–36.
8. Charlevoix, V, 73.
9. *NY Col. Doc.*, IV, 255–258; *Cal. A &WI*, XV, 356–357; Drake, *Border Wars of New England*, 117–120.
10. Ibid., 120–127.
11. Belknap, *History of N.H.*, I, 145; Drake, *Border Wars of New England*, 131–134.
12. *Cal. A&WI*, XVI, 95.
13. Ibid., 94; *N.H. Prov. Papers*, II, 299–300.
14. Belknap, *History of N.H.*, I, 145; *Narratives of the Indian Wars*, 272.
15. *NY Col. Doc.*, IV, 340, 347–351, 435, IX, 682; Chalmers, *A Collection of Treaties Between Great Britain and Other Powers*, Vol. I (Treaty of Ryswick), 332–340.
16. Ibid., IX, 690.
17. Ibid., IV, 349–350; IX, 690–691.
18. The 1702 Treaty of Montreal would secure Iroquois neutrality for over fifty years.

CONCLUSION: KING WILLIAM'S WAR AND THE FUTURE OF NORTH AMERICA

1. The population of the English colonies was approximately 210,000 while that of New France about 12,000.
2. "Projects Against the English," *NY Col. Doc.*, IX, 725–728.
3. Ibid., 511.
4. *Cal. A&WI*, XV, 246.
5. Ibid., XVI, 97.
6. *NY Col. Doc.*, IX, 492.

Bibliography

Acts and Resolves of the Province of Massachusetts Bay. Vol. I, 1692–1714. Boston: Wright and Potter, 1869.

Anderson, Melville (trans.). *Relation of Henri de Tonty*. Chicago: Claxton Club, 1898.

Anderson, Melville (trans.). *Relation of the Discoveries and Voyages of Chevalier de La Salle from 1679 to 1681. Chicago*: Claxton Club, 1901.

Arnold, Samuel G. *History of the State of Rhode Island*, 2 vols. New York: Appleton & Co., 1859–1860.

Baker, Alice C. "The Adventures of Baptiste," *Proceedings Pocumtuck Valley Memorial Association*, IV (1905), 342–360.

Bayard, Nicholas, and Fletcher, Benjamin. *A Journal of the Late Actions of the French at Canada . . .*," London: Richard Baldwin, 1693.

Baylies, Francis. *A Historical Memoir of the Colony of New Plymouth*. 2 vols. Boston: Wiggen & Lunt, 1866.

Belknap, Jeremy. *The History of New Hampshire*, 3 vols. Dover: J. Mann and J.K. Remick, 1790–1812.

Birch, Thomas. *A Collection of the State Papers of John Thurloe*, 7 vols. London: F. Gyles, 1742.

Bodge, George M. "Soldiers in King Philip's War," *NEHGR*, XXXVII (1883), 61–76, 170–189, 278–285, 362–375.

Bouton, Nathaniel. *Documents and Records Relating to the Province of New Hampshire, Vol. II: 1686–1722*. Manchester: John B. Clarke State Printer, 1868.

Brandão, José António. *"Your Fire Shall Fire No More." Iroquois Policy Towards New France and Its Native Allies to 1701*. Lincoln: University of Nebraska Press, 1997.

Brandow, John Henry. *The Story of Old Saratoga and History of Schuylerville*. Saratoga Springs, New York: Robson & Adee, 1906.

Brodhead, John Romeyn. *History of the State of New York*, 2 vols. New York: Harper & Brothers, 1853, 1871.

Bryce, George. *The Remarkable History of the Hudson Bay Company*. London: S. Low, Marston & Co., 1900.

Brymner, Douglas (ed.). *Supplement Report on Canadian Archives 1889*. Ottawa: E. Dawson Printer, 1901.

Brymner, Douglas (ed.). *Report on Canadian Archives 1895*. Ottawa: E. Dawson Printer, 1896.

Calnek, W.A. *History of the County of Annapolis*. Toronto: William Briggs, 1897.

Campbell, Charles. *The History of the Colony and Ancient Dominion of Virginia*. Philadelphia: J.B. Lippincott and Co., 1860.

Cartland, John Henry. *Ten Years at Pemaquid*. Pemaquid: Private printing, 1899.

Chalmers, George (ed.). *A Collection of Treaties Between Great Britain and Other Powers*, 2 vols. London: J. Stockdale, 1790.

Charlevoix, Pierre-François-Xavier de. *History and General Description of New France*, 6 vols. Paris: 1744. (trans. and ed.) John Gilmary Shea. New York: Francis P. Harper, 1900.

Church, Thomas. *The History of King Philip's War*. Boston: Solomon Southwick, 1716.

Clowes, William. *The Royal Navy: A History from the Earliest Times to the Present*, 6 vols. London: Sampson, Low, Marston, and Co., 1897–1902.

Colden, Cadwallader. *The History of the Five Indian Nations Depending on the Province of New York in America*, 2 vols. New York: 1727, 1747. Cornell, New York: Cornell University Press, 1958.

Collection de manuscrits contenant letters, mémoires, et autres documents historiques relatifs à la Nouvelle-France, recueillis aux Archives de la Province de Québec, ou copies à l'étranger, 4 vols. Québec, 1883–1885.

Collections of the New-York Historical Society for the Year 1869: Clarendon Papers. New York: New-York Historical Society, 1870.

Collections of the State Historical Society of Wisconsin, vol. 5. Madison: The Wisconsin Historical Society, 1907.

Documentary History of the State of Maine. 24 vols. Portland: Bailey and Noyes, 1869–1916.

Documents Relating to the Colonial History of the State of New Jersey, 33 vols. Newark: Daily Advertiser Printing House, 1880–1928.

Drake, Samuel. *The Border Wars of New England*. New York: Charles Scribner's Sons, 1897.

Eccles, W.J. *Canada Under Louis XIV, 1663–1701*. Toronto: McCelland and Stewart Ltd., 1964.

Eccles, W.J. *Frontenac: The Courtier Governor*. Toronto: 1959. Lincoln: University of Nebraska Press, 2003.

Fernow, Berthold (ed.) *The Records of New Amsterdam from 1653 to 1674*, 7 vols. New York: Knickerbocker Press, 1897.

Girouard, Désiré. *Lake St. Louis Old and New and Chevalier de La Salle*. Montreal: Poirier, Bessette, & Co., 1893.

Goodwin, Maud Wilder. *The Dutch and English on the Hudson*. New Haven: Yale University Press, 1919.

Gosselin, A. (ed.). *Journal de l'expedition D'Iberville en Acadie et a Terre-Neuve*. Evreux: Imprimerie de L'Eure, 1900.

Green, Samuel (ed.). *Diary Kept by Captain Lawrence Hammond*. Cambridge: John Wilson and Son, 1892.

Green, Samuel (ed.). *Two Narratives of the Expedition Against Quebec, 1690*. Cambridge: John Wilson and Son, 1902.

Guerin, Leon. *Histoire Maritime de France*, 6 vols. Paris: Boulanger et Legrand, 1851–1856.

Hall, Michael G., Leder, Lawrence H., and Kammen, Michael G. (eds.). *The Glorious Revolution in America: Documents on the Colonial Crisis of 1689*. Chapel Hill: University of North Carolina Press, 1964.

Havard, Gilles. *The Great Peace of Montreal of 1701*. (Trans. Phyllis Aronoff). Montreal: McGill-Queen's University Press, 2001.

History of King William's War and the Consequent Negotiations between the French and Indians, in America. Ottawa : Canadian Institute for Historical Microreproductions, 1993.

Hough, Franklin. *The Pemaquid Papers*. Albany: Weed, Parsons & Co., 1856.

Hull, John T. *The Siege and Capture of Fort Loyal and the Destruction of Falmouth*. Portland: Owen, Strout & Co., 1885.

Hunt, George T. *The Wars of the Iroquois: A Study in Intertribal Relations*. Madison: University of Wisconsin Press, 1967.

Hutchinson, Thomas. *The History of the Province of Massachusetts Bay*, 3 vols. London: M. Richardson, 1765–1828.

"Hutchinson Papers," *Collections of the Massachusetts Historical Society*. 3rd series, I. Boston: Mass. Historical Society, 1825.

Jaenen, Cornelius. *The French Regime in the Upper Country of Canada during the Seventeenth Century*. Toronto: Champlain Society, 1996.

Jameson, Franklin J. (ed.). *Original Narratives of Early American History: Narratives of the New Netherlands, 1609–1664*. New York: Charles Scribner's Sons, 1909.

Jameson, Franklin J. (ed.). *Original Narratives of Early American History: Early Narratives of the Northwest 1634–1699.* New York: Charles Scribner's Sons, 1917.

Janvier, Thomas. "The Sea-Robbers of New York," *Harper's Monthly Magazine,* Nov. 1894, 813–827.

Johnston, John. *A History of the Towns of Bristol and Bremen.* Albany: Joel Munsell, 1873.

Jones, George H. *Convergent Forces: The Immediate Causes of the Revolution of 1688 in England.* Ames: Iowa State University Press, 1990.

Kenyon, W.A., and Turnbull, J.R. *The Battle for James Bay.* Toronto: Macmillan, 1971.

Kingsford, William. *The History of Canada,* 10 vols. London: Trubner & Co., 1888–1898.

La Hotan, Louis-Armand de Lom d'Arce, Baron de. *New Voyages to North America,* 2 vols. London: 1703.

Lajeunesse, Ernest. *The Windsor Border Region.* Toronto: University of Toronto Press, 1960.

Lanctot, Gustave. *A History of Canada, 1600–1763,* 3 vols. Trans. Josephine Hambleton and Margaret Cameron. Cambridge: Harvard University Press, 1963–1965.

La Potherie, Bacqueville de, Claude-Charles. *Historie de l'Amérique Septentrionale,* 4 vols. Paris: Nion & Didot, 1722.

l'Incarnation, Marie. *Word from New France: The Selected Letters of Marie de l'Incarnation.* Trans. and ed. Joyce Marshall. Toronto: Oxford University Press, 1967.

Lincoln, Charles H. *Narratives of the Indian War, 1675–1699.* New York: Charles Scribner's Sons, 1913.

Lotbiniere, Rene-Louis Chartier de. "Vers burlesques sur le voyage de Monsieur de Courcelles gouverneur et lieutenant general pour le Roy en la Nouvelle France en l'annee 1666." *Le Bulletin des recherches historiques,* 33, #5, 264–282.

Markham, Clements. *The Life of Captain Stephen Martin.* London: Naval Records Society, 1895.

Massachusetts Historical Society Collections: Correspondence of Fitz-John Winthrop. 6th series, vol. 3. Cambridge: John Wilson & Son, 1889.

McDonald, Kevin. "'A Man of Courage and Activity': Thomas Tew, Anglo-American Piracy, and the Manhattan to Madagascar Trade Network, 1690-1720," U.C. Santa Barbara, 2005.

Munsell, Joel. *The Annals of Albany,* 10 vols. Albany: Munsell and Rowland, 1850–1859.

Murdoch, Beamish. *History of Nova Scotia*, 3 vols. Halifax: J. Barnes, 1865–1867.

Myrand, Ernest. *Sir William Phips Devant Quebec, 1690*. Quebec: Demers & Frere, 1893.

Natstock, Joshua. *A Journal of the Proceedings in the Late Expedition to Port Royal*. Boston: Benjamin Harris, 1690.

Neal, Daniel. *The History of New England*, 2 vols. London: J. Clark, 1720.

O'Callaghan, E.B. *History of New Netherland; or New York under the Dutch*. 2 vols. New York: D. Appleton & Co., 1855.

O'Callaghan, E.B. (ed.). *Documentary History of New York*, 4 vols. Albany: Weed, Parsons & Co., 1849–1851.

O'Callaghan, E.B. (ed.). *Documents Relative to the Colonial History of the State of New York*, 15 vols. Albany: Weed, Parsons & Co., 1856–1877.

O'Callaghan, E.B. *Papers Relating to Count Frontenac's Expedition against the Onondaga, 1696*. Albany: Weed, Parsons & Co., 1850.

Owen, Daniel E. *Old Times in Saco*. Saco, Me.: Biddeford Times, 1891.

Parkman, Francis. *Count Frontenac and New France Under Louis XIV*. Boston: Little, Brown & Co., 1902.

Preston, Richard, and Lamontagne, Leopold. *Royal Fort Frontenac*. Toronto: University of Toronto Press, 1958.

Prowse, D.W. *A History of Newfoundland*. London: Macmillan, 1895.

Purple, Edwin, *Geneological Notes Relating to Lt. Governor Jacob Leisler*, Private Printing. New York: 1877.

Quint, A.H. *The Journal of the Rev. John Pike of Dover, New Hampshire*. Cambridge: John Wilson and Son, 1876.

Rawlyk, George A. *Nova Scotia's Massachusetts*. Montreal: McGill-Queen's University Press, 1973.

Reed, Charles. *The First Great Canadian: The Story of Pierre Le Moyne, Sieur D'Iberville*. Chicago: A.C. McClurg & Co., 1910.

Report on the Boundaries of the Province of Ontario. Toronto: Hunter, Rose and Co., 1877.

"Report from Committee on Boundaries of Ontario," *Journal of the House of Commons*. Vol. XIV Appendix. Ottawa: Maclean, Roger & Co., 1880.

Robichaud, Robert, and Mullock, John. *The Weather of Atlantic Canada and Eastern Quebec*. Quebec: Nav Canada, 2001.

Sainsbury, W. Noel et al. (eds.). *Calendar of State Papers, Colonial Series, American and West Indies, Preserved in Her Majesty's Public Records Office*, 45 vols. London: His Majesty's Stationery Office, 1860–1964.

Steele, Ian K. *Warpaths*. New York: Oxford University Press, 1994.

Thornton, J. Wingate. *Ancient Pemaquid.* Portland: Brown Thurston, 1857.

Thwaites, R.G. (ed.). *The Jesuit Relations and Allied Documents,* 73 vols. Cleveland: Burrows Bros. Co., 1896–1901.

Trigger, Bruce G. "The Mohawk-Mahican War (1624–1628): Establishment of a Pattern," *Canadaian Historical Review*, 51 (1971), 276–286.

Tyrrell, J.B. *Documents Relating to the Early History of Hudson Bay*. Toronto: Champlain Society, 1931.

Verney, Jack. *The Good Regiment*. Montreal: McGill-Queen's University Press, 1991.

Vinton, John A. *The Giles Memorial.* Boston: Dutton and Son, 1864.

"Wadsworth's Journal," *Collections of the Massachusetts Historical Society.* 4th series, I. Boston: Mass. Historical Society, 1852.

Walker, Hovenden. *A Full Account of the Late Expedition to Canada.* London: G. Strahan, 1720.

Wallace, J.N. (ed.). *Twenty Years of York Factory: Jeremie's Account of Hudson Strait and Bay*. Ottawa: Thorburn and Abbott, 1926.

Watkins, Walter K. *Soldiers in the Expedition to Canada in 1690.* Boston: Private Printing, 1898.

Webster, J.C. (ed.). *Acadia at the End of the Seventeenth Century: Letters, Journals and Memoirs of Joseph Robineau de Villebon, Commandant in Acadia, 1690–1700, and Other Contemporary Documents.* St. John: New Brunswick Museum, 1934.

Westover, Allan. *La Salle's Fort St. Louis at Starved Rock, Illinois.* Illinois State University: Midwest Archeological Research Center, 1984.

Whitmore, William Henry. *Memoir of Sir Edmund Andros*. Boston: T.R. Marvin & Son, 1868.

Whitmore, William Henry (ed.). *The Andros Tracts: Being a Collection of Pamphlets and Official Papers,* 3 vols. Boston: Prince Society, 1868–1874.

Williams, Alan F. *Father Baudoin's War*. St. John's: University of Newfoundland, 1987.

Williamson, William D. *The History of the State of Maine.* Dallowell, Maine: Glazier, Masters and Co., 1832.

Willson, Beckless. *The Great Company*. New York: Dodd, Mead and Co., 1900.

"Winthrop Correspondence: Winthrop Papers, Part IV," *Collections of the Massachusetts Historical Society*. 5th Series, VIII. Boston: Mass. Historical Society, 1882.

"Winthrop Papers: Part V," *Collections of the Massachusetts Historical Society,* 6th series, III. Boston: Mass. Historical Society, 1889.

Acknowledgments

This work would never have happened without the support and encouragement of my family. I am very fortunate in this regard and my sincere thanks go out to all of them, especially my beautiful wife, Pam. Nor could I have done this without the help of my old friend Ernie Botos, and as always, a special shout-out to Folgers. I also could not have done this without the help of several excellent institutions, many of which have helped with my previous works; the Massachusetts Historical Society, the Champlain Society, the University of Arizona Library, the Bailey-Howe Library at the University of Vermont, and Dartmouth's Baker Library were all of great assistance in this endeavor. And to the numerous others, from my colleagues at work to friends of friends who expressed interest and passed on words of encouragement, my thanks as well. Although you may not know it, your timing was often impeccable.

Index